W9-DHT-941

American Chronicle

American Chronicle

THE AUTOBIOGRAPHY OF

Ray Stannard Baker

[*DAVID GRAYSON*]

* *
*

NEW YORK

Charles Scribner's Sons

1945

Printed in the United States of America

THIS BOOK IS
MANUFACTURED UNDER WARTIME
CONDITIONS IN CONFORMITY WITH
ALL GOVERNMENT REGULATIONS
CONTROLLING THE USE OF PAPER
AND OTHER MATERIALS

PRINTED IN THE UNITED STATES OF AMERICA
AMERICAN BOOK—STRATFORD PRESS, INC., NEW YORK

Contents

The publishers wish to acknowledge with thanks permission of the Estate of Theodore Roosevelt to print the letters of Theodore Roosevelt to Ray Stannard Baker on pages 192, 194, 199, 203, 300.

American Chronicle

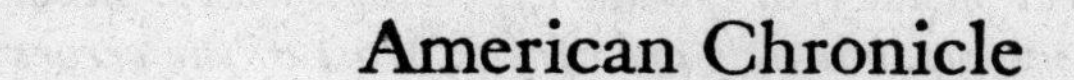

"Ideals in politics are never realized, but the pursuit of them determines history."

LORD ACTON

"The great malady of public life is cowardice. Most men are not untrue, but they are afraid. Most of the errors of public life, if my observation is to be trusted, come not because men are morally bad, but because they are afraid of somebody. God knows why they should be: it is generally shadows they are afraid of."

WOODROW WILSON

CHAPTER I

I Enjoy Life in Chicago

MY LIFE as a newspaper reporter in Chicago began in 1892. I had left the University of Michigan in June of that year, hoping to earn enough during the summer vacation to complete my law course. At that time Chicago was calling itself grandly the "news center of the Western World." "I Will" was its solemnly adopted motto. The people were furiously at work creating the vast pageant of the World's Fair, and the city, stimulated by one of the most glamorous advertising campaigns ever known, was thronged with workers and visitors: it seemed boundlessly prosperous.

I was not at all prosperous. My ignorance of the newspaper world was equalled only by my interest in it; but if my income did not at first average four dollars a week, I was enchanted by everything I saw or heard. I was as clean a slate as life ever had to write upon.

The bright banners, the music, and the tinsel of the World's Fair, gorgeous as they were, soon faded. They were followed with dizzying haste by another pageant, sombre and threatening, that of the depression and panic of 1893–94, nowhere else so severe as in Chicago. It was marked by unprecedented extremes of poverty, unemployment, unrest.

Every day during that bitter winter the crowds of ragged, shivering, hopeless human beings in Chicago seemed to increase. I reported the establishment of huge soup kitchens where I watched the long lines of the miserable unemployed waiting to be fed. Sometimes I talked with a man here and there, and often visited the police stations and "flop-houses" where they spent the winter nights. I attended the mass meetings called by citizens to deal with the crisis. I watched what the labor unions, the churches, and the social settlements were trying to do. I listened to the fiery prophecies of the soap-box orators on the Lake Front. Each of them had his own devil, each his own utopia.

I wrote three or four times as much every day as the *Record* could or would publish.

"We can't make Chicago look as though everyone was starving and homeless," remarked the sagacious city editor.

I cannot, in all honesty, remember that my interest at that time was prompted by benevolence. While I was truly sorry for the miserable men I saw, I was also angry and contemptuous. My attitude was that of the frontier where I had grown up. Bums, tramps! Why didn't they get out and hustle? Why didn't they quit Chicago? There was still plenty of room on the frontier. Why didn't they go to work anywhere, at anything?

"In the sweat of thy face shalt thou eat bread," said the stern old Presbyterian Bible on which I had been brought up.

But if I was not then primarily moved by pity, I was fascinated by what I was seeing and hearing. What a spectacle! What a human downfall after the magnificence and prodigality of the World's Fair which had so recently closed its doors! Heights of splendor, pride, exaltation in one month: depths of wretchedness, suffering, hunger, cold, in the next. It was wholly beyond my understanding, but it seemed to me profoundly significant and interesting.

I had begun with a determination based upon a combination of ardor and ignorance to work upon what, in my innocence, I called my "Great American Novel." This was to center around the career of a certain half-starved "potato-car boy" with whom I had had a chance meeting one bitter night in the wintry streets of Chicago and whose simple story, as I slowly unravelled it, had strangely fascinated me. My book was to present a complete picture of American life as it had burst upon me since I had come to the city in the spring of 1892, with special reference to all the evils that plagued the body politic. It was to be an abstract and epitome of modern civilization in the last decade of the nineteenth century. No less than that!

As a matter of fact, and in spite of all the misery I saw around me every day, I was positively enjoying myself.

I had moved from a hall bedroom in North State Street, where I had had to do my reading standing on a chair under the single dim gas light, to a more comfortable front room in a brick house kept by Mrs. Leusmann at 270 Huron Street—as befitted a man who had seen his salary shoot up from twelve dollars to fifteen dollars a week.

My hours of employment on the Chicago *Record* were eleven a day, from one o'clock in the afternoon until midnight—sometimes, when a great "story" was afoot, much later. I usually slept until about nine o'clock; and when I slept I slept—so that the piano of Mr. Campbell Tipton, the young composer in the adjoining room, even when he pursued a fugitive theme most hungrily, never disturbed me. I went out to breakfast at a little German restaurant in North Clark Street where I could get, for ten cents, a cup of coffee and a huge square of coffee cake sprinkled with sugared nuts and served by a blooming, red-cheeked German girl. As I sipped my coffee and ate my cake I read the "story" I had written the day before in a moist copy of the *Record*, and rejoiced when I found it on the first page with large headlines.

I shall never forget the blessed two hours, or three, after I returned to my room; hours that I had to myself and could be quiet. I sat at a little table in the window where I could look down into the occasionally sunny street and watch the unending drama being enacted there. Sometimes I started a story in the Kipling manner, sometimes I played the sedulous ape to Robert Louis Stevenson. It was always easy enough to get into a story; the trouble was to get out of it. My characters, once they began to come really alive, commonly refused to fit into the neat little plots I made for them, but would be going off by themselves to do what they pleased. After a few days of discouragement I usually tore up everything I had written and asked myself indignantly why it was, with the world rushing madly to destruction before my very eyes, I continued to piddle around with silly little made-up stories. With that I would turn to my memorandum books or write an impassioned paragraph or two for my Great American Novel—being careful to lock them up safely in my trunk when I went to the office.

I enjoyed these mornings very much indeed.

On Sundays I often took long walks up the Lake Shore, or down it—not so good as a tramp in the open country, but still full of ease and pleasure. I went to the theater as often as I could. I saw the great Rejane play in *Madam sans Gêne.* I saw Sarah Bernhardt in *Gismonda,* and Henry Irving and Ellen Terry in *Hamlet* and other plays. I went three times and held my sides while Etienne Girardo (a naturally solemn little man whom in later years I came to know well) presented *Charlie's Aunt.* There were many good lectures, two of which I remember clearly; one by Conan Doyle, the other by Hamlin Garland. I met "Sherlock Holmes" at that time, and Garland, in after years, became a good friend.

It was a time when the very atmosphere we breathed was full of the marvels of hypnotism and faith healing and mind-cure, to say nothing of spiritualism. I attended a number of "demonstrations" and seances. One in particular I recall, though with compunctions.

Mrs. Leusmann invited me, with her other roomers, to meet a hypnotist whom she knew. I was delighted; I had been wanting to meet a real living hypnotist. Hadn't I been reading Du Maurier's *Trilby,* which was just then being published, and shuddering over the awesome power of Svengali? Didn't I know an earnest young man who was crossing his legs every night when he went to bed and trying to "dream true" in the manner of Peter Ibbetson?

My first glimpse of Mrs. Leusmann's hypnotist was somewhat disillusioning. He did not look in the least like Svengali; he was a little rotund man as mild and inoffensive as any young fellow I knew, but he soon demonstrated his powers by putting the pale young lady who lived on the third floor back, quite to sleep. He proved it by sticking pins in her arm.

I was much pleased when he wanted to hypnotize me, having already blocked out a story in my mind which would require a minute description of the process. The accomplished young man placed me in the easiest arm chair in the room, directing me to relax completely, my head resting back and my eyes half closed. I followed all the directions implicitly because I really wanted to know what happened. The hypnotist placed his chair in front of me, made passes with his hands and informed me that I was now going to sleep. I was to lie still, I was to be easy and natural, I was going to sleep. He gradually approached closer and closer to me, waving his hands gently and rhythmically back and forth. I could feel his warm breath on my face as he repeated over and over:

"You are now going to sleep. Close your eyes, you are asleep."

When I looked into his china-blue eyes, not four inches from mine, and listened to his dreamy voice, I felt something strange going on inside me. I resisted desperately for a minute or two, and then, suddenly, exploded with laughter. It was a terrific outbreak, since it had been sharply repressed.

When I looked around at the gathered company, I could see the horror in their faces. I had committed an unforgivable sin. They did not know, and I could not tell them, that it was entirely unpremeditated. The poor little hypnotist was pale with anger.

"You are antipathetic," he said savagely, "you are utterly antipathetic."

He could not have used fiercer language if he had called me a burglar.

I could see plainly that I was disgraced. I had spoiled the party; and I soon went upstairs to my room.

"I'm always laughing at the wrong places," I said to myself, ruefully.

But in the back of my mind I was already working over the story I had thought of, changing it from a tragedy into a comedy, fitting it to the experience I had just had—all with keen delight.

The delight continued the next morning when I walked down to the office. It was one of those rare winter days in Chicago, crisp air and sunshine, that made even the dingy streets and the sooty smoke rising upward from the chimney tops somehow beautiful to see. I heard a boy singing at the top of his voice "After the ball is over, After the break of day"—and every time I thought of the little round hypnotist, his china-blue eyes and his angry denunciation of me as "antipathetic," I could not help laughing aloud.

In short, everything I saw interested me, and everything that interested me I wrote about. For a reporter who remained still undisillusioned, this was a state of bliss.

CHAPTER II

Marching with Coxey's Army

ONE DAY IN MARCH, 1894, I was gloriously translated into a wholly new but nonetheless exciting field. I was called into the office of Charles H. Dennis, the managing editor of our paper. Up to that time I had seen very little of him: he was in quite another, and far more rarefied, ring of the editorial heavens. Although a rather shy man, and quiet, with the reputation of being a prodigious worker, he was much, and warmly, regarded by his staff.

I was considerably awed by the summons into his office—and anxious, too.

"How long will it take you to get ready to go to Massillon, Ohio?" he asked me.

I knew little or nothing about Ohio. I had never heard of Massillon. I had never, indeed, been farther east than the state of Michigan, but I gave a response that would have fitted into any properly dramatic story of newspaper experience. Afterward I put it into a story myself!

"In ten minutes, if necessary."

"There is a queer chap down there in Massillon named Coxey," said Mr. Dennis, "who is getting up an army of the unemployed to march on Washington. He is going to demand legislation to cure all the ills of the nation. We hear that he is getting a good deal of support. Go down there and see what it all amounts to."

When I went out of Mr. Dennis' office my head was swimming with excitement—and pure joy! I had my first assignment directly from the managing editor and an order for one hundred dollars cash in my hand for immediate expenses. I was to take the night train—a sleeper, mind you!—and explore a new world. Best of all this assignment would enable me to go on with my study of the problems of unemployment and social unrest. I remember going down the stairs saying over and over to myself:

"Was there ever a luckier fellow than I am?"

The next day in Massillon I hired a horse and buggy and drove over four or five miles of the muddiest roads I think I ever saw, to Coxey's farm. I had already learned that he was one of the leading men of the countryside, that he was not only a farmer and breeder of blooded horses, but that he owned and operated a large quarry that produced "silica sand," which he shipped to Pittsburgh for use in the steel mills.

I found two men sitting in the front room of the largest farmhouse I had seen. On the dining-room table between them there was a huge pile of letters, telegrams, and newspapers. One of the men was Jacob S. Coxey, mild-looking and of medium size, with rounding shoulders, an oily face, a straw-colored moustache, and gold-bowed spectacles. He did not impress me as a great leader of a revolutionary movement.

The other man was too good to be true. He was strongly built with a heavy moustache, and a beard with two spirals. He wore a leather coat fringed around the shoulders and sleeves. A row of buttons down the front were shining silver dollars. Cavalry boots, tight-fitting, well polished, came to his knees. This was Carl Browne of Calistoga, California. He handed me a card with his written signature, at the end of which was a grand flourish and the words, "The pen is mightier than the sword."

He reminded me immediately of some of the soap-box orators and venders of Kickapoo Indian remedies I had seen on the lake front in Chicago.

Coxey and Browne told me in all seriousness that they expected to start from Massillon on Easter Sunday, March 25, with at least twenty thousand marchers and to arrive in Washington on May Day, where they intended to present their petition on the steps of the Capitol.

I had as yet seen no army and ventured to inquire where it was—since March 25 was only ten days away.

"Look at all these letters!" said Coxey with a wave of his hand.

There were hundreds of them—perhaps a thousand or more. Most of them were poorly written, some were on the letter paper of labor unions, clubs of the Knights of Labor, Populist organizations and the like

"With millions of men out of work and starving in America, and other millions striking for a living wage," said the expansive Browne, "our problem is not to recruit an army, but to prevent a rush to Massillon that will overwhelm us."

I picked up one letter and drew out of it, to my astonishment, a check for five thousand dollars. Coxey seemed somewhat embarrassed, but explained to me that they had received many checks—quite a number of large ones bearing the names of prominent citizens of New York and Chicago. When he had banked them, however, they came back dishonored. However, he showed me one letter, received that morning from a poor widow in Iowa, which contained a dollar bill.

All this did not, of course, increase my confidence in the "petition in boots," as Coxey called his enterprise. I was to be further astonished and perplexed. Browne, who was plainly the voluble showman of the two, took me out into Coxey's dooryard where there were wonders at every turn. It soon appeared that Browne was not only a showman but an artist, a poet, and a philosopher.

He showed me a large oil painting of the Christ he had just completed. It bore an extraordinary resemblance to himself, including the two spirals in the beard. This, he said, expressed his faith in theosophy. He believed that when a man died his soul went into one great reservoir and his body into another, to be used over again in future human beings. In this way a man might have parts of the souls of several dead worthies. Browne declared that he had within him a portion of the soul of Christ and a portion of the soul of the Greek orator Callisthenes. Above and around the portrait he had inscribed these words:

"PEACE ON EARTH
Good will toward men!"
HE hath risen!!!
BUT
DEATH
TO *INTEREST* ON BONDS!!!

He showed me also many other paintings, drawings and cartoons which were to be carried as banners on the march. One of them represented Coxey in the act of dosing the sick chicken of honest labor with a big bottle of "eye-opener"—that is, the Coxey plan for the "resurrection of the nation." Numerous transparencies carried mottoes like these:

"Peace on earth, good will to man, but death to the Shylock of interest on bonds."

"We workmen want work, not charity: how can we buy at the stores on charity and cast-off clothes?"

It appeared also that the name of the army was not to be the "Petition in Boots" but the "Commonweal of Christ." And Browne pooh-poohed Coxey's figures of twenty thousand for the army at the start.

"There'll be nearer one hundred thousand," said he.

When I inquired mildly who was meeting the expense of these large preparations Browne said—I am quoting from my report to the *Record*, made at the time:

"Brother Coxey has plenty of this world's goods and he is obeying the Savior's injunction to 'sell all he hath and give to the poor.' It shows how thoroughly he believes in the work."

I learned later that Coxey was seriously involved, especially in his investments in blooded horses, for one of which he was reported to have paid ten thousand dollars. Moreover, the steel industry, which furnished the market for "silica sand," was in the deep doldrums of the depression.

Both Coxey and Browne parried my doubts with airy assurances. They seemed to me to be living in an unreal world of their own feverish enthusiasm.

"How," I asked Browne, "are you going to feed and house one hundred thousand men when you get up into the mountains?"

He handed me a little printed bulletin which they were circulating widely throughout the country, pointing out certain passages for me to read.

"Fall in, let everybody send or bring all the food they can . . . Join the procession, you who have bring to those who have not."

They evidently believed in divine guidance:

"We are acting from inspiration from on high. We believe that the liberty-loving people comprising this indivisible and undividable

American Union will respond in such numbers to this call of duty, that no hessian Pinkerton thugs, much less State militia or U. S. troops can be hired for gold to fire upon such a myriad of human beings, unarmed and defenseless, assembling under the aegis of the Constitution, upon the steps of the Nation's Capitol, to assert their prerogative, shielded as they would be by right and justice, and guided by Him in the interest of good and higher government, and thus will take place that final battle, long foretold; for it will be, as noble Lester [he meant Elbert] Hubbard once wrote: 'That plain of Armageddon, dimly seen by ancient seer when the brute nature and immortal soul of man close in final contest, which shall herald the dawning of the era of love and tenderness, when nations shall know the fatherhood of God and live the brotherhood of man.' "

One of the good omens cited by Browne was the fact that a baby had just been born to Coxey and given the name "Legal Tender."

When I inquired about what, specifically, they intended to do in Washington I was assured that the plans had been carefully worked out. Two bills had been drawn up and introduced into the United States Senate by Peffer of Kansas, a leader of the discontented farm elements of the mid-west. The first bill called for the issue of $500,000,000 of treasury notes, making them full legal tender for all debts, public and private. This money was to be used to set the four million unemployed men in the country to work macadamizing the roads all over the United States. The second bill, called the "non-interest-bearing bond bill," demanded that Congress grant to the States, counties, townships, municipalities, towns or villages the right to issue bonds, without interest, not to exceed one half of the assessed valuation of their property. When these bonds were deposited in the United States Treasury, it was made mandatory upon the Secretary to issue up to their face value in full "legal-tender money."

These bills stemmed, of course, from the earlier demands of the Greenbackers and the Populists for "easy money"—which, with the growing agitation for the "free coinage of silver," commanded the support of a large number of depressed and poverty-stricken people in America.

Coxey and Browne had complete faith in the cure they suggested, and believed that if they could march into Washington with an army of public opinion large enough behind them, they could force the immediate passage of their bills—and all the evils that Americans suffered could at once be remedied. They had both been much encouraged by speaking campaigns in the neighboring industrial and mining districts. Browne had mounted his huge painted cartoons attacking the "Money Power" and the "Octopus of the Rothschilds" on a platform wagon which was lighted at night by a kerosene flare. Great crowds of workingmen had cheered them lustily.

I remember going back to Massillon thinking this the craziest enterprise ever I had known in all my life. Everything about it was crazy, including, for the time being at least, the two leaders. I did not believe that any army, large or small, would ever start. And if it did start, I felt sure it would soon be starved out, or wrecked by inner dissensions. But my business as a reporter was to telegraph the facts as I found them: and this I did. I remember writing one of my early despatches while a number of seedy-looking young fellows, led by a cornettist whom Browne had enlisted, practiced at the top of their voices, just outside my window, a song that Browne had written—the air being "After the Ball":

After the march is over,
After the first of May,
After the bills are passed, child,
Then we will have fair play.

It wasn't possible, but there it was! I began to wonder, sometimes, whether I had really been seeing and hearing what I wrote about. I was—or believe I was—the first out-of-town correspondent in the field, most of the earlier reports having been sent by Robert P. Skinner, editor of the local paper, the Massillon *Independent*, who, during the Great War, made a fine record as Consul-General in London. I recall meeting Coxey one afternoon coming from the post office with a large gunnysack half full of mail and telegrams. He had a broad smile on his face:

"We're beginning to hear from your articles in Chicago," he said.

It struck me all in a heap. So I was helping to launch this crazy enterprise! My articles, published in that hotbed of unemployment, which I had heard called "the metropolis of discontent," were bringing in recruits for a crusade in which I did not, myself, in the least believe. This set me to thinking, for the first time, of that vague something I had heard called the "power of the press." Here was I, all unconsciously, a part of it. What was I doing with my share of that power? I need scarcely say that I did not settle that query at the moment. And I kept on sending the facts.

Within the next few days, so widely spread had become the reports from Massillon, other newspaper correspondents began appearing, some of the best known in the country, like Charlie Seymour of Chicago, Babcock of the New York *World*, Beach and Austin of Pittsburgh and many others. The telegraph lines began to hum with the all but unbelievable news of what was happening in Massillon. All sorts of wild prophecies were published; denunciatory editorials began exploding like bombs in newspaper columns already afire. A few photographs gave convincing evidence of the grotesque preparations—and pictures of Coxey and Browne, judiciously placed in the proper hands, appeared in newspapers from New York to San Francisco.

One of the earliest results was the appearance of some of the strangest human beings I, for one, had ever seen. Many of the cranks of the country seemed to have scented spoil and to have started for Massillon; some, like The Great Unknown, coming with a flourish in Pullman cars, others riding on the lowly brake beams. Every day, to those of us who were closely watching the developments, was a fresh repast of wonder and delight.

One of these recruits was "Doctor" Cyclone Kirkland, a little man who wore a battered silk hat. He was an astrologer who professed to be able to predict hurricanes, and who soon began writing an epic poem on the Coxey march after the style, so he declared, of the Odyssey. He told me he thought it would be a "hummer in a cyclonic way." Like the Ancient Mariner he waylaid anyone he happened to meet and read a canto or so of his masterpiece. I am regretful to report that sometime later when we arrived in Pittsburgh the astrologer was beguiled by a dime museum manager to appear as one of his attractions. For this offense he was court-martialed by Browne and discharged.

Another recruit was a Negro minstrel singer giving the name of

"Prof." C. B. Freeman, who laid claim to being the loudest singer in the world, a gift he willingly demonstrated on the spot. He told Coxey that he had a wife and six children, but that he regarded it as his duty to "lebe all an' follow de Gen'l."

Another was a half-breed Indian who came wearing at least a few of his feathers and explained that he was a scout or forerunner who would go ahead of the army and spy out the land. We noted that he always returned in time for supper.

Browne, the showman, delighted in characters such as these. He knew that they would attract attention—and possibly be "publicized," as he said, by the newspapers. One of them in particular was a three-weeks' wonder. He was a bluff, well-dressed man who made a speech in the public square in which he supported the Commonweal leaders, using the most striking and picturesque language in denouncing the money power. From that time on he was one of the Commonweal's greatest attractions. He was known as Louis Smith, The Great Unknown, and his wife, who met the Commonweal in Pennsylvania, was promptly dubbed the "Veiled Lady." His identity was disclosed by the newspaper men a score of times; he was set down as an anarchist, a circus ringman, a German military officer in disgrace. In the army he ranked next to Browne and his services were at first invaluable in controlling the motley array. He became more and more of a mystery until the march was half over, when he tried in the absence of Coxey to usurp the place of Browne, and was summarily deposed. It was then that he was found to be a "Dr." Bozarro, or Pizarro, who had formerly traveled through the country with a band of Indians, advertising a patent medicine.

It was all very interesting and amusing, but as Easter Sunday drew near some of us who had been reporting the assurances of Coxey and Browne that the army would "positively march" began to wonder and to doubt. Everything seemed to be in readiness, including the huge band wagon of the prairie schooner type which bore on its side the words "Commonweal of Christ Brass Band—J. J. Thayer, Conductor," and two marvelous new banners, one a picture of Coxey as the "Cerebrum of the Commonweal," the other of Browne as the "Cerebellum of the Commonweal."

But there was no army; at least no privates. I recall going to see the two leaders on the morning of the day before the march was to begin. Both seemed in a trance of exaltation—awaiting the predestined miracle. They were receiving the usual number of letters and telegrams, which they considered highly encouraging. The writer of one letter I saw offered to shave the bogus checks which were coming in so plentifully. Browne told me he thought it a "hoax" (pronounced in two syllables). Their faith, in short, was colossal!

This dilemma led to an amusing discussion in our group of newspaper correspondents. Charlie Seymour of the *Herald* started the discussion: he had a racy, if sometimes macabre, humor, and I recall the problem he plumped at us—his face inscrutably solemn, his cigar held at an angle in one corner of his mouth.

"What are we going to do if this army blows up and doesn't start?"

This precipitated a discussion as to which would make the best "story"—an immediate and disastrous failure, or a grand and noisy start with the breakup later. All of us, I think, believed in an early debacle. The point was a pretty one, involving the ultimate art of our profession.

"I say," said Charlie Seymour finally, "that this army has got to march. We've said it would, and it must."

He paused.

"Our honor," said Charlie Seymour with a glint in his eye, "is at stake!"

"How are you going to do it?" someone asked.

I never knew how much in earnest he really was: but his proposal brought a roar of laughter.

"I've been talking with the fellow that owns the circus"—a small circus that had its winter quarters in Massillon—"and he says a lot of his roustabouts are getting pretty hungry waiting for the spring season to begin. He says he thinks he could get a hundred or so of 'em for a dollar apiece to march with Coxey, say four or five miles, half way to Canton. If the army starts, that's all we want."

"Where's the hundred to come from?" inquired a voice.

"And you a newspaper correspondent," exclaimed Charlie, "and never heard of an expense account!"

The idea proved irresistibly amusing, but it led away into a discussion of the fertile subject of expense accounts, of what was legitimate and what was not—of daring forays made upon editors who, remembering their own degenerate days in distant fields, winked their reluctant approval. But like most discussions among newspaper men —who rarely agree upon anything—these arguments, while delightful, never got anywhere. We did not hire the circus roustabouts.

As a matter of fact, the miracle happened. On Saturday I saw a freight train rumbling into Massillon. It was made up mostly of coal car empties and nearly all of them, as soon as the train stopped, dropped a load of hungry-looking men in ragged overcoats buttoned up to the chin. I learned that others came in on trains later in the night, and in the morning I saw them climbing out of the wagons of farmers who were driving into town to see Coxey's army start off. Some of them carried bundles covered with bandana handkerchiefs or meal-sacks, but the majority seemed to have no belongings whatever, except what were on their backs. In my report to the *Record* I remarked that "a pitchfork used on any of the straw stacks within miles of the city would have set a tramp to swearing."

Coxey and Browne had prepared for this emergency and the first thing we saw when we went to the appointed assembly ground on Sunday morning were hundreds of men eating the first square meal they had had, probably, in many days: huge cups of hot coffee, good bread, and unbelievable slices of ham which they themselves roasted on forked sticks over large fires which also warmed their shivering bodies.

The spectacle that followed would have satisfied even the most exacting of newspaper correspondents, of whom there were now enough to make up a small army of our own—some forty or fifty, including the newspaper artists.

At eleven o'clock the "Commonweal of Christ Brass Band," from its place on the red, yellow, and black wagon, began to play a march. Carl Browne, who had added a delicate white lace necktie to his costume of buckskin jacket and sombrero, pranced out upon Coxey's white stallion, Currier. "Windy" Oliver, the bugler, mounted on a horse with a red saddle, blew "attention" and the Commonwealers tumbled for the first time into ranks. After much preliminary squabbling among enthusiastic recruits as to which should carry the banners, the Great Unknown shouted in a voice that could be heard half way to Canton, "Everybody March."

The column moved, and Coxey's army was on its way to Washington. Mr. Jasper Johnson Buchanan, a gentleman of color, led the way, carrying the national flag. He winked his eye and said in a loud aside:

"That there man'll have me sawing wood yet. I ain't tired now, but I'm soon goin' to be."

Carl Browne rode just behind the colors and was followed by Oklahoma Sam of Three D ranch, a real cowboy, with lariat and spurs and a ten-gallon hat, who rode back and forth on his bay nag to the worshipful delight of the small boys.

Coxey rode in a phaeton and bowed right and left as he passed through the crowds. Hugh O'Donnell, who had been a leader of the workers at Homestead, Pennsylvania, during the great steel strike of 1892, was another prominent member of the cavalcade. Behind the band wagon, which was decorated with a picture by Browne of the Three Graces, marched the rank and file of the army—three or four hundred strong. The Three Graces, representing "Faith, Hope and Charity," were relatives of Coxey—one of whom wore spectacles. Browne called the picture symbolic.

A harder lot of men could not well be imagined, but they seemed to be enjoying the novelty of the experience. Banners to the number of twenty-five or thirty, with all sorts of mottoes and allegorical pictures, were borne by the marshals. The picture of Browne painted as Christ, with the words, "Peace on earth, good will toward men, but death to interest on bonds," attracted more attention than any other. One of the much-observed attractions was Mrs. J. S. Coxey with little Legal Tender Coxey, all unconscious of his fame, in her arms. Another figure in the parade was Jesse Coxey, son of the General, who rode Onvaleer, a splendid bay stallion. He was clothed in blue and gray, representing, as Browne explained, the unity of the North and South.

The commissary wagons were drawn by heavy draft teams and one of them bore the following legend in big letters:

SELL WHAT YOU HAVE AND GIVE
TO THE POOR

When the column marched up the main street of Massillon, banners flying and band playing, it was cheered by thousands of people who had been coming into the city from all directions since early morning. A large number of horsemen, carriages, and marchers followed the procession, and cars on the Massillon & Canton Electric railroad, loaded to suffocation, travelled abreast of the procession.

Before the Army arrived in Canton snow began to fall, but it did not drive away the spectators gathered there to watch the triumphant entry. Tents were pitched near the fair grounds and the men built campfires and cooked supper, after which they found beds in the big tent and lay "spoon fashion" under the straw to keep warm.

A march of eight miles in roads swimming with mud, and with the temperature near freezing, would have been enough to take the spunk out of old soldiers, but there was astonishingly little complaint. Coxey declared that the men were "marching for a principle" and that nothing could daunt them. Both he and Browne regarded the success of their expedition as assured.

One observer on that day could not get over the shock of astonished wonder that he felt. The whole enterprise had seemed preposterous: it couldn't happen in America. And yet here it was sloshing its way through the rich farm country of central Ohio, on its way to Washington to reform the social and economic ills of the nation. What was more, we had already begun to hear of "armies" being organized in the west, stimulated by the publicity given to Coxey, to join in the "advance on the Capitol." Some of them, notably Kelly's army, were reported to have seized entire railroad freight trains and to be coming east with thousands of men.

Other miracles soon developed. Instead of beginning to disintegrate immediately, as we had anticipated, the army grew in numbers, and at each stopping place the crowds were larger and more enthusiastic. The problem of the commissary, which every sane observer predicted would be insuperable, solved itself immediately and completely. Coxey had started with only enough in his wagons for a day or two, but at each town where a stop was scheduled, there appeared an impromptu local committee, sometimes including the mayor and other public men, with large supplies of bread, meat, milk, eggs, canned goods, coffee, tea—a supply far more generous and varied than even Coxey and Browne had expected or imagined.

The army arrived in Pittsburgh on April third. Lentulus returning with victorious eagles could not have had a greater triumph. Brass bands, marching delegations from labor unions, uncounted thousands of spectators in the streets! I shall never forget as long as I live the sight of that utterly fantastic, indescribably grotesque procession swinging down a little hill through the city of Alleghany singing with a roar of exultation Coxey's army song (composed by Browne) to the tune of "Marching Through Georgia":

> Come, we'll tell a story, boys,
> We'll sing another song,
> As we go trudging with sore feet,
> The road to Washington;
> We never shall forget this tramp,
> Which sounds the nation's gong,
> As we go marching to Congress.

I wonder if there was ever anything quite like it in this or any other country!

From Pittsburgh the army proceeded southward to Uniontown. At nearly every stop Coxey made a speech and Browne exhibited his panorama of cartoons. Many new recruits presented themselves, but few were now accepted. Mere tramps and hangers-on had been mostly eliminated. Considering its heterogeneous make-up and the absence of any real authority on the part of its officers, the discipline was remarkable.

I tried to get really acquainted with these men. I knew that no reporter going to them, notebook in hand, seeking interviews, would get anywhere at all. So I marched with the army nearly every day for a few, at least, of their hard miles. I liked walking: I liked country roads and country scenes, especially with the spring coming in. I rested with them, sitting at the roadsides, or leaning on the rail fences. I began to know some of them as Joe and Bill and George. I soon had them talking about their homes in Iowa and Colorado and Illinois—and Chicago and Pittsburgh—and the real problems they had to meet. I had known just such men in my boyhood. To call them an army of "bums, tramps, and vagabonds," as some of the commentators were doing, was a complete misrepresentation. A considerable proportion were genuine farmers and workingmen whose only offense was the fact that they could not buy or rent land—having no money—or find a job at whicn they could earn a living. Moreover, I soon made up my mind that there could have been no such demonstration in a civilized country unless there was profound and deep-seated distress, disorganization, unrest, unhappiness behind it—and that the public would not be cheering the army and feeding it voluntarily without a recognition, however vague, that the conditions in the country warranted some such explosion. The new "armies" gathering in various parts of the country, mostly in the west—my own newspaper, the *Record*, had published a map showing that eleven of them were on their way to support Coxey's invasion of Washington—were further evidence of the conditions that existed.

I remember feeling guilty regarding some of the things I had written in my earlier despatches—before I began to understand. One night after I had telegraphed my report I sat down and wrote a personal letter to Mr. Dennis, my editor. A few days later I was surprised to find that he had used it in an editorial, with this introduction:

From the *Record's* thoughtful and able correspondent, who has followed the fortunes of Coxey's remarkable army from the time of the enlistment of the first straggling recruit until the present, comes this letter, dated at Alliance, O., March 28:

"The army is meeting with a surprisingly warm reception at all these little towns. The entry last night into this city was really triumphant. The country seems to be full of sympathizers in the movement. Browne told me this morning that the advance agents at all the camping points between here and Pittsburgh had already collected more food and clothing than the army could possibly use. Taking into consideration the grotesque and outlandish appearance of the army, it is really surprising to see how well it is treated. I have stopped making predictions. The whole thing is so utterly improbable, that no one can tell what will be the outcome. I shouldn't be surprised to see the Commonweal march into Washington. I am beginning to feel that the movement has some meaning, that it is a manifestation of the prevailing unrest and dissatisfaction among the laboring classes. When such an ugly and grotesque fungus can grow out so prominently on the body politic there must be something wrong. The national blood is out of order, and Coxey, Browne, and the other Commonwealers seem, seriously considered, to be but the eruption on the surface. I don't like to think of the army with a sober face, but it seems to me that such a movement must be looked at as something more than a huge joke. It has more meaning than either Coxey or Browne imagines."

The correspondent is right. The continual turning of the people to Washington for aid, of which the Coxey army is merely a caricature, is pathetic and portentous. The country is sick just to the extent that its people try to lean on the government instead of standing upright on their own feet.

I had also become intensely interested in Browne. He was new to me: a singular character that I might sometime put into a story or a book. I delighted to watch him. There was something positively childlike in his love of make-believe, the romantic completeness of his faith in himself, the innocence of his self-deception, and his word-intoxication—the "languorous languor of the lingering day." The spectacle of him speaking at night from his wagon with the kerosene flare uncertainly lighting his grotesque cartoons, his coattails flying in the wind, while he demolished the Rothschilds and the Rockefellers, is a scene I cannot forget. The authority of his ignorance!—and yet somehow, somewhere, a kind of sincerity. If Coxey had not been there as a balance wheel, the army would never have marched: and yet when I think of the army, I think first of Browne. He was a kind of brief abstract and chronicle of the time; but when I saw him heading a great public movement, and trying to do the thinking for it, I was sorry for our civilization.

Browne had no reticences: everything he knew he said, and much that he did not know. He told me his life story with romantic flourishes, especially of the loss of his wife, "who died," he told me, "a victim of the moloch of gold usury." The string of large amber beads which he wore just under the collar of his leather coat—I had already seen them—had been hers.

We stopped a day or two in Uniontown, Pennsylvania. The army was worn out, and the long, hard march over the Alleghany Mountains lay ahead of them. Soon after we began to climb we found snow a foot deep on the rugged roads. Quite a number of the ill-clad Commonwealers, marching in ragged shoes, were forced to drop out. Contributions of food in that sparsely settled country nearly ceased:

mountaineer farmers, as poor themselves as any Commonwealer, seemed never to have heard of Coxey or his army. One night in particular, after going hungry most of the day, I saw the weary marchers crawling supperless into their wet tents.

Even the correspondents who were following the army, now reduced in number to ten or twelve, were forced to share in the hardships. There were no adequate "stopping places" in the little mountain settlements, and no telegraph offices from which to send our despatches. The Western Union sent us three linemen, who climbed the poles when we stopped, tapped the lines and sent out messages from barrel tops or drygoods boxes set up in little stores or hotels. One night we drew lots as to which of us should take all the despatches and try to reach a telegraph office some miles away on the railroad which ran on the further side of the Potomac River. I was one of the two to be chosen. I recall our efforts to find a boat in which to row across the river, and how, it being a dark night, we were near capsizing on a sunken tree trunk. When we finally reached the railroad, and stumbled a mile or so into the little town, we found the station closed and locked. It was nearing midnight but finally, after arousing most of the inhabitants, we routed the telegrapher out of his warm bed, got him to his office, and sat by his side until we were sure our precious messages were transmitted. It was four o'clock in the morning before we returned to the army.

One difficulty confronted Coxey and Browne during much of the route through Pennsylvania and Maryland. They found toll gates on all the pikes. When the keeper came out to collect the fares, the doughty Browne would plunge forward on his big horse and demand that the army be allowed to pass free. Invariably this request was refused, and then Browne would order forward the standard bearer and call upon the "minion of the bloated bond-holders and corporations," as he denominated every toll-collector, to permit the passage of the Stars and Stripes. When this demonstration had been made Coxey would come forward and quietly pay the fares and then, if the toll-gate keeper happened to be a woman, Browne would dismount and shake her hand and beg her pardon.

Beyond Cumberland. Maryland, the roads were reported to be so bad that Coxey chartered two enormous boats for navigating the

Chesapeake and Ohio Canal, the army being billed as "perishable freight" at fifty-two cents a ton. With the spring coming on and the dogwoods and judas trees in bloom, cowslips in all the little brooks that ran down into the canal, and innumerable wild flowers on the hillsides, I found it a rarely beautiful and interesting trip. It took about three days to travel as far as Williamsport, in Maryland.

The correspondents, having to follow the army, chartered a smaller canal boat, which they named *The Flying Demon.* In one of his speeches Browne, irritated by some of the despatches that were being sent out to the newspapers, had referred to us as "the forty argus-eyed demons of hell." This had led to the immediate organization of a Commonweal of Correspondents called "The Argus-Eyed Demons," and we broke out with badges and banners in imitation of the marchers. Finding our own clothing growing hopelessly soiled and even ragged, we bought uniforms of corduroy and a blanket each, which we rolled and wore over our shoulders like Civil War recruits. There being no place to sleep on our canal boat, we bought a number of bales of straw which we spread on the deck and into which we crept, shivering, at night. I think few of us slept at all: I remember the songs we sang, the stories we told, the sky-larking—those starry spring nights, while our canal boat crept through the still water.

One evening when we stopped at a canal station two or three of our men celebrated ashore and came back hilarious with a bottle or two. Most of us had crawled into the straw and were trying to get some rest. Soon after the boat started we were awakened by loud cries of "Fire, fire." The entire stern end of the boat seemed to be ablaze. One of our men from Pittsburgh, awakened from a sound sleep, was so panic-stricken that he ran and jumped into the canal, and straightway began shouting, "Help, help, I can't swim." We tried to stop the boat and couldn't. It was pitch dark, and only by luck were we able to get a rope to the man overboard and drag him dripping into the boat. The now-chastened celebraters had thought it would be a grand joke to set off a package of "Greek-fire" on the after deck.

Before the voyage was over we had all grown so frowzy and unshaven, even ragged, that we could easily have been mistaken for members of the Commonweal.

After the hardships of the long marches over the mountains the Commonwealers enjoyed the canal voyage as much as we did. They sunned themselves on the decks, lazily watching the barefoot boy who trotted along the towpath whacking the mule. Most of the time the two leaders sat at an improvised desk on top of the cabin of the "flagship," where the "General" kept a typewriter at work, and Browne found ample opportunity for promulgating written orders, an occupation in which he took especial delight. He also wrote a poem or two.

The nearer we approached to Washington, the greater grew the crowds. It seemed certain now that the army would succeed in reaching the Capitol. Would there be riots? What would the government do? Would Congress listen to them? Coxey, whose resources, owing to the increased commissary and other expenses, were evidently being strained to the limit, secured a walled tent which was set up as soon as the army reached a town, and a fee was charged to visitors. On Sundays, as an added attraction, Carl Browne preached. He would mount an old box or wagon, open a little red Bible, and deliver a sermon on theosophy which usually began with an original poem and soon ran into the subject of good roads and non-interest-bearing bonds.

To add to the martial aspect of the army Browne conceived of "peacing" it, as he said. Stout oak sticks, obtained at a sawmill in Frederick, each with a little white banner, were issued to all the marchers.

On April 26 the army reached Brightwood Park, within sight of the dome of the Capitol and was joined by two branch armies, one recruited in Washington by "Citizen" Redstone and the other from Philadelphia led by a character in a high silk hat, named Christopher Columbus Jones. Such reinforcements added to the conviction of the two leaders that they might soon be dictating to the Congress of the United States. They seemed dazzled by the prospect. Coxey told me with every appearance of supreme elation that he intended to "keep clamoring at the doors of Congress" until his bills were passed.

At last the great day came, a day of excessive heat and dust and crowds. At ten o'clock Miss Mame Coxey, the General's daughter, appeared on a white horse, attired in red, white and blue. She was supposed to represent the Goddess of Peace, and under her leadership the Commonweal marched up Pennsylvania Avenue, with all of its grotesque trappings.

Immense crowds lined the streets, including among their number many senators, congressmen, and other public officials. A large police guard had been provided.

The army finally halted near the B Street entrance to the Capitol grounds. Here other crowds had collected, not only in the street but on the lawn and even up the steps of the House of Representatives. Mounted police officers were stationed just beyond the low stone wall that bordered the Capitol grounds.

None of us had been informed exactly what Coxey and Browne planned to do—except that they intended to speak from the Capitol steps. I saw Browne dismount from his horse. Coxey, stepping from his carriage, stooped to kiss his wife—to the vociferous cheering of the crowd.

I made a lightning decision to follow Browne, knowing that his dash to the Capitol steps would probably be more spectacular than that of Coxey.

It was. Browne darted across the street (with me at his heels), easily jumped up on the low stone wall, and slipped between two of the mounted policemen. I heard a shouted order and the entire guard instantly turned their horses and dashed into the wildly shrieking crowd. No police arrangements could have been worse. In his sombrero hat and leather-fringed coat buttoned with silver dollars, Browne was a conspicuous figure, but he was able to dodge through the shrubbery. The police were hampered alike by their horses and by the panic-stricken people. Some of them completely lost their heads and used their clubs right and left.

Just before reaching the open grounds near the Capitol building two unmounted police officers sprang at Browne. The first he struck with his shoulder and knocked to the ground. The other grabbed him by the collar and threw him down. The chase was over.

At the last moment, just as Browne was seized, I saw something burst from his neck and fall to the ground. I made it out at once—Browne's precious amber beads. The string had been broken. I have never been able to explain quite why it was, in the midst of all that excitement, that I should have stopped to pick up a few of those beads and put them in my pocket. But I did.

Coxey had no such riotous adventure. He was a mild-looking business man, indistinguishable in that crowd, and when all the police charged down upon Browne, Coxey slipped aside and reached the Capitol steps.

Was this ruse planned beforehand? I did not know, and never found out.

Before Coxey could read his petition the police were upon him and prevented his addressing the people.

Late that afternoon I thought of poor Browne and wondered how he was taking his imprisonment and what his plans were. After all, I had been seeing him now for nearly two months and had become not a little interested in him. Besides that, when I remembered the events of the morning, I felt a kind of admiration for the man which I had never felt before. I did not know he had it in him!

So I went down to the District Jail and after considerable argument was admitted to the cool corridor. I saw Browne sitting on the bed in his cell. Blood had dried on his hair and neck. His elbows rested on his knees and his head was buried in his hands; he was a picture of complete dejection.

The turnkey let me into the cell and I sat down by his side. When he turned to look at me I placed in his hand the amber beads I had picked up during the melee. When he saw them his shoulders began to heave and he sobbed like the child he really was.

"You're the only friend I've got left in the world," he blubbered.

For several years afterward, Browne called on me every time he came to Chicago. He also wrote me many letters signed with a flourish and the motto "The Pen is Mightier than the Sword." The last time I saw him he was wearing a frock coat and silk hat and looked like a United States senator—and knew he did.

As for the Commonweal, it vanished in thin air.

CHAPTER III

"If Christ Came to Chicago"

I RETURNED TO CHICAGO after my adventures with Coxey's army much elated. I had been away nearly two months. I knew that my reports, accompanied by a series of photographs which I had taken with my own camera, had been much appreciated by the editors. The photographs in particular had been a wholly unexpected contribution. It was in the days before half-tone reproduction was used in newspapers, and every photograph had to be drawn-in by a good artist on a silver print—a cumbersome and expensive process—but the *Record* had used many of my pictures.

The journey itself had opened my provincial and pioneer eyes to a wholly new America, *old* America. I had seen groups of people, ancient citizens, like the Amish and the Mennonites of Pennsylvania, whom I had never even heard of before. I had had glimpses of the large population of foreigners in the mines and factories of Ohio and western Pennsylvania where a great strike was in progress. I had also seen, for the first time, something of the Old South with its distressful Negro population. I had visited two American cities of distinctive importance—Washington and Pittsburgh. I had spent every spare moment I had in Washington in visiting the wonders there, especially the Capitol and the White House. I had even caught sight of President Cleveland driving down Pennsylvania Avenue behind a spanking pair of horses.

I am amused now when I think of the intense interest with which I looked up the Barbara Frietchie house at Frederick, Maryland, the very window from which the "old gray head" had looked and from which she had flung her "country's flag"—she said! At Hagerstown I met a famous Confederate general, H. Kyd Douglas, a distinguished and handsome old man, who took a group of us to visit the battlefield of Antietam. To this day I have, in my mind, a map of that battlefield—its rolling hills, its green fields, its stone walls—as I saw it that spring morning. Few things I know can exceed the joy of such early explorations, or dim the memory of them.

But all of these adventures put together did not give me the satisfaction I felt when I thought of the march with Coxey's army. It had been a grand adventure in itself, and it had increased my knowledge of the exciting and vital problems of unemployment and social and economic disorganization that then confronted America. It seemed to me that I had discovered some new things for myself and that I had added immeasurably to the value of the material upon which I hoped to base my Great American Novel. Why shouldn't my "potato-car boy" march with Coxey, wonder at Browne, and suffer the defeat at the Capitol?

I had fully determined, as soon as I returned to Chicago, to go to work seriously on my novel. I had now not only all the material I had gathered on the Coxey trip, but I had also been greatly interested in another and scarcely less fantastic reform movement that had been going on in Chicago for a number of months. Great crises so often have strange flowerings. I had been sent to "cover" the story of William T. Stead, the famous English journalist and reformer who had set himself the task of reforming the moral, social, and economic conditions in Chicago. No less!

I knew of Stead's campaigns in England in many good causes, and of his imprisonment in Holloway jail for his attempt to reform, even slightly, the age-old evils of prostitution. He had written a sensational book called "The Maiden Tribute in Babylon," which had forced action in Parliament. He was a fiery orator, with strong religious convictions, a virile, sturdy man with a bushy red beard, and unusually large blue eyes, set widely apart.

I had been much stirred by my first meetings with him and impressed with the journalistic skill with which he had gathered the facts regarding the conditions in Chicago. I wrote a long interview setting forth his findings and was not at all prepared for what I found the next morning—or, rather, what I did not find. My fine article, written at white heat, had been cut down to two or three colorless paragraphs.

"It was all true, every line of it," I argued earnestly with the editor when I reached the office.

"But, Baker," he responded with the ironical look he often had, "we don't want to publish all the truth on one day. What should we do for next Monday and Tuesday?"

I don't know that there was any general agreement to "play down" Stead, but I soon found that none of the important papers in Chicago were giving him much if any space. He was beginning to talk about unjust taxation, and corrupt franchises, and boodling aldermen; he even dared to criticize the richest men in Chicago—naming names. And of all things, he was attacking the churches!

I was considerably cast down by the failure to publish my article, which I thought was about the best that ever I had written. That evening I cheered up; I had a new thought.

"If the *Record* won't use it, why I'll work it into my Great American Novel."

Where could I have found better material? All day I could not get the idea out of my mind—and it led that night to a ridiculous incident. I had been kept later than usual at the office and was hurrying homeward—I think running part of the way. I remember the echoing of my own footsteps in the deserted street. Suddenly I was confronted by a policeman, stepping out of the shadows.

"What's the hurry?" he asked.

I was taken completely by surprise, and as at several times in my life when I have been startled, I blurted out exactly what I had in my mind.

"I'm writing a book," I said, "and I'm hurrying home to put down some new thoughts I have."

He looked me over, witheringly.

"So ye're running up State Street," he remarked, "at two o'clock in the marnin' to write a book."

He had huge red jowls and a menacing eye. I could see that I was on the way to being taken in as a suspicious person. There were all too many suspicious persons in Chicago in those days. At that moment, fortunately, I remembered the reporter's badge that I wore on the vest under my coat. When the officer saw it he looked at me again. These crazy newspaper reporters!

Even a policeman in the golden era of Bath-House John, Hinky Dink, and their associates in the maladministration of Chicago had his doubts. I might be putting something in my paper. At any rate he came to the only explanation that could possibly have occurred to him.

"Drinkin' eh!" he remarked, "Well, get along home wid ye."

He did not know of the heady liquor I had had!

I come now to the most extraordinary of all my meetings with Mr. Stead.

"Do you know the writings of your great poet, James Russell Lowell?" he asked me when I came in.

"Why yes," I said, "some of them."

"Do you know his Parable which begins:

> "Said Christ our Lord, 'I will go and see
> How the men, My brothers, believe in Me.'"

He did not wait for me to reply. I had never before seen him in a mood of such intensity and vehemence.

"What would you say if Christ came to Chicago?"

I was dumfounded.

"And what do you think He would do? Walking about and looking at things as they are today—the poor, starving derelicts who tramp the streets, the rich men, yes and the rich churches, that will not hear their cries. What do you think He would say and do if He walked down through Custom House place and saw the houses of ill-fame in that neighborhood? What would He do if He knew that they were protected by the police with the wages of degradation that those poor women earn?"

I don't remember that I said anything at all: what could I say?

"I'm writing a book about all these conditions—which you and I have seen and known—and I am calling it, *If Christ Came to Chicago*.

Not long afterward I had a copy of that book in my hand, and I wrote the news review of it for my paper.

It was an extraordinary production. It was bound in paper and had nearly five hundred pages; on the outside cover there was a reproduction of Hofmann's famous painting of Jesus, with uplifted scourge, driving the money-changers from the temple. But the faces of the angry Jewish traders had been wholly changed. The one nearest at hand, with the rings in his ears, who is hastily raking his scattered gold into his open treasure chest, had been replaced by the face of Charles T. Yerkes, the rich and powerful trolley-car magnate of Chicago, and the treasure chest had become a north-side streetcar. The other faces, a strange assortment indeed, could be identified as the caricatured portraits of some of the richest and most notable business and political leaders of Chicago, among them the head of the gas trust with his huge bag under his arm, and the leader of the City Council running away as fast as he could.

Stead said to me regarding this picture:

"There are plenty more who ought to have gone in, but we didn't have room for them. These are the people who have polluted the temple, by which I mean the city government, and they should be driven out one and all. In the words of Christ: 'My house has been called a house of prayer and ye have made it a den of thieves.' "

If this was not sufficiently sensational, Stead had for his frontispiece a map of the heart of the Red-Light district of Chicago. The brothels were colored in red, the saloons in black and the pawnbrokers and lodging houses in hatched-gray. On other pages there were lists of all the houses of ill-fame in that district, with the names of the "madames" who kept them—and even more startling, the men and women who owned them. For days before the book was actually published the advance news regarding that map, and the caricature on the cover, had spread over Chicago like another Chicago fire. It was referred to by one commentator as a "map of sin." Seventy thousand copies were printed, and gobbled up, so we heard, on the day of publication—even though the news companies refused to sell it.

The book itself, which was loosely written, was divided into five parts, all dealing with what the author had seen of the most disreputable aspects of the life of Chicago, this mingled with religious preachments and appeals to the people of Chicago to arise, organize, and meet the crisis facing them.

It may be imagined what a sensation such a book caused in the city—just then so proud of the impression that its Fair had made upon the world. Stead, however, did not remain to breast the storm it raised: on the day of its publication he was on his way back to London.

The difficulty was that the indictments made in Stead's book were generally true; and everybody knew they were true. The harlots were there, paying their wages of sin to corrupt policemen who passed on part of the loot to boodling aldermen and politicians; the gamblers were there, robbing Chicago of millions of dollars a year; the rich and greedy public-utility magnates were there, stealing franchises; the sleepy churches were there, unaroused to their duty. If Christ were to visit Chicago, Stead remarked that He would prefer to visit the City Hall, with all its wickedness, to remaining among the churches.

The brilliant editorial writer on our newspaper, the *Record,* who called Stead the "queerest guest this city ever sheltered," did not criticize his findings, but remarked:

"If by his own peculiar cauterizing process he can help burn out the blemishes on Chicago's lofty forehead he is welcome to try. Yea, even though he precedes the performance with the contortions and locutions of a mountebank.

"It is his unpleasant characteristic to drag truth from her well only on such occasions as she may come up shrieking."

I never met Stead again, but I continued to watch his activities down through the years. I tried especially to determine, if I could, what result his sensational campaign in Chicago really had. The one practical suggestion he had made, for the organization of a strong group of public-spirited citizens in all walks of life, modelled upon the Civic Church of London, came into being as the Civic Federation of Chicago—a "clearing-house of reform," which did good work for several years.

I learned from Stead a number of things, some to commend, some to avoid, that were of value to me in the years so soon to come, when I was to play a part in developing the so-called "literature of exposure." He was one of the vanguard of a new and powerful impulse in social criticism which Matthew Arnold had called "The New Journalism."

Stead himself tried to explain everything he saw in religious terms—religious terms that became sometimes hopelessly confused with his own spiritualistic experiences and beliefs. He never seemed to think anything through: he says himself in a passage quoted by his daughter in her book:

"I know I always jump to conclusions: I never ponder: when I do I go wrong."

Stead saw with hope the rise of a remarkable young man, who promised to become a great leader in American journalism. This was William Randolph Hearst. He went at him, as he went at every problem that really engaged him, with directness and vehemence, and tried to convert him to the teachings of Jesus Christ. I should like to have been there to hear what was said! Stead emphasized the opportunities in journalism for such a young man, who had both brains and wealth. What could he not do to enrich American life! He impressed on Mr. Hearst when he met him (this is Stead's own account) the importance of giving a "soul" to "sensational journalism." By a soul, he meant a "moral purpose in some social movement or political reform."

He did not stop to ask whether the young man he was arguing with had any "soul."

Years later Stead was one of the distinguished company of passengers who met their death on the *Titanic* when it collided with an iceberg in the north Atlantic, 1912.

All of these things that I was seeing and hearing during the winter of 1894 excited me intensely. I was not at all satisfied with Stead's answer to the problems he had seen so clearly, nor yet with Coxey's. It did not seem to me that either of them understood what the fundamental conditions really were, or the difficulties of meeting them. I did not myself! I remember with what zest I set about writing a story, possibly for a chapter in my book, in which the principal character was one of the money-changers in Hofmann's picture, as caricatured by Stead. What became of him? What did he do? Where did he go? What did he think? How did his friends and neighbors respond? What did they say to Jesus or do to him afterward?—all points to which the scriptural narrative remained oblivious. It was an idea quite bizarre enough to fascinate me even in those furious early days. I was vastly absorbed and interested, but soon found myself lost in a maze of conjectures. What *would* the money-changers do after they were driven out? Where were the followers of Jesus who would keep them out by devising a better way of life, and practicing it themselves? And what was that better way of life?

At times I became bitterly critical of the educators I had had in college. Why hadn't they told me about, or at least referred me to, the books that would have helped me in understanding the things I was seeing? I had had excellent courses in the physical sciences (then new fields for wonder and for thought), I had had good mathematics, I had run more or less hastily through a few of the best old books, I had dabbled in languages and in history, but the study of human relationships, whether sociology or economics, was then practically unknown. I did have a course in "moral philosophy" conducted by a good old man, a superannuated professor kept on by the trustees because he had no other means of support, which derived largely from the "shalts" and the "shalt-nots" of the Bible. As for the world of business and industry, I understood, dimly, that it was operated according to the immutable gospel of Adam Smith. "Enlightened selfishness" would solve all the problems!

There were indeed a number of disturbing books in circulation, among them Bellamy's *Looking Backward,* allowable to read because it was only a fantasy, and Henry George's *Progress and Poverty,* which bordered on the dangerous. I also read, and was greatly drawn to, an account of Robert Owen and his social experiments. I should not, as I realized later, have blamed my educators. They themselves did not know; they were no more awake to the new problems than, say, students of the natural sciences before Darwin.

But I was temperamentally impatient. I wanted explanations promptly. I wanted to know what *I* should do to help save the world.

I have thought since that it was fortunate for me that there were so few books in the field of social relations and most of those utopian fantasies, or else the application of religious dogmas or aspirations to a new world which nobody had really explored. It was fortunate because I was thus forced, if I wanted to understand, to "look at it again" as old Dr. Beal had taught me in college.

CHAPTER IV

Bloodshed

WITHOUT MY KNOWING IT I was being educated with dizzying speed as to conditions in the new world I had entered. In a former volume I described one of the best courses I ever took—an introductory laboratory course it was—in which I had myself for a time been one of the unemployed. I had known at first hand some of the realities of that period, even reaching the point of not knowing where my next meal was coming from. I can recommend this enlightening experience for any youngster just out of college and in the beginning too sure of himself, as I was. Stead and his lurid book had constituted an excellent second course. The remedy he proposed was religious, but he had gone off and left Jesus, as men have always been going, to do the scourging alone—and most of the loving and forgiving. Nothing much had happened. The city had indeed been scandalized, but it showed no evidences of any real conversion. The good people of the town were perhaps working a little harder than usual to feed the hungry and house the destitute, but the power of the corrupt politicians and the greedy exploiters—and the gamblers and the prostitutes—seemed quite undisturbed.

Coxey and Browne, I could see, had tried another method of approach. They also believed in magic—the magic power centered at Washington. A couple of bills passed by the Congress and signed by the President would turn the trick—and all would be well again. I had seen them jailed for walking on the grass at the Capitol. There had again been commotion and excitement, this time on a national scale, but so far as I could see, the Power at Washington had scarcely fluttered an eyelid.

I had wondered what would happen next. When neither religion nor statesmanship serves to quiet social unrest, what happens? I should have been shocked if anyone had, at that moment, given me the correct answer. What but bloodshed?

Three days after I returned to Chicago from the Coxey trip and, before I had had time to write a line on my novel, I was asked to go down to the town of Pullman and see what the trouble was. I had never been in Pullman, but a year or so before I had read a glowing account of the wonderful contribution that George M. Pullman had made to the solution of the problems of labor and capital. He had gone out of the crowded city and built a beautiful model town for his working people, quite the finest in the country—"a town from which all that is ugly, discordant, and demoralizing is eliminated." It had its own attractive small houses and apartments for the men who worked in the great shops where Pullman cars were produced. It had its own hotel, its own arcade for stores, and its bank, its churches, and its schools, all built to an architectural plan. Everything else—water supply, gas, an adequate sewage system—was provided and operated with thoughtful intelligence by the company. And paid for by the workers. Playgrounds were even furnished for the children. Workmen did not dare to enter the only bar in the town, which was in Pullman's hotel, where liquor was served only to visitors.

I remember the portrait of the benevolent-looking, bearded man, Mr. Pullman himself, that went with the article. I regarded the experiment as one of the most promising I had ever heard about, and I hoped one day to be able to meet the man who was responsible for it. It seemed that here was a leader not only with vision, but with true generosity of spirit. He might be the Messiah of a new age.

I found everything at Pullman in the wildest confusion. "Three thousand men," I wrote in my report of May 12, "stopped making palace cars for George M. Pullman yesterday forenoon and spent the day in discussing their wrongs in the streets of the 'model city.' "

I saw this notice posted in the buildings of the great plant:

THE SHOPS ARE CLOSED UNTIL FURTHER NOTICE

WILLIAM A. MIDDLETON, *Foreman*

I learned also that the workmen had organized and were affiliated with the powerful new American Railway Union, headed by a brilliant young leader, named Eugene V. Debs, which had just won a triumphant victory in a strike against the Great Northern Railway.

All such controversies, I knew, had two sides. I tried to see George M. Pullman, and other officers of his company. I was told that during the depression the company had been losing money, and that the shops had recently been operated only to keep the workmen busy. To this the workmen responded that the company was just about to pay its regular dividend, and asked why the employees should bear all the losses due to hard times. Pullman himself was reported to have said that "no man who participated in the strike would ever be allowed to resume his position in the Pullman shops."

It was thus that the issue was joined. I reported that if the strike continued, "most of the workmen will be unable to meet their rent, and the evictions from the company's houses which must necessarily follow will undoubtedly be met by the most determined resistance."

I found that the strikers, unable to meet in the model town, were holding tumultuous all-night sessions in happy-go-lucky, unregulated Kensington, just across the border. If no liquor was to be obtained in Pullman, there were forty-six saloons and plenty of go-easy amusement in that neighborly resort which thrived on all the extravagances forbidden in the model city.

The reporter traveling back that night on the suburban train to Chicago had felt in the very air a sternness of purpose, a deadly determination, that had been wholly lacking in either of the two movements he had just been seeing—Stead's or Coxey's. These men meant business! This was war!

I had no idea on that May day of how completely the incidents I had begun to report would continue to absorb me. I devoted most of my time and all of my interest during that summer and fall to "Debs Rebellion." It was one of the greatest industrial conflicts in the history of the country—perhaps the most important of all in its significances. The issues it raised were carried through to the Supreme Court of the United States with a resulting decision that had a profound influence upon the labor movement in America. It led to a rapid growth of the Socialist party, with Debs himself becoming a socialist and a national figure, the candidate at five elections for President of the United States.

I first met Eugene Debs about the middle of June. He had come to Chicago for the convention of the American Railway Union, and the chief subject of discussion was the month-old strike at Pullman and whether or not the American Railway Union should support it.

The company had not yet evicted the workmen for non-payment of rent, but literal starvation was likely soon to do it. There had been meetings of the older trade unions of Chicago—I had attended some of them—and plans had been made to raise a relief fund, through contributions from working people, but the money actually contributed was scarcely more than a drop in the bucket. Bitterness was increasing. One minister of Pullman, Mr. Oggel, from his Presbyterian pulpit had made a sharp attack on the strikers: Mr. Carwardine from the Methodist pulpit had quite as sharply defended them and had dared to criticize the company. Tales of injustice and oppression rose like noxious fumes out of the town: complaints of the charges Pullman levied for water and gas, charges for rent on houses and churches, and of the constant and expensive supervision of everything connected with the town.

Debs himself had at first been opposed to the strike. Compared with the vast issues that confronted him in his relationships with western railroads it seemed a trifling issue. It ought to be settled by arbitration. But Debs was a sensitive and warm-hearted man. I remember thinking he resembled Bill Nye, the humorist, another mid-westerner. He had the same gangling height, the same thinning hair and blue eyes. He was somewhat awkward, with an embarrassed gentleness of manner and a gift of explosive profanity. James Whitcomb Riley had written of him:

> And there's Gene Debs—a man 'at stands
> And jest holds out in his two hands
> As warm a heart as ever beat
> Betwixt here and the judgment seat!

I had liked him almost on sight, for I felt his unselfish devotion to the cause he was interested in. It was not primarily unionism, the organization, that absorbed him, as it did Gompers, but the human problems of the workingman. He was not so much concerned with the "aristocrats of labor," like the locomotive engineers, but with unorganized railroad workmen. He was for "clasping hands with the whole working class." When he refused a job that would have brought him several thousand dollars a year, in order to work for seventy-five dollars a month with the American Railway Union, he said:

"I have a heart for others and that is why I am in this work. If I rise, it will be *with* the ranks, not *from* them."

Years afterward, when he knew, better than most men of his time, what defeat was and what prisons meant, he placed these words at the beginning of his only book, called *Walls and Bars*:

My Prison Creed

While there is a lower class I am in it;
While there is a criminal element I am of it;
While there's a soul in prison I am not free.

Though Debs had not wanted the Pullman strike, he was much moved and angered by the stories told by the striking workers. When he rose to speak at the convention he made a powerful and persuasive plea:

"The time has come to strangle the Pullman monopoly. You will never be stronger for the conflict than you are now and you can go into it with a bright prospect of winning."

His union gave Pullman five days to consider a settlement. Pullman's reply was: "We have nothing to arbitrate." He also said:

"The workers have nothing to do with the amount of wages they shall receive; that is solely the business of the company."

The battle began immediately. The powerful railroad unions refused to haul Pullman cars, and when the railroad managers tried to hire non-union men, or sought the protection of the police and large numbers of deputy marshals, the rioting began. All southern Chicago seemed afire. I saw long freight trains burning on side-tracks. I saw Pullman cars that had been gutted by fire I saw attacks by strikers on non-union men, and fierce conflicts between strikers and the police and deputies.

As a reporter I could and did set down, as facts, what I saw: but I could not, in the least degree, make up my mind what ought to be done. My opinion, of course, was of little or no importance to anyone

—except to me. At times I found my sympathies going out strongly to the starving strikers in Pullman, some of whom I had begun to know personally. What other remedy had they to meet injustice and oppression except to strike? If neither religion nor statesmanship could solve the difficulties, how could a rich employer, a rich city, a rich nation be aroused? And were not other branches of organized labor warranted in helping the Pullman strikers? Was it not a nobly generous thing to do?

I asked myself these questions over and over again. And yet, when I saw huge mobs running wild, defying the officers of the law, attacking non-union workers, putting the torch to millions of dollars' worth of property—I was still more perplexed. Could such anarchy be permitted in a civilized society? I remember going out to the lake front one day in early July, and seeing long rows of military tents, and soldiers marching. President Cleveland had sent in the regulars to restore order. I knew of the controversies that had been going on as to such a course of action. I was with Governor Altgeld of Illinois when he visited Pullman and had seen how deeply he had been moved by the sufferings there. I knew that he was opposing Cleveland's action. And yet I can remember asking myself:

"What else, after all, can be done at this stage? Hasn't order somehow got to be restored?"

I was deeply stirred, and these more or less clumsy questionings were the best I could do at the time.

Early Sunday morning, July 8, 1894, I went out to Hammond, Indiana, which was then—as now—one of the great railroad junction points for the Chicago district. We had heard that a battle with the strikers was impending.

When I had arrived I found that battle already in progress. Sunday morning crowds choked the railroad yards. The "tracks from crossing to crossing," as I reported, "were strewn with overturned freight cars, battered and burned coaches, twisted rails and broken switches." I heard hoarse voices shouting, "Heave ho! Heave ho!" and saw that a crowd of men had thrown a hawser across the top of a Pullman car and were in the act of tipping it over to block a main railroad track. Hundreds of men were tugging at the rope. The heavy car would lift up on one side and then sag heavily back again.

"Heave ho! Heave ho!" shouted the hoarse voices.

The vast crowd held its breath.

Suddenly I heard what seemed to me to be firecrackers exploding. A moment later a spectator, who was standing near me, slumped to the ground, and I saw blood spurt from his breast. Then another man fell. I looked up the track and saw a locomotive moving slowly down upon the mob. Blue-clad soldiers covered the fender, and the running boards, and the top of the cab. They had their rifles lifted and were firing directly at us.

Instantly there was a panic, men running and women screaming.

I sprang aside behind a freight car and then, remembering that the soldiers might fire under the car, I climbed up on the iron ladder at the end of it. At that moment I saw a long wooden splinter fly from the car not an arm's length from where I clung. A rifle bullet fired from the locomotive had come through both sides of the car. I jumped down and started to run across an open space toward a row of small houses. As I ran, I saw two men carrying the poor fellow who had fallen beside me—one by his arms and the other by his legs. I saw blood dripping at every step.

When I got around to the rear of the first house, I saw another man, very pale, sitting with his hands clasping his thigh.

"Are you hurt?" I asked. He did not answer but lifted his thumbs from the wound and I saw the blood spurt out.

Nights later I woke in a cold sweat, sitting up in my bed, with that scene before my eyes, asking myself what I should have done, how I could have helped.

What I actually did do, in that moment of fierce excitement, was to ask the man who was holding his leg, what his name was and where he lived. I then stepped over to the man I had seen brought away by his friends. He was dying. A workman who stood by said to me,

"He was no striker. He was just an onlooker."

Another man said to me, "When I picked him up he said, 'Where is Mina? I was hunting for Mina. I had nothing to do with the mob.' "

I am amazed, reading those old reports, how completely I set forth the facts as I saw them, and how little there was in any of them of what I myself felt and thought—but that would have been literature.

In that single battle, one man had been killed and seven wounded, and not one of them was a striker.

All these things I reported.

That battle broke the strike. Debs was promptly arrested and locked up in the Cook county jail. I went to see him on Sunday morning. Several friends were there before me, one of whom, named Hogan, was a stout railroad fireman and a director of the American Railway Union. The iron door opened and Debs came out, a tall, stooping figure in shirt sleeves. When he spied his devoted friend Hogan, he put his hands on his shoulders, and stooping over, kissed him.

I found Debs not only unshaken by his imprisonment but as ardent and confident as ever. He gave me a copy of an appeal to the people which I was glad that my paper was willing to publish in full. Under Lawson and Dennis, the *Record* was a thoroughly honest newspaper, willing to print the facts, no matter what its editorial opinion might be. Afterward I was called into court to identify that document.

There followed interminable court proceedings. It seems to me I spent weeks that hot summer and fall in musty courtrooms, listening to an unintelligible drone of voices—to the weariness of the flesh, and the contamination of the spirit.

In the meantime the strikers at Pullman continued, more or less forgotten, to starve in their model houses. I went out many times during late July and August and reported as well as I could what I found—the attempts to open the Pullman shops, the attitude of the company, the arguments of the men, and the like: but the strike was over, nominally at least, and public interest was shifting to new subjects. My reports, much cut down, went into the inner pages.

One day I tried a new method altogether. I had, by now, become well acquainted with some of the workmen and their families. I could feel and perhaps share a little in their problems. I began telling their stories, exactly as I heard them:

"The broad-shouldered Swede lives at 522 North Fulton Street. His name is Andrew F. Rall and he has not been in the country long enough to speak any English. He and his wife and five little white-headed children are crowded into two small rooms, for which he is charged ten dollars a month rent. He owes thirty-eight dollars to the Pullman company and the milkman has a bill of four dollars. No one else would trust him or he would have been still deeper in debt. The five dollars which he had when the strike began was soon spent, and for more than two months he has not had a cent, depending entirely upon the relief committee. Yesterday morning he and his family sat down to the little oilcloth-covered table in his front room and ate a loaf of bread—the last in the house—and drank some water. Yesterday afternoon the children were whimpering for something to eat and the mother was urging them to be quiet until the father came home. She did not know that he would bring an empty basket.

"Hardly less pitiful is the case of Andy Onda, a Greek, who lives with his wife and four little children in room 8, tenement block H. He made only $1.50 a day when the shops were running, and when the strike came on he was wholly out of money. He owes about sixty dollars for rent and supplies. Last Saturday he received his last supplies and yesterday afternoon his wife baked some hard biscuits on a neighbor's stove—having no fuel of her own—and when they were gone there was not enough left in the house to feed a mouse, to say nothing of four moaning children. Neither Onda's wife nor any of the children have any shoes to wear. Last week their water supply gave out, and being back on the rent the company would not repair the pipes, and Mrs. Onda has been compelled to carry water upstairs. Until recently she was accustomed to get fuel at the Pullman dump, but the company has placed its watchmen around that source of supply, and no striker's wife is allowed to approach. Every vestige of material suitable for burning has been picked up, and yesterday strikers with baskets were carrying away the refuse of the burned cars at Burnside."

One morning, a day or two after I began writing these stories, hot out of life, I was called into the office by the editor.

"See what your stories have been bringing in," he said.

He showed me several checks and a number of bills—contributions of people in that city who had been moved by what was happening in Pullman. I can recall, to this day, the wave of intense pleasure, complete satisfaction, that swept over me. It came to me powerfully that people, after all, were wonderfully decent, all kinds of people, if only you could get to them. I learned also, then and there, although I did not define it in words until later, that common human suffering, and common human joy, if truly reported, never grow stale.

There followed an experience that I have always looked back upon with amused pleasure. I took the money that had come in and went down to Kensington with it. I bought fifty bags of flour, I bought salt pork and beans, I bought good coffee and tea and sugar —and many other things, in quantity. I had them loaded into the largest truck I could hire and rode over to Pullman sitting beside the driver, feeling like a kind of benevolent king. I knew where the suffering was worst. I stopped at the door of the Onda family and the Rall family, and the Booth family and the Olaf Olson family, and stocked them all up with good food. What crowds gathered, and followed, and cheered! What thanks were showered upon us!

I wrote an account of this experience for the next day—and more and more checks and money flowed in. I soon begged to be let off as an almoner, and on August 23 the *Record Relief Fund* was instituted. Mr. Lawson, the publisher, himself contributed one hundred dollars. I wrote the announcement:

"In obedience to the request of many of its readers and because it is deemed a merciful duty the Chicago *Record* has taken up the cause of the hungry and distressed people of Pullman, and today has established the Chicago *Record* Pullman Relief Fund. No appeal is necessary to touch the heart of great Chicago. It is enough to say that thousands of innocent children and good women are suffering in the town of Pullman for the want of food and clothing. Any sum of money from five cents upward will be very acceptable and hurriedly placed where it will do the most good. . . ."

The money so received did a world of good temporarily.

The Pullman strike painfully dragged itself to a close. The strikers went back to their work, having gained nothing by their suffering. Debs was in jail for three months. The American Railway Union was beaten and disrupted.

I tried to watch Debs along through the years. In 1897 I wrote an article about him for *The Outlook* of New York giving his plans for a new co-operative commonwealth—which was both socialistic and utopian. He had come to the conclusion that "labor unions cannot be maintained without strikes. Strikes involve a resort to force. Corporate power has learned to meet force with force, and with the leverage of unlimited means and the ability to invoke the aid of the law, the workmen can never win." He proposed, as his solution, a co-operative colony in one of the newer states of the union. But he was soon to be fully engaged in organizing the Socialist party.

All reformers I met in those stirring days seemed to have got themselves promptly into jail, and all for trivial offenses not based on the merit of the issues involved. Stead had spent three months in an English jail, not because he had risen in his wrath and demanded laws to protect young girls from being sold into prostitution, but on a minor legal technicality. Coxey and Browne had not been punished for trying to get legislation that they thought would cure unemployment, but for walking on the grass of the Capitol lawn. Debs was punished for contempt of court.

Here were things I saw and knew and felt. They added to my knowledge, still more to my questionings. Great things to think about, as great and as interesting as any in the whole world—with no time in the life of a hard-working reporter to think about them. Here, indeed, was the material for many novels, and no time at all to write any one of them. Moreover, events would not stand still and wait to be thoroughly examined and written about: they rolled majestically onward, absorbing and terrifying, confused and complicated.

What was a man to do?

CHAPTER V

Youthful Unrest

I CAME NOW UPON troubled times of my own; for my honeymoon as a newspaper reporter ended with the Pullman strike. All along from the beginning, even when I could not earn enough to live on, I had been wonderfully fortunate. I had been able to work on subjects that interested me profoundly ever since my days in the university—the new problems of unemployment and the relationships of labor and capital. I had been able to see and, in some measure, play a part in the most important and dramatic manifestations of these problems—the Stead exposures in Chicago, Coxey's army and the popular uprisings which grew out of it, and finally, the "Debs rebellion." Looked at afterward, at least two of these were significant and culminating aspects of the panic and depression of 1893–94. I had learned much from all of them: I felt that I had mastered most of the material upon which I proposed to found my Great American Novel. Everything had seemed to be coming my way (except sufficient increases in salary) and I felt greatly elated.

Quite imperceptibly the commonplace began to replace the spectacular. The Debs strike, which had shaken Chicago to its foundations, had been the crescendo. I could see nothing beyond it; and yet I felt that even though the cowed and beaten workmen had crept back into the Pullman shops, the railroads were operating again, and the evidences of fire and riot had been removed, nothing had been much changed, let alone settled.

The people of Chicago were profoundly relieved to have the trouble ended. They were happy to see factory chimneys again beginning to belch black smoke, the unemployed trooping back to work with full dinner pails, and money, the sure barometer of prosperity, beginning to proliferate as in times past. Sensitive newspaper editors, who had been interested and even anxious about the conditions that had existed through 1894, shifted comfortably back to the old familiar subjects and sensations.

I returned to murders, in which the people of Chicago, supreme in this as in many other fields, had become connoisseurs.

"Half protruding from a dry-goods box the terribly mutilated remains of a man were found at dawn yesterday morning near the corner of 63rd Street and South Park Avenue. They were taken to Rolston's morgue and positively identified two hours later as Alfred D. Barnes, the head janitor at the Hiawatha flats at 258 37th Street."

I wrote many bloody columns about this janitor of the Hiawatha flats. I wrote about fires and robberies and gambling and corrupt politics. I went to see the assassin of Mayor Harrison "hanged until dead" in the Cook county jail, a grisly business, unintelligible to me, from which I did not recover for many days. I went back to the reporting of lavish banquets and charity balls and grand opera, with Chicago in the gala boxes again looking preposterously rich and comfortable.

I might have borne up under greater events for some time, even if they were no longer new to me, but I began to suffocate under the pressure of daily trivialities, which absorb so much of the lives of newspaper men. Some days the only comfort I got was to cut out of the paper, not my own writings but bits of new poetry—the requiem of Robert Louis Stevenson beginning "Under the wide and starry sky," and Kipling's "Christmas in India"—"Dim dawn behind the tamarisks—the sky is saffron yellow"—and to paste them in my scrapbook. I was also gathering such admonitions to courage as "They conquer who believe they can." It was easier to put them into my scrapbook than into my life.

When I tried to go on with the writing of my great novel something seemed to have gone out of me; the more I forced myself, the more paper went into the wastebasket.

My father, who was also my dearest friend and confidant, with whom I corresponded regularly, occasionally made observations about the newspaper profession which nettled me—probably because they hit too near the mark. "The plateau of mediocrity," he quoted from an article he had been reading, "is reached by many newspaper men but they rarely get any further."

This hurt. I assured him that it did not apply to me! "I'm on my way up," I wrote him grandly. "If my strength and grit hold out I'm going to make my influence felt before I get through with it."

To make the situation still more difficult, an overwhelming new interest had come into my life. I wanted to marry the girl I had known for so many years and regarded so dearly, but how marry when I was not earning enough to support a wife? And how write a novel when I was spending so much of my spare time writing love letters?

I suppose these have been the problems faced from time immemorial by ambitious youngsters. I tried hard to work them out, and came finally to these conclusions, I even wrote them down:

First, even if the heavens fall, I am going to marry J——.

Second, I have got to have more money. I am going to make it in some way, somewhere.

I was on duty long hours; I often wrote three or four thousand words in a single day; but there were two or three hours in the morning before I went to work during which I tried my hand at stories or worked on my novel. These hours were precious to me, delightful, almost sacred. I had not succeeded in producing a single manuscript, whether prose or verse, that I myself really approved, but I had strong hope that something worth while, sooner or later, would emerge.

I now turned these precious hours, and all the spare time I could get during the day, to outside work. I began to write Sunday "feature stories" for the Chicago *Tribune* and *Chronicle,* our own paper having no Sunday edition. I illustrated some of them with photographs which I took with my own camera. The prices I received were ridiculously small, but they were something added to my income. A little later, as I found I could do such work, I tried, with varying success, the New York *World* and the *Sun,* both of which paid me more than the Chicago papers. I also salved my conscience and kept up my interest in the subjects to which I was most devoted by writing a number of articles and editorial paragraphs for two weekly publications, *The Outlook* and *The Independent* of New York. These concerned mostly the work of the reform and civic organizations of Chicago, and Jane Addams and other progressive leaders.

My closest friend in Chicago, one of the truest men I have ever known, was Hollis W. Field. We occupied the same office at the *Record*. He was the editor of the "bull dog," the country edition of the paper—a dull job to which he had become the loyal slave. Feeling ourselves overworked and underpaid, we both decided to work harder than ever, with a gambler's chance of getting any pay at all, by writing a novel. No Great American Novel! Just a good common thrilling story that would sell. What we wanted was money.

I shall never forget the evenings we spent, and the earnest discussions during long walks, plotting our book. It was to be the story of a man who "breaks his birth's invidious bar" and "grapples with his evil star"—in other words a hereditary handicap. Poor Field: I did not know it at that time, but he had just such a handicap himself, though not the one we used in our story. Our novel, which we called *An Interrupted Destiny,* was to be filled with hair-raising incidents, "not a dull moment in it!" We wrote alternate chapters and ruthlessly criticized each other—which was good for both of us. It was altogether a beautiful experience, a true adventure in friendship.

What really fearful labor during most of one year we put into it —writing, revising, copying. How our hopes rose and fell. I remember once, when we calculated how much we could possibly make out of it on the lowest conceivable royalty basis, of my shouting exultantly:

"Why, that's enough to marry on!"

We finally sent off the manuscript, with fear and hope, to Harper and Brothers. It came back promptly with the usual impersonal rejection, worded with icy courtesy. It seemed as though the world had come tumbling about our heads. Neither of us had the heart, at the moment, to start it off again. It lay in my desk for several months. One Sunday I took out my copy and read it straight through. I came out of it with the strangest and most paradoxical of reactions. One was of utter discouragement and remorse for all the time we had spent in working on it: the other was a kind of reluctant approval of the editor who had rejected it. I saw, as never before, all of its limitations and deficiencies, its forced humor, its crude attempts to realize situations and characters that could have been great—if we had been greater writers. It was, in short, pretty terrible! I remember sitting in my room, tears in my eyes, and tearing that manuscript chapter by chapter into the smallest possible fragments, and pushing them down into my groaning wastebasket with my fist. I think Field felt very much as I did about the book. Knowing now what he must have suffered in the writing of it, I never thought of it in later years without a sense of tragedy. I do not know what became of his copy of the manuscript.

I find many references in my letters written at that time to my efforts to increase my income: for I took the girl in Michigan fully into my confidence.

"I'm paying out so much now that I don't have a cent left by the time payday comes around. If I had to raise the money out of my salary I couldn't possibly get enough ahead [for our marriage] within the allotted time."

Sometimes I philosophized about the situation: "It's hard, sometimes, to think that money must be allowed so much say in our matters, but it's as it is, and there is no way out of it."

"You can't imagine how provoking it is to feel that you need only a little money—and can't even get that."

A little later, however, I find myself exulting over an income of seventy dollars in one week, from outside work—riches!—nearly three times my salary. It brought the wedding perceptibly nearer.

I suspect the editor knew that I was growing restless. I think he also knew something of the extra work I was trying to do. One day he said to me:

"Baker your last few stories have been unusually good. You are improving every day."

Honeyed words! With what delight I repeated them in my next letter to "the girl." It was wonderful to have someone as much interested in them as I was, to whom I could on occasion boast of my successes.

For the first time since I had been on the paper Mr. Dennis and I began talking about other than business matters—books, magazines, newspaper features and so on. I told him that I now had time for few books, but that I did read a good deal of poetry.

"You don't need poetry," he said: "you've got enough of that already in your work." He probably meant I had too much; I knew I was often too lyrical.

He spoke of finding much of interest in the London *Saturday Review*—it was full of "stirring odorous English"—and advised me to read it. Sometime later, when I got a little more money, I acted upon his advice and subscribed for the *Review*. Much of it seemed to me stodgy or written with a kind of British superiority that I found irritating, but there were occasional articles or reviews so founded in sound scholarship, so broad in their treatment, so lean and resonant in the beauty of the English, that they were worth the entire subscription price.

I shall never forget Mr. Dennis' final words on one occasion:

"You should keep right on writing: it will be of great pleasure and profit to you in the future."

His words did me no end of good.

A little later I was much amused and pleased to discover that Mr. Dennis, for all his warning to me, was not himself free from a sly liking for good verse. We were discussing John Vance Cheney, a Chicago poet with a delightful, if limited, gift of song. Mr. Dennis quoted aloud a quatrain which so charmed me—it began "The weasel thieves in silver suit, The rabbit runs in grey"—that I rushed out to an old bookshop in Clark Street and straightway purloined these verses out of a volume I found there, by memorizing them on the spot. I could neither afford to buy the book nor to let the verses go.

Not long afterward I had my first "promotion," which consisted of being sent "downstairs" and given a desk of my own, and what was still more thrilling, an advance in salary. Mr. Dennis was greatly interested in the special features of his paper. He was, indeed, one of the earliest and most successful promoters of newspaper "columns." Eugene Field's "Sharps and Flats" had long had a place on the editorial page of the *Record* and was a widely known success. He had more recently set George Ade to writing "Stories of the Streets and of the Town" with illustrations by John T. McCutcheon. It became immediately popular. Ade was rarely gifted with humor and had the light touch which goes with discursive narrative. His "Fables in Slang" were first published in his column.

Mr. Dennis had thought of a new column which he hoped would

be of particular interest to the thousands of workers in the factories and mills of the city. It was to be filled with that "everyday news" not usually published, in which he was always keenly interested. The column was to bear the title "Shop Talk on the Wonders of the Crafts," with this subsidiary quotation, "Here is the Master Key: Skilled Hands and Industry." If I remember correctly, Malcolm McDowell, an unusually interesting reporter, had begun writing it, and I was now assigned to carry it on.

While I was much more interested in social and civic problems, I took hold of the new work with great enthusiasm. These studies I felt would give me a clearer insight into the heart of the industrial process, the very thing I needed most in authenticating my Great American Novel. And wonder of wonders, I was to be relieved of night work, which would enable me to spend my evenings at home—with my wife; if ever I had one.

I imagined myself poking around with delight in all the workshops and mills of that great city, making acquaintances here and there with a few genuine workers—I would know them by their slow, competent ways, and the look in their eyes. Perhaps they would invite me to their homes where I could meet their families and come to understand them—not from the outside or above, but deep down and within. I also had visions of crossing the line and getting acquainted with the bosses, the white-collared managers, and even—by some miracle—coming to know the all but mythical gods of the machine, who dwelt in Lake Shore Drive or at their heavenly summer places on Lake Geneva. What an opportunity!

My first Shop Talk dealt with the making of mirrors. I visited the best shops in Chicago and talked with both workers and employers. I spent a good deal of time on it, and completely enjoyed the experience. I can recall the well-concealed excitement with which I turned in my manuscript to the editor. But alas! alas! from this time forward I had to do one of these articles *every day,* six days a week. I wrote upon every conceivable industrial subject, Saws and Saw-Making, Olive Oil, Wood-pulp and Paper, Drop Forging, Making Bessemer Steel, Peanut Oil, Diamond Cutting, and scores of others. The articles were usually about a column and a half long, some fifteen hundred words. I had also to see to getting the picture material to go with them. Instead of poking around as I had dreamed of doing, I had to run. Sometimes I tried to run faster than I possibly could—and fell down. It was only occasionally I could talk with a workman: they all seemed to work with one eye on the boss. I was usually "shown around" by some manager who rarely became really interested. I had to rely largely upon descriptions in technical and other publications. I did, however, have my eyes with me, and I kept them open. That helped.

If this had been the only task I had, I might gradually have learned to separate the significant from the insignificant and at least once a week have produced a really fine piece of work. But a newspaper office is an exacting master. It is full of alarms and emergencies. I was often called aside to other tasks. During most of one summer, while George Ade and John McCutcheon made a trip to Europe, I took over their "column" and wrote "Stories of the Streets and of the Town." I was made one of the dramatic editors of the paper on a night's notice, being blissfully ignorant of nearly everything connected with theatres and actors, except the fascinating business of sitting in the top gallery and watching the plays unfold. The experience taught me far more than I taught the public. I even took over the financial column for a few days while the editor was away, knowing far less of the stock market and the prices of wheat than I did about the theater. I was also called upon from time to time to write editorials.

All these pressures, everything done at top speed, almost nothing well or thoroughly done, soon began to plague me seriously. I found myself growing careless. I could turn out a "Shop Talk" or even a "Story of the Streets" and fill my allotted space with less and less preparation. No one seemed to mind: no one criticized: and since nothing I wrote was ever signed, I heard nothing, or almost nothing, from outside the office. Moreover, I was kept so busy that I had almost no time to myself to read an occasional book, or tramp into the country, still less to do the outside work I considered absolutely necessary to increase my income.

I sometimes thought, with a wry face, of my father's comment. With such hard-driven tasks as these, how reach even the "plateau of mediocrity"? I began to read everything I saw in books or magazines regarding newspaper work, and even the more ambitious "journalism," often copying down the best passages I found, especially those that would confound my father by glorifying my profession. I was at the age when the resounding prose of Thomas Carlyle especially pleased me, and I remember copying down a passage I found in *French Revolution*:

> Great is journalism. Is not every Able Editor a Ruler of the World, being a persuader of it; though self-elected, yet sanctioned by the sale of his Numbers? Whom indeed the world has the readiest method of deposing, should need be: that of merely doing *nothing* to him: which ends in starvation.

Another good one I liked was from my much-regarded "Leaves of Grass":

> And I say that genius need never more be turned to romances,
> (For facts properly told, how mean appear all romances)

I began to think I was not cut out for a reporter at all. While I felt that I was learning a good many things from my daily experiences, I was certainly not doing work that really absorbed me: in which I felt any great pride. Yet I knew it was writing or nothing for me.

One day I was astonished to find a paper-covered book on my desk called *Shop Talk on the Wonders of the Crafts*. It contained all the articles I had written up to that time. The *Record* had brought it out as one of its quarterly publications and the selling price was twenty-five cents. My name was not on the title page, but it was my first book—published without my knowledge or consent. It was followed the next year by two other books containing my "Shop Talk," also a volume of *Stories of the Streets and of the Town,* containing among others, those that I had written. These books must have had enough sale to warrant their continued publication.

CHAPTER VI

I Marry but Resist the Temptation to Settle Down

On January 2, 1896, I was married. My wife was Jessie Irene Beal, the daughter of my old and highly regarded botany teacher at the Michigan college. We were nearly the same age and had been friends since we were fifteen years old. We had both been graduated from the college and had many common friends and common interests. She knew well of my precarious finances and was willing to take the chances.

We reached Chicago on one of the coldest mornings of the winter, and drove three miles in a hansom cab, with the driver up behind, to the little apartment I had rented. It was a wild extravagance, but one that we felt was justified by the occasion.

It was, I think, one of the smallest apartments known in that neighborhood of Chicago, up a long flight of stairs from 44th Place. The neighborhood had been recommended to me by the agent as being inhabited by "respectable and God-fearing people." He might have added that everyone in it was scratching as hard as ever he could to make both ends meet. Many years later, when my wife and I were visiting in Chicago we decided to make a sentimental journey to the apartment where we had spent our honeymoon. When we arrived at 44th Place we found a large fat Negro woman leaning out of our front window! The whole neighborhood was occupied by colored people.

The problem of furnishing our new home had been much discussed between us. How could it be done without spending all our small savings? I knew how much my wife had looked forward to having everything fresh and new and exactly right: but she willingly agreed to let me purchase, from a friend who was breaking up housekeeping, a miscellaneous outfit of furniture for seventy-five dollars.

It can be imagined what it was like. Although, I knew, she was sharply disappointed, she went at the task of settling it in our rooms without a word of complaint. It was most fortunate for me that she had come from frugal-living Quaker stock and had been brought up in the home of a college professor who, until late in life, had never had a salary of more than eighteen hundred dollars a year (plus a house on the campus).

Just before we were married I had been bold enough to ask for an increase in salary from the newspaper, explaining why I needed it. It was the first and only time in my life I ever made such an appeal. The editor responded with good will and warmth, remarking that I deserved it, but when I drew my first pay envelop I found that the advance was only $2.50 a week. My wife and I immediately made several resolutions to meet the situation. First, we decided to live strictly within our income and never buy anything until we had the money in hand to pay for it. We also determined to save a little something, even if only a dollar or two, every month. No doubt we were unusually fortunate during all those early years, in having no serious illnesses or accidents, and we were able to live up to these resolutions.

Perhaps if we had had a generous income at the beginning we should have lost some of the warmly remembered experiences of working together, and of saving up, week by week, to purchase this little rug, this chair, that set of kitchen utensils. By the time our first child was born we had put aside enough money to pay all the bills in cash. With even a little extra money we might not have had the good fortune to work with our own hands putting down the clean, but irregular and provoking, Chinese matting in the bedroom and hall, or hanging the pictures, or doing a score of other common tasks in which, in the after-look at least, we took much pride. I can remember, but this may have been at a later time, the pleasure we had in building a bookcase out of an old drygoods box and covering it with imitation leather, made secure with brass-headed tacks. We were proud of that bookcase; it served us well for many years, and it now lives a retired life in our attic.

We might never have had the highly amusing anxieties and alarms many times related since then, with our first guest, a jolly old lady who was unusually fat. We had to get her through the crack left by the door of our so-called guest room opening against the foot of the bed, and make sure afterward that she could squeeze between the bed and the clothes press.

I was fortunate in all those months in having work at the office which I could do in the daylight hours. So far as my writing was concerned I seemed to be living in a comfortable haze of routine, with the sun rising, paradoxically, late in the afternoon when I arrived at the apartment to find my wife in the kitchen, wearing a long apron, getting supper. It was then that life began! We read books together, we went to see Joe Jefferson play *Rip Van Winkle* and other good or great plays for which I could usually get free tickets, we put on our best clothes and went to grand opera to hear the de Reszkes and Emma Eames and others, and we enjoyed together a number of old friends and made a few new ones. In all those earlier years I never sent off a story or an article without reading it aloud to my wife. She says I always asked her:

"Is it interesting all the way through?"

In short, our life in those early months was altogether a grand experience. What a thing it was to have a home of our own!

We were soon to discover, like all other enchanted dwellers in Arcadia, that our Eden had its serpent. It seemed at first quite unobtrusive and harmless, but it grew presently to be quite a monster.

When I was a boy on the frontier I often heard a phrase which described the experience we were having: we "had married and settled down." In those prolific old families in the new country, it was the commonly accepted process, when the son or the daughter married, to "take up" a nearby farm, or settle in the village. Even if some of the younger generation "pulled up and went west," they still "settled down." This was usually accompanied by a "renewal of the ties" with the Presbyterian or some other church, and, when elections came around, by voting the Republican ticket—thereby living happily ever after. So many times in my life, especially at the great critical moments, I have felt that early life on the frontier, and the strong family traditions in which I grew up, reasserting themselves. I have always, at heart, been a countryman.

So it was that the serpent tempted us to settle down in our Eden of mediocrity. Now that we were really quite happy why not be content? If my salary was still small, I knew that my work was much appreciated by my superiors and that I would in all probability be called up presently to better positions and a larger income. It would no doubt be possible to satisfy my itch for writing, as my father had suggested, by doing stories, and perhaps acceptable little verses, on the side. I might even, give me time, realize my dream of a Great American Novel. If we had a real family we should need more room; we dreamed of having a little place in the country, at least in the suburbs, where there was a tree or so and a bit of a garden. We wanted what we vaguely thought of as more leisure. Wasn't this patient acceptance of a comfortable place on a good newspaper staff the best way of getting what we most desired? Many of the best friends we had were pursuing this safe and satisfactory way of life —or so it looked to us.

The serpent began to tempt me, wearing the guise of a most excellent Presbyterian minister, whose church I attended for a time and whose sermons I occasionally reported for my paper. I had become rather well acquainted with this fine old minister and one day he drew me into his study and made a moving appeal to me to come into the "church of my fathers" especially "now that you have a family."

"We want your help," he said, "and we will give you ours."

I was taken considerably by surprise. I had in fact for some time been doing considerable reading and thinking about religious matters. Although I had become critical of many church practices, and especially of the attitude of the church toward the social problems in which I had recently been interested, I felt, deep down, the essential truth of the teachings of Christianity. My wife, whose father was a devoted scientist, nurtured on Darwin's doctrine of evolution, had also been much disturbed by the "higher criticism" of the Bible and the teachings of the church. It was a period in the life of the nation when religious controversy was near its height. President Andrew D. White of Cornell University had called the notable book in which he discussed this controversy, *The Warfare of Science with Theology.*

I was, in short, much at sea as to what I should believe, and this warm-hearted invitation had at the moment a power of appeal that astonished me. It would be so comfortable to make port in the safe harbor of the old church—and stop questioning, and stop thinking.

I was, I believe, on the very brink of accepting the minister's suggestion, but I rallied enough to ask, somewhat weakly, for a copy of the creed I would be asked to accept if I became a church member. The good old man gave it to me, I thought, with reluctance. He was on the point, I felt sure, of making explanations and interpretations, but he finally handed me the little booklet without comment.

As I hurried down the street afterward I had the strangest feeling of having escaped a most insidious temptation. I was still more convinced of this when I read the creed he had given me—and this even though I knew and felt the value of the organization of good will which the church seemed to me to represent. At least, I knew I was not then ready to unite with any church. I felt that I must try to clear my own mind concerning the great questions involved. I passed through a period in which I liked to quote mournfully from Matthew Arnold's "Dover Beach." I felt myself on a "darkling plain."

One of the books I had read with deep interest was Henry Drummond's *Natural Law in the Spiritual World*. I regarded it so highly that I kept it for some time, as I wrote to the girl in Michigan before we were married, next my volume of Emerson which contained the essay on *Compensation*, and not far from my *Leaves of Grass*. Incongruous company!

I read, I even studied, Andrew D. White's book, of which I have spoken. A few years later when I was in Berlin I recall going out to walk in the Tiergarten with Dr. White, who was our Ambassador there, and of carrying a large yellow sun umbrella over his head, for it was a warm day and he was then an old man. We sat down on one of the benches under the pleasant linden trees and I remember how delighted the fine old scholar was when I asked him a question or so about his book, and how earnestly he discussed the questions I raised.

"You are young," he said. "You are entering a new world: a scientific world. It will be different from this one, far different; I wonder if it will be any happier?"

I read other books in my search for truth. The best, at least for me at that time and in that mood, was Benjamin Kidd's *Social Evolution*. I liked especially his remarks on Democracy:

"The fact of our time which overshadows all others is the arrival of Democracy. But the perception of the fact is of relatively little importance if we do not also realize that it is a new Democracy. There are many who speak of the new ruler of nations as if he were the same idle Demos whose ears the dishonest courtiers have tickled from time immemorial. It is not so. Even those who attempt to lead him do not yet quite understand him. Those who think that he is about to bring chaos instead of order do not rightly apprehend the nature of his strength. They do not perceive that his arrival is the crowning result of an ethical movement in which qualities and attributes which we have been all taught to regard as the very highest of which human nature is capable find the completest expression they have ever reached in the history of the race."

In spite of all this reading, however, I could not seem to come clear. I grew tired of thinking on the subject: I wanted to get something settled and concluded, to go somewhere, or get into something, like the church, where I could rest in well-established acceptances, and go about the urgent business of earning a living. I could not seem to do it.

A long time later, when I was at work on *Woodrow Wilson; Life and Letters* I came upon passages in Wilson's early letters which deeply interested me because they recalled my own struggles. They were a part of his correspondence with Ellen Axson whom he was afterward to marry. Poor girl! She was then "poring over Kant" and, although a faithful daughter of the Presbyterian manse, was studying the conflicts of the old religion and the new science. Wilson did his best to reassure and comfort her. He declared that for him, so far as religion is concerned, "discussion is adjourned."

He had permanently settled everything in his own mind—and the problems of religion were never again to disturb him. His was an immovable faith in God: he rested upon it and drew strength from it. "All things work together for good," he wrote Ellen Axson, who was doubtful about it. He believed absolutely in the immortality of the soul. In a talk I had with him after the close of the Great War, the time of greatest stress in his entire life, I heard him reaffirm his unshaken faith.

I was a warm admirer of Woodrow Wilson, but this attitude of mind bewildered me. I could not doubt that this rock-like faith and the moral acceptances and certainties that went with it were great elements in his career. A "shield and buckler" he called his religion.

"Does it frighten you to know," he had written Ellen Axson, "that the city has temptations for me? It need not. I am quite sure that my religion is strong enough to make the temptations harmless."

I could feel a certain envy, even at this later date, of such unquestioning faith, such moral certainties, but how could a scholar of Wilson's character and attainments go through such a revolution in human thought as that which had been in progress during all his studious earlier years, and retain, quite undisturbed, the beliefs and the faith of his Scotch-Presbyterian forebears? Of course he had had no thorough early education as a scientist and his specialized later schooling was that of a lawyer who, generally speaking, looks backward to authority, not forward, like that, say of the doctor, to new exploration and discovery. But how could a truly thoughtful man "adjourn discussion" on one of the most important, and indeed, interesting problems then baffling the human mind?

I was tempted, I remember, to write an essay "In Defense of the (Partially) Closed Mind." What an advantage it was, say to a statesman, to have one great segment of human inquiry permanently settled. Never any more doubt or controversy! What a conservation of intellectual energy, that could be devoted, unhampered, to politics or to war. Was not the measure of the efficiency of an engine based upon the size of the hole through which its steam was discharged?

I soon found, however, that my pretty essay began to develop a *reductio ad absurdum*. If a partially closed mind was of use to a statesman, why not to a merchant who wanted to make money: why not to a robber who wanted to steal it?

And if it was advantageous to adjourn discussion on religion, why not on politics, why not in the dismal field of economic practices and institutions? Men I have known have done all three and lived. But is there not danger that the steam of the intellectual engine, reduced to a hole so small, will block up or blow out? And at what point does the closed mind produce the fanatic?

All of which illustrates the futility of indulging in little essays.

CHAPTER VII

I Establish My Own Personal Journal

I FOUND THAT even though married I was now facing a serious personal dilemma. I was perhaps getting on as a writer, since my stories and articles were being published and paid for, and I was comfortably settled in what seemed a permanent position on the editorial staff of the *Record*. Between the two I was now making a fair income, but I was still not writing about the subjects that interested me most nor about the things that lay deepest in my thoughts.

I tried sending away stories of the kind I liked best to write, but nearly all of them came back promptly. I even submitted little semi-editorial essays to the editors of the *Record*, hoping I could get a chance to discuss some of the things I was concerned about; but I found little encouragement. Most of the essays related to public affairs, social conditions, or even to politics, in which I had begun to be interested, but I soon found I was trespassing on the fields of the newspaper experts in these subjects, or else I was not conforming to the general editorial policy of the paper. I may say that this policy, in the case of the *Record*, was tolerant and highly intelligent, and my comments were probably regarded as incompetent. But I was interested, and really wanted to say something.

I thought, for example, that I was correct in my opinion that the great political struggle of 1896, and the policies of McKinley in 1897, grew in large part out of the crisis of 1893–94, of which I had been a fascinated observer. Coxey had failed in seeking relief from Congress: Debs had failed in the "direct action" of great strikes by the working class: and the problems had now been thrown, quite normally in a democratic system, into politics. Bryan was the representative of the underprivileged, with a remedy based principally upon tinkering with the national money system—which was also Coxey's chief appeal.

To the youngster in Chicago who was busy planning his Great American Novel, this new development seemed of the greatest importance and interest. It was the expected next stage. His "potato-car boy," now growing up, would naturally find his stumbling steps leading him into the campaign, cheering with the noisiest of them for the coinage of silver on the basis of sixteen to one, without really understanding what it was all about—and yet getting, somehow, a little beyond Coxey. From the background, but clearly enough, I had heard my father fulminating, as only he was capable of doing, against Bryan and all his works, incidentally making every contract he drew up payable "in gold coin of the United States of present standard of weight and fineness." I had decided that I must put my father, under another name, of course, into my Novel. He was priceless!

In one way or another I heard most of the important leaders in that famous campaign of 1896. I heard McKinley speak and did not like what he said, especially about the tariff; I heard that dull, sad old politician, Vice-President Adlai E. Stevenson, who was soon to retire to private life. I was in and out of the Chicago Wigwam during the Democratic National Convention of 1896 and I heard part of Bryan's famous "cross and crown" address which nominated him for the presidency. I decided then and there that he was the greatest popular orator I had ever heard, and I was further confirmed in this opinion by a later experience—I think on the same day—that I shall never forget.

Bryan's headquarters were at the Palmer House, then the most famous hotel in Chicago. Strangers who came to the city, especially those from the West, inevitably visited its vast barbershop, known far and wide for the silver dollars laid in as part of its marble floor, and now worn quite bare and smooth. What a sensation, to walk on dollars; like a breath of the Old West!

I had been sent around to see what happened when the hero returned to his headquarters after his triumph. When I reached his rooms, known as the "bridal suite," I found them literally crowded to the doors with excited followers of the "peerless one," bronzed farmers and ranchmen of the Middle West rubbing elbows with red-faced city politicians. They were standing on every chair in the rooms, even on the sofas and desks. The only thing they had respected was the huge bridal bed of black walnut which was overhung, high up, by an ornate canopy. Tobacco smoke, gathering since the convention began, and daily renewed, now thick and rank and foggy, permeated every part of the rooms.

Almost immediately I heard wild cheering, and Bryan and the excited group that surrounded him swept down the corridor.

"Speech, speech," roared the crowd.

Bryan looked around for a place to stand and, finding none, stepped up and into the middle of the bridal bed.

What a picture he made there in that smoke-befogged room, with the crowd all around him yelling and stamping like Comanche Indians. It was an unsteady footing; he swayed up and down and back and forth, but he was not in the least disturbed in the easy flow of his oratory. I thought I had never seen a handsomer man: young, tall, powerfully built, clear-eyed, with a mane of black hair which he occasionally thrust back with his hand. His face was still glowing with his recent triumphs.

There could not have been a speech more perfectly adapted to the moment and the occasion. It was not the grandiose oratory of the convention floor; he was here among old friends, stanch supporters out of the West, loyal men he loved. He had a beautiful, deeply modulated voice, and he talked to them with an intimacy of feeling, a fire of devoted emotion, an imparted sense of complete dedication to a sacred cause, that could not have been excelled. The essential impression he made—one that I could never forget in later years even when he was the target of the bitterest attacks—was one of deep sincerity.

When I tried afterward to write a report of that speech, I was surprised to find how little there was to get hold of. It had appreciation and devotion and inspiration, and a "clarion call to battle," as he himself expressed it, and it went straight into the hearts of his hearers—without hurting their heads. He was a great popular orator, but a very different one from Woodrow Wilson, who aroused, disturbed, and swayed people's heads, often without reaching their hearts. I have sometimes been tempted to write a chapter on the delays in human progress caused by admirable men who believed sincerely, tenaciously, powerfully, in things that were not so; but I have fortunately, thus far, refrained from yielding to this temptation.

I was, in short, being stirred during these days by many things I could not discover any way of writing about as I should have liked to write about them. Who cared for the opinions of an unknown, unimportant, young reporter?

I devised one method as naïve as it was ineffectual for getting around this difficulty. I laugh now whenever I think of it. I chose a pen-name and wrote off my feelings in letters to the editor of the *Record*, which were promptly printed in the Readers' column. When I was disgusted with D. B. Hill's campaign for governor in New York state, I exploded in one of these letters, giving President Cleveland some excellent advice. I urged him to refuse to lend his support to Hill:

"Not only would such an action be incompatible with the dignity of the (presidential) office, but it would be positively unjust and traitorous to the interests of the whole people, a great majority of whom have no confidence whatever in Mr. Hill nor his Tammany Hall backers. Grover Cleveland is right in keeping quiet. What we need in this land are statesmen great enough to rise above party when they are in office. We have a great superfluity of mere politicians."

I can't tell what satisfaction I felt in setting forth what "we need in this land" and in expressing my ripe opinion of "mere politicians."

I signed this letter "Lloyd Barrington." I also used other *noms de plume* which I have now forgotten. I never had a response, except once, from any of these letters: but they mercifully let off some of my steam. The one response I did have astonished me greatly.

"Baker," called the editor as I was going out, "here's a letter from a man named Barrington that I clipped out of the Readers' column this morning."

I was transfixed. So my secret had been discovered! I gulped and made no response.

"It really makes a good point, and it's down your alley," said the editor, "write an editorial paragraph about it."

What a relief! I remember going chuckling down the corridor. I remember also the unction with which I spoke about the "highly interesting and provocative suggestions in the letter of Mr. Lloyd Barrington." And gloated over it when I saw it printed.

But these letters were not enough: they did not begin to touch all of the things I was thinking about and reading about—and longing to write about. I had, for quite a long time, carried little memorandum books in my pocket in which I jotted down ideas for stories and articles, copied names I came across which I might use in the many novels I intended to write, or put down what I called "arresting phrases." Some of my notes concerned what I would do if *I* were the editor of a newspaper; what *I* would play up or play down; what *my* editorial policy would be. At times I thought seriously of getting out of Chicago—I did not like the city anyway—and "taking over" a good paper in a small city or town, one that I could edit exactly according to my wishes. My soaring fancies, however, always crashed upon the rock of my poverty; how own a paper when I had no money?

One day it came to me suddenly, and like a bright light, that I might establish a kind of "inner paper," which would cost me no money and in which I could write what I pleased and when I pleased. It seemed to me a beautiful idea, and I began at once to think of all the things I could put into it—things I could not at present possibly say in public—the half-thought thoughts on religion and politics and social reforms which needed clarification in my own mind, and the bits and strays and glimpses of my daily life that I might wish to use in some grand future book.

I went that very day into a stationer's store and bought a leather-covered blank book, with removable fillers, about three and a half by six inches, which would carry easily in my pocket. I put at the head of the first page: "Ray Stannard Baker. His Inner Journal," and followed it by a passage I had marked in my copy of Emerson's essay on "Spiritual Laws":

"He that writes to himself writes to an eternal public. That statement only is fit to be made public which you have come at in attempting to satisfy your own curiosity."

I began at once to put into this little journal all sorts of gatherings of the day, odd bits of overheard dialogue; descriptions of interesting faces, landscapes, buildings—anything and everything that impressed me. Often I tried to make sketches to go with what I wrote but this proved a complete failure since I had no gift in that art. One day I was out on an assignment with a raw young fellow who had come in as a member of our art department. He told me that he had never taken any lessons and was wholly self taught. I never knew his equal as a sketcher. He carried little packets of drawing paper in his pocket and wherever we went, on streetcars, or on foot, even in a theater or at a baseball game, he was forever sketching—and tearing up the sketches, or most of them, soon after they were made. If he ran out of paper he drew on his frayed cuffs. It was amazing how much life he could capture in a few swift lines.

It struck me that what I was doing was also sketching, literary sketching: and the more I thought of the idea the better I liked it. Why shouldn't a writer make a practice of sketching, just as an artist did, not for publication, but to train his eye, and his brain, and his hand? I redoubled my sketching and began following my friend's example of tearing up all I wrote.

I have continued this agreeable and useful practice ever since, nearly fifty years, and still believe it to be the best possible discipline for the writer. Looking back, I can say honestly that it was the most fruitful discovery in literary method I ever made. The Journal proved practically valuable as a storehouse of literary material, for after a few years I used larger books (300 pages, 7 x 9 inches) and ceased to destroy my "sketches." The total number of books is now about seventy. The later ones run from forty thousand to forty-five thousand words each; the earlier were smaller. I should not be surprised if the total number of words was around two millions. These books were not primarily diaries, but notebooks, and they contained, in addition to what I wrote, much copied material, and scraps out of books, magazines and newspapers. They were, in short, a veritable rag-bag of literary odds and ends, experiences in which I have been momentarily interested or which I thought might sometime be usable in books I planned to write—those innumerable books that flamed for a moment in my imagination only to die down and be forgotten.

I am appalled when I think of the sheer bulk of this self-disclosure. Everything I am I have here set down. *So much I wish were different!*

But if I had tried to make myself out something other or better or wiser than I really am, I should have lost the sense of freedom, relief, assuagement, that has come, increasingly with the years, in setting down spontaneously exactly what I saw, heard, thought, felt, at the moment when the impression was sharpest. I have never written by habit—the vice of the diarist—but only when I needed, or longed, to write. Nothing in my life, nothing whatever, has given me such continuous requital, such a sense of living more deeply and understandingly into the heart of things. Here I have written away my sorrows by the complete expression of them, as one to his nearest friend: here I multiply my joys by describing them; here I grope in my thinking toward a fuller understanding—setting down, without the fear of an immediately critical audience, all my doubts, my roving speculation, my flashes of mystical penetration—everything.

What if the thoughts are immature and the observations often trifling? Who cares? They will meet no eyes but my own. I am not seeking to convince anyone else that I am greater, or different, or more amusing, or more thoughtful, than I am: I am trying, since I am the only person I have to deal with when I write, to *realize* myself—just as I stand in this world, with all my qualities, limitations, virtues, interests.

Just to open any one of these books sends my mind back upon the events of the day or week or the month so that I re-live and re-enjoy them, thus, as it were, doubling the length of my life, extracting twice as much from my days as most men do. If events were happy how pleasant the revival; if sad or evil or tragic, how rich the consideration of the strange fate that sways one's life. How rewarding are the comparisons of one's ills with the common ills of men, the brooding upon the briefness of existence—the little day, the short hour, the long rest. And thus, through the consideration of *this* day, I think of future days, wherein it will be good to live: where there will be many interesting adventures, contacts with friends, and fine music and bracing talk—and good things to see and smell and *eat*. No, I do not want to put even the ill away, but to write it clear, set it in time—my time—and in space—my space—so that it takes on finally a kind of majesty and beauty, however much at the moment it may have hurt. I am continually surprised how it is that one can be acutely sensible to the imperfections, limitations and tragedies of life and yet enjoy it all so greedily, and desire not to put it away and forget it, but to reflect upon it and write about it. For this is a strange matter: it is possible afterward to enjoy a sorrow, delight in a sadness, become tranquil in considering a tragedy, and out of failure and loss rise to new heights of aspiration, bracing one's life for the strong events of a new day.

Sometimes I look ruefully at all the writing in these many books, so much for my own pleasure and my own discipline, with no return from any audience: no material income. I might have been making some money! I suppose it somewhat resembles the lonely practice, day after day, of the musician. I keep the fingers of my spirit in training to express the life of my soul. I play for myself. It remains the greatest comfort and pleasure of my life. And it all grew out of my frustrated gropings back there in 1897.

In the beginning I imagined that my idea of an "inner journal" was original with me; at least I knew personally of no writers who used just such a device. But I was soon to find that the "commonplace book," the "intimate diary" has been known and used by many of the best and noblest of writers, especially the poets and the essayists—and by not a few who were not so noble. The journals of our own Emerson, Thoreau, and Walt Whitman are all but as fascinating to read as their regimented books and poems. For as Epictetus says, "A lute player when he is singing for himself has no anxiety." It is this unedited freedom, this stark vision of the man's soul, that sends us eagerly to the note-makers and the diarists.

My own notebooks down through the years have proved invaluably useful to me. Most of the books which I have written under the name of David Grayson were based upon suggestions and notes and even whole chapters from these "sketch-books": and one of them —*The Countryman's Year*—was made up wholly from extracts selected from my notes. In writing this autobiography I am constantly being informed and corrected by entries I made long ago when the incidents or the events were fresh in my mind.

CHAPTER VIII

Making Money—Though an Author

WHILE I HAD DISCOVERED an ingenious method of letting off my superfluous steam in letters to the editor of the *Record*, or in writing voluminously in my "Inner Journal," in which I found keen enjoyment, there was still such a thing in the world as the necessity of earning a living, especially now that I had a wife. In short, I had to earn more money, and keep on earning it. The Great American Novel in which all my hopes had been centered, could not be finished, probably, for a year or so—and where could I find a publisher for such a book, and how make any money out of it? The stories and verses I had been trying were unlike anything I saw published in magazines or newspapers and did not satisfy even me. I liked well to experiment with them, and I had faith that I really had something to say, but how could I sell them? I tried a few on the magazine publishers and they came back with startling promptness, with printed rejection slips.

One day a group of us in the office had a lively discussion as to the most popular family magazine in the country. The one man who had the reputation of having "broken into the magazines" argued stoutly that it was the *Youth's Companion.*

"I'll wager," he declared, "that in three out of every four homes, say in Iowa, you will find the *Youth's Companion.* And the whole family reads it."

Another man present had a friend who had received fifty dollars for a single story accepted by the *Youth's Companion.*

Fifty dollars for a story! I sat down that very evening and wrote to the editor of the *Youth's Companion.* I had in reply the first really friendly letter I had ever received from an editor. After many slings and arrows of outrageous rejection slips it was balm to a bruised spirit. It was written in long-hand and signed, anonymously, "The

Corresponding Editor"; for the *Youth's Companion* was as old-fashioned as a quill pen. "The Corresponding Editor" enclosed a two-page printed leaflet entitled "The Youth's Companion Story," which is or should be a monument or a classic in the annals of the publishing business. All magazines, if they are successful, arrive at a formula, a kind of chart of prosperity, based on the reports of the subscription manager, after he has looked over the latest returns from the advertisers. This is the chart for "sure-fire success," which is to be sedulously followed. Don't experiment. Don't originate: repeat! But few magazines I think ever set down their formula so explicitly in black and white as the *Youth's Companion* in the leaflet I have before me as I write. Proof that it was based on a keen sense of what the average reading American in the latter part of the nineteenth century wanted and would pay for needs only the evidence of the really remarkable business success, over a long period of time, of the *Companion*. Millions of Americans grew up on the stories and anecdotes in this, their favorite weekly journal.

This leaflet and a supplement I received later left the author in no doubt whatever as to what he was expected to write.

"Detective stories cannot be taken. Crime, if used at all, should be sedulously kept in the background and all its unpleasant or unwholesome details carefully omitted. The moral tone of the stories must be irreproachable.

"We do not want anecdote or reminiscence, but a real story with a well devised plot, and at least one strong incident.

"Stories must not fail to entertain from beginning to end. They may portray character or describe adventure. They may be pathetic or humorous. But they must always have incident, movement, and dramatic effectiveness.

" 'The Companion' seeks to be acceptable to the widest possible audience. Therefore it excludes both theological and political stories, as well as all matter which might tend to revive sectional feeling between North and South, or to arouse bitterness between rich and poor.

"In tales of adventure authors should bear in mind that a plot may be of interest, absorbing interest, without having a trace of sensationalism or a suggestion of melodrama. Neither bloodshed nor evil passions should be made the most prominent features. In stories of pathos we beg our contributors to turn their art toward brightened endings. 'The Companion' wishes to convey cheer; final impressions of death or calamity are not desired."

I recall my snort of exasperation after my first reading of these specifications.

"What is a man to write about anyway? No politics, no religion, no labor problems, no bloodshed, no love stories—and nothing but happy endings. What they really want is a fiddler who is willing to play on one string."

I had at the time, I think, somewhat glorified ideas of what the real objective of the author should be.

"Look in thy heart and write."

"A new picture," as Emerson said, "composed of the author's eminent experiences."

"Give me," as Whitman chanted, "to sing of the Great Idea."

I laid the leaflet aside for several months and the grocery bills, and the rent, and the life insurance payments, continued their inexorable weekly and monthly parades. One day I was surprised to receive another letter from the Corresponding Editor suggesting that I might like to consider writing a story dealing with newspaper life. This was the first time, I think, that I had been "pursued" by an editor. "Pursued" was a word used by my friend who had "broken into the magazines." This request was also accompanied by a sheet of specifications, among them:

"Although the adventurous side of the profession should be mainly drawn on for material, adventures are not exclusively desired, and any story of newspaper life will be gladly considered.

"An ethical purpose is desirable, but the moral must be revealed by the story itself, not by any comment of the writer."

I was, of course, genuinely interested in newspaper work and was beginning to think I really knew something about it. So I cleared off the dining-room table on Sunday morning and wrote the kind of story I thought the *Companion* might like—I think at one sitting—and sent it down to Boston. The responses I received made a great impression on me. They were really courteous; they made me feel that I was somebody!

MY DEAR SIR,

The manuscript of your "newspaperman's story" reached me safe to-day. Thank you for submitting it. I will let you know the decision as soon as possible.

Cordially yours,

THE CORRESPONDING EDITOR.

In those days many editors kept a writer's manuscript for weeks —or months. I had a decision from the *Companion* in ten days:

MY DEAR SIR,

I take pleasure in letting you know slightly in advance of the regular routine, that your story of newspaper life, "Pippins," is to be retained by the *Companion*. In the ordinary course a cheque in payment should reach you early next week.

With cordial thanks for sending in so good a story, I am, my dear sir, very truly yours,

THE CORRESPONDING EDITOR.

How I loved that word "cheque"!

At that time an author sometimes waited months or years for his payment; but the very next day I received this letter:

We enclose the cheque of Perry Mason & Co., for fifty dollars, in payment for your story entitled: *Pippins*.

I would not relate, except in strict confidence, what I did with that "cheque." After looking at it for some time, I kissed it!

I was off. I could make nearly as much in one forenoon at story writing, and that with keen pleasure, as I could in two weeks of hard work at the office. Why shouldn't I try it?

I did try it—I wrote thrilling adventure stories about firemen and locomotive engineers and lumbermen and river drivers I had known when I was a boy in the north woods. Nearly all of them were promptly accepted. It was a curious thing to me that, once I was familiar with the *Companion* formula, I felt quite free in it, and was surprised to see what lively and interesting stories could be turned out. I came to agree with one of the comments in the *Companion's* leaflet:

"Even very able writers err in treating as a trivial problem the creation of a rounded story within a 3000 word limit."

This success whetted my ambition. I began to be eager for other dragons to slay. I even ventured to send an article to *McClure's*, then the sensation of the publishing world. I had been fascinated by an article in it on Abraham Lincoln by Ida M. Tarbell and wrote the editor that an uncle of mine, Lieut. L. B. Baker of Michigan, had been in command of the party that pursued and captured J. Wilkes Booth. My uncle, I said, had interesting reminiscences of his experiences, and a number of documents and pictures. I asked if *McClure's* would like to see the account as given by Lieut. Baker.

They would, promptly. I went at it immediately and thoroughly, but not without much trepidation. In a surprisingly brief time after I sent the manuscript I had a letter from Miss Tarbell herself. Was it believable? I did not know it at the time, but it was the beginning of a life-long friendship. "You have produced a very interesting paper," she wrote, and followed it up in a later letter with the glad news that "Mr. McClure was very much pleased" and would use the article in the May number (1897). "A check will be sent you in due time."

I considered this a perfect story, with a happy ending.

I hit immediately while the iron was hot with suggestions for stories of the secret service of the United States during the Civil War. My father's cousin, General Lafayette C. Baker, had been chief of that service and my father, in the earlier years of the war, had been attached to it. I have already spoken of the many stories I heard my father tell during my boyhood there on the frontier. I thought then, and I think still, that he was the best story-teller I have ever heard, and the stories themselves unsurpassed for vigor, suspense, and complete reality.

After I had written quite a list of short stories for the *Youth's Companion*, the Corresponding Editor suggested serials. When his letter came I was about to go home to Michigan with my wife and little daughter for the regular two weeks summer vacation. Instead, I remained in Chicago, quite alone in our apartment. I got up early every morning, drank a cup of coffee, and sat down to the littered dining table. It was warm summer weather and I worked in my shirt sleeves in the half-darkened room. I went nowhere and saw no one: I did not even answer the doorbell. I just wrote. It was a story of the north woods, all the background and characters of which I knew well. I remember few experiences as a writer that have given me a greater abandonment of delight. Everything came easily and naturally: incidents, bits of description, dialogue that I did not know were there leaped into my mind—just when I needed them, and just where they belonged. In one week I had completed a five-part serial, copied it out on the typewriter, and mailed it to Boston. I spent the second week of my vacation in Michigan, and not long after I returned I received a "cheque" for $250.

A little later I was "pursued" by the editor for a Memorial Day story. I remembered an incident from one of my father's wonderful narratives, told when I was a boy. I expanded it into a story. When it was completed and read aloud to my wife we both liked it so well that instead of sending it to the Corresponding Editor I packed it off to the editors of *McClure's Magazine*, with whom I was beginning now to be acquainted by correspondence. To my astonishment, it was immediately accepted and I had a check for $70: more than the *Companion* had ever paid me for a single contribution. But I straightway began to be sorry for the good and friendly Corresponding Editor whom I would thus disappoint. So I sat down and wrote another Memorial Day story for him. This also was promptly accepted: and that year I celebrated Memorial Day with stories in two magazines.

As I have intimated, I had grown fond of the anonymous Corresponding Editor who wrote me such delightful letters. I used to try to imagine what he looked like. I thought of him finally as a distinguished old gentleman with a broad beard parted down the middle like James Russell Lowell, possibly balancing a pair of glasses between his finger and thumb. When I first went to Boston I had the disillusionment of my life. The Corresponding Editor was not one man, but several, and the one with whom I had corresponded most energetically was a fresh-faced youth two years younger than I, named Ellery Sedgwick, who afterward became owner and editor of the *Atlantic Monthly*, and a good friend of mine.

The stories I wrote, though they were limited in their scope, were intensely interesting to me. Several of them dealt with the adventurous life of railroad men. I obtained, with considerable difficulty, permission from the Burlington Railroad Company, to ride with the engineer in the cab of the locomotive of their famous night express, the Burlington Fast Mail. I don't think either the engineer or the fireman at first much liked my presence, but we were soon on the best of terms. What an experience it was! All night long plunging through the darkness, a thin rain slashing at the cab windows, the headlight feeling out the mysterious depths ahead of us, glistening on the rails, leaping here at a suspicious bit of forest, there outlining sharply for a second or two a sleeping farmhouse, then, as the great train slowed down, lighting the crowded way through the freight-sheds and sidings of some indistinct little town. From time to time the cab glowed with the light of the firebox and I could see the dark fireman swinging forward and backward as he threw in the coal. The engineer, with his elbow on the window seat and his left hand on the throttle, drove the great train all night long through the raining darkness of Illinois. I remember getting off at the little stations, stopping for a cup of coffee, listening to the good rich railroad jargon when the conductor came up with his little lantern, or the brakeman ran ahead to turn a switch. I spent all of Sunday with Bullard, the engineer, and his friends in Burlington—good and interesting men, all of them. What stories they told me and how fascinated I was in the way they lived and how they looked at life. I returned to Chicago Monday morning in time to go to work in my office. Out of that experience came a number of good stories, one of them called, "How Potts Saved the Night Express."

When this story was published in the *Youth's Companion,* I received a number of interesting letters about it, including a delightful one from the daughter of Harris the fireman, which pleased me very much. And afterward, to my surprise, I had requests from the publishers of several college and school text books, and one or two anthologies of short stories, asking permission to publish it. As an example of the occasional unlooked-for recompenses of the author, I received a great deal more for the privilege of these reprintings than the *Youth's Companion* originally paid me. And what amusement I afterward had, with this, as with other stories and essays reprinted in school texts, in the questions and comments that the eagerly educative editors posed for the students who read the stories:

"What words and phrases did you notice that contributed especially to your sense of danger?"

"At what points in the story did you feel the greatest suspense?"

"On the basis of what you have learned in this story, make a list of the qualities which you think a railroad engineer should possess."

And the requests for diagrams showing "the position of the freight and the express in relation to each other at the time Potts discovered the danger," and so on and so on—when I had written off the story without a thought of using any particular "words of sound, words of feeling," or with any "devices" for producing suspense, or a sense of danger.

But alas, and alack, the sheen of this writing honeymoon, as of all honeymoons, was destined soon to be dimmed. One day it occurred to me that the *Youth's Companion* had purchased a considerable number of my stories and had not published more than one or two, and I wondered if I were overdoing my welcome. So I stopped writing stories for the Corresponding Editor and began trying to see what I could do in the same field of swift adventure for *McClure's Magazine*. Not long afterward I had a letter from the gentleman in Boston "with the double beard and the eye glasses" asking why I wasn't submitting any more manuscripts. I wrote immediately telling him naïvely what my reason was. I shall never forget the amusing reply I had. It ran something to this effect:

"Bless your soul, my dear fellow, we can take a story a week from you as long as you are willing to write them and we continue to like them."

He then went on to tell me of the bright particular star in the firmament of the *Youth's Companion*. This was C. A. Stevens, who had been writing stories for I forget how many years, some being published under his own name and others under pen-names.

This letter had the strangest effect upon me. What a life—to write stories within the formula of the *Youth's Companion* during all my remaining years! My heart beat one, and struck bottom: then and there I resolved never to write another story for the *Youth's Companion*. Such a resolution was, of course, foolish, and I did not wholly live up to it, but it expressed something deep in me that I did not then fully understand. It seemed to me at that moment as though my whole plan of life, so far as I had one, had gone awry.

CHAPTER IX

I Enter a New World: New York and the Magazines

LOOKING BACK ALONG the accumulating years I can recall few incidents that gave me a warmer glow of exaltation than the letter I received on March 12, 1897, from S. S. McClure, the editor of *McClure's Magazine*. I had been somewhat low in my mind, wondering whether, now that I was married, I could make a living from my pen, wondering indeed whether I was getting anywhere at all as a writer. And there, on that morning, in my box in the editorial office of the *Record* was Mr. McClure's letter.

I had been a devoted admirer of *McClure's Magazine* from the beginning, in June, 1893. I had bought every number as it appeared and read every line in it. All through my boyhood on the frontier my father had taken the old *Scribner's Monthly* (afterward *The Century*), and *Harper's Magazine* with the little boys blowing bubbles on the cover, and Littell's *Living Age* (of which I recall in after years the innumerable bound volumes on his bookshelves), the *Christian Union*, and *St. Nicholas* for the children. I had read them all with keen interest. I shall never forget George Kennan's articles on Siberia or Frank Cushing's explorations among the Zuni Indians.

But *McClure's* was something new and different. The *McClure* articles were not merely about people, aloof and critical objectivity, but the people seemed to be there in person, alive and talking. That very first number contained a series of pictures of various celebrities taken at different ages from boyhood up; of William Dean Howells with a dozen or more portraits, beginning at the age of eighteen. These were called "human documents" and they truly gave the reader more of the life of the subject than many pages of text could have done. Equally interesting were the "real conversations" between famous men—like that between Howells and Professor Boyesen, in which we heard from their own mouths what they were thinking and feeling. At that time I thought it a great literary discovery: later I was not so sure.

The new method of dealing with the latest discoveries of science was even more fascinating to me. It gave the reader himself the sense of exploration in an undiscovered country which the editors called "The Edge of the Future." It was the very place where I, for one, wanted to travel. In this first number I found an article, richly illustrated, on evolution. It was called "Where Man Got His Ears," and was written, wonder of wonders, by Henry Drummond, whose *Natural Law in the Spiritual World* I had read some years earlier with such interest. Then there was an article on "Europe at the Present Moment," by deBlowitz of the London *Times*, probably the most famous living newspaper correspondent. His portrait, with gorgeous side-whiskers and a signature almost as unintelligible and much larger and more sprawling than that of Horace Greeley, accompanied the article.

This does not begin to be all I found in that first number; stories by Joel Chandler Harris, author of "Uncle Remus," and Gilbert Parker and Mrs. Robert Louis Stevenson, and graphic accounts of two of the most famous of men living at that time, the first, "A Day with Gladstone, from the Morning at Hawarden to the Evening at the House of Commons," by H. W. Massingham, and the other of Count de Lesseps, the builder of the Suez Canal, by R. H. Sherard, both wonderfully well illustrated.

In short, the new *McClure's* was something fresh and strong and living in a stodgy literary world. The numbers that followed—I am astonished in looking them over these long years afterward—contained about the best in the entire field of English writing during that decade: Kipling's *Captains Courageous* and *Stalky* and many short stories and poems. Stevenson's *Ebb Tide*, Anthony Hope's *Rupert of Hentzau,* and many stories by Conan Doyle, Stephen Crane, Hamlin Garland, Howells, Bret Harte, Marion Crawford and others. And there were Ida M. Tarbell's *Lincoln* which became a legendary magazine success, and the *Reminiscences* of Charles A. Dana, one of the most famous living editors, and General Miles' *Memoirs*—and many other unusual and interesting features.

To say that I was awed at having a letter from the founder and editor of such a magazine was to put it mildly—a man who, presumably, knew Kipling personally, and Howells, and Conan Doyle and all the others.

"I like your scheme and suggestions very much indeed," he wrote referring to the stories I wanted to write on the Secret Service.

"Would it be possible for you to come on to New York to see us? It would, I think, facilitate matters if you could see us and also Miss Tarbell, and perhaps we could together plan out a series of articles."

If a dream ever came true, this was it! A few days later I had a letter from John S. Phillips, who was Mr. McClure's associate, enclosing a "pass" on the New York Central Railroad for my trip. It took my breath away. So this was the magical way they did things in New York.

I had never been in New York in my life. I was so eager to see what the East was like that, as soon as it began to be daylight, I propped up my head on the pillows in the sleeping car to take it all in.

"The trip down the Mohawk Valley and along the Hudson River was charming," I wrote to my father. "It is almost a continuous town from Utica to New York City. The places have the dignity of age and an air of comfortable contentment, with a trace of dilapidation, of which there is no example in the West. The farms are small, scrawny, cobbly yards with endless stone fences. Some of them are tipped up on one side at such an angle that I should think the cattle, if any are raised, would have to be provided with tar heels. The barns are all brick, red and big, and the houses are weather-gray and small. Why don't some of the farmers move out to Polk county where a plow will strike into the ground without rasping on a rock?"

I found when I arrived that Mr. McClure had suddenly dashed off to Europe, as was his custom, but I had long and delightful talks with John Phillips and August Jaccaci, the art editor, and Ida Tarbell and others of the staff. I went out with them to the jolly table at the old Ashland House where they lunched together, a spot that still glimmers bright in my memory. It all seemed like a marvelous new world, with a quality of enthusiasm and intellectual interest I had never before encountered. Even with S. S. McClure absent, I suppose I was in the most stimulating, yes intoxicating, editorial atmosphere then existent in America—or anywhere else. The editors suggested that I give up my place in Chicago and devote my entire time to the writing of stories and articles. They even outlined a wonderful book which they declared they could make out of my secret service material—I began using the word "material" from that hour! —and they would publish it in the new book department they were then building up, and pay me a ten per cent royalty.

I went back to the quiet little city of Chicago with my head swimming, resolved to resign immediately from the *Record* and embark in my own frail craft on the stormy literary seas of New York. When I talked the whole matter over with my two best and most sensible friends, my wife and my father, I calmed down. Even if my father's favorite motto had been, "When in doubt, charge!" he was a sound and cool-headed adviser. "Don't go off half-cocked," said the old soldier. "Wait until you see the whites of their eyes." And my wife reminded me that we were expecting our first baby that spring.

So I kept my dependable place with the *Record* and began writing harder than ever—my father's secret service adventures and other stories for *McClure's,* thrilling tales of adventure for the *Youth's Companion,* and short articles for *The Outlook, Harper's Weekly* and other magazines.

I never worked harder, I think, in my life: and while I was enjoying my work, the old problem of earning enough really to live on remained unsolved.

After looking forward for months—yes, years—to the beatitude of matrimony I was considerably astonished to discover, in my innocence, that nothing much had been changed. It had only grown more so. I had felt that if only I could earn enough money to get married all things afterward would somehow work out easily and happily. And there, in reality, month after month, marched the familiar army of expenses: for rent, for clothing, for day-by-day living, now doubled or even trebled. Everything for two rather than one—and soon there were three.

I remember the shock of wonder and surprise I had when my wife and I went down to Siegel and Cooper's store to buy a baby-carriage, and calculated how many thousands of words I would have to write in order to pay for it. Our baby herself, who was blue-eyed and fat and happy—altogether quite satisfactory—had cost me, at the lowest calculation, about seventy thousand words, a small volume like Emerson's essays. All the various unnamable fixings that went with a baby I put down at ten thousand words, the equivalent of two or three substantial short stories. After a hard day's work at the office, or an even harder evening, when I sat at the cleared corner of the dining table in our apartment to write a new story, I used to count up my total wordage for the day and, for my own amusement and the edification of my wife who sat nearby nursing the new baby, I made estimates of what these words might buy—if we chose to be recklessly extravagant:

> One porterhouse steak.
> One year's subscription to *The Century Magazine.*
> A trip by boat to Grand Haven, Michigan.

And so on and so on.

My wife, I soon discovered, had been endowed with the precious gift of sales resistance.

"But we don't need a trip to Grand Haven or a porterhouse steak. Have you got enough words for a small graniteware frying pan, and a dozen kitchen towels?"

Just ahead we saw indistinctly looming (fate blessedly dims our eyes, bemuses us, at that time of life) the problems of more room to live in, schools for—yes, for the children—more books and magazines, something of music and of art, something more of interesting social life. My trip to New York and the encouragement I received had served not to satisfy any of these longings, only to stimulate them. It had given me new ambitions as well as new hopes.

During all that busy year I kept up a steady and growingly intimate correspondence with the *McClure* people:

"We like the new Secret Service story very much; we will be glad to use it and have put it in hand for illustration. You make a good suggestion about having an introductory paragraph. Won't you write that out for us."

"The fire story, as I told you, we all like very much indeed. We are putting it into the March number. Send us more of those stories of firemen."

In January, 1898, there were again invitations from Mr. McClure and Mr. Phillips to join their staff, and in February I left Chicago, with not a few regrets, to enter the new world. My father approved and my wife was so completely satisfied with the new member of our family that she was prepared to be contented anywhere, east or west, north or south. For she said of the little girl, whose name was Alice:

"If I had to select a baby, I'd get one exactly like this."

CHAPTER X

I Discover the Great American Renascence

DID THE GREAT ONES of the Elizabethan period, I wonder, know that they were living in an era that historians of the future would call a renascence? Did Shakespeare realize it, or Bacon, or Milton? Did Raleigh the explorer, or Harvey the scientist? Did Petrarch and Dante, Leonardo and Michelangelo, know that they were a part of the greatness that came to be called the Italian renascence? Or were they all, breathing the keen air of a new world, so busy living, creating, enjoying, suffering, fighting, that they knew only that life was good and hard and great, and every moment rich in adventure, exploration, discovery?

Looking back, in later years, I have thought of the period in America, including the last few years of the nineteenth century and the early years of the twentieth, as the American Renascence, even the Great American Renascence.

Was there a world outside of America? If there was, I knew next to nothing at all about it—as a reality. I had indeed read and deeply enjoyed a good many books of exploration and discovery, but I read them as I would Marco Polo romances. I knew something of European history—the old tyranny of kings, the absurdity of aristocracy, the futility of feudal wars—out of which America, the wonderful, had stepped proudly into the enlightenment of the Bill of Rights and the Declaration of Independence. I was a true geocentric American.

I had, however, made the valuable discovery—I did not know at the time how valuable it was—that we were not absolutely perfect. Had I not lived in Chicago? Had I not known of the political corruption there, and the economic greed, and the social heedlessness? Had I not marched with Coxey's army, and seen the rioting and the bloodshed of the Debs rebellion? But were these not, after all, mere blemishes on the rugged countenance of America, easily to be removed when we had time to turn from the enormous labor of taming a continent?

When I went to New York to join the staff of *McClure's Magazine* in the spring of 1898, I found myself, suddenly and joyously, in this new world, full of strange and wonderful new things, and I at the heart of it, especially commissioned to look at it, hear about it, and above all, to write about it.

Our American attitude toward world affairs, for example, was just then undergoing all but revolutionary changes. Only a few days before I arrived in New York, our garment of secure and aloof provincialism was rudely torn to shreds by the crisis of the war with Spain. The *Maine* was blown up in Havana harbor on February 15, 1898; every newspaper I saw during my first weeks in the East blazed with the news of it. Dewey won the battle of Manila on May 1 and in July the Americans, with Roosevelt and Wood leading their hurrahing cowboys, had entered Santiago. In August the war was won, and America had acquired an empire.

We had determined that spring of 1898—the sheer bumptiousness of us!—to publish the greatest special edition of a monthly magazine ever made, and I can remember the thrill I had—I was temporarily absent from New York—when I received a telegram from one of my associates:

"Making war number. Good subjects for you. Come quickly. Wire."

Theodore Roosevelt was the outstanding hero of the hour, and I went out to greet him on his return from Cuba with his weary troopers and their sunburned horses. I accompanied him from his home at Oyster Bay to Montauk Point where the Rough Riders were camped; I had long talks with him confirming the admiration I already felt, and I wrote one of the earliest biographical articles about him, published in November, 1898. I was to write about him many times afterward, not always so uncritically. Later I visited General Wood at Santiago and wrote of his life, and his remarkable service in the reconstruction of Cuba; I talked with Admiral Dewey, and sat with Admiral Sampson on his battleship while he told of the great battle in which Cervera's fleet was utterly destroyed. When I went to Cuba I saw the torn and battered hulks of the Spanish warships lying beached near the port of Santiago. My article on Admiral Sampson was published in *McClure's* in September, 1899, and the one on General Wood in February, 1900.

If I am to judge by my own profound reactions to these stirring events, America as a nation began at that time to awaken suddenly to a sense of a swiftly expanding world in which, whether we liked it or not, we should have to play our part.

Everywhere there were signs, if one had eyes to see them, of the growing pains of a new age, which might powerfully affect the destinies of America. In 1894, there had been the Chinese-Japanese War; in 1896, the Ethiopians trounced the Italians—I recall my fascinated reading of all the details—and in 1897, came the Greco-Turkish War. In 1898, we fought our own war with Spain and in 1899, Americans were almost as much interested in the Boer War in South Africa as in our own war in the Philippines, which ended that year with the capture of the Filipino leader Aguinaldo. And finally in the last year of the century we were deeply concerned with the Boxer insurrection in China in which our own soldiers played a part. In short, there was a widespread awakening in America to new world interests and responsibilities.

But there was another awakening, equally alluring, to stimulate the imagination of a responsive editorial office. This also concerned a new world, then just opening to the discoverer and the explorer—I mean the world of science and invention. I wonder if there was ever another brief period in history when there was such an outpouring of marvelous new inventions and scientific wonders. In my boyhood—not so long ago either—the world I lived in knew nothing of most of the world-shaking inventions that have now become unexciting commonplaces. I remember going to a much-advertised "Electrical Lecture," in the district school house at St. Croix Falls, in Wisconsin, where I grew up, to see a contraption of batteries set up, one in the girls' cloak room, the other at the most distant corner of the schoolroom (probably sixty feet away) with wires connecting them, over which we could actually *talk*—even with the door closed. What a miracle! It was our earliest acquaintance with the telephone.

But the real deluge of wonders did not come until later. Edison was busy working at Menlo Park—the phonograph, the incandescent lamp, the moving picture, and scores of other wonders. Swedish

André had invented a new kind of balloon which he said could fly to the North Pole. He had the courage of his convictions and perished in putting his invention to the test (1897). We at *McClure's* were intensely interested in *that* and in March, 1898, only a few weeks after my arrival in New York, published an article about it called "Where is André?" Not long afterward we had the astonishing news of the discovery of radium by Professor Curie and began at once to plan an article about it. We had already published two articles about another new scientific wonder, the discovery by Professor Roentgen, of X-rays. In some ways this seemed the most astonishing of all the recent discoveries and we made much of photographic illustrations taken *through* animals and even human beings.

We had two of the earliest comprehensive articles about the automobile, which was then called the "horseless carriage." Few people believed that it was anything but a pleasure toy. One of my own early articles (published in *McClure's* July, 1899) dealt with "The Automobile in Common Use." I remember going over to New Jersey to talk with Thomas A. Edison about it and of taking a ride in one of the strangest looking vehicles—half old-fashioned buggy and half new-fangled mechanical monstrosity—with which Edison was then experimenting. I started my article with a flourish:

"Five years ago there were not thirty self-propelled carriages in practical use in all the world. A year ago there were not thirty in America. And yet between the first of January and the first of May, 1899, companies with the enormous aggregate capitalization of more than $388,000,000 have been organized in New York, Boston, Chicago, and Philadelphia for the sole purpose of manufacturing and operating these new vehicles."

I was a fascinated spectator at the finish of what was then regarded as a stupendous achievement—"a trip," as I wrote, "of 720 miles, from Cleveland to New York, over all kinds of country roads." And I could remark, as a contrast, that "less than four years ago—in November, 1895—only two cars out of six finished a 53½-mile endurance test at Chicago and the winning car averaged only 5¼ miles an hour!"

In this early article I enumerated many of the advantages of the wonderful new invention:

"It is lighter than the present means of conveyance when the weight of the horse or horses is counted in with the carriage.

"It cannot possibly explode.

"It will climb all ordinary hills, and on the level it will give all speeds from two miles an hour up to twenty or more."

We were also intensely interested in the earliest efforts to conquer the air. *McClure's* began as far back as 1894 with an article on the "Maxim Airship," which was built on the principle of the kite. This was followed by the earliest thorough expositions of other experiments: "The Flying Man," an account of Lilienthal's "wings" patterned after those of a bird, and an article on O. Chanute's further developments in the art of gliding. We published "The First Flight of Count Zeppelin," in November, 1900; and in September, 1901, I remember, we printed an article by one of the most distinguished scientists of Harvard University, Professor Simon Newcomb, called "Is the Airship Coming?" If ever a cautious and doubtful scientist threw cold water on the hopeful experiments in a new art, Simon Newcomb did it in this article. He admitted grudgingly that while "the problem of a dirigible balloon might be within the power of inventive genius, we could not hope that it would become a vehicle for carrying passengers and freight under ordinary conditions." He could see no future at all for the airplane.

The other day while writing these lines I saw in the newspapers the news of a celebration of the birthday of Orville Wright, the pioneer of flight in America. I discovered that he was one year younger than I am! What a world—when such mighty developments can be crowded into one man's life.

There was another field of the awakening which seemed to me of more immediate importance, as far as America was concerned, than it did to Mr. McClure and Mr. Phillips. It was the sudden and widespread economic revival which swept across the country after the Spanish war in 1899 and 1900.

I had become greatly interested in the economic conditions in the country and the social problems that grew out of the panic of 1893. I had been through the mill myself as one of the half-starved unemployed. I had been deeply interested in various reform movements, especially in the Single Taxers, and I had felt that the uprising of the West led by W. J. Bryan was correct enough in its diagnosis, however inadequate it might be in its remedies. I have often referred to the Great American Novel, in which I intended to present all these alarming conditions and problems, and to which, after 1894, I had devoted a great deal of thought and labor. In short, I had built up quite a structure, in my own mind, upon that foundation of poverty and social unrest. I was prepared, or thought I was, to write a devastating book!

But in 1899, I found the whole edifice of my vision and my ambition crumbling around me, for the country suddenly ceased being poverty-stricken and became superlatively prosperous. It had entered an era of "Unparalleled Prosperity," as I called it a little later. All the mills and factories had started up, the vast numbers of the unemployed had swiftly disappeared, men were working at higher wages than ever before in America. The banks were full of money, foreign commerce was increasing.

I am amused now, remembering how all this development startled and baffled me. I even resented it! But there it was, a reality, a fact, and the more I looked at it the more significant it seemed and the more I wanted to study it carefully, not only to enlighten the public, but to clarify my own mind. I spent all my spare time for many months digging into the statistics, reading *The Manufacturers' Record, The Iron Age, The Tradesman, The Engineering and Mining Journal, The Northwestern Miller, The National Provisioner, Bradstreet's, Dun's Review,* the annual "Financial Review" of *The New York Times, The Railway Gazette, The Marine Review,* and others. I interviewed many of the foremost business men in the country. I made two trips into the West to study the conditions at first hand.

My own editors at *McClure's* were not as excited as I was, though they published two articles, one in December, 1899, the other in May, 1900, which were called "The Movement of Wheat" and "The New Prosperity." I wrote a number of other articles which I was glad to have printed in the then largely circulated *Harper's Weekly* and in Albert Shaw's *Review of Reviews*. I began one of my articles with a leaf directly out of the book of my own experience in the New West:

"A witty Western writer, summing up the marvels of growth, expansion, and prosperity of the year 1899 in the United States, made this his telling climax:

" 'And every barn in Kansas and Nebraska has had a new coat of paint.'

"To anyone who knew the great unpainted West of 1896 and 1897, with its bare, weather-stained houses, its dilapidated barns, its farm machinery standing out in the rain, its ruinous boom-towns, its discontented inhabitants crying out for legislation to relieve their distress, this bit of observation raises a picture of improvement and smiling comfort such as no array of figures, however convincing, could produce."

I was surprised at the response which I received from these articles and I was glad enough to have Frank N. Doubleday, then the dynamic young publisher who had come into the *McClure* organization to organize a book department, suggest that I publish the articles in book form. The book was, I remember, rushed through the press, as though the era of prosperity might evaporate before it could be sold, and it appeared in March, 1900. The following list of chapter headings will indicate what it contained:

I. The Beneficence of Hard Times
II. How Prosperity Came
III. Influence of Speculation and Trusts on Prosperity
IV. Effects of the Prosperity Wave at Home
V. Expansion of Foreign Commerce
VI. American Commercial Invasion of the World
VII. Iron and Steel
VIII. Prosperity on the Great Lakes
IX. A Self-Reliant South
X. The Rise in the Price of Meat
XI. Corn, Wheat, and the West
XII. Coal and Coke
XIII. Wool and Lumber
XIV. Labour
XV. The Edge of the Future—The Country's Greatness

I was cautious enough not to go all out in my description of the new prosperity. I was myself somewhat suspicious of it. I remembered too vividly what had happened in 1894, and I said in the conclusion to the book:

"And yet, the country must expect another backset, another period of hard times, tight money, mortgages, discontent, and distress. It will come in the natural course of events. The pendulum swings as far one way as it does the other. The conditions of prosperity now prevailing will result in enormous expansion of credit; everyone will over-invest, over-lend, over-manufacturer, over-produce; and then, having trodden in high places, there will be a gradual failing of confidence, liquidation here, and a crash there—then panic and hard times again. This must certainly be expected in time, but only the wise man will be prepared for it."

I also felt that the conditions as I described them "should not lead to self-complacency."

"The American has need of his own 'Recessional'—lest we forget our own grave national deficiencies and national faults. We can feed ourselves, we are great and powerful; but we have our own galling Negro problem, our rotten machine politics, our legislative bribery, our municipal corruption, our giant monopolies, our aristocracy of mere riches, any one of which is a rock on which the ship of state, unless skillfully navigated, may go to its destruction. And, then, great as we are in money, and commerce, and power, we have yet our greater fame to make in music, art, literature, science. In these branches of human achievement we are only just beginning; we have still much to learn from scholarly Europe."

It is well I added this "Recessional" to my conclusions. So much of the glamor of that "new prosperity" was fool's gold! It bred colossal new fortunes, it created Big Business, it widened the power, often a power used unscrupulously, of the owners of railroads and trusts. It meant little or no improvement for the common man. Three years later I was devoting all my time and energy to exposing Big Business in *McClure's Magazine*.

For a book of its kind, *Our New Prosperity* had an unusually large sale and much discussion in the newspapers. It seemed clear evidence of the great interest, not unmixed with doubt, that ordinary Americans were beginning to feel in the economic problems of the country.

One thing this new development, and the book I wrote about it, did for me personally—it ruined forever my plan for the Great American Novel. There was so much more in the American scene than I had dreamed. I felt I did not know enough to write such a book, or indeed at that time, any book. I was not ready for conclusions, or remedies. Was there any sure or comprehensive conclusion, or any one remedy?

The loss of a compelling interest in my life, such as the Great American Novel had come to be, was a serious one for me personally —as I was soon to learn.

CHAPTER XI

The New Journalism

IN NO FIELD was the American awakening more marked than in the field of journalism. Pulitzer's *World* was already a great popular success, and Hearst was rising on the journalistic horizon like an ominous cloud. That keen-sighted Englishman, Matthew Arnold, had been watching a similar development abroad, and had written in the *Nineteenth Century* of the meteoric rise of William T. Stead, the editor of the *Pall Mall Gazette,* afterward the founder of *The Review of Reviews:*

"We have had opportunities of observing a new journalism which a clever and energetic man has lately invented. It has much to recommend it; it is full of ability, novelty, variety, sensation, sympathy, generous instincts; its one great fault is that it is *feather-brained.* It throws out assertions at a venture because it wishes them true; does not correct either them or itself, if they are false; and to get at the state of things as they truly are seems to feel no concern whatever."

However different the methods pursued and the results achieved, the same forces that produced Pulitzer and Hearst and Stead in the newspaper field produced S. S. McClure and John Brisben Walker, of *The Cosmopolitan,* in the magazine field. The immediate creative impulse was an extraordinary sense of newness in the world—fresh interest in world affairs, the thrill of new discoveries and inventions, the "new prosperity," and in it all and through it all, an awakening sympathy for the world's down-trodden and oppressed.

It is not insignificant that two of the most practical-minded of peoples, the French and the Americans, had more or less instinctively capitalized on these new interests with the first great World Fairs: in Paris in 1889; in Chicago in 1893; and again in Paris in 1901. In the last two, both of which I attended, the sense of a new earth with vast unrecognized treasure in it was the keynote, challenging to the spirit of man. The emphasis, as never before, was upon machinery, inventions, the miracles of transportation and communication, and upon strange people with strange customs from strange and distant lands.

The deeper-seated influences behind the new journalism were even more significant. For the first time in history great masses of the people were becoming literate. They were reading more than ever before with a boundless new human curiosity that had to be satisfied. Matthew Arnold, in the article I have referred to, saw clearly the rising power of democracy with "abundance of life, movement, sympathy, good instincts." While he charged it with being "feather-brained," like the new journalism, there it was, a gathering power in the world, demanding new knowledge and new rights.

In the entire field of the magazine, *McClure's* was the outstanding and pre-eminent example of this new journalism. Its leadership was not only gifted with rare qualities of intelligence and creative imagination, but the medium itself was far better adapted than the newspaper to the accurate and thorough-going presentation of the new world. Since it was published only once a month, it could take time: it was not required to print "spot news"; it could in some measure at least avoid being "feather-brained."

I once heard one of the cleverist journalists that ever lived in America, and one of the most casuistical—I mean Arthur Brisbane, the editorial mouthpiece of the Hearst newspapers—give this advice to a young newspaper man:

"If you would succeed in journalism, never lose your superficiality."

He had as proof the tangible evidence of his own success; he was said to have become the highest paid writing journalist of all time.

When I joined *McClure's* I found, or thought I found, everything different from the world of haste and superficiality that was the newspaper. When I was commissioned to write an article regarding General Leonard Wood, who led the Rough Riders at Las Guasimas, and was then in command of the eastern provinces of Cuba, I went to Santiago and spent several days with him. I accompanied him on his tours of inspection, even as far as Guantanamo, talking with his officers and soldiers and with the Cuban leaders who were co-operating with him. I went to Havana to meet General Brooke, then governor-general of the island, and his staff, some of whom were sharply critical of Wood. I wanted to find out how well based this criticism might be, and how much consideration I should give to it in my study. After my return, I journeyed to Boston and Buzzard's Bay to meet Wood's family and early friends—I wanted to know fully his deeper rootages. I made a trip to Washington to talk with Mrs. Wood and with many army men who were his friends, or indeed his critics—for his meteoric rise from army doctor to commanding general in a twinkling of the eye was resented by many military men.

I came back to New York literally saturated with my subject. I had been working on it, intensively, for five or six weeks. I had made an expensive trip to Cuba, I had written an unusually long article—it was the day of the long article—so that the cost to the publishers was far greater probably, than magazines, up to that time, had ever spent on such work.

This thoroughness of preparation was true also of Ida M. Tarbell's great series on Abraham Lincoln, and later, her *History of the Standard Oil Company.* It was especially true of the later so-called "exposure" articles, perhaps the most original and successful development of *McClure's,* which demanded especial care as to accuracy and fairness that comes of complete mastery of the subjects treated. I do not know the exact figures, but I should be surprised if many single articles in *McClure's* did not cost from $1500 to $2500—in those days fabulous prices.

But what a boon to the writer! To be able really to take his time, saturate himself with his subject, assure accuracy by studying the subject at first hand and by consulting every possible expert, and then, above all, to be able to write and rewrite until the presentation should not only be clear to any reader of reasonable intelligence, but be interesting. *Interesting! Interesting!* For everything, at *McClure's,* given thorough knowledge of the subject, turned upon the quality of the writing. We maintained no society of mutual admiration in those good days. We were friends indeed, but we were also uncompromising critics of one another. I have always regarded John S. Phillips as the most creative editor I ever knew. He could tell wherein an article failed and why; he could usually make fertile suggestions for improving it; he was willing to give the writer all the precious time he needed for rewriting his story or his essay or his article. One of the warmest satisfactions, and to the writer certainly the most valuable reward of this method of striving for dependability and thoroughness, was the criticism or commendation that came in, not from casual readers but from men who were themselves experts in the field, and whose comments had especial value in further establishing the truth of the author's report. Among many letters I received regarding the article I wrote on General Wood, there were two, both from men who knew and cared for the truth of the matter, that pleased me deeply. One was from the young Lieutenant Colonel of the Rough Riders, Theodore Roosevelt, who had served under Wood in Cuba, and the other was from Captain E. G. Bellairs, the experienced Associated Press correspondent in Havana.

S. S. McClure was called the "genius" of the magazine he established; but the explanation is not as simple as that. He had indeed a highly creative mind, and a great deal of excitable energy, but the success of *McClure's* was based upon the fecundity of S. S. McClure, as edited and condensed by J. S. Phillips, and guided and bounded on the business side by the clear-running intelligence of Albert Brady. The three together—who had been friends since their college days—made the perfect publishing organization. "S. S.," as he was called familiarly by his associates, was all intuition and impulse, bursting with nervous energy, one of the most unorganizable, impatient, and disorderly men I ever knew. During a somewhat excited conference in his office I remember how he suddenly sprang to his feet, jumped up on the radiator and leaned far out of the window. We all started up and after him. It was four or five stories down to the street! Before any of us could reach him he was back in the room, slapping the coal dust off his hands, and laughing impishly:

"That's the most direct way to the street," he remarked, "but the stairs are safer."

Especially in his earlier days he had extraordinary qualities of imagination: a vivid sense of what was really interesting to people—what people would read and pay for. He early established a Newspaper Syndicate, buying novels and stories of famous writers, mostly English, and selling them to a long list of American newspapers for

"Sunday features." He had all sorts of ideas for advertising them, for advance notices, for vivid headings. He would dash off to Europe to call on Stevenson, Kipling, Conan Doyle and others, and come back to sell their manuscripts to editors in Chicago, or St. Louis, or San Francisco, whether they wanted them or not. After the magazine was founded in 1893 he literally erupted, like a live volcano, with ideas. He would descend on the office, or write from Europe, enclosing in his letters fat packets of newspaper articles, headings, editorials, usually not cut out but torn out, jagged, scored and underlined, as suggestions for "stupendous new series of articles." Everything with him in those days was "stupendous." Soon after I joined the staff I received several such letters, written from France or Switzerland, some of which seemed to me utterly fantastic. And yet there were, here and there, flashes of extraordinary penetration, suggestions that John Phillips winnowed out and developed into solidly framed and authentic articles or stories. McClure's instinct for that which was really alive, timely, interesting, also enabled him to pick out many stories and articles by unknown writers which proved unusually successful. It always seemed to me, after we began publishing the so-called exposure articles, that it was not the evils of politics and business, or the threat to our democratic system, that impressed him most, but the excitement and interest and sensation of uncovering a world of unrecognized evils—shocking people!

Many of Sam McClure's ideas were the ancient and more or less banal stand-bys of editors who sought large circulations. It was a simple formula: he told people more about things of which they were already hearing a good deal. He satisfied newly awakening wonder, which had usually been stimulated by bits and strays of news published in the newspapers. Really new things about which people had not yet begun to speculate interested him little or not at all.

"Baker," he once asked me, "who are the three best-known heroes in America?"

While I was turning this amusing question over in my mind, he responded instantly:

"How about Abraham Lincoln, Napoleon Bonaparte, and Jesus Christ?"

Without waiting for me to comment, he continued torrentially:

"Miss Tarbell has already written great series on Lincoln and Napoleon. What we have got to do now is to publish a new biography of Jesus Christ."

He meant it, and went at it with enthusiasm and determination. He induced a famous author to begin work on a manuscript and interested himself, with the assistance of August F. Jaccaci, who was the able art editor at *McClure's,* in a series of paintings made in Palestine by the French artist, J. J. Tissot. He bought at a pretty price from the French agents the rights to use these pictures in color, and they were published in the magazine. When the first biographer chosen failed to produce the study required, he engaged Dr. John Watson, a noted leader of the Scotch church, who had written many popular stories under the name of Ian Maclaren ("The Bonnie Briar Bush"), and sent Corwin Knapp Linson, an able American artist, to Palestine to paint a new series of pictures. These were gorgeously reproduced in color, thus attracting some of the fresh interest which was lacking in Dr. Watson's biography.

S. S. McClure saw everything big. When *McClure's Magazine* began to be successful, he planned wonderful new magazines, three or four of them; he had a vision of establishing the greatest publishing house in America. He brought in Frank N. Doubleday, who had made a brilliant beginning at *Scribner's,* and organized Doubleday, McClure & Company. He and his associates even planned to take over the great old publishing house of Harper and Brothers.

Quite off-handedly one morning, S. S. appointed me to be editor of one of his new magazines, and later of *McClure's Magazine,* all without any plan of reorganization and, so far as I could learn, without consulting his indispensable associates. He used to appoint—or try to appoint—Miss Tarbell quite regularly to such editorships. In later years, there had been so many editors of *McClure's* appointed that a meeting and dinner was suggested to bring them all together. My friend Sam Adams (Samuel Hopkins Adams) who came to *McClure's* in later years, suggested that we hire Madison Square Garden to hold them all.

In those early days S. S. McClure was an exciting and colorful figure, but like so many "geniuses" he seemed to have been cast in a special mold, capable of certain ranges of super-normal action and unusual achievement, but without the gift of growth. So often such men become tragic figures, unhappily imitating themselves, trying vainly to repeat their early successes.

John S. Phillips was a man of a wholly different sort—a perfect counter-balance to S. S. McClure. He was thoughtful, sensitive, critical, with a deep love for the genuine, the thorough, the sincere in literature and art. There was nothing flamboyant about him. He had a strong sense, in which S. S. McClure was deficient, of co-operation with his associates. From the very beginning I felt that he was my friend. Many years later, The Players' Club of New York gave him a testimonial dinner, which I deeply regretted I could not attend, but for which I wrote a brief letter expressing my feeling of regard:

"I remember with astonishment that I began my association with J. S. P. almost forty years ago. He was my editor and, all along, my friend. I think I got into this precarious world of the printed word largely as a result of his perfected art of editorial midwifery. He has had many a lusty infant to his credit! I have had dealings in my time with a good many editors; I never knew one who had so much of the creative touch, a kind of understanding which surprises the writer himself with unexpected possibilities in his own subjects, and by his gift of literary taste suggests felicities of expression which the author would have liked to think of first."

One other associate and great friend of those days at *McClure's*, and afterward *The American Magazine,* was Ida M. Tarbell. It is difficult for me to express the growing admiration and affection I have felt for her down through all the years. In November, 1937, Mrs. Baker and I attended her eightieth birthday party given by our mutual friends the Finleys (Mr. and Mrs. John H. Finley of New York), and I can perhaps express a little of my feeling, by quoting the entry I made the next day in my notebook:

"It will be forty years next spring since I first met Miss Tarbell and I say now as I have said many times in the past, that I have never known a finer human spirit in this world. She is beautiful with virtue—so generous, so modest, so full of kindness, so able, so gallant—and yet with such good sense and humor. What a worker she has been all down the years! So fearless as a writer, so honest, so interesting, with such ability to infect her pages with her own shining love of truth that those who read her once cannot but read again. She lives so warmly in the hearts of her friends that they take new courage in a discordant universe; are reestablished in their faith in the human race, learning anew what it can be, at its best."

The last time I saw her—she was then eighty-two and struggling with some of the handicaps of age—she was as fine and brave as ever; she was "learning" she said, "the technique of being eighty years old." She told me she believed as strongly as ever she had, in the "upward spiral of human development." And this in spite of the greed, the corruption in high places, the brutality of war, which she had spent her life in fighting.

I should also refer to two other remarkable men, both vivid men and vital, who came into the McClure organization in those early years. The first I have already mentioned, Frank N. Doubleday, who was then only thirty-six years old, and was presently to organize the great publishing firm of Doubleday, Page and Company and build up one of the most interesting and beautiful printing plants—The Country Life Press—ever seen in America. I was one of his earliest authors and a good friend always: he published my first book in 1899.

The other was John H. Finley, who had been at Knox College where McClure and Phillips had graduated, and was afterward its President. He came into the group at McClure's in 1899, at the age of thirty-six. He was to have a truly notable career as an educator and editor, becoming finally the editor-in-chief of the New York *Times*.

I have wondered if there could have been a more interesting editorial office than ours, one with more of the ozone of great ideas, touch-and-go experimentation, magic success. We were all young. In 1898 when I joined the staff, S. S. McClure was about forty years old, Phillips was several years younger. I was only twenty-eight, the youngest of the group. Frank Norris, who was an assistant editor, was about my own age.

Many of the ablest contributors were still scandalously young. Stephen Crane, of *The Red Badge of Courage,* who contributed many stories and articles, was only twenty-seven. He was often in our office. I recall finding him one day sitting on top of my desk with his knees drawn up to his chin and his long arms clasping his legs—a pale, slim, tired-looking young fellow, full of half cynical, half pessimistic talk, but always interesting.

William Allen White, not yet thirty, who later became a dear friend of mine, was writing his boy-town stories, *The Court of Boyville,* one of the most delightful of all his books. And Lincoln Steffens, who had been an early contributor to the magazine but was not yet a member of the staff, was thirty-two. We published our first story by O. Henry, then thirty-six years old, in 1899, and the first by Jack London, who was, I think, only twenty-three, in the following year. Some of the earliest writings of Willa Cather and Kathleen Norris were to come later. Nor shall I ever forget the delightful chronicles of that most fascinating of little girls, "Emmy Lou," by their equally delightful author, George Madden Martin of Kentucky. Booth Tarkington, whose first novel, *The Gentleman from Indiana,* was published as a serial in *McClure's* in 1899, was only twenty-nine years old. I well remember the excited reading of his manuscript by various members of our staff. A fresh breath of life: a book full of the America of the Middle West.

Several of the famous English novelists who contributed to *McClure's* in those early days were still young men, writing on new themes, with fresh vigor. I had a shock of astonishment when I first saw Rudyard Kipling. I had been a devoted admirer of his writings from the first story I had read—I think one of the "Plain Tales from the Hills." I have already chronicled my studiously written report, in Scott's seminar at Ann Arbor, of "The Children of the Zodiac," which he contributed to *Harper's Weekly* in 1892. In my mind he had become almost a classic of the blessed and accepted past. And here I was shaking hands with a slightly built young man, rather solemn looking, with bushy dark eyebrows and a thick moustache—only five years older than I was! I think I had expected, through some vague sense of his association with India, to find him with the tranquil look of a Hindu pundit—and, possibly, a turban on his head. That brief meeting I found disillusioning; for no one should ever meet an author whom he has worshipped. He has already given the best of him, the best he has to give, in his books: he cannot be expected to give more in a few minutes of unpremeditated talk, however pointed or arresting it may be. Kipling was not at all tranquil. Something had gone wrong in our office, and he was evidently bent upon relieving his mind with British thoroughness in his talk with the editors—I think S. S. McClure and John Phillips were both there. He was testy and irritable, he was sharp and cynical, not at all the great man, one of whose finest poems, "The Recessional" we had republished only a few months before in *McClure's*; not even the tart humorist whose stories, *Stalky and Company,* we were about to serialize. In fact I could never quite replace the halo of the magic poet and story-teller that Kipling himself had snatched from his own brow: even though I lived to become an admirer, this side worship, of his great novel of India, *Kim,* which we began publishing in *McClure's* in 1901.

Those brilliant early years at *McClure's* I shall never forget, the men I came to know, the vitally interesting discussions we had, the laughter we laughed. I recall especially the daily luncheons in the little private dining room in the old Ashland House, sometimes with one or more distinguished guests. One day Admiral Peary, the discoverer of the North Pole, was there—a grave man talking quietly, all but monotonously, of the most astonishing experiences. Other days came Bliss Carman, the poet, who recited with unction one of his own poems; and Marconi, fresh from his early triumphs; and Hamlin Garland, still smelling of the pennyroyal of his journey through Alaska; and Parson Wagner, who wrote *The Simple Life:* and Charles Dana Gibson, the artist, who created the "Gibson Girl," then at the height of his fame; and others too numerous to mention. All these, and the discussions we had of the tasks we each had in hand, the men we were meeting, the fascinating new ideas we were eager to develop and explain—no, I shall never forget those early days at *McClure's.* I shall not forget them even though I was soon to discover the limitations of the McClure method so far as I, as a writer, was concerned.

CHAPTER XII

Seen in Germany

I WAS ASKED, in the early spring of 1900, to go to Europe on a roving commission. My only definite assignment was for an article on the building of the largest steamship in the world, the *Deutschland* of the Hamburg-American line, then nearly completed at Stettin in Germany. George Varian, a highly accomplished illustrator, was to go with me to make the pictures. After the visit to Stettin, we were to travel about Europe, seeing what we could see.

What could possibly have pleased a young writer more than this! I had longed for years to go to Europe but had never had either the time or the money. On this trip I was to receive my usual salary and all my expenses were to be paid. Above all, I was in large measure to choose my own subjects to write about, the things that interested me most, or that I considered vitally significant.

The only hesitation I had was in leaving my wife and family. When I raised that problem, S. S. McClure advised that I take them with me, generously offering to help with the expenses. He argued that I could settle them down somewhere in Switzerland where he himself had a temporary home, thus making a European headquarters for Varian and me. My wife did not, however, dare to venture a wintry voyage across the ocean with two young children, and we therefore broke up our home at Bronxville and she was warmly welcomed at her home in Michigan.

Varian and I sailed on the old *Fürst Bismarck* on March 15, 1900. It was a stormy winter voyage. We lay tossing about in a blinding snowstorm for twenty hours off Sandy Hook, and arrived in Hamburg two days late. Varian at once proved his superiority over me by being an imperturbably good sailor. He never missed a meal. I found that his father had been a British sea captain and that he had himself sailed before the mast. His grandmother was a Brazilian Spaniard, and he an American citizen. I found him a devoted and conscientious worker, modest and straightforward; I could not have selected a more agreeable companion for such a trip.

I spent a considerable part of the rolling voyage in my berth reading books about Germany and studying a German grammar and word-book. Several years before, in Chicago, I had taken a course in the Berlitz School of Languages and was able to manage simple conversations in German, and to read a little. While on the voyage, and after arriving in Europe, I used my amateur German remorselessly on everyone I met. I have no doubt that many of them laughed in their sleeves (some not entirely in their sleeves!) but I could laugh at it as heartily myself, and I found the continual practice highly helpful. My amusing and floundering efforts to improve my German made me two or three good German friends on the ship, one of whom was of much assistance to me later.

I also had time on that long voyage to consider our plan of campaign. I had secured a number of potent letters of introduction to noteworthy people in Europe, among them Ambassador Andrew D. White in Berlin and Ambassador Joseph H. Choate in London. I had letters to Professor Ernst Haeckel, one of the most distinguished scientists then living in Europe, to Lord Kelvin, the great English physicist, to Sir William Huggins, the astronomer, and to Sir John Murray, the oceanographer, and to many others. I tried to define my own objectives as a reporter of the things I saw; I wanted, if possible, to discover some sure fundamental principal by which I could test what was really significant among the vast and confusing activities of a newly awakening Europe.

"I am trying hard," I wrote to my wife, "to get clear ideas of the *meanings* of things over here: why Germany is making such progress, how much is due to her system of bureaucracy, how much to her splendid educational methods, how much to her national resources." And above all, as I wrote later, I wanted to understand the "new impetus in scientific research and discovery."

I was soon to find that I was most deeply interested in what I had called the "bureaucracy" of Germany, which proved to be the beginnings of the momentous conception of the totalitarian state, and which, fourteen years later, was tc upset the world and keep it upset for more than a generation. Next to this, I was most deeply interested in talking with the scientific and industrial leaders of the new Germany, who, even at the time that their explorations and discoveries were vitally assisting the development of totalitarianism, were themselves jealous of their individual freedom and often sharp critics of the growing bureaucracy.

I am amazed in re-reading, after many years, the articles and letters I wrote describing what I saw and heard and *felt* in Germany. They are all there: the fundamental ideas upon which the Emperor William went to war in 1914; and the genesis of Adolf Hitler and *Mein Kampf*. If I had been a great prophet!—but I was not a prophet, I was a reporter, trying as faithfully as I could to set down what I found. Nor do I know anyone else who, at that time, could or would have dared to predict the mighty potency of the new nationalistic totalitarianism, the bloody wars which it would precipitate, or the revolutionary changes in world politics which it would stimulate.

"The Englishman," I wrote, "has gone to sleep content with his own commercial supremacy and greatness; the American is not yet fully awake to his own power; the Frenchman frets himself with visions of a greatness that is gone; but the German is fully alive to every world-condition, establishing banks and businesses in South America, buying islands of Spain, boldly taking the lead in the Chinese troubles, extending his colonies in Africa, preparing to absorb Austria and possibly Asia Minor, building a splendid new navy, stretching the lines of his merchant marine around the world, and putting his manufactured products into the homes of every nation on earth."

I saw also, and clearly, the struggle that was going on in Germany between the powerful New and the stubborn Old.

"Fifty years ago the German was the world's typical dreamer, musician, poet, scholar; then he became the world's philosopher, scientist, and educator, and now he is appearing as a great man of affairs, of world politics, of giant industries."

I saw also that the change was not without tragical possibilities: there was seemingly a "bottomless chasm" between the two struggling conceptions: the old Germany of "free thought and high culture set over against a government that will not permit free speech, a free press, or free assemblage for the discussion of certain questions of administration and politics—a government that punishes with an iron hand for lèse-majesté. Here is a vast and bloated militarism standing in contrast to a professed desire and a real need of peace, a huge army and navy costing millions in taxes and taking half a million men from agriculture and the industries, when there are not enough laborers to till the fields."

Everything that Varian and I saw as we traveled about Germany seemed to illustrate and fortify these general impressions. At Stettin we saw, under the guidance of Captain Albers, not only the mighty *Deutschland,* but also the truly wonderful activities of the Vulcan Shipyards, where the vision of the new Germany had been given life in the stupendous development of every phase of modern shipbuilding. I suppose that there was not anywhere in the world at that time another such exhibit of the modern Vulcan at his forge, as that at Stettin in the year 1900.

From Stettin we traveled, with our eyes and ears open, to Berlin, Leipzig, Jena, Dresden, Munich, Vienna and to other cities. Vienna seemed to us a kind of "shabby Berlin," having "neither the interest of the ancient cities which we had seen nor the splendor of the new." Afterward we went on to France and England.

More than half my articles, I find, dealt with the new Germany, and the governmental implementation of the ideas upon which it was founded. I wrote about the Kaiser, whom we saw every day or two dashing down Unter den Linden behind a pair of splendid horses, traveling like the wind, touching his glistening silver helmet to the cheering people in the streets. I wrote about the German soldier who was then in process of a training which was more comprehensive than any, perhaps, ever before devised. We were told that army training grounds were forbidden to visitors but we walked out, two or three times, to the vast Tempelhofer Feld, and the gates being open, we walked in and watched the extraordinary thoroughness with which the raw recruits were being transformed into goose-stepping private soldiers. We saw the bayonet practice, the tilting with muffled lances, the building of pontoon bridges—everything. Varian was able to make excellent sketches, which were reproduced when our articles were published.

From the beginning I felt a warm liking for the German people—especially those in the smaller towns and in the country. I took many long tramps and it was a delight to meet the peasants, the country teamsters, and "all the little boys and girls with rosy cheeks and flaxen curls." They always had a smile for the stranger, a "Guten abend," or a tip of the hat. I remember in later years the contrasts I found, tramping in the French country, between these and the dour northern peasants. Even in England, which I have always loved, I found no hospitality equal to that in some parts of Germany. These were, it seemed to me, honest, docile, simple-living, hard-working people, caught in the fierce currents of the European awakening, the result of a Germany that had been outdistanced in achieving political unity and economic competency. There had been too little time to develop a sturdy middle class, much less a vigorous democracy. Their leaders, who saw clearly the problems of European rivalry, the swift disappearance of far-distant islands and continental tropics suitable for colonization, sought to meet the conditions by governmental short-cuts. The leaders would establish a dictatorship from above, not a democracy laboriously built up within; they would work by force of arms, not by reason and co-operation. No dictator ever had finer, or stronger, or more docile human material to work in. I quoted in one of my articles from an address by the Kaiser:

"The soldier should not have a will of his own, but all of you should have one will, and that is my will. There exists only one law, and that is my law; and now go and do your duty, and be obedient to your superiors."

This spirit I found everywhere rampant in German life and I filled my articles with specific illustrations of it. Having myself been brought up on the American frontier I had, in that most democratic of all democracies, breathed the bracing air of individual freedom, and I began actually, in Germany, to feel suffocated.

As to organizations or parties to meliorate or combat these conditions, the socialists for example, the Kaiser expressed his intentions (in an address to his troops at Potsdam) in no uncertain terms:

"For you there is one foe, and that is my foe. Considering the existing socialistic difficulties, it may be necessary for me to command you to shoot down your own relatives, brothers, and parents, in the streets, which God forbid, but you must obey my orders without murmuring."

What I saw in Germany, and sought to describe, was the development of a powerful new political and social system which I felt, instinctively, was inimical to our own. Only a few years later I was to see the bloody fruition of those ideas and that system on the battlefields of France and Italy. I was to live through another thirty years' war.

The other aspect of the new Germany, of which I have spoken, also interested me profoundly. This was the development of science and scholarship, and the vast new industries which were beginning to grow out of them. Here in these oases of intellectual freedom, still unhampered and even encouraged for their own ends by the totalitarian over-lords, I found everywhere notable human beings, working freely and happily in their own fertile fields. Varian and I visited the Physical and Technical Institute at Charlottenburg, and met Professor Kohlrausch and Professor Day and Professor Hagen. I went to Dresden to visit Professor Nobbe and to see his experiments in the fertilization of plants. I spent many days in Jena looking into the new developments in the glass industries where the Zeiss lenses were made. I met its genius, Professor Abbe, an inspired philanthropist, then fully as much interested in a new profit-sharing system as in experiments in glassmaking.

"Were it not for the German professor," I wrote, "Germany would never have reached her present high place among the nations, either intellectually, industrially, or commercially. Delve into the history of many of the greatest business enterprises of the empire—for instance, the sugar-beet or the coal-tar industries—and you will find a quiet, plodding, painstaking, preoccupied German professor; and if you seek for the causes for the astonishing perfection and economy with which many German factories are today operated, you will find a German professor with a staff of scientists working side by side with the men who operate the machinery, keep the books, and sell the completed products."

Jena interested Varian and me more than any other town we visited. Besides the Zeiss industries it was the home of Professor

Ernst Haeckel, who was at that time, perhaps, the profoundest scientific mind in the nation.

We were entranced by the town itself, its ancient university, its shady streets and lanes. We found at the inn where we lived, the Hotel zum schwarzen Baeren, the veritable atmosphere and tranquillity of old Germany. We slept in great plump beds, that looked like flowery dumplings; we had only candles to light us, and we were warmed—a little—by the tall, ancient tiled stove that stood in the corner. In the sunny nook in the oak-raftered beer room, we sat in the very seat, at the very table—as we were perhaps overemphatically informed—where Martin Luther met the Swiss students on his way to Wittenberg.

"The street outside," I wrote my wife, "bears the name Luther Strasse. Bismarck also stopped here once and up the street a little way lived at one time both Schiller and Goethe. Here Fichte and other famous Germans spent much of their lives. Near Jena, Napoleon fought one of his most famous battles and won perhaps his most notable victory. It is only a little town set deep among the hills along the Saale River, but queer and crooked and old. Every corner is a surprise, every nook a whole history. The buildings lean up against one another and sag out into the streets and there are glimpses of queer paved areas through ancient stone arches. Only a step from our inn runs the river and this morning the women were out with their washing, kneeling on little wooden piers and gossiping and frightening away the ducks. All this with coming spring, green leaves and blossoms, makes it a veritable place of enchantment."

Surprisingly soon we began to be acquainted; we were invited to a delightful beer garden on a hilltop where jolly German families sat half their Sunday afternoon over a few steins of beer, singing their German songs; we found a welcome at the houses of German students corps and attended several bloody duels at the country inn at Wöllnitz; and better than anything else I remember the long tramps I took, usually alone, through that beautiful German countryside, with cherries in bloom along the roadways, and peasants at work in the fields. Once we walked eleven miles to Weimar, and spent most of the day in and around Goethe's old home and the little park on the Ilm. It greatly stimulated my interest in Goethe. I already knew

Lewes' biography. I now re-read it, and I found Eckermann's *Conversations* one of the most suggestive books a young writer can read.

Varian and I, in all these experiences and wanderings, found we had much in common and became devoted friends. Since I had been brought up on the frontier, I had never had the opportunity to see famous works of art or hear really good music. What a fortune it was to visit the rich old galleries at Munich, Vienna, Paris and London with an artist who could guide me among the masterpieces. And we heard together some of the greatest music—I remember especially "The Marriage of Figaro" in the royal opera house in Berlin—and we saw Henry Irving in "Waterloo" and "The Bells" in London, and Coquelin as "Cyrano" in Paris.

I found then, and have acted upon my discovery ever since, that earned or incidental sight-seeing is far more enjoyable than sight-seeing as an occupation, even for a few weeks, let alone a whole summer. If a man is working hard, say in Munich or in Paris, he will choose only the things he wishes most to see or hear, his visits will be concentrated, he will never be "lost in a whirl of madonnas" or "bored by cathedrals" as I once heard an American tourist—and that in the cathedral of Notre Dame in Paris—express it. We went to the Passion Play at Oberammergau, stopped for the night with Judas Iscariot, and were all but frozen to death sitting for seven hours in the chill mountain air—for the new theater was not then constructed. But we enjoyed it.

I bought a miniature set of chessmen in a folding board and we occupied an occasional hour playing that great game. I came to know all of Varian's people, and he mine. Having no children of his own, he was interested in my little daughter, and I recall rainy evenings in German hotels when he made charming sketches of "Little Red Riding Hood," the "Babes in the Woods," "Jack-the-Giant-Killer," the "Pied Piper" and others, while I sat near him writing new versions of the famous old stories which, with his pictures, I sent home to Alice.

Varian and I soon found that everything at Jena was dwarfed into insignificance compared with our meetings with Professor Haeckel—the long talks we had, the little walks in the flowering gardens around his laboratory, the lectures I attended in his classroom.

Varian outdid himself. He made many sketches of the famous scientist with his dome of a head and his silvery white beard—sometimes with his mounted chimpanzees and orangoutangs and platipuses around him—all of which pleased Haeckel very much indeed.

We walked up to call on him, spring mornings, through Schiller's lane, where a hundred years before Goethe and Schiller often walked arm in arm, going out from Schiller's house. Here we found the benches on which they sat, and here the stone table; the inscription above told about it in Goethe's own words (to Eckermann):

"At this old stone table have we two often eaten and exchanged good and great words."

Here in this garden, also, Schiller wrote his *Wallenstein*, in 1798. A more peaceful spot, I thought, richer in historical significances, was nowhere to be found in the world. Varian and I sat there many times, having walked up from the zum Baeren.

It was here, in this very garden below the zoological laboratory, that Goethe "saw in imagination the great scheme of life, the developing process of nature, when Darwin was a mere boy; and . . . it is curiously interesting that Haeckel should have come to work out the great theory of evolution in the spot where Goethe dreamed it, even using some of the same instruments which Goethe had used in his investigations half a century or more before."

I found Haeckel speaking of Goethe constantly, both in his conversation and in his books; it is certain that the great scientist owed much to the great poet. Forty years earlier Haeckel had been one of the few thinkers of Europe who supported the theories set forth in "that extravagant book," the *Origin of Species.* What Huxley did to establish Darwinism in England, Haeckel did on the Continent. He and the distinguished co-discoverer of the theory of development, A. R. Wallace of England, were the last of the great militant evolutionists.

Haeckel usually met us at the doorway of his laboratory, "a great and genial presence—a man of robust build, both erect and strong, with a thick white beard and keen blue eyes set about with wrinkles of humor. The shake of his hand was warm, and his voice full and hearty. He wore a broad-brimmed black hat with a dome-like crown. He called it his 'Creation Hat,' and told us that two just like it were sent to him every year by a man whom he had never seen, who admired his *Natural History of Creation.* As he opened the cabinets in his museum he introduced a big chimpanzee as 'your nearest relative.' He remembered how he came by the baby chimpanzee in the next case. It had belonged to a traveling menagerie, and it had agreeably chosen to die just as the menagerie was coming into Jena.

" 'It is not often that a professor of zoology has such a fine chimpanzee die at his front door,' he said."

After we began to be well acquainted I ventured to ask Haeckel as to the new developments in Germany which we had been seeing. It was plain at once that he was deeply conscious of the mighty changes that were going on, and anxious about them.

"Here in Germany," he said, "the tendency is all toward the centralization of power in the government, the removal of individual responsibility, and the working together of large masses of men as one man. In America, the tendency has been different: there the individual is developed, he has great power and responsibilities—the man is the unit. Who shall say how these great influences will work out? Here we have military selection—all the young men being taken at a certain age, removed from productive labor or study, and put through exactly similar training for one or two years. In America there is no such influence. How will such training or lack of it develop the race?"

Re-reading my account of Haeckel and his work, after forty years, I see more clearly the cogency of his prophecies. He saw plainly the "terrible new struggle" that was on its way.

"Then there is a still more powerful influence at work: the earth is now almost wholly inhabited; there are few new places for immigration and the development of virgin land—the two influences which have had so great a share in the progress of the world during the last few hundred years. The contest must now change. Instead of discovering and settling new continents, there must set in a terrible new struggle for existence between the older nations, for instance, in commerce and trade, and the strongest, most easily adaptable, most resourceful nations will win."

Professor Haeckel spoke of the retrogression of the Latin races during the past few decades as a striking instance of this new struggle

—especially the retrogression of once-powerful Spain. He called attention to the sudden upward progress of Japan.

My conversations with this fine old prophet, and the ideas they suggested, were to linger in my mind and to help guide me, a little later, in coming to certain valuable, if painful, decisions regarding my own life and work.

It was clear to me that Haeckel saw the imminence of this new world struggle and feared it, especially its possible disruptive effects upon the free life of the intellect and the "blessed quiet of laboratories and libraries" (as Pasteur described it). He believed, also, that science was then reaching its apogee—a mistake that other great scientists have made.

"The nineteenth century," he said, "has been the golden era of science—there will never again be so many discoveries of profound importance."

And this with Einstein just around the corner! And Marconi and the Wright brothers! And Madame Curie!

It was a joy I shall never forget, the writing of my article there in the sunny corner of the zum Baeren, with Varian finishing his sketches; of going up from time to time to call on Professor Haeckel to make sure of certain difficult points; and finally of submitting my completed manuscript to him. I think he took pleasure in reading it, suggesting various slight changes, and adding the Latin names of several species of animals which I had intentionally omitted. He sent the article back with a letter which I have preserved to this day and prize highly.

Varian and I had many other interesting experiences in Germany and later in France and England but there is not room to enlarge upon them here. Throughout our expedition, we did all our work on the spot while the subjects were fresh in our minds and the labor, arduous and exacting as it was, came as near heavenly satisfaction as one is likely to find. But it could not last. We drove too hard, tried to do too much and do it too fast, and in the last days in Germany I fell ill. While not serious, for it was in part sheer weariness and satiation, the illness resulted in a personal crisis of which I shall speak in a later chapter.

I found on my return that I had written twelve articles while in Germany, and several others in France and England. The most important of them were published in *McClure's Magazine*, others in the *Outlook, Collier's Weekly* and in *Pearson's*, the *Windsor* and the *Idler* in London. Mr. Doubleday suggested that he bring out the German series as a book. This considerably surprised me, for I had no idea that I had written enough to make a book: and had certainly never thought of publishing them in book form. It was called *Seen in Germany*, and had a considerable immediate sale. A large edition was afterward used by the Chautauqua Reading Circles which were then popular in the United States.

One aspect of the response to this book was new to me. In earlier days when I wrote for a newspaper I never had the feeling that I had any readers—or that those who did read cared anything whatever for what I was doing. Of course I wrote anonymously, and the occasional letters I received were usually sharply critical—abusing me for what I said, or did not say.

This book brought me many letters and comments and inquiries. I may possibly be excused, since this was a first experience—and I am after all writing an autobiography—if I refer particularly to the letter which gave me the warmest pleasure of all. I knew it was sincere and that it was the word of an authority on Germany and German affairs. It came from Andrew D. White, American Ambassador in Germany, who had so warmly demonstrated his interest and friendship when I was there.

I have just read *Seen in Germany* through from cover to cover with the greatest interest, my only criticism being that it ought to have been twice as long. Come again and give us a second volume, and, indeed, a third volume in the same style on kindred subjects. To tell you the truth, I was fascinated by the book and found myself neglecting various duties until I had finished it. In spite of an experience begun forty-five years ago and extending over long periods at various times since, you have taught me many new things and suggested new and, I think, fruitful trains of thought.

There are so many important and interesting things more awaiting your attention here! Come again. With renewed thanks, I remain,

Very sincerely yours,

(signed) AND. D. WHITE.

I do not pretend that my book on Germany was either exhaustive or thorough. I remember, a year or two later, of meeting an able man in Constantinople—Dr. Peet, who had been for thirty years treasurer of the American Board of Missions in Turkey—with whom I sat up half the night talking about conditions in the Near East. It was the most convincing exposition of the whole subject that I had ever heard and I urged him to write out his impressions and conclusions. I felt sure that they would easily find a publisher in America. I have many times recalled his response:

"When I had been in the Near East for six months, I could have written a good book about it. Now that I have been here thirty years, I could not possibly do it. The mountains have too many foothills."

I had seen some of the mountains, few of the foothills.

CHAPTER XIII

New and Difficult Decisions

I HAD RETURNED to America from my European trip not only ill but much depressed. It was an illness not serious enough to put me to bed, or to prevent me entirely from going on with my work; but I was unaccustomed to any such limitation. I had been brought up hardily in the cold north country. I had lived much out of doors. I had been able to work long hours without weariness. I have no memory of being really tired until after I was thirty years old. Even though I fortified myself with my father's bold motto, "Admit nothing to be a hardship," I was irritated and even worried.

When a man begins to take himself too seriously he discovers presently, if he has even a rudimentary sense of humor, that he is making himself ridiculous. But I could not, somehow, laugh off the fact that while I knew I had attempted to do too much in Europe, driven too hard, the difficulty lay far deeper than any physical illness. I find references in my letters to my dissatisfaction with my work and the kind of life I was leading.

"I have been spreading too much, trying to do the impossible," I wrote from Europe. "I live in a whirl: I get no time to think."

One dismal morning in London I took the first passing bus in the Strand and rode to the end of the line. I did not know where the bus was going and I did not care. It stopped finally at a dingy, bare little park, in a squalid neighborhood, and I got out and sat down on a wooden bench. I was as completely miserable as I had ever been in my life. I remember, presently, taking out my pocket notebook and writing these words:

"Primary things: I have not yet learned the primary things. I know how to work: I do not yet know how to live. I have no central guide. I have no dominating purpose."

In thinking of it since I cannot but smile at the pathetic figure I must have appeared and yet it was as deeply sincere an expression of my feeling as anything I ever wrote.

That afternoon when I returned to my lodgings I wrote to my wife that I intended to resign my position on *McClure's* as soon as I returned to New York. I regretted that my pleasant relations with the men at *McClure's* must be severed, but I had fully made up my mind.

"You may think," I wrote, "that this is an unwise step for a man who has a wife and babies living on the words he writes, but you must trust me."

At any cost I felt that I must be free. I must have a few months to think things over and try to decide what I wanted to do, and to be.

In the earlier years I had had, so far as my work was concerned, a great central purpose. I was putting everything I saw or felt or thought into my Great American Novel. It absorbed everything I had in me. That bubble had burst—and nothing had appeared to fill its place. Moreover I had begun to feel that my life was being ordered, not by myself, but by other people; not for my purposes, but for theirs. I recall the sense of admiration, and indeed envy, I felt when I came to know such a man as Professor Haeckel in Germany. He was on fire with his work. Neither money, nor fame, nor power, nor privilege, could tempt him: he had freely and happily given his life to it. I thought then that the only really happy men in the world were the scientists, the artists and the saints. Inspired workers! I think so still.

I had no such dominating passion: and I did not know where to find one, or how. I could throw away what I had, but could I find anything better?

No question of the success of the European expedition had arisen. The editors seemed wholly satisfied.

"You have done splendid work," John Phillips wrote me. "I am surprised at your great success. The trip has paid you and us."

He even suggested that Varian and I remain longer in Europe and complete several further studies we had in mind. All this approval made my own fully determined course more difficult to pursue. These men and women at *McClure's* were my warm friends as well as my associates: and there was certainly no editorial group in New York more stimulating to a young writer than this. When I tried to explain why I wanted to resign, they would scarcely listen to me.

"You are tired: you are ill: what you need is a rest."

John Phillips, as I could have anticipated, made the most understanding of comments.

"I am glad," he wrote, "that you are thinking so seriously about your work and your future, for something good will come of it. I believe that you can do better than you have ever done, and I believe that we can help you to that end. The thing that is best for you would, no doubt, be best for us as your editors and publishers, and I cannot think for a moment of your severing your connection with our house.

"A great many writers have combined the editorial and the productive sides of literature, and I am not sure but that you could do this with unusual success, for you have the capability of winning friends among people you see, as well as the ability to write. Think of this, too, when you are doing your thinking."

This was very much the same advice that my father had given me some years earlier—to make sure of a respectable money-making occupation, and do my writing as a polite avocation. I had rejected it promptly, even indignantly, for I had then no dependents: it was now a much more persuasive temptation. The editors followed up their arguments most effectively by giving me a substantial increase in salary, which I had not requested. They even dated it back for several months, so that I had in hand an unexpected sum of money—which at that time I really needed.

I have set down these somewhat intimate personal facts with hesitation but they seem to me necessary to explain my problems at that time.

It was clear to me that help was needed in the McClure office. S. S. McClure was ill and under the care of a physician and a nurse. He occasionally dashed into the office from Europe, remained a few days, and dashed back again. John Phillips was not well and was absent much of that summer. Jaccaci, the art editor, had gone to England for a rest. Albert Brady, the able businessman of the triumvirate that founded the magazine, had died, partly as the result of too much work and worry. For most of the members of the staff, long continued overwork, nervous tension, and excitement had begun to extort the price of high-flown ambition and swift success. It appeared clear to me that I was following rapidly in their footsteps. Why, and what for? Did I want that kind of success, at that price?

Nevertheless, I agreed to postpone my own plans for the time being and do what I could to help. My work became a busy miscellany of editorial tasks, dully performed, of which I can remember almost nothing. When one is ailing and unhappy all the zest oozes out of life. One precious experience, however, still lingers warmly in my memory, since it helped me to see more clearly what I myself wanted to do.

I went to Georgia to see Joel Chandler Harris—"Uncle Remus"—who had already written for our magazine and from whom we hoped for further contributions. I liked him on sight. His face bore the seal of good humor and good health and a pleasant outlook on the world. Around his eyes the years had worn little wrinkles of amusement. He was deliberate in his movements and slow and drawling in his speech. He seemed to me one of the simplest and most genuine human beings I had ever met.

On the floor of his sitting room, when we entered, I saw a large metal terrapin—the gift of an admirer of the "Br'er Terrapin" stories told by "Uncle Remus." This he moved slowly across the room with his foot to the chair where he was to sit. He then pressed down on the terrapin's head and the back flew up, disclosing a large sanded spittoon for his accommodation as a chewer of good strong Georgia tobacco. He soon overcame the slight impediment of speech which bothered him among strangers and began telling me stories in the delightful patois of the Southern Negroes. The stories came as naturally as his breath and he often laughed at them himself until the tears ran down his face. They were the old familiar stories of the Negro cabins—a folklore as old as Aesop—so old and so simple that no one up to that time had ever thought of writing them down.

I knew something already of the folklore of the South: and on this very trip. Mr. Harris, having given me a letter to an old friend at Eatonton, I was able to visit several ancient Negroes who had come up in the ante-bellum South and knew the old stories. I heard several of them, notably "Br'er Rabbit and the Tar-Baby," which had been made famous in Mr. Harris' books.

The author of "Uncle Remus" was a matchless writer of the spoken story—a difficult art, indeed. The original-folklore narrator had to aid him all the flexible and expressive accessories of the Negro voice, he could add the emphasis of changing facial expression and of gesture, he could interject eloquent pauses. Moreover, he had impressive stage-settings—night, the brightness of an open fire, shadowy, fascinated faces ready to express the common thrill. Those are parts of the story as much as the spoken words, and it was the triumph of Mr. Harris' art that he could represent them all. His versions were closer to the real story than any verbatim copy could possibly have been, for he told not merely a story about a rabbit and a fox, but he presented also, with life-like reality, the Negro who told it, and what he felt and thought about while he was telling it; he showed us the rapt listeners swept by superstitious fear, by laughter, by tears; no mere philologist could have taken hold of the hearts of generation after generation of readers as Uncle Remus has done. That triumph was left for the literary craftsman who knew how to make his stories quiver with life and human emotion.

Harris' own story, however, interested me at that time far more deeply than any he ever wrote: he told how he had come up in a "poor-white" family through the hard years of the Civil War, with little or no education except what he himself got from an old Southern classical library; how he began work in a country printing office at eleven years of age, and grew and grew and grew: becoming wise in the best and most curious knowledge of Negroes, of dogs, of horses; of the way of the red stream in the swamp; of the folk of the woods. As for his literary style it was an integral part of him; he was as unconscious of it as he was of the tone of his own voice. The author of "Uncle Remus" did not go to the publishers; he gave what he had, and they came to him. And here he was living quietly "At the sign of the Wren's Nest," writing what he liked best to write.

"Success such as Harris has had," as I wrote later, with a wistful thought of the serious problems I was myself facing, "often sends a young writer flying to New York where he is promptly petted, befooled and stimulated into an over-production that shortly ends him. But Uncle Remus was not to be tempted away from his Georgia home. So far from having his head turned by his successes, he looked upon the flurry of fame which his stories brought him in the light of a joke—a rather unreal and somewhat annoying joke. He was not convinced that he was a genius, nor did he begin to feel the responsibility of a great mission resting upon him."

Although Joel Chandler Harris, the Georgia countryman with

his love of simple things and the quiet life, was far removed—in character, in training, in intellectual interest, in nearly everything—from the distinguished German scientist, Professor Haeckel, the two had in common one of the greatest gifts bestowed upon human beings. Both were men possessed, centered, absorbed. Both knew what they wanted to do—and were doing it. Both were essentially happy men, with a kind of tranquil assurance and contentment I did not know, and wanted to know—passionately.

While this experience was intensely interesting to me and, from the point of view of the publishers, highly successful, since I made an agreement with Mr. Harris for his entire literary output, it increased rather than diminished my restlessness. It seemed to me that I was no longer doing anything of any account. I was not more than half alive. I knew that my associates in the office considered me most unreasonable—a kind of pathological case! Wasn't I succeeding as a writer? Weren't my articles and stories being accepted and published in the magazines? Didn't I have two books already in print—not great books, I knew well enough, but making a good start—and another, my *Seen in Germany*, almost ready? Didn't I hold an editorial position that promised better things in the future? What more could I possibly want?

One of my devoted friends in the office was my most vocal critic. He had a hot temper and after one of our arguments he cried out:

"Damn it all, what a temperamental ass you are."

I came back at him as sharply as I knew how:

"Why do you think that money is the only thing in the world?"

With this I stormed out of his office and into my own. I sat down in my chair.

"What a fool I am," I said, "what a fool."

A few minutes later I heard someone tap on my door. It opened just a crack. There was my friend with his hand shading his eyes as if I were a long distance away. He was smiling broadly. No warmer hearted man ever lived.

"If you'll forgive me for calling you an ass," said he, "I'll forgive you for thinking that lucre is my graven image."

I jumped from my seat and we shook hands as warmly as two old friends ever did.

"After all, Baker," he said, "you know you *are* an ass."

When I tried to respond he put his hand over my mouth.

"Come on out to lunch," he said.

And out we went arm in arm—with nothing really settled.

I spent all my spare time in a weary treadmill of doubt. What was it that I ought to do? Should I not accept the gifts of the gods and stop complaining? Wasn't I making a good living in a precarious profession? What more could anyone ask for?

While I was in Europe, John Phillips had outlined in one of his letters the kind of articles he wanted for the magazine. They were first of all to be *important*. "An article must have great human interest or a great news interest." "It must answer a great craving for knowledge on the part of the public." Above all it must be *important*.

I remember asking myself bitterly, "Important to whom?" Not necessarily important to *me*; when I was thinking of so many things I should like better to do. To whom then? Why, to the magazine, in building up a huge circulation—beating the world! And why build up a huge circulation and beat the world? So that rich advertisers would pay high prices for reaching the public that was being attracted by the important articles. This naturally would bring in large profits to the owners of the magazine with which they could establish new magazines and a great publishing house—to make still more money. And break down physically in the process.

I felt that I was more or less disloyal even to think such thoughts —but there they were: I thought them. What possible interest could I have in any such process? I was being as hard driven as I ever was as a newspaper writer—and I was scarcely freer to follow my own bent.

I remember, in my bitterness, that I thought of the great American advertiser as the modern Mæcenas, upon whose trickling favors such writers as I were dependent for our livelihood. I even wrote doggerel odes addressed in the Horatian manner to Ivory Soap and Pettyjohn's Breakfast Food and Pond's Extract—my inspirers and providers—heading them with couplets from Horace himself:

> Get money, money still
> And then let Virtue follow, if she will.

It can readily be seen what a state of mind I was in.

That winter (1900), having grown quite hopeless, I took my fate into my own hands. I left New York and *McClure's*, and went to Arizona.

CHAPTER XIV

In the Arizona Desert

I KNEW LITTLE or nothing about Arizona. I had no reason for going there except to get as far away as possible from New York. I wanted to cut entirely free from the work I had been doing. In the desert one could be quiet and think—or could he?

And yet, I could not have borne the expense of the long trip to Arizona and the months of freedom I demanded, I could not have taken my wife and little daughter with me, if it had not been for the truly generous interest of my editors in New York. They astonished me by assuming, as though it was the perfectly normal thing to do, that I should be paid my regular salary while I was away, and they offered also, if necessary, to help with my expenses. It quite bowled me over.

"But," I said, "I am not going to write anything at all, if I can help it. If I do write anything, it will be what I myself want most to write—probably nothing at all important, probably nothing that you would print in *McClure's Magazine*."

"Try it out for a few months, do only what you yourself want to do, get well physically, and we'll talk it over when you get back."

What good friends they were—and what hopeful editors!

We left Tucson for the Santa Catalina mountains early in the morning. The stage driver had two old horses and an open wagon: the road, always upward, was rocky, crooked, dusty.

At noon we stopped at a lonely desert corral with a huge mountain rising sheer behind it. Except for a sparse growth of cactus and mesquite and greasewood there was scarcely a living thing to be seen. Here we ate the luncheon we had brought with us, and the stage driver changed his horses.

It was forty miles northward to the ranch at Oracle and nearly a mile up; it took us all day to make it. We found the weather-beaten ranch house there on the mountainside, a wooden building with wide porches and a number of little cabins, in one of which we were to make our home. At the doorway we were met by the warmly hospitable ranchers, Mr. Dodge and his wife, who were from Nova Scotia, and who had come to that wild country to raise cattle and angora goats.

I remember little or nothing of the early days at the ranch. We arrived tired and dull, worn out by the long journey. Our little daughter had not been well, I was myself ill in body and wretchedly depressed in mind. At first the desert wastes, the great bare mountains, the wild and rocky arroyos seemed forbidding and even hostile.

One morning I heard a tap on my door and when I called out "Come in," there appeared a grizzled old Mexican, smiling apologetically:

"Ceniza."

He had no English at all with which to answer my inquiries; he could only repeat "Ceniza, ceniza." He came in with his pail and shovel to take up the ashes in our little iron stove and to build a bright new fire, since the mornings were sharply cool.

It was still early, but I got up quickly, threw on my clothes, and stepped outside. The sun was just coming up over the mountains. All the broad desert was glowing with light—pale yellow tones and lilac and amber. In the limpid morning air I could see, thirty or forty miles off, that sentinel of the desert, Piccachio Peak, rising abruptly upon the horizon, its summit glowing with gold.

I stood there for some time with the strangest sense of returning life, eagerness, appetite. I walked down the slope toward the great corral where the goats were herded. There I turned, facing the morning sun, and found myself, I don't know why, running up the hill at top speed, so that I arrived at our cabin panting, quite out of breath.

That was the beginning of my renewal. I think it was that very morning that I went down to the horse corral and met the cowboy who kept his horses there—a bluff shaggy man who had come from Kansas. We were soon acquainted, and deep in the lore of the range, and of cattle and horses—and horses. As a boy I had ridden with delight, often long distances. I had even learned to shoot partridges from the back of a western pony my father had owned—but all I knew, or thought I knew, was as sounding brass compared with what I heard that morning. My cowboy knew horses, as the rancher told me, "from the innards outard."

He caught one of his horses, saddled and bridled it, and loaned me a pair of wheel spurs, which I did not want and thought I should not need. It was a lean bay mare with a good eye. My father, who had been a cavalryman in the Civil War, always said:

"When you get a horse, get one with a good eye."

What a morning ride that was, in the full, warm, winter sunshine, with such a sense of freedom as I cannot well describe. There were no roads in that desert, one went where he pleased or where he could, up mountain arroyos full of immense round boulders, across bare ridges and open spaces where there were only cactus clumps or sprawling mesquite trees. I really began to see the living things of the desert—jack-rabbits running ahead of me with swift grace, and cotton-tails sitting up to watch as I approached, feeling safe so long as they saw only the horse, dodging instantly into their holes when they caught a glimpse of the rider.

I saw that curious but beautiful bird, the Mexican road-runner, darting in and out among the cactus clumps. Most surprising of all, on that very first day, I saw the last and only herd of antelope known in that desert—a buck with five or six does. I saw the buck standing alert, head up to watch, a beautiful sight, then with sudden alarm leading his flock in a flight swifter than the wind. They were a long way off that morning—but I saw them. What days afterward I spent skulking in the sagebrush, wriggling over sandy ridges on my belly, stalking that flock!

It was a grand morning, full of new wonders, above all new *feeling*. I came back with an appetite for dinner such as I had not had before in many months.

I bought the horse I had ridden on that first day, for the unbelievable price of fourteen dollars. I felt myself a robber in doing it: I was soon to learn that a horse trader in Arizona was not different from a horse trader in Wisconsin. That little mare cost me twenty-two dollars a month to feed and keep! Every ounce of grain and meal and all the hay she ate had to be hauled in expensively over the rough trails from Tucson. But Tucson was also in the desert and had its supplies from Kansas or Iowa—hundreds of miles away. I soon became inordinately fond of that wise little mare, and fed her, I think, better than any other horse in the southwest. I broke all the cowboy rules and rubbed her down myself—for the joy of it—until she shone. Some weeks later I rode her to Tucson, forty miles in one day, and back again two days later: and she seemed as fresh when we got home as she was when she started. When we left Oracle in the spring I sold her for twenty dollars—which was considered a bargaining triumph.

A horse is a better companion in the desert than a dog. A dog is too human, too uneasy, active, nervous, intense. He never lets nature alone—chases birds and rabbits, scratches after kangaroo rats, barks emptily, as men do, at game he knows he can never catch and would not know what to do with it if he did catch it. A horse is wise and patient: she will go when and where she is told to go: she will stand and wait.

I rode almost every day, usually alone: I explored the mountains and the desert for miles in every direction, once going as far as the San Pedro River, where I visited the old mine at Mammoth. On the return I tried to ford the deceitful river and got into quicksand. I had presence of mind enough to slip off the mare's back and cling to a saddle strap. Little Betts snorted and floundered and swam for her life. I was wet to the skin, but lucky, they told me, to get out at all.

Sometimes we made up picnic parties and rode up the arroyo into the mountains: a wild and beautiful country. My wife took her birdbook and her manual of botany, and little Alice rode on a burro. I had been told that a certain almost mythical rancher named Castro had plenty of burros and might let me have one. The next time he came into camp—wearing the largest hat that ever I had seen, and the most elaborate chaparreras and tapaderas, with huge silver conchas on his horse's bridle—I approached him with some awe. Si señor, he had burros.

"How much are they?" I asked.

"You catch um," said he, "two bits. Me catch um, four dollars."

"You catch um," said I, "I pay four dollars."

That very afternoon he came in dragging behind him at the end of a lasso one of the most obstinate, unreasonable, stupid, ridiculous, but adorable and gentle and amusing little beasts that one could have imagined. We spent no end of time fitting up a saddle and bridle and trying in vain to train him to follow the simplest instructions. We never succeeded in getting him to do anything or go anywhere without systematic prodding from behind. But Alice adored him and delighted in riding on his back.

As for my wife, I did not at first realize the difficulties and hardships she was having to meet in sharing my life in the desert. She had a dread of strangeness and little of my appetite for adventure. In my masculine absorption in my own problems, I was scarcely aware of the real sacrifices she was making. But we had one enthusiasm in common: our interest in the remarkable plant life of the desert, then so strange to us.

She had been trained by that best of botanists, her father, Dr. Beal, to whom I owed so much as a student in college. She was much more patient as an observer than I was, but we both found delight in many of our explorations and discoveries and, incidentally, new enjoyment in each other. I sent to Washington for government bulletins on the desert flora and fauna which proved most helpful. One of them, I remember, was by Professor Merriam and described the life on San Francisco Mountain, a bleak, lone peak in the northern part of the state, which showed the zones from the semi-tropical at the base to the semi-arctic on the summit. I believe he discovered certain rare species not found elsewhere south of Greenland. I was on fire with the idea of visiting that mountain and climbing to the stormy top of it with Professor Merriam's manual open in my hand. There seemed something strange, wild, symbolic, about it. I could not manage it that winter: but it has been a vision I have had ever since. I shall probably, now, have to save it up for one of my imagined future lives.

At first I had paid little attention to the great herd of angora goats, more than a thousand of them, that provided the principal occupation and anxiety of the ranchero. I saw them often going out in the early morning, a vast smudge of dust on the horizon, or came upon them miles away on the desert moving restlessly up and down, back and forth, literally consuming every green thing that grew except such as were armored, like the cactus, with spines.

Gradually I began to get acquainted with the herders, who were, I decided, a separate species of the genus cowboy. One was a strange, lonely Frenchman. No one knew where he had come from or why he was there: no one even seemed to know his name—he was called Gill—but he was the best herder in the camp. He seemed to have an uncanny understanding of the psychology of the herd—the sudden panics they had, the indescribable outbreaks of irritation and hostility, the obstinacy of their determination to go west when they should be going east. I never knew another human being who could stand perfectly still, his hands crossed upon the staff he carried, as long as he could. What did he think about? Once or twice I joined him at the little fire he made of dry cactus stalks to heat a can of tea. He had nothing to say: but he offered me a cup of the bitter black concoction which he poured, hot, from his can.

Kidding time came in the early spring and brought with it the most anxious activity of the year. The herd instinct in the angora goat seems to be stronger than the maternal instinct, and when the ewes dropped their kids on the desert, they were likely to move on irresistibly with the herd and leave the shivering little kids bleating and trying to stumble after them. All hands were called upon to help. We followed the herd on horseback, picking up the kids and putting them into gunny sacks tied across our saddles. We carried them into the dim corral sheds, grotesquely lighted here and there with lanterns.

The problem was to find the mothers of the kids. Most of the ewes were bleating pitifully, but no one of them, after nosing the various kids we presented to them, would take any but her own. When she was sure, the bleating ceased and she was soon fondling the kid as it sought her over-distended and painful udder.

When the shearing began, our speechless French herder, who had begun reluctantly to tolerate me, showed me how to use the shears. When I proved adaptable he found me an extra pair which I used on the smooth backs and sides of the goats, under his severe eye. But I had to turn the goats over to him to finish off.

All these things I lived through—the strange and fugitive beauty of the desert and the mountains, the primitive realities, the sky and the sand, so easily dissolving in mysteries and visions. All the quiet common things of the earth I came to love, and the simple and useful human beings—life going on, going on. It all gave me a depth of satisfaction I find it hard to express. All things were somehow beautiful to me: I longed to understand them better.

During all the early weeks in the desert I had avoided writing anything, even letters. I read no books. I rode or tramped to weariness every day, I ate prodigiously, I slept soundly.

I had a theory about thinking—that thought was like happiness, not to be had by direct assault. Thought was the by-product of an abundant, various, opulent life. The whole of a man's nature, not his mind alone, went into it. Thinking was not a part of life: it was all of life.

Presently, I began again to write in my neglected notebooks, trying to understand what all the things I saw and thought and felt might really mean, and it was not long before I had what would have made a small book about the desert. A paragraph or so may indicate what I was seeing and its relation to my own life.

The way of the desert is the way of the defiant spirit, always and everywhere, of meeting disaster by living inward and downward. Everything in the desert, whether plant or animal, does this. In an arroyo near our ranch I have traced the roots of a mesquite tree forty feet under ground and in places these roots are larger, harder, gnarlier than branches above. They dig themselves in, they grip for dear life upon the barren soil. If there is too little water they seek out every drop and store it up. The cactus does the same above ground, filling its thick leaves and stems to the uttermost. Cut open a bisnaga cactus and often you can press out a cup or so of pure water. Nature, defeated of ease and comfort, here turns inward upon herself, determined at all events to live. At the same time, these hard-pressed desert plants, like hard-pressed men, arm themselves with thorns and spikes, or cover themselves with gum, like the incense bush, or exhale a fetid odor, like the bladder pod.

I not only began writing again, but reading again. I had brought with me several books I had long wanted to read, mostly biographies. Among them were the diary of George Fox, the founder of Quakerism (not the copy I read so faithfully, and annotated, some years later), and a brief biography of Pasteur, as holy a man as any of the saints, living a life as completely consecrated.

"Pasteur was a priest," said his biographer, "the priest of an idea."

Most of all and most urgently, I considered, from the safe retreat there in the desert, the world I had been living in since I had gone to Chicago eight years earlier to become a writer. I considered what my own place in it had been. I could see, in spite of certain outward successes in my work, how completely I had failed. I had no inward unity: I was trying to march to victory with a civil war going on in my soul.

My mind went back to my father, as always the datum plane of my thought. When my father, after the Civil War, had felt dissatisfied with the life he was living, he went West to the frontier where there was new land to be opened, and roads to be built, and rivers to be bridged or dammed. His father before him had done the same thing, and *his* father before that—for eight generations of our family. My father had failed bitterly after the Civil War; as a merchant and as a small manufacturer he had lost his health and all his money. He went West to the frontier just as his ancestors had done: and there he found great and satisfying work, as satisfying spiritually as it was materially. My mother faded away under its rigors: he gloried in it. For it seemed to him quite the greatest thing in the world to clear away the forests, root out the stumps and build roads, churches, schools, houses, for the eager people who were to come crowding in. He suffered personal sorrows and reverses, he faced a severe physical limitation, but all his later life he knew the equanimity that comes from living the kind of life he loved, and doing the kind of work he could do best. He seemed to me always a strong, sure man, self-directed, united within himself, and therefore a contented man.

He did not know, and neither did I as a boy, that we were living on the "last frontier." There was no longer anywhere in America, or indeed in the world, for the ambitious or the discontented to go for free land, free forests, free rivers, for free opportunity which had been the goal as well as the precious possession of the pioneer.

I was literally the first of my immediate family, since the original ancestor arrived in Boston in 1630, to go East instead of West. To go East to grow up with the people, rather than West to grow up with the country. I went first to live in Chicago, then in New York, and was later to go to Massachusetts, which had been the home of our "original settler." With this the circle was complete.

What a different world I knew from that of my ancestors! They had the wilderness, I had crowds. I found teeming, jostling, restless cities; I found immense smoking, roaring industries; I found a labyrinth of tangled communications. I found hugeness and disorder. I found, after the clean forests and the open plains, confusion and dirt and poverty and crime. I found dishonest politics and greedy business men. While we were not without evil enough there on the frontier, it was not concentrated and complex and overpowering.

In short, it was a crowded world I had found: how was I to live in it? How was a man to look at it: what was he to do? Was it possible for any man, especially a man with my pioneer backgrounds, to live happily in it?

When in Germany I had heard the grim prophecy of one of the greatest scientists then living, Professor Ernst Haeckel, who saw clearly the vast social and national changes then in the making. The first World War was indeed only a few years away.

"There must set in," Haeckel had said with the calm assurance of the scientist, uncolored by his own hopes or fears, "a terrible new struggle for existence."

He had seen that there were few habitable places in the world left for immigration and the development of new human society—the two influences which had had so great a share in the progress of civilization during the last few hundred years. He could see ahead only a bitter struggle for survival.

All of these things had been fermenting ceaselessly in my mind. I could not at first think clearly about them. I kept getting in my own way, considering my own desires and fears and hopes, longing to believe the world something other than it was, unwilling to face the realities I was beginning to see so plainly.

I can recall vividly almost the instant when the problem, at last, began to come clear to me. It was in the early spring, there on the desert: the poppies had begun to bloom and there was a kind of sweetness I had not felt before in the desert air. I was riding horseback westward from the ranch house along a rough desert trail. I said aloud to myself:

"It *is* a crowded world. There is no longer, anywhere, any escape for me, or anybody else, from living in it."

This simple conclusion, which I had been so long in reaching, seemed to glow with reality. It was true: and I accepted it, to my own astonishment, without another argument or objection. In the afterlook it may seem that I ought to have come to such a simple conclusion without so much hesitation and such personal misery. It may have been what I ought to have done: I am telling here what I did do. I know how difficult it often is for a man to hack his way through the jungle of his personal desires, his fears, his traditions, his prejudices, his hopes, to an objective perception of reality clear enough to act upon.

I asked myself instantly:

"This being true, what am I to do about it? What is my function as a writer in a crowded world—that is, a writer not wishing merely to amuse people, but, in the practice of his art, to make them see and think, and thus to help fit them for living in this inevitably crowded world?"

I am perhaps making this process of illumination and decision clearer than it was to me forty years ago: nevertheless the ideas were there, and I was prepared to act upon them. It was something like an old-fashioned religious conversion. I had such a sense of conviction and of inner unity, a new purpose in life, as I had never felt before.

This acceptance of reality, and these decisions, however poorly I may have acted upon them, were, I think, the most important in my life. They established the pattern upon which, at times uncertainly and with many failures and few complete successes, I have acted ever since.

Having accepted the fact of a crowded world, even an overcrowded world, did not the prime test of the individual lie in his practice of the art of living in it? This led to a sharp inquiry as to what were my own personal qualifications and gifts for the test ahead of me. I had to consider what I was not, as well as what I was. I was not a leader, not an organizer, not a preacher, not a business man; *I was a reporter*. I had certain definite gifts for seeing, hearing, understanding, and of reporting afterward what I had seen and heard and, so far as might be, what I understood. I had certain clear scientific interests: I liked the exploration of new places and new things: I was curious about ideas. I especially liked people, almost all kinds of people. I liked to know how they lived, what they loved, why they laughed. I was keenly interested in writing down everything I saw and heard.

What seemed to me then the supreme problem confronting mankind was the art of living in a crowded world. The part I could best play in it as a writer—but this I worked out more slowly—was to become a "maker of understandings," as I soon began to phrase it. I was to help people understand more clearly and completely the extraordinary world they were living in—all of it, without reservations or personal prejudices—and in the process to make them understand one another, which I considered the fundamental basis for the democratic way of life. I believed these things at that time; I believe them more firmly with every passing year. If men can really be made to understand one another they can live together peaceably, even in a crowded world. But I have learned with the years how difficult real understanding may be, especially if it asks service and sacrifice as the price of living happily in a crowded world.

When I left the desert, as I shall presently relate, I began trying to live in accordance with my new "illumination," and soon found it, as many a man has done, a difficult business.

CHAPTER XV

California and "The Water-Lord"

IN APRIL OF THAT YEAR (1901) I arrived in California. My wife and little daughter, when we left Arizona, had gone eastward and homeward, and I westward to new country.

Beyond any other spot in America I had longed to visit California. It was the newest and quite the most glamorous of the American frontiers. It possessed the magic of new fortunes that had allured my restless forebears—the untamed water powers, uncut forests, unmined mountains, unbelievable monsters of trees, and fields so varied and so rich that they grew everything from the wheat of the North to the citrus fruits of the semi-tropical South. And what scenery it had—snow-clad mountains, strange, unexplored and dreadful deserts, waterfalls of surpassing beauty.

I remained in California for five weeks, and was as happy as ever I had been in all my life, but I did not see California. I lived in a dingy room in a cheap boarding house in the Westlake section of Los Angeles and wrote steadily during all that time. I had taken the cheap lodgings because my money was running out: the Arizona adventure had cost far more than anticipated. But it was no hardship; I was writing again. Every morning early I was at my desk. I wrote until noon and in the afternoon I tramped endless miles, living in a world of my own, far busier than the streets I walked in, sunnier than the parks I visited, brighter than the little lakes and ponds I saw. For I was full of new plans, I was living new stories and articles, inventing new characters, eagerly building up sentences, paragraphs, chapters, and committing them to memory as I tramped, so that all I had to do when I got home was to copy them down in the manuscript under my hand.

That spring it seemed to me I had everything! I had the robust physical health that had come from a winter in the desert; I had put down the inner civil war which had been destroying my soul. I knew now—or seemed to know—what I had to do in the world during all of my remaining years.

There were to be two novels: the first dealing with the struggle of men with the hard bare land—men against nature. I had already found a name for it: I called it *The Water-Lord.* I intended to make it the most searching and poignant presentation of the spirit of the pioneer yet written in America. No less than that! I felt I knew, in my own life and in my backgrounds, what pioneering was: I believed I could make other people see and understand it. I had resolved to write about the most difficult of all the problems that had faced restless Americans on their way to the settlement of a continent—the desert, that most resistant and unconquered of all land.

The second of the two novels was to deal with the other problem I had seen so clearly in the desert: the struggle of men with other men: the Art of Living in a Crowded World. This was to be the greater of the two, and since it would deal with problems not yet clearly understood, would involve much new labor.

I had, in short, recovered all the elation I had felt in the early days in Chicago when I was planning my elusive Great American Novel. Everything I now saw or heard or felt or thought would find a place in one or the other of these books. It seemed at the moment, so great was my exaltation, a perfect plan, to be happily executed—perhaps even speedily executed. What a time it was—when I did not yet know that all the best of my books were to remain forever unwritten.

I knew, of course, the difficulties I was facing. Money, money! I had to live while I carried forward these great plans: I had a family, precious to me, that I must support. I was already under obligations to the editors in New York for the advances they had so generously made. I considered, if it had not been for their timely assistance, I could not have spent those priceless months in the desert.

While I had solemnly agreed with myself that I would do no writing whatever during the winter, except in my notebooks, I had thought out what seemed to me an excellent plan to clarify the work on my novels. I would set down, in broad outline, what I had learned regarding the desert country, and at the same time satisfy my editors in New York with a number of articles and stories. It was a rare device for killing two literary birds with one stone.

My outline for these articles was as follows:

1. The Great Southwest: an effort to give some understanding of the vast and then little known domain of Arizona, New Mexico, West Texas and the eastern part of Southern California.

2. The Desert. This I longed most of all to get at. I felt the desert deeply both as a reality and as a symbol.

3. The Tragedy of the Range. The era of cattle, sheep, goats, the "hoofed locusts" of the dry country, as John Muir had called them, wherein every green and growing thing that was not armored like the cactus, had been consumed, as though devastated by fire. The first contact of man with the land is always destructive: he wastes before he replenishes.

4. The Green Land. I would tell what could be done by bringing in the water to these desert wastes. It was near the town of Phoenix that I first saw this marvel—the brown line of running water that marked the desert from the sown. On one side dry land, dry from the beginning of time; on the other a field of green alfalfa, luxuriant beyond belief, deeper than a man's thigh, overhanging the fences, dripping wetly down into the ditches. The great field beyond the ditch seemed to stretch for miles, the vivid green of it comforting and blessing one's weary eyes. It had seemed a vision of infinite peace: the culmination of contentment after years of labor and of struggle: I could not keep the tears from my eyes.

I wrote all four of these preliminary articles in the dingy bedroom of that Westlake boarding house. My letters of the time contain many references to the joy I had with them: the freedom I felt: the hope they bred in me.

I had determined from the beginning that for once in my life I would write exactly the kind of articles and stories I wanted most to write, not trying to fit them to the "requirements" of any magazine, nor caring whether they were publishable or not. I knew well enough from my own experience on the editorial staff at *McClure's* that they were not what we considered "*McClure* articles." They were not, certainly, "important": they were not primarily "timely." I had only one hope, that they might prove so interesting, so significant, as to breach the *McClure* formula. I doubted it, but I hoped. When they were finished I packed them up and sent them to the editors. I included with them a single short story for which I had found the background at a rodeo I had attended at Tucson. It was called "The Roping at Pasco's." I had an immediate response as to the story: they liked it very much and would publish it at once. Concerning the four articles in which I had invested my very life, there was ominous silence.

I had planned several other little stories like "The Roping" which would interpret various phases of the life of the desert country and would also help me along with my novel, but I did not go on with them because I had letters from Mr. Phillips and Miss Tarbell urging me to return as soon as possible to help again with the editorship of the magazine.

"Your work here," I was told, "would be done under pleasant auspices and in a very easy manner."

I was in no doubt about the pleasant auspices: these men were my good friends: but "a very easy manner" in the office at *McClure's*! I shivered at the thought of the roaring days in store for me, the long, hard hours, the weary nights. I felt, however, that I must do something, and at once, to discharge the great debt I owed to the publishers.

I left for the East in May, stopping over in San Francisco for several days to do a few editorial errands. I had been asked to call on two men, as different in every way as any two that ever I knew. The first was Jack London, then in the beginning of his meteoric literary career, in whom Eastern editors had suddenly become interested; the other that most gifted and original of living American naturalists and explorers, John Muir of the California mountains.

I found some difficulty in reaching Jack London though he had written directions quite fully. I was to "look about for a freakish house built of terra cotta" and I was to "find my way in somehow." He further whetted my interest and curiosity by telling me that he "expected a group of five or six people" whom I would "certainly find interesting—a little group which read old English plays now and again. Gelett Burgess will be among them in the bad company of two or three good socialists." I had already met Gelett Burgess, he of the "Purple Cow," and I had heard of the "interesting girl, a Russian Jewess, also a Socialist," whom I identified as Anna Strunsky.

Cameron King, associate editor of the *Advance,* an organ of the Socialist party, was also to be there.

I climbed the hill in Oakland according to directions and was soon lost in a maze of back streets: but I knew the freak house instantly when I found it. I am certain that there was not another like it in America. It had been built by an imaginative Italian musician, of highly colored stucco with the bottoms of blue and yellow glass carboys set in around the front entrance. Over the door a bar of the music of "Home Sweet Home" had been worked into the stucco, with flourishes. It seems that the inventive Italian had neglected to make room inside the house for a stairway to the second floor: but this had caused him no anxiety: he built a kind of ramp rising up the wall outside of the house which seemed to serve perfectly well.

I have always liked the first sharp impressions I get of men, when my mind is alert and full of curiosity. Jack London radiated vitality; he had curly hair, eager and lively blue eyes, powerful shoulders and a chest not easily confinable in any mere coat, so he was not wearing one. He was younger in years than I had supposed, only twenty-five, six years younger than I was, but he seemed to me considerably older, for he had had a rough and turbulent life, fighting his way upward out of poverty, trying to "break his birth's invidious bar." He had been married for only a year or so and had settled down to what he called a sober life in the freak house with the bar of "Home Sweet Home" over the doorway. Here he was passionately reading books on history and economics, and indeed poetry and plays, trying to make up, in weeks or months, for the educational deficiencies of his earlier years. He took me into the closet-like study where he worked and showed me the neat little piles of various socialist publications. When he had come up struggling out of the abyss to which his early life had condemned him, he had taken a swift and angry look at a world which had mauled him so unmercifully, fooled him, cheated him—he told me about it with bitter virility—and had become forthwith a militant socialist, with a flaming purpose of making over that world, and doing it immediately.

"Are you a socialist?" he demanded impetuously.

"No," said I.

"Why not?"

"I don't know enough."

"What do you mean?"

"Well," I said, "I want to be reasonably sure when I accept a utopian remedy for making over the world . . ."

"Utopian," he cried out, "it's intensely practical . . ."

"Hold on," I said, laughing, "hear me out and then let's go to it."

To my surprise I found myself putting into language for the first time some of the things I had been thinking about during the winter on the desert: it is for this reason, probably, that I recall these incidents so clearly.

"You see," I said, "I'm not a reformer. I'm a reporter. I have only begun to look at the world. I want to see it all more clearly and understand it better, before I pledge myself to any final solution for the evils we both see. I'm not sure yet that if either you or I made over the world, it would be any better than the one we now have. We don't know enough."

He came back at me hotly, and we had it, give and take, until dinner time. We both enjoyed it, I think, and got exactly nowhere. He was speaking out of his own bitter past, out of his own stormy temperament—and I out of my past and my temperament. The difference between us lay probably in the fact that he wanted to reform me, and I did not want to reform him. I wanted to see how he worked: how he had come to be what he was, for I knew that I should have to go on living in a crowded world with many people who differed from me far more radically than Jack London. In later years I have often reflected what a dull, uninteresting, unamusing world this would be if we all believed the same thing: thought the same thoughts!

The reading that evening turned into a comedy I delight in remembering. Jack had secured from the libraries in Oakland and San Francisco several ancient editions of Elizabethan plays, some of them printed in miserably small type and illustrated with old-fashioned engravings. After considerable jolly conversation we calmed down to the serious business of the evening—which was to beard culture in her lair. We took up one of Ben Jonson's plays, I think *The Silent Woman*, and having chosen parts began reading it. Some of us had several parts and often lost our places, had to be reminded that it was our turn, found it difficult to master the archaic English. We got sleepy. I have never, anyway, been able to make sense out of a book thus read, turn by turn. I want to take a good book into a quiet corner, like a dog with a toothsome bone, and give it my undivided attention. We became steadily more earnest, more serious. We concealed our yawns and waked up quickly when we missed our cues. We began to realize how difficult it was, even if we found culture in her lair, to drag her forth.

I don't know how long we should have persisted, if Gelett Burgess, with his God-given sense of humor, had not suddenly closed his book with a bang.

"I don't know how it goes with the rest of you," he said, "but I can't make a damn thing out of this play."

We all roared with laughter, Jack as much as any, and banged our books.

The next day I went for a sail with Jack on the bay. He had his own neat little craft and was here completely in his element.

I understood him better, there with the wind in the sails and his hand on the tiller, than I had the night before when he and all of us were lumbering through the dry wastes of Ben Jonson. How beautifully deft he was, and what joy he had in it! His head was bare and his loose shirt open at the throat, a pattern of physical perfection. He told me innumerable stories full of sweat and blood, and brutal poverty, and profanity and rum, some of which I saw afterward in his stories and novels. I remember especially his account of a wild night in Japan, after too much hot *sake,* when he and his friends ran through the paper partitions in the house where they were staying and wound up by arousing the village and fighting the entire Japanese population while they backed away to their ship.

I urged him to send us, at *McClure's,* some of his stories, which he promised to do.

My other visit, to John Muir, was as different an experience as one could have imagined. I had, that winter, been reading with delight some of Muir's essays and I had heard of his response to a friend who asked him why he did not kill off the destructive butcher birds around his home.

"Why should I kill them," he asked, "they are not my birds?"

I thought I should like a man who could say that.

Somewhere, I think in Eckerman's *Conversations,* Goethe contrasts "talent" with what he calls "nature." The "nature" is the man possessed, "more full of prescience, of deeper insight and wider scope." He is the man on fire, the noble human being. I thought of that comparison when I began to get acquainted with John Muir. Jack London had "talent." Muir was a "nature." He was sixty-three years old that spring, a wiry man, all muscle and sinew, fitted to climb mountains, brave dangerous glaciers, live weeks at a time on the dry bread he carried in his knapsack and the tea he brewed over an open fire, sleeping on the cold ground under the spreading branches of fir trees. In the midst of a storm in the high Sierras, he told me, he once climbed to the top of a huge tree that was beating about in the winds. There he hung, chanting the wild Scotch songs he knew in his youth. When I had looked into his eyes I knew he could have done just that thing: I seemed to know why he had done it: the ecstasy that had been in him.

All my life I have been looking for and treasuring men who are all of a piece: possessed men, sure men, inwardly united, men who expend themselves fearlessly and utterly in some great cause, great exploration, great art. I have found not a few of them—mostly scientists, poets, artists, saints. Muir was one of them. In my estimation he stands side by side with Thoreau as the greatest of American naturalists.

I spent a weekend with him at his home in the Contra Costa hills. We took long tramps: we talked early and late. Since that time I have always had a portrait he gave me with his signature hanging on my study wall where I can look up at it often.

I cannot here give any full account of what we talked about, or of how much he taught me. I will put down only a few of his sayings, and a little story about a dog.

We were talking about snakes.

"Poor creatures," he said, "loved only by their creator."

He loved the mountains. "Up there," he said, pointing, "up there is my home." He did more than any other man to preserve the mountains of the West for posterity, in parks and reserves.

To him all the earth was full of friends. "How many hearts with warm red blood in them are beating under cover of the woods, and how many teeth and eyes are shining! A multitude of animal people, intimately related to us, but of whose lives we know almost nothing, are as busy about their own affairs as we are about ours: beavers are building and mending dams and huts for winter, and storing them with food; bears are studying winter quarters as they stand thoughtful in open spaces, while the gentle breeze ruffles the long hair on their backs; elk and deer, assembling on the heights, are considering cold pastures where they will be farthest away from the wolves; squirrels and marmots are busily laying up provisions and lining their nests against coming frost and snow; and countless thousands of birds are forming parties and gathering their young about them for flight to the Southlands; while butterflies and bees, apparently with no thought of hard times to come, are hovering above the late-blooming goldenrods, and, with countless other insect folk, are dancing and humming right merrily in the sunbeams and shaking all the air into music."

He was essentially a poet, highly gifted in writing of his experiences and of what he saw and heard and thought about.

Emerson enjoyed Muir on his western trip, and Muir paid his highest compliment to Emerson by comparing him with the grandest of trees. "He is the Sequoia of the human race." Famous botanists who came to the Yosemite—Asa Gray, Torrey, Sir Joseph Hooker—all sought out Muir, not only for his extraordinary knowledge of the plant forms of his valley, but for himself, his quaint philosophy, and his abundant humor.

Muir's attitude toward Nature was that of one who stands with bared head. A man who goes to nature "must be humble and patient and give his life for light; he must not try to force nature to reveal her secrets, saying proudly 'I'm a great man! Trot out your wonders: I'm in a hurry.'" He must look long at nature, he must always be "letting the blood circulate around it," awaiting the slow coming of his conclusions.

On one of the mornings of my visit we went for a tramp into the hills. He had at that time a beautiful Collie dog. It was not the dog "Stickeen," which was with him on the Alaska glaciers and of which he afterward wrote a charming story: but it was a dog of almost equal intelligence. He called her "Colleen."

Colleen went with us, running wildly about on every side in dog-like enjoyment, and finally settling down to a leisurely trot, with tongue lolling out, just in front of us. I commented on her beauty.

"She's a remarkable dog," said John Muir, "and we're so much together that she understands all I say."

I must have looked a little incredulous, for John Muir said: "I'll show you. Watch her closely now while I am speaking."

With that he began telling me in his ordinary tone of voice and without talking directly to Colleen of the bad habits she had, how she barked at the birds, and if one wasn't watching, would even chase cats. Well, you should have seen Colleen! Her tail, which she had been carrying proudly aloft, began to droop. John Muir continued in a rather sorrowful voice to relate other bad habits. Colleen drew in her tongue, hung her head and was soon as dejected looking as any dog I ever saw.

John Muir glanced around at me as much as to say, "Now, do you believe it?" and then he began to tell what a fine and noble dog Colleen was: how she could travel all day without weariness, how she could herd a flock of sheep, and what a good watch dog she was at night. In a moment Colleen's head began to lift, her tail rose like a plume, she stepped with pride, and presently looked around at us. If ever a dog smiled, Colleen at that moment was smiling.

When anyone tells me that dogs can't understand human speech, I respond with this story of John Muir: but of course John Muir understood dog speech.

When I left John Muir I went homeward down the green hills with a higher appreciation of the nobility of the human race.

I arrived in New York eager to hear what the editors would say in regard to the articles on the Southwest that I had sent them. Several of the office readers commended them in the warmest terms—but they were not "*McClure* articles." As I have said, I had expected just this reaction, but I was, nevertheless, much cast down. How could I go on writing for a magazine which would not print the kind of work I most wanted to do?

After thinking about it for some weeks I put my rejected articles under my arm and walked down Fourth Avenue to Union Square, where I turned in to call on Richard Watson Gilder of the *Century Magazine.*

At that time the *Century* was probably the most notable of American journals. It represented, with *Harper's, Scribner's* and the *Atlantic Monthly,* a distinguished literary tradition, scarcely challenged as yet by the newer *McClure's* and *Cosmopolitan.* One could literally feel the difference in the atmosphere of the editorial offices. Our offices at *McClure's* were little glassed cubicles, a hard yellow table, a harder yellow chair, and perhaps a bit of a sectional bookcase. Only the Editor's own cubicle was somewhat larger and made a few spartan concessions to Comfort and to Art. It had a rug on the floor and a picture or so on the wall.

Richard Watson Gilder's office at the *Century* somewhat resembled the spacious study in a gentleman's country house, a gentleman who was interested, more or less platonically, in Literature. It radiated easy circumstances and leisurely living. Books everywhere, and portraits of distinguished contributors, framed paintings of notable *Century* illustrations, a fine old-fashioned globe in the corner.

When I went in, a rather slight, gray-bearded old man with pleasant eyes stood talking with Mr. Gilder. Robert Underwood Johnson was also there and Mr. Drake, the gifted art editor. I was introduced to the bearded old man: John Burroughs. I was somewhat overcome, since I had not expected to meet the man whose early books on natural history had delighted me. I blurted out the first thing that came into my mind:

"When I was a boy I read and greatly enjoyed what I think was one of your earliest books, *Pepacton.*"

He smiled at me and said:

"Do I look as old as that?"

It seems that they were discussing the kind of subject rarely heard in the cubicles of *McClure's.* It was not because we had no men who could have discussed it with discrimination and with wit, but in the bristling and busy atmosphere of our cubicles, it could not easily have emerged. The subject was the literary expression of disdain or pride: and I shall never forget the quotation that Mr. Gilder gave as one of the best examples he knew: the response of King Henry of France to the "bravest of the brave," his general, Crillon, who had failed to arrive in time for the battle.

"Go hang yourself, brave Crillon: we have fought at Arques and you were not there."

When I told Mr. Gilder about my articles on the Southwest, he shook his head doubtfully.

"I am afraid," he said, "that they are too much for us."

But he kept them to read and to my surprise telegraphed me a few days later asking me to come to see him. When I entered his office he took me warmly by the hand.

"Those are fine articles," he said, "we want them."

To my further surprise the *Century* sent Maxfield Parrish to the Southwest to make the illustrations. His paintings, published in color, were the most vivid representations I have ever seen of the desert country, perhaps even a little too vivid.

The *Century* advertised the articles widely, and were so well pleased with the response they had from the public that they asked me the next year to go to the Great Northwest to write another similar series, and sent the gifted young painter, Ernest L. Blumenschein, with me to make the illustrations for them.

This experience greatly encouraged me; I was learning that I wrote better and with greater ease and joy when I was writing about what interested me most.

CHAPTER XVI

I Watch the Birth Pains of a Famous Invention

To SAY THAT I WAS DISHEARTENED, after my glorious winter in Arizona, to have to sit down to an editorial desk in New York, was to put it mildly. I said so in letters written at the time: I wanted to "shake the dust of New York off my feet"! I wanted, more than anything else in the world, to get down to work on the novels I had planned. My head was full of them; and here I was in the bright spring weather, living in a city boarding house—my family was in Michigan—and spending all the long days at work which I did not like, and for which I felt I was not well fitted.

I was firmly determined upon one thing: I was going to get out of the city and live in the country as soon as I possibly could. The city interrupted and confused me. I not only longed to live in the country, but I thought it would give me the leisure I required to carry on my own work. A way opened for me sooner than I expected. Tramping in Westchester County, I came across an interesting old farmhouse, which I fell in love with on the spot. It was on a quiet country road that led from the village of Pleasantville on the east to Chappaqua on the west.

"It is a most picturesque old place," I wrote my wife, "with orchards around about and the most charming country scenery. The house, which was built in 1816, is covered with split shingles and has an open fireplace and a huge end chimney."

My wife, who arrived soon afterward with our two children, was delighted with the place. We had no near neighbors except two pleasant old ladies who lived in a little house just across the road and kept chickens. They had them all named. One fine old hen, a crested Wyandotte, they called Thanatopsis, and the majordomo of the flock, a noble and truculent rooster, had the strange name, "Barriers Burned

Away." It seems that one of the old ladies was fond of the novels of E. P. Roe, a writer even then mostly forgotten, and had named several of her favorites after his books, because, she said, one could never tell how they were going to turn out. The only problem in their placid lives, or so it seemed, was the necessity from time to time for putting some member of their cherished flock into the pot. We used to see them sitting on their porch, rocking gently back and forth and discussing whether they should sacrifice Henry Wadsworth Longfellow or John Greenleaf Whittier. When the decision was reached I went over with my sharp hand-axe and while the two old ladies sat with their eyes closed and their fingers in their ears I did the bloody deed.

While we all delighted in the Westchester countryside, and I found much joy on Sundays in tramping the country roads, the experiment was not a success. It took me an hour and a half to get from my office to our home—three exhausting hours every day—and often when I was delayed at night I missed finding any of the ancient one-horse carriages at the station and had to walk the dark roads, a mile or more from either Pleasantville or Chappaqua. I had hoped to make a garden and dig in it, to work in the meadow with the haymakers, but there was no time. I was so weary every night that I got little or nothing done on my writing. Worst of all, I was spending all I earned in mere living expenses—getting nothing ahead with which to make any literary experiments.

"If only I could have a small steady income, and a little time to myself," I wrote my father, "I could do the kind of work best suited to my tastes and my talent. I see now, as never before, how much hard work and thought it requires to write any really good thing; I have no time for any such work or thought: the rent comes due, the grocery and coal bills must be paid. My money obligations are a constant drag upon me."

Had I any warrant, beyond a passionate desire, in thinking I could do better writing than I had done before, or that it would be more valuable in the "making of understandings" (to which I had committed myself) than high-class and well-informed journalism? And was there any vital difference between the two?

Journalism, for the time being at least, had a strong fascination for me—that is, *writing* journalism, not the confusion of an editorial desk. The world was so new and freshly interesting to me, so many things to see and hear, such men to meet, so much to learn and write about: would I not be better equipped if I continued for a year or so longer with my magazine articles and stories? I could at least be sure of making a living—perhaps even save something—and at the same time dig deeper into the world I wanted to understand. Or, was this reasoning a mere temptation to scatter my energies?

When the bright opportunity came that winter to escape my editorial desk and write about one of the most extraordinary events of that or any other year, I snapped at it eagerly. News had come to us that the young Italian inventor named Marconi, then little known, had arrived secretly in Newfoundland to try to get wireless signals across the Atlantic Ocean. Several years before we had published an article about the "shy, modest, beardless youth" who had come up to England from Italy to experiment with "electric waves." He had called himself an "ardent amateur student," but his work, though original and important, had attracted little attention. How could any sensible man—the kind who prides himself upon "keeping both feet on the ground"—accept the crazy idea of sending messages through space, with no wires to carry them? In these trustful later days when the public is more than willing to seize upon scientific marvels even before the inventor is sure about them himself, it is difficult to recall the cold skepticism which, even forty years ago, paralyzed the acceptance of such "astonishing statements" as Marconi had made.

I can well remember my own excited curiosity as I traveled through Nova Scotia and thence by train around the north shore of Newfoundland to St. John's, the capital. I had hastily gathered together everything I could buy or borrow on the work of Herz, Branley, Sir Oliver Lodge, Edison, and Alexander Graham Bell. These I studied on the long, slow journey northward.

It was in the dead of winter, just before Christmas, that I arrived in St. John's. The weather was bitterly cold and raw, with lowering clouds rolling in from the sea. I recall the sense of unreality I felt when I struggled up Signal Hill, where the inventor had set up his instruments in a low room of the old barracks. As I approached the gloomy, wind-swept building, I saw a wire reaching upward toward a dark object beating about among the wild clouds. It was Marconi's great kite. An ocean cable, marvelous as it is, maintains a tangible and material connection between speaker and hearer: I could grasp its meaning. But here there was nothing but space, a pendent wire on one side of a broad, curving ocean, an uncertain kite struggling in the air on the other—and thought passing between!

When I went into the low, warm, dim room my credulity was even further tested. The inventor was a tall, slender youth, shy and almost boyish looking, with a thin moustache, and glowing eyes. He was at that time only twenty-seven years old, four years younger than I was: it was unbelievable. I was further astonished when he showed me, gravely, the apparatus with which he was performing his miracles. I had read, on the way up, of the cost of laying the first Atlantic cables: the immense and complicated equipment, an ocean steamship as a workshop, the costly installations in both England and America. I don't think Marconi's instruments could have weighed more than a few hundred pounds, and his kites and the wire from which they flew may have cost two or three hundred dollars. He told me that he and his two assistants, Mr. Kemp and Mr. Paget, had everything ready in three days' time.

The only difficulty he had encountered resulted from a miscalculation of the rough power of the winds of the north Atlantic. The kites were huge hexagonal affairs of bamboo and silk nine feet high, built on the Baden-Powell model. The first one he had sent up snapped the wire and blew out to sea. He had had the same experience the next day with a fourteen-foot hydrogen balloon which he sent upward through a thick fog bank. It also broke away and was lost. On Thursday, December 12, a day destined to be important in the annals of invention, Marconi had tried another kite, and though the weather was so blustery that it required the combined strength of the inventor and his assistants to manage the tetherings, they had succeeded in holding the kite at an elevation of about four hundred feet. He was then prepared for the crucial test. Before leaving England he had given detailed instructions to his assistants for the transmission of a certain signal, the Morse telegraphic S, represented by three dots (. . .), at a fixed time each day, beginning as soon as they received word that everything at St. John's was in readiness. This signal was to be clicked out on the transmitting instruments near Poldhu, Cornwall, the southwestern tip of England, and radiated from pendent aerial wires attached to masts two hundred and ten feet high. If the inventor could receive on his kite wire in Newfoundland the electrical waves thus produced, he knew that he had found the solution of the problem of transoceanic wireless telegraphy. He had cabled his assistants to begin sending the signals at three o'clock in the afternoon, English time, continuing until six o'clock; that is, from about eleven-thirty to two-thirty o'clock in St. John's.

I was much impressed by the matter-of-fact way in which he told me of that supreme moment, when he had sat waiting in the old barracks on Signal Hill, with a telephone receiver at his ear. It must have been a moment of stress, expectation, anxiety—the supreme moment in his life—but he did not show it in any way when he told me about it. Was it a masterly self-control, I wondered, or was it a supreme confidence in the delicate instruments which he had made with his own hands?

"I believed from the first," he told me, "that I would be successful in getting signals across the Atlantic."

He had waited patiently, but for a while there were no signals. Who indeed, standing on that bleak hill and gazing out over the waste of waters to the eastward, could have believed enough in the ingenuity of man to accept the possibility of such a miracle?

But Marconi adjusted his delicate instruments: and again waited. Only two persons, at that momentous hour, had been present in the room. Mr. Kemp told me that the inventor himself sat absolutely still, showing not the least excitement. Presently he looked up and said:

"See if you can hear anything, Mr. Kemp."

Mr. Kemp took the receiver, and a moment later, faintly and yet distinctly and unmistakably, came the three little clicks—the dots of the letter S, tapped out in England. At ten minutes past one more signals had come, and both Mr. Marconi and Mr. Kemp assured themselves again and again that there could be no mistake. During this time the kite had gyrated so wildly in the air that the receiving wire was not maintained at the same height, as it should have been; but again, at twenty minutes after two, other repetitions of the signal had been received. The miracle had happened; the problem was solved.

So secret had been the preparations of the inventor, and so little importance was attached to his experiments, that not a single newspaper correspondent had been sent to St. John's from the outside world. On the particular day of success even the ubiquitous local reporter at St. John's had been absent. I was the only writer who was present during any of the experiments. On my very first visit at the old barracks Mr. Kemp had the telephone at his ear and I heard him cry out, "Coming in again."

Marconi quickly took over the instrument and remarked quietly, "Yes, stronger than ever."

Even after he had been successful, the inventor hesitated to make his achievement public, lest it seem too extraordinary for belief. After withholding the great news for two days, certainly an evidence of self-restraint, he had given out a statement to the press, so that on Sunday morning the world knew, and doubted; on Monday it knew more, and believed. Many, like Mr. Edison, awaited the inventor's signed announcement before they would credit the news. Sir Cavendish Boyle, the Governor of Newfoundland, had reported at once to King Edward; and the cable company which had exclusive rights in Newfoundland, alarmed at an achievement which they thought threatened the very existence of their business, had demanded that he desist from further experiments within their territory, and handled Marconi's own paid cablegrams with reluctance. This was at once an evidence of the incredible stupidity of the money-making mind, and the future commercial possibilities of Marconi's invention.

As I write these words at my quiet home at Amherst, Massachusetts, it is again nearly Christmas time, and only forty years from that day in Newfoundland when I saw Marconi receiving those signals across the Atlantic. I have only to look up to see my indispensable radio set, before which I sit every evening to hear the reports coming in, one after another; from London and Cairo and Chungking and Melbourne. I never listen without thinking of what a marvel it is: "What hath God wrought"! All in forty years; and so much of it based upon the work of that shy youngster, twenty-seven years old, whom I went to see. The world would seem even more unintelligible than it does now without that discovery; and the work of Marconi and of other scientists and inventors in that broad field.

It has seemed to me sometimes, as I sit here quietly listening to the account of the battles of this second world war and the stupendous economic, political, and diplomatic problems growing out of them, that without the radio and the universal enlightenment that it encourages, there would be little hope of coming to any real understanding of the new art of living in a crowded world. And without understanding, how construct a lasting peace?

Marconi left St. John's with his assistants on Christmas day and invited me to accompany him. The Governor of the island, Sir Cavendish Boyle, placed his private car at the inventor's disposal, and sent his cook along to prepare the Christmas dinner. It was a trip I shall certainly never forget—the wonderful dinner we had, the grand conversation.

It seemed as if every fisherman and farmer in that wild country had heard of Marconi, for whenever the train stopped they came crowding to look in at the frosty windows, wondering most at the inventor's youthful appearance. Telegrams and cablegrams arrived by the score—every evidence of the sensation that the triumph at St. John's was awakening in the world.

We spent most of the day on the Newfoundland train, and all evening, talking about his experiments, and his life, his enthusiasms, his plans for the future. I think I must have asked hundreds of questions, quite as ingenuous—in the afterlook—as this one:

"And you can send messages through hills and in all kinds of weather?"

"Easily. We have done so repeatedly."

"Then if neither land nor sea nor atmospheric conditions can stop you, I don't see why you can't send messages to any distance."

"So we can," said the inventor—"so we can, given a sufficient height of wire."

I think Marconi enjoyed talking about his work fully as much as I enjoyed hearing him.

We crossed the straits of Belle Isle between Newfoundland and Cape Breton in the night steamer, the *Prince Edward*. The passage had the reputation of being one of the worst in the world and that winter night a wild storm was blowing. I am not the poorest sailor in the world, nor yet the best, and I held on with both hands all night long. I never before or since made a sea passage in a ship that seemed to roll clear over and recover its equilibrium by standing on its head. Alas for the gorgeous Christmas dinner I had eaten—alas, alas!

In the morning when I crawled out at Cape Breton, I was a specimen of complete emaciation, embarrassed even to face my friends of the night before. I was vastly reassured when I saw Marconi. His face was of a pale yellowish green and he looked like a worn old man.

The article I wrote about Marconi's work appeared in *McClure's Magazine* for February, 1902, and was widely quoted as the first fully verified account of the new invention and its revolutionary possibilities. What pleased me most was Marconi's own written comment:

"Mr. Baker's article is the first good popular account of my recent work in wireless telegraphy.

"Guglielmo Marconi."

Early that spring (1902) I went again to Europe. I had several editorial commissions to look into, and I wanted to see Marconi and follow up his experiments. I had become deeply interested in him and his work. I traveled down to Cornwall, where he had his principal laboratory and was rapidly developing methods for the commercial use of his discoveries. When he took me into his transmitter room, he gave me cotton wadding to put into my ears, and colored spectacles for my eyes. The noise of the transmitter was absolutely deafening and the flashing sparks between the huge brass transmitter knobs were all of a foot long, as thick as a man's wrist, and unbearably bright. Marconi worked early and late, with a passionate disregard for time or for his own health. He rode a motorcycle at breakneck speed back and forth between his laboratory and the little hotel in Poldhu where we stopped. He was all energy and nervous tension: but he lacked the steady, quiet, methodical industry of Thomas A. Edison or Alexander Graham Bell.

I was to have one more visit with Marconi, nearly seventeen years later. It was in 1918 just before the close of the Great War. I was in Rome and Thomas Nelson Page, then American Ambassador to Italy, invited me to go with him to Paris where President

Wilson and the American Peace Commission were soon to arrive. When I reached the compartments on the private train which the King of Italy had reserved for Mr. Page, whom should I find but Marconi: and we all traveled together to Paris.

I was shocked at his appearance. Although he was then only forty-four, he looked like a worn old man. He had lost the sight of one eye, and his hair was thin and gray: his eyes that had impressed me in the earlier time as glowing with life, looked dull and tired. And our talk, how different from that triumphant day on the Newfoundland train!

He had had every honor that the world can heap upon its dearest heroes: university degrees, the medals of famous societies, the Nobel prize. He had won great wealth: he was a senator of Italy, and probably the most distinguished Italian citizen—and he was unhappy.

I had welcomed the trip to Newfoundland to see Marconi and his experiments, and gladly went to England to follow them up. All of these diversions were fascinating. They presented new fields to be explored, vital new men, leaders in science and art, statesmen, builders, dreamers, to be met and written about; but I had firmly resolved that after my visits with Marconi at Bournemouth and Cornwall I would return directly to New York and "go to work."

Before I was ready to start home from London, I had a most urgent summons to "one more grand adventure," as I called it in a letter written at that time.

Ellen M. Stone, an American missionary in Turkey, had been captured by brigands in the wilds of Macedonia. The kidnaping had caused a great sensation in the press. Missionary organizations, after immense efforts, succeeded in raising a ransom of some $65,000, which had recently been paid over, and Miss Stone and her companion had been released. Mr. McClure, scenting a sensational magazine feature, had hurried down to Bulgaria, where he urged Miss Stone to let him print her story in *McClure's.* I was to go to Salonica, where she was then recuperating, close the arrangements with her, and see that the narrative was immediately forthcoming.

At Salonica I met Dr. John Henry House, who had long been a missionary in Turkey and was in charge of Miss Stone's affairs. We had many long talks. He and his large family lived in a house just under the ancient city wall, and I shall not soon forget the hospitality of his welcome, or the comfortable, homelike, American atmosphere it radiated. Such friends I made there and such stories I heard told! He was the kind of man I liked—and have always admired and trusted. It was not because of his religious views; although these were dominant and appealing aspects of his personality. I had also liked Professor Haeckel of Germany, who had, I think, no religious beliefs at all; I had liked Jane Addams of Chicago, who loved human beings. I was afterwards to follow and to trust Woodrow Wilson. Many other devoted men and women I have known and loved: my friendships with them I treasure among the highest and finest rewards of my life.

All these men and women had certain common qualities: all were devoted to noble objectives outside themselves: all deeply sincere. Men not possessing, but possessed. And finally, all had creative imagination, or if it seems a better word—vision, to which they were unselfishly devoted.

I never knew any other man, I think, who lived so completely and genuinely by what he called "communion with God" as Dr. House, without fear, without personal ambition. His vision was of a new kind of missionary work. He was not contented with the older objective of changing men's religious beliefs and affiliations. He wanted to change their lives. He organized the American Farm School in the open country north of Salonica and brought in students of several Balkan nationalities, taught them new methods of agriculture in a land where there had been scarcely any changes in five hundred years. He taught them to work together, taught them how to live honestly and helpfully, and sent them back to their own villages to pass on the torch of education and of progress.

After I returned to America I corresponded for many years with Dr. House. I became (a too-little helpful) trustee of his school, and have watched with admiration through many years, its successful growth. He died a few years ago at the age of ninety—a life wonderfully rounded out, rich in friendships, soundly useful throughout, and to the end, happy.

A great new problem soon arose. Miss Stone wanted above everything to return to America—and so did I. Difficulties developed in securing the necessary passports, and it was suggested that I might be able to help through Mr. Leishman, the American minister to Turkey, if I went to Constantinople.

I started immediately, and had a series of incidental experiences extremely interesting to me.

The one adventure I desired most of all, perhaps because it was the most improbable of realization, was to see the Sultan of Turkey. As the result of a series of fortunate happenings, I found myself standing on the palace terrace which rose above the roadway that led from the Yildiz Palace down to the Mosque where the Sultan went to worship on holy days. It was the Mohammedan feast of Bairam.

I have not the space here to describe all the extraordinary things I saw and heard on that day, but I must put down the glimpses I had of the Sultan himself, which I can never forget.

Preceded by his women in closed carriages, several of his sons, and some eighty great generals and officers of the army, and the Chief Eunuch of the Court, marching on foot, came the Sultan himself. He was driven slowly in an open carriage, facing forward, with his Minister of War sitting opposite. This was Abdul Hamid II, the absolute ruler of 25,000,000 people, the Defender of the Faith, monarch of the Huymet-i-senize, the Glorious Government—known elsewhere as the "Great Assassin."

Every splendor of the generals and the troops was forgotten; every eye was fixed on the little, old, round-shouldered man in the carriage. A shout—a well-trained and evidently long-practiced shout, curiously lacking in fire or spontaneity—went up from the troops. The old man raised his hand in salute. He wore a red fez, his face was a sickly white, like parchment; his nose was that of an old eagle, long, hooked, high-bridged—the Armenian nose, his subjects whispered in contempt. His eyes, what one saw of them, for he turned his head neither to right nor to left, were deep-set and black. Those who knew him best said that he had a peculiar way of moving his eyes without moving his head, as if he were always seeking to look behind him, to pry out secrets, to surprise hidden motives. His beard was deep blue-black, as were his eyebrows. Naturally, they would be gray, but he dyed them, for the Sultan must never look old. To his generals he left all the pomp and display of gold and lace and tinsel; he himself was clad wholly in black, like a eunuch, without ornamentation of any kind. "The Raven" he had been called, and the raven he looked. Not really an old man—only sixty years old—but if he gave one impression more than another it was that of age and great weariness.

When I returned to Salonica, the passport arrangements had been completed and Miss Stone and I took the train northward. The compartment in which we traveled was guarded on both sides by Turkish secret agents, who remained until we reached the Serbian border. We learned that the Government was fearful that some attempt might be made by the revolutionaries to seize Miss Stone again.

We traveled across Europe to England and sailed on the *Deutschland* for New York.

CHAPTER XVII

I Plan Out a New Life of My Own

YEARS AFTERWARD, I read, in a portentously serious book discussing the period of the so-called "literature of exposure" (1902–1909) and the "insurgents" and "progressives" who followed that movement, quite a flattering account of my own work as a "flaming crusader." I was naturally much pleased with it—at first. I liked my looks in such a portrait; I seemed, after all, a far more important person than I had imagined. But presently I began to laugh—remembering how little at the time I felt like a "flaming crusader." I find no evidence of it in re-reading the letters I wrote at the time, nor in the notes I made in my intimate journal. What I do remember and what I do find in my notes, is a consuming interest in the new world I had come into since leaving my boyhood home on the frontier. I had a sharp appetite for life: I liked people—all kinds of people—and I wanted, above everything, to get down on paper what I heard and saw and felt and thought about them. I did not want to reform the world; there were plenty of others willing and eager to do that! I knew I did not know enough to do it: what I wanted was to understand it.

I wanted to understand it and put it all into the two books I had planned while on the Arizona desert in 1901. Why did American human beings do what they were doing? Where were they going, and how were they planning to get there?

My chief difficulty all along had been to find time and quietude to do the work I had in mind. I was living the same kind of distracted life on the magazine that I had formerly on the newspaper. I remember the impatience I felt returning from Europe that spring (April, 1902) on the fine ship *Deutschland*. I had time, during the long calm days, to think, and my thoughts did not comfort me. I was not doing the kind of work I wanted most to do, I was not living the kind of life I wanted to live. I actually felt a kind of irritation that I should be expending all my precious time on a subject—the story of Ellen Stone, the missionary who had been a captive of brigands in Macedonia—which was so far removed from the themes I considered my own. It even vexed me that I should find Miss Stone's adventures so interesting!

I came to know and enjoy two men on that ship. One was a thoughtful looking man, distinguished in his bearing, at first rather formidable. A judge perhaps? A famous doctor? A college president? I could see that he was not to be taken by storm: he even seemed to respond grudgingly to the good-morning salutations of the deck promenade. One sunny day, he pointed out to me a whale he had seen spouting far off to the north and responded to my questions with comments, at first somewhat hesitant, that let me into the world of the seas as I had never known it before. I think I must have shown my eager interest, for he began to tell me about the famous scientific expedition of the "Challenger," and of all of the wonderful things the explorers had found. It was the first of several infinitely fascinating talks. I soon learned to my astonishment that I had been talking with Alexander Agassiz, son of the great Agassiz of Harvard, and one of the most accomplished American naturalists then living. He himself, if I am not mistaken, had led the "Challenger" expedition. I told him of how often I had heard my old teacher, Dr. Beal, tell of his work in Louis Agassiz's laboratory and of how thoroughly he had infected me with the Agassiz method of study—"look at it again." His talks were so rich in interest that I thought that they might easily be made the basis of a fine magazine feature; but it was not this that moved me most deeply. I remember thinking that he was a man on fire with his subject, and able to devote his time to it—which to me at that time seemed the pinnacle of felicity.

I also made the acquaintance, partly by accident, partly because I was attracted by his extraordinary black eyes, of a spare, pallid little man who sat near me at the ship's table. I could not at first make him out. I thought he might be a musician, or possibly an artist. He turned out to be Santos-Dumont, the Brazilian aviator, one of the earliest builders and experimenters with dirigible balloons, whose own story we were able to publish a few months later in two articles in our magazine. He had recently won a coveted prize for sailing his huge angular "ship" around the Eiffel Tower in Paris. He told me that he had been interested in aeronautics as long as he could remember, beginning by flying kites. When he and other boys played "Pigeon flies," he refused to pay the forfeit when he put up his hand at "Man flies."

"The more they laughed at me for thinking a man could fly, the happier I was."

The impression I got, and strongly, was that here was still another life absolutely centered and devoted, a man who had met innumerable difficulties and dangers and had driven through them to success.

Both of these men, it seemed to me, had a recipe for satisfaction in life, yes, for happiness, that I did not know. So had Dr. House whom I had so recently met in Turkey.

Upon arrival in New York I had a telegram telling me of the birth of our second son, Roger, our third child, and I hurried homeward immediately. During my absence, my family had been living in Michigan near the home of my wife's parents. Here the answer to the problem of what I should do rapidly took shape. I recall coming upon a quotation from Herbert Spencer which I find in the notes made at the time—and which, in the words of the Friends, "spoke to my condition."

"The best definition of happiness," he said, "is freedom to exercise one's own faculties."

That was what, exactly, I wanted most to do—exercise my own faculties. I began receiving letters from S. S. McClure telling me that he was again raising my salary and urging me once more to accept the "responsible editorship of *McClure's Magazine.*" A little later an eloquent appeal came from Albert Boyden, then the managing editor, who was my dear friend, for "great articles to sell the magazine." I saw clearly that I was at the parting of the ways.

Near the grounds of the Michigan State College, where Dr. Beal was still a professor, a small settlement had been started on an old Michigan farm. It was not even, as yet, a village; it had no post office, no school building, no church—and the nearest markets were three miles away in Lansing. Here I bought a small white house with room for a garden behind it, and we moved in. One of the chief advantages it had for me was the open farming and forest country all about and the delightful and interesting country roads, leading off toward the vast Chandler marshes, as well as eastward up the Cedar River through a number of small farm villages. It was a country I had known well as a student.

The new home satisfied two of my most urgent requirements: it was a quiet spot where I could work, and it was inexpensive to maintain. This latter was important to me, for I knew it might be a year or two before I could again earn a good living. And even if I did finish a novel in that time, how could I know that it would sell? Another great advantage was that the new home pleased and satisfied my family; it was near the campus residence of my wife's people and other old friends.

I shall never, certainly, forget the feeling of joyful independence I had when we were settled in the new home. I fitted up one corner of my bedroom for a study. On the wall over my roomy desk I put up portraits of my father, and Walt Whitman, and Tolstoy with his long beard, also a photograph signed for me by John Muir, and smaller pictures of Rudyard Kipling and Robert Louis Stevenson. At the back of the desk I pinned a number of quotations which I had come across in my recent reading. I called them "things to think about" and I changed them from time to time.

One from Bagehot, whom I was then devouring:

"The reason why so few good books are written is that so few people that can write know anything."

"Every man can do his best thing easiest," from Emerson's *Uses of Great Men.*

This from Whitman:

> I think heroic deeds were all conceived in the open air,
> and all fine poems also;
>
> I think I could stop here myself and do miracles;
>
> I think whatever I shall meet on the road I shall like,
> and whoever beholds me shall like me;
>
> I think whoever I see must be happy.

To have everything easily at hand and familiar, I also set up a few books at the back of my desk; some of them were more or less permanent working associates:

Rural Rides, by William Cobbett, especially the introduction, which I always felt was first-class advice to the writer.

Walt Whitman's *Leaves of Grass.*

Emerson's *Essays* and *Representative Men.*

William Penn's *Some Fruits of Solitude.*

Thomas Jefferson's *Morals of Jesus*—but this may have come to me a little later.

Others changed with my enthusiasms from month month. Boswell's *Life* was there for some time, and Pepys' *Diary,* and Cellini, and Don Quixote—all good, long, satisfying books. Kipling, Stevenson and Barrie gradually disappeared, giving place to George Meredith and George Gissing and W. H. Hudson. George Borrow gave me great satisfaction for several years, and Thoreau and Huxley. As soon as I found it, I added my now indispensable *Meditations of Marcus Aurelius.*

With what fondness I recall that old desk in the corner of my small bedroom. It was the first desk I ever had that was big enough, where I had everything I needed near at hand either in the capacious side drawers, or in the small filing cabinet, and where I could spread out my elbows and work as long as I wanted to without interruption —theoretically without interruption, for there were three lively children in the house! What a thing it was, also, to have everything I most desired securely in the future—fresh, new, radiant—as unspoiled as the white paper on which I wrote, as unused as the ink in my pen.

And it was thus, one golden spring day, all free and happy, with enough money in the bank to keep me and those dependent on me free for a year (as I thought) I began my second novel—although the first, *The Water-Lord,* was not yet finished.

Chapter I
Joseph the Pioneer and John His Son

It was fortunate that, at that time, I could not know all the tribulations I was to have with that book.

CHAPTER XVIII

The "Muckraking" Period—I Talk with President Roosevelt

I HAD MADE the decision to remain in Michigan and to go forward with my own writing without definite consultation with the editors in New York: I expected that it would mark the end of my direct connection with *McClure's Magazine.* I actually thought my future was settled! For it seemed to me that I was now securely anchored in a home seven hundred miles from New York where I could not be reached or interrupted. I did not count sufficiently upon S. S. McClure and John Phillips and the other friends at *McClure's.* S. S. had a way with him! While he wrote that my decision was a blow to him, he insisted upon sending to me regularly half the salary I had been receiving, with the understanding that "we are to publish your novels on the same basis that we publish Booth Tarkington's, Stewart Edward White's, and others. I believe you will make a great success at fiction and if you wrote a good novel for me I should set about to sell 100,000 copies."

So the serpent in my new Eden!

At first I wrote on my novel with ease and delight. I found I had a firm grasp on the principal characters (except the heroine) and the earlier chapters went off with a bang. I tramped up and down the country roads, thinking my story, and rushed home to put down upon paper my fresh-minted contrivances. I loved the freedom I had, and the solitude. I was soon literally overwhelmed with what seemed to me the richness and importance of my material. It was certainly the Great American Novel I had dreamed about. One hundred thousand copies!—why not three hundred thousand? Why not translations into many foreign languages? Why not a play based upon the book? I was so eager to awaken the American people to a clearer understanding of the new problems and dangers they faced—as I saw them—that I was even strongly tempted to let the *Magazine* go ahead and print the early chapters, as I was foolish enough to do with a later novel. I was as sure as this that I saw my way through to the end. It was some friendly djinn that stayed my hand: I did not yield to that temptation.

I find myself embarrassed when I make these naive confessions—but there they are truthfully set down—and when all is said, those days were among the most engrossing of my life.

I have spoken perhaps too often of the training I had in scientific method under my old professor, Dr. Beal.

"Look at it again."

"Go slow."

"First be sure, then talk."

But highly as I still regard these principles, there were times in my life when I wanted to curse the thought of them. For I had a kind of swift facility as a writer and was constantly being delayed, tripped up, by the necessity of making absolutely sure of what I had seen or heard. Afterward I would discover that I had so much new material, all so interesting and important, that I could not without prodigious labor subdue it to the limitations of a single story or article, or even a novel. My novel, which had been flowing along as beautifully and abundantly as a spring freshet, suddenly slowed down.

My purpose all along had been to present the explosive new economic and social and perhaps political forces that affected American life. It may be recalled that I had begun in Scott's seminars at Ann Arbor to read and write about strikes and lockouts which then (in 1892) were ominous forerunners of the coming economic crisis. When I went to Chicago I found myself in the midst of the storm and later, as I have recounted, I marched with Coxey's Army of the unemployed, and "covered" the great strikes at Pullman, and the so-called "Debs rebellion." Afterward, when I joined the staff of *McClure's Magazine,* I found that if I really went on with the novel I had planned I needed a much more extensive knowledge of American economic and business conditions than I then possessed. So I made as thorough a study as I could of the economic situation in the country as it then existed (1899) and published a book about it, called *Our New Prosperity* (1900).

I kept on, as I could, enlarging my background of knowledge—even though I could not always persuade the editors at *McClure's* to publish my articles on these subjects. They did use a biographical account I wrote of J. P. Morgan (October, 1901), and another on "What the U. S. Steel Corporation Really Is and How It Works" (November, 1901). I also wrote an article on the great struggle between the titans of finance for the control of the Northern Pacific Railroad, which *McClure's* did not care to publish—but it came out in *Collier's Weekly* (November 30, 1901). I was especially interested in this last because it opened to me the business and financial side of the railroad situation in the Northwest—of which, during the Debs strike of 1894, I had come to see and know the workers' side. I had met Debs and many other labor leaders personally; I not only felt them as strong and able human beings, but I knew, or thought I knew, the powerful incentives for organization behind their movements, and their demands for more wages and more freedom.

It was because I needed a similar close acquaintanceship with the leaders on the other side of the battle line that I had gone with fear and trembling to see J. P. Morgan—the giant of them all. I also met other leaders, among them Charles M. Schwab of Steel and Hill of the Great Northern Railroad (but I could not get to Harriman). I worked hard and long to try to understand, thoroughly and honestly, what they were trying to do and why; what things looked real to them.

Yet I had not gone far with my novel there in my sunny room when I began to find that I was still not as clear as I had supposed upon certain of the inside arrangements and relationships, either of labor or of capital. While I had made first-hand studies of several great strikes, and had read everything I could get hold of relating to labor problems, including Sidney Webb's great book on the British labor movement, *Industrial Democracy*, I felt that I needed to know a great deal more regarding the actual practices and policies of labor organization in America.

Accordingly I dropped my work and dashed off to New York and Chicago and elsewhere to see the leaders themselves. I met Samuel Gompers for the first time in Washington, and found him a very different type from Debs. He was a determined, indefatigable, cool-headed organizer, contrasted with Debs, the ardent, idealistic, emotional evangelist. I made careful memoranda of all I heard and saw for use in my novel.

I turned part of my material into a kind of basic explanatory article which I hoped *McClure's* would publish, thus helping to relieve, somewhat, my obligations to them. It was called "How Labor Is Organized."

At that time American opinion, so largely based upon the convictions of an earlier preponderant individualistic agricultural life, was generally hostile to labor unionism. It did not care to understand the underlying forces that were driving labor to organize. I considered that my article was *news* (though it was not in itself a very good article), but the editors at *McClure's* thought it too general. I took it over to Walter H. Page, the brilliant and forward-looking editor, indeed the creator, of the new *World's Work*—and he was glad to publish it (August, 1902).

At that time I never thought of these articles, either on the capitalistic or the labor side of the new problems, as "revolutionary" or "crusading." They were fact articles on conditions which keenly interested me personally, and when published they also interested a great many other people—judging by editorial comment and by letters received. They were in no way essentially different from the articles later blasted by the highest possible authority—President Theodore Roosevelt—as being the work of "muckrakers."

During that fall, while I was busily at work on my novel, a great strike was under way in the Pennsylvania coal fields.

So I went in October to Wilkes-Barre and met John Mitchell, the able leader of the miners. He was not at all the man commonly presented in the newspapers I saw—the "wild-eyed radical," the "disturber of the peace." He seemed to me a singularly steady-headed man, with some of the qualities of both Gompers and Debs.

I met quite a group of writers and students, to say nothing of radical leaders in other fields, who sensed the historic importance of what was happening there. Two men who were there were well known in liberal gatherings, Henry D. Lloyd, whose *Wealth and Commonwealth* was one of the earliest contributions to the real "literature of exposure," and Clarence Darrow of Chicago, even then the champion of the underdogs of the world—often without bothering to inquire whether the over-dogs had any case at all. I recall gatherings in dingy hotel bedrooms filled with tobacco smoke, in which the issues were discussed with a passionate certitude not warranted, as it seemed to me, by any real or deep knowledge of the facts.

I used the same methods, as a reporter, that had proved so successful at the time of the Pullman strike in Chicago. I tramped out to the miners' homes, I went down into the mines where the men worked, I sat in at several of their long-winded meetings, and listened to their bitter discussions. I found the newly organized miners not only at war with the powerful owners of the mining properties, but even more angrily with the large numbers of their fellow workers who would not "come out" and support the strike. They hated these "scabs" to the point of murder.

I have always liked, best of all, to study minorities. Majorities may have power; minorities often have understanding. Majorities are commonly interested in property; minorities in ideas.

It was easy enough to see the glaring injustices of the coal fields—low wages, company houses, company stores, poor schools, wretched living conditions: these had not only been widely publicized by the leaders of the strike, they were generally admitted. I did not need, at first anyway, to study these aspects of the situation. But why, if all these things were true, should 17,000 of the men in the anthracite fields, a sizable proportion of all the miners, doggedly refuse to support the strike? Why should they prefer to go on working in danger to their lives?

What men I met during those fiery weeks! What stories they told me: what dramas of human suffering, human loyalty, and human fear I saw: all brilliantly lighted against the scorched and dusty background of the Pennsylvania hills.

My article was a vivid series of case histories. It neither offered conclusions nor suggested remedies. I was unprepared for the enthusiasm with which it was received by the editors in New York. S. S. McClure wired me, "Your article tremendous," and even came down to Scranton to see me and to plan for vivid photographic portraits of the men whose stories I had told—remarkably fine looking men they were. He afterward sent down my old friend of the German trip, George Varian, to make pictures of the miners' homes. And finally we had earnest discussions there and later in New York as to an introduction to the article which we had decided to call "The Right to Work." I was strong in my opinion that it should be clearly stated that I had treated only one aspect of a highly complex problem. It was true only as far as it went; I did not wish to be making ammunition for mere stupid opposition to all labor organization, or even all strikes.

After completing my article, I hurried back to my home in Michigan quite on fire with the wealth of new material, new characters and, above all, new understandings of the human elements in the vast problem I was interested in. I had written to my wife that I intended to remain at home and "write gloriously all winter long." I went at my work with enthusiasm, and a month later I was telling my father:

"I am deep in the writing of my novel." Even as late as February, 1903, I was still holding my own.

"The Right to Work" was published in January, 1903, and I soon began to receive editorial clippings regarding it and letters from all over the country. S. S. McClure himself wrote to me on January 23: "Everything has borne out the truthfulness and value of the article you wrote, and I am sorry we could not get the whole thing into one issue. I hear a great deal from the article."

That January number of *McClure's* also contained two other memorable articles, one by Lincoln Steffens on "The Shame of Minneapolis" and the other by Ida M. Tarbell, the third in her great *History of the Standard Oil Company.* Until the magazine was in "dummy" form it never seemed to have occurred to the editors that three of the articles it contained had a notable resemblance and were actually discussing the same general subject—a subject that was just then beginning to disturb the consciousness of the American people. One of the best proofs, of course, of the value of these articles was the extraordinary demand for the magazine on the newsstands and the sudden increase of subscriptions. Mr. McClure wrote me on January 13: "From all I can hear your article and the other two articles in the January magazine have been the greatest success we have ever had."

This reception of the three articles, as well as the forethought that had gone into each one of them separately, resulted in an extraordinary stroke of editorial perception. I think it was the restless, but eagerly intuitive mind of S. S. McClure that made the discovery that these articles rested upon a heretofore unrecognized groundswell of public interest. At the last moment an unusual semi-editorial was inserted on the final page of the magazine commenting, for the first time I think, on what was later to be known politely as the "literature of exposure," impolitely as "muckraking." It began:

"How many of those who have read through this number of the magazine noticed that it contains three articles on one subject? We did not plan it so, it is a coincidence that the January *McClure's* is such an arraignment of American character as should make every one of us stop and think. How many noticed that?

"The leading article, 'The Shame of Minneapolis,' might have been called 'The American Contempt of Law.' That title could well have served for the current chapter of Miss Tarbell's *History of Standard Oil Company*. And it would have fitted perfectly Mr. Baker's 'The Right to Work.' All together, these articles come pretty near showing how universal is this dangerous trait of ours. Miss Tarbell has our capitalists conspiring among themselves, deliberately, shrewdly, upon legal advice, to break the law so far as it restrained them, and to misuse it to restrain others who were in their way. Mr. Baker shows labor, the ancient enemy of capital, and the chief complainant of the trusts' unlawful acts, itself committing and excusing crimes. And in 'The Shame of Minneapolis' we see the administration of a city employing criminals to commit crimes for the profit of elected officials, while the citizens—Americans of good stock and more than average culture, and honest, healthy Scandinavians—stood by complacent and not alarmed."

The public response to these articles, by any test, was astonishing. I doubt whether any other magazine published in America ever achieved such sudden and overwhelming recognition. Partly by chance, partly by a new technique of reporting which demanded thoroughness of preparation and sincerity of purpose—and gave the writer the time and the freedom to cultivate those virtues—we had put our fingers upon the sorest spots in American life.

We might well have expected response and approval from students of public affairs, from liberals and radicals and "agitators," but everybody seemed to be reading them.

I was myself surprised to receive a letter from the President of the United States. At that time Theodore Roosevelt was probably the keenest living judge of trends of American opinion. He had been reading my articles and watching the response they were awakening. He asked me to come to lunch with him at Oyster Bay on July 11, 1903. He had not only seen the labor articles, but he had heard that I had been in Arizona and wanted, he said, to talk with me about the great new irrigation project in the Salt River Valley, where a huge new dam, afterward to be called the Roosevelt dam, was in process of construction.

"At times," he wrote me, "I hear rumors of crookedness in connection with the Government irrigation work especially in Arizona. I have been utterly unable hitherto to get any definite statement in reference thereto. It has occurred to me that you may be able privately to tell me something about this Government irrigation work in Arizona, if you happen to know anything wrong about it."

It is quite unnecessary to say that I was tremendously excited by the President's invitation, or that I took the morning train from Long Island City, as directed. I was so eager to help him in any way possible that I got together a large package of notes and memoranda—also maps and pictures—and a veritable article of several thousand words on which I spent several days of hard work, setting forth in detail the exact situation in the Salt River Valley as I had seen it. Then I recalled suddenly that it might not after all be the irrigation projects that he really wished most to know about—and I spent another day or so writing a memorandum on the situation in the Pennsylvania coal fields. I was determined to be fully prepared: I could and would be able to give the President of the United States several hours of sound enlightenment and instruction!

On the train to Oyster Bay I found Mr. Shaw, Roosevelt's Secretary of the Treasury, Mr. Bonaparte of Baltimore, and Mr. Kohlsaat of Chicago.

We got into a dilapidated old public carryall drawn by a decrepit horse and drove over the pleasant three miles to Sagamore Hill.

"The country reminds one," I wrote in my diary, "somewhat of a quiet corner in the English downs country: the chestnuts, all in bloom, marked the hillsides, and we met many people out driving in their carriages. As we went up the hill toward the President's house I wondered what a foreign nobleman would have thought of this, the modest country place where the chief executive of a great nation was conducting the affairs of government.

"A maid opened the door and we went into the President's library. On his desk I saw a gold-miner's pan, a silver dagger, a portrait of his father, many books both old and new. There were skins on the floor—evidences of the President's prowess as a hunter. After a time Mr. Roosevelt came in—robust, hearty, wholesome, like a gust of wind. He was clad in knickerbockers, a worn coat, and a disreputable pair of tramping shoes. After greetings he literally burst out:

"'I want to read you a letter I have just received regarding conditions in the South.'

"I thought he looked with special glee at Mr. Bonaparte, who was from Baltimore. The letter was from Booker T. Washington, calling attention to an enclosed clipping which, Mr. Washington said, related a true incident. The President read this clipping with the greatest gusto. It seems that a Florida colonel, meeting Booker Washington, had shaken his hand.

"I've wanted to meet you, suh. I believe, suh, you are the greatest man in America.'

"'Oh no, I'm not the greatest man.'

"'Well, who's greater?' pursued the colonel.

"'President Roosevelt.'

"'Who? Roosevelt! No, suh: he's the greatest demagogue in America.'

"'Why? Why do you call him a demagogue?'

"'Why, suh, why? Didn't he invite you to dinner with him at the White House?'

"At this the President laughed uproariously. Then he asked us if we recalled the incident of the Indianola Post Office, how the people there had deposed a worthy Negro post-mistress because of her color, how he had abolished the post office, and how they were now getting their mail from a post office three miles away.

"'And what do you think?' he exclaimed. 'They are having it distributed by a *Negro carrier*. How is that for consistency!'

"When the lunch bell rang we went in and I was presented to

Mrs. Roosevelt, Miss Alice Roosevelt, and Commander Cowles and his wife, who is the President's sister. It was a very simple lunch, served by a maid. At first the President talked postal affairs with Mr. Bonaparte, asserting over and over again that he wanted the investigation then in progress to be thorough.

" 'I don't care whom it hurts,' he said, 'we must get to the bottom of these scandals.'

"He then turned abruptly to me and said,

" 'Baker, who is the chief devil down there in the Salt River valley?'

"Since I had never considered the situation in terms of devils, I hesitated a moment—and the President burst into a vigorous, picturesque, and somewhat vitriolic description of the situation, implying that if he could catch the rascals who were causing the trouble he would execute them on the spot. Several of the statements he made seemed to me to be inaccurate, or at least exaggerated, but when I tried to break into the conversation—boiling inside with my undelivered articles and memoranda (one of which indeed I tried to draw from my pocket)—the President put one fist on the table beside him, looked at me earnestly, and said:

" 'Baker, you and I will have to get together on these subjects.'

"As we went out of the dining-room, standing and waiting while the President stepped ahead of us—the only bit of ceremony I saw—the President joked with Mrs. Roosevelt about passing before her.

" 'My wife insists on maintaining the dignity of my office,' he said, 'she will not even let me be a gentleman.'

"As the time drew near for leaving, I began to wonder when the President would ask me for the information upon which I had spent so much time and hard work. I had my heavy brief case in hand when I went up to say good-bye—and my grand plans for enlightening the Government of the United States vanished in a handshake.

"Mr. Bonaparte, Mr. Kohlsaat and I walked down together, some three miles, to Oyster Bay. I carried my heavy case, filled with my memoranda, and papers, and maps and pictures—and the sun was hot."

CHAPTER XIX

Subterranean Mysteries of American Life

I FOUND IT MORE and more difficult, as the months passed, to keep down to my novel. I was tormented with interruptions. While S. S. McClure could write me in February (1903) that "I don't think it best for you to leave your work; I think it best for you to finish your novel," he could also write me frequently—and insistently—suggesting a confusing miscellany of subjects, some of them of interest, but all diverting me from the work I wanted most to do.

My difficulties, I must here confess, were not wholly due to interruptions, but partly to the dissatisfaction I sometimes felt in trying to write fiction when the world seemed literally on fire with critical, possibly revolutionary, movements in which I was deeply interested.

I finally went to Chicago to study the labor-capital situation there. It was most complicated, involving many secret arrangements which I am sure I should never have been able to untangle if it had not been for the friends I had made there while a newspaper reporter, especially friends among labor leaders who had been connected with the Pullman strike of 1894. I discovered an extraordinary situation, one that I had never expected to see, for here the workers in certain industries were so completely organized that the "scab" seemed to have disappeared entirely. I found that organized labor and organized capital had joined forces and formed what was in effect a complete monopoly in various industries, thus enabling them to prey upon the public.

I asked Milton Booth, secretary of the Coal Teamsters Union, if there were any non-union workmen in the industry which he represented.

"No," he replied, "unless they are in the hospital."

I asked John C. Driscoll, secretary of the Coal Team Owners' Association—the corresponding organization of employers—if there were any independent operators in his branch of industry.

"You'll have to look for them with a spy-glass," he said.

On one side stood the men who drove the coal wagons, each with his little button in his cap, organized in an impregnable union, and over against them, also marshaled in close order, stood the men who owned the teams and the wagons, and, oftentimes, the coal. Both sides had crushed independent competition. The fundamental industry of a great manufacturing city—coal—thus lay absolutely at the will of these two unions. The teamsters had salved their sores with increases in wages, the coal dealers and the team-owners had fattened their bank accounts with an increase in profits, and the defenseless, unorganized public had paid the bill.

This situation I was able to authenticate with many special instances and I even discovered the actual written agreements upon which the combination rested. I wound up my article with this paragraph:

"We have been sighing for labor and capital to get together; we have been telling them that they are brothers, that the interest of one is the interest of the other. Here they are together; are we any better off?"

This article, which I called "Capital and Labor Hunt Together," was published in *McClure's* for September, 1903, and awakened immediate and widespread discussion. I was now so intensely interested, feeling that I was really getting down to a deeper understanding than I ever had before, that I began immediately with an inquiry into the situation in New York City, where a great building-trade strike had been in disastrous progress.

Here I discovered unexpected new ramifications into the vitals of the American system—how we governed ourselves, or failed to, and why and how we were misgoverned. It was not enough to find the labor-leader "devil" on the one hand or the capitalistic "devil" on the other, and lock him up: it went far deeper than that.

And yet the man I found, the "key man" on the labor side, might easily have qualified as a kind of devil. He was riding down Fifth Avenue in New York City on a handsome white horse. He was wearing a broad-brimmed hat, and the highly decorative regalia of his order, and he was leading a tumultuous labor parade. His name was Sam Parks. His face was thin and sharp and had a curious pallor.

I learned straightway that he was only six days out of Sing Sing Prison, and that he was dying of an incurable disease. Later when I went to his office, at his invitation, I got little more than explosive profanity, and came away thinking him one of the roughest, toughest human beings I had ever met.

I thought to myself that if Sam Parks had really dominated for months the building industry of the greatest American city in the time of its most spectacular growth, it was an irresistible conclusion that he was either a genius of extraordinary force, or else he must represent some vital basic condition which had forced upward from the mass the man who best represented it.

I began to look into the career of the man. He was one of the four walking delegates of the Housesmiths' and Bridgemen's Union, duly elected by his 4,500 fellow workmen to conduct their collective business with their employers in New York. He had a seat and a vote in the Board of Building Trades, a central body composed of delegates from each of thirty-nine trades connected with the New York building industry.

This Board was built upon the lines of our representative political system: so that a visitor from Mars, examining the wise constitutions and by-laws of these unions and this central body, might conclude that we had reached the millennium of perfection in the self-government of our workingmen.

According to all the rules, Sam Parks, the faithful servant of his constituents, was worrying along on the wages of an ironworker, reporting regularly to his union, meeting the employers in the quiet, dignified manner of a business man, and never calling strikes when there was any other way out. In reality, I found that Sam Parks was riding about in his cab, wearing diamonds, appearing on the street with his blooded bulldog, supporting his fast horses, "treating" his friends.

The money he received from the union treasury probably did not begin to equal the amount he got from the employers. Behold the extraordinary spectacle of builders and manufacturers summoned by this former coal heaver to come to the saloon of his appointment and pay him hundreds or thousands of dollars to secure permission to go on with their business! This happened not once but many times, as the evidence presented to District Attorney Jerome abundantly showed. And if a builder was recalcitrant his jobs were "struck" and the men kept out until he "settled."

Sometimes Parks spent the spoils liberally "setting up" for his friends at nearby bars. I heard a housesmith excuse him thus:

"Sam Parks is good-hearted all right; if he takes graft he spends it with the boys."

The more closely I examined the situation the more striking appeared the parallel between the government of the trade unions and American city politics. Why not? The union was a voluntary elective association and its offices were prized places. It was, therefore, subject to all the approved American electioneering methods. Sam Parks was the Croker of the building trades. Other bosses there were in other trades: Carvill of the derrickmen, for instance, who was second only to Parks in his appetite for the money of the employers, and Murphy of the stonecutters, who stole $27,000 of the union's money and was then in Sing Sing.

Such were the conditions of bossism I found in the unions. But I knew well that where bribes were received bribes must be paid. As soon as I began to study the employers' associations I found that there had long existed a more or less regular schedule of bribe money paid to corrupt officials of the city building department. Often the bribes were contemptible five-dollar bills for breaking little laws, and sometimes as high as $2,000 paid to high officials for breaking big laws.

Bossism and venality had existed in New York for a long time, and might have continued much longer if another element—an outside, unrelated influence—had not entered the field and disturbed the evil equilibrium of the industry. This was the appearance in the building field of "Big Business." It was represented by the Fuller Company, itself capitalized at $20,000,000, but owned and operated by a still more gigantic corporation known as the United States Realty and Construction Company, with a capitalization of $66,000,000.

I traced the management of the new company, and found it, as I related in detail in my article, backed by representatives of the Standard Oil Company, the United States Steel Corporation, and many of the greatest railroad corporations. Banking and other huge financial interests, including the greatest life insurance companies, were behind the Fuller Company, also the most powerful of the real estate men who knew when and where buildings were to be built, and who knew these things *first*.

The Fuller Company, fresh from bitter strike experiences in Chicago, had learned the simple business lesson that the labor unions had come to stay quite as surely as the big corporations, and that it was better to work with them than to fight them. It went out of its way to win labor—or at least the labor bosses; and since the company did not a little of its work on a percentage basis, it simply charged the added expenses to the owner. In other words, "took it out of the public."

We can now get back to Sam Parks, the hero of this story. It was a significant fact that the Fuller Company brought him from Chicago when it came. There was evidence that he was on their payroll long after he became a leader of the union: that while he was drawing wages from his union to look after its interests, he was also drawing money from the Fuller Company to look out for *its* interests.

But the Fuller Company, as a labor leader expressed it to me, "went the old builders one better at their own game." Instead of buying delegates occasionally, it was able to own a supply outright! This idea of being friends with labor, good or bad, had kept the Fuller buildings going throughout the great New York lockout and strike. The Company had made good its claim to getting its buildings done on time—at any cost of money or honor.

Was this attitude of unfailing friendliness a sign that the Fuller Company recognized more clearly the rights of labor, or that it was thrilled with any new conception of the brotherhood of men? Not a bit of it. It believed as firmly as ever that the workingman was created for the natural use of the employer, but recognizing that if it could not use the workers individually as in older times (play them off against one another and secure lower wages), then they must be used as a union—but *used*. Instead of fighting organized labor it appeared as its best friend, and the foolish union, greedily swallowing the bait, accepted the immediate advances in wages as evidence of a surrender to its demands. It did not see that it was being employed as a tool by a mighty corporation to crush its competitors, it went onward for some time, at least, proclaiming the Fuller Company its dearest supporter.

I soon came to the conclusion that Sam Parks did not cause the great strike in New York; he was the visible sore of the disease, the invisible germ of which was circulating in the blood of the American people.

I quoted District Attorney Jerome in my article: "'This corruption in the labor unions is simply a reflection of what we find in public life. Everyone who has studied our public life is appalled by the corruption that confronts him on every side. It goes through every department of the national, state and local government.'

"And this corruption in public life is a mere reflection of the sordidness of private life," I said in my article. "See what we find on every side of us—men 'whacking up' with their butchers and grocers, employers carrying influential labor leaders on their payrolls, manufacturers bribing the superintendents of establishments to buy their goods.

"In short, if we want self-government—not the name, but the real thing mentioned in the Declaration of Independence and the Constitution, we have got to work at it ourselves."

I closed my article with a quotation from Henrik Ibsen, whose plays I was then reading:

"And men still call for special revolutions, for revolutions in politics, in externals. But all that sort of thing is trumpery. It is the human soul that must revolt."

It was with intense and growing interest and even emotion that I wrote the articles setting forth the conditions I had found, first in the coal fields of Pennsylvania, then in Chicago, then in New York. I could not myself have believed that such conditions existed anywhere in the world, let alone in America. And these, I found, were not sporadic evils, they were deliberately organized and generously financed; *they actually represented the American way of life in many of its most important activities.*

It came to me personally with withering certainty that I myself was on the wrong track. I could see that the conditions in the country were immediately and sharply critical: and that I was not fully aware of them, nor doing what I could or should to make the public understand what I was finding.

It was a beneficent if painful discovery: I c
been too eager to force my material into a prec
form. I resolved then and there to stop the wo
on with the inquiries I had started and get my fi
soon as possible, so that they would reach and int
possible number of readers. I think my decision was partly
feeling that was growing in our office at *McClure's* of a po
new interest, a common purpose. Ida Tarbell's articles on the Standa
Oil Company, upon which she had been working for many months, were beginning to get the recognition they deserved, and Lincoln Steffens, full of enthusiasm in his campaign of investigation of the "shame of the cities," was a constant inspiration to me. Never shall I forget the memorable editorial discussions and conferences we had.

About that time I came across a passage in Walt Whitman that I copied out and pasted on my desk where I could see it every day:

"For facts properly told, how mean appear all romances."

Why bother with fictional characters and plots when the world was full of far more marvelous stories that were true: and characters so powerful, so fresh, so new, that they stepped into the narratives under their own power?

Another thing these new explorations did for me personally: they made me more and more suspicious of glib reformers—men who, having stopped looking and thinking, found sanctuary in easy conclusions and proposed to change the world—the "system" they sometimes called it—in accordance with some more or less nebulous or utopian plan. I knew some of them well. One of the characters in my novel, one of the few I really delighted in, was quite willing to change the whole world without knowing or changing himself. I was perfectly well satisfied that if he could achieve the Utopia he so eagerly advocated, he would soon be discontented, and begin also to reform that. What was wanted, so it seemed to me, was a far more complete and accurate diagnosis of the diseases that affected the body politic—a far better understanding upon the part of the people, as a basis for the necessary changes. There would thus be plenty of well-equipped reformers and lawmakers when they were needed.

I spent the next two or three years working harder than ever before in my life, trying to see, to understand, and to get what I ed written down. I felt that I had got hold of something that far bigger, more significant, more interesting—or had it got ld of me?—than any literary plans of my own.

I cannot attempt, of course, within the limits of this autobiography to describe all of my findings—anyone who may possibly be interested can read the articles in the dusty old magazines—but a brief summary may help in explaining what happened in my small corner of the so-called "exposure" movement.

In *McClure's* for December, 1903, I had an article called "The Lone Fighter"—in which I celebrated the work of one brave and honest man I had found in Sam Parks' union in New York.

"One such man," I wrote, "no matter how obscure, quiet, simple, can get results amazing in their importance; one such man is worth about four thousand so-called respectable citizens who stay at home and talk about the shame of boss-rule . . . If this republic is saved it must be saved by *individual effort*."

In the winter of 1903–04 I was in California, which was then supposed to have the most complete organization of labor of any state in the union. In San Francisco I found a wholly new and extremely interesting situation, existing, so far as I knew, nowhere else in the country, in which the ancient master, the employer, had been hopelessly defeated and unionism reigned supreme.

"The employers of San Francisco are flat on their backs," a prominent contractor told me; "when a labor leader makes a demand we give in without a word. We can't do anything else."

This the workers had been able to achieve not only by strong organizations of their own and by striking, but by seizing control of the political machinery of the city and electing one of their own leaders as mayor. As a result, they had demanded and secured what were said to be the highest wages paid anywhere in America—or, for that matter, in the world.

The article covering my findings in California, published in February, 1904, I called "A Corner in Labor: What is Happening in San Francisco where Unionism Holds Undisputed Sway."

A little later that spring (1904), in the mining camps and smelter towns of Colorado, I looked into the worst conditions of industrial anarchy then anywhere existing in America. Here neither capital nor labor obeyed the law and the local governments were unable to control the situation, or prevent riots, bloodshed, destruction of valuable property. I called my article "The Reign of Lawlessness: Anarchy and Despotism in Colorado" (*McClure's,* May, 1904).

In later articles I tried to present other aspects of these complicated and dangerous problems. Many of the conditions I reported were then absolutely new to the American people as a whole, and were therefore, at that time, highly sensational. I endeavored earnestly to see and set forth without prejudice, not only the point of view of the workers, but, with equal thoroughness and understanding, the side of the employers and the public. In the July *McClure's* (1904) for example, I published an article on the new employers' association movement, which I called "Organized Capital Challenges Organized Labor." I was greatly interested and instructed to find an able and intelligent group of business men hard at work trying to understand what the real trouble was, and how it could best be met. These men corresponded with the better and more thoughtful type of labor leaders, suggesting ways by which capital and labor might devise means for solving their common problems, not by war, but by discussion and co-operation.

No one of the articles I wrote at that time more deeply aroused my interest and sympathy than the one I called "The Rise of the Tailors" which appeared in *McClure's* for December, 1904. It concerned the effort of a number of far-sighted and idealistic labor leaders to organize the most poverty-stricken, unrecognized, and undefended laboring people in the country—masses of new immigrants who spoke little or no English, who were remorselessly exploited and cheated at every turn. They were the Russian Jews of the slums of New York, and Southern Italians, and Poles and Portuguese and Greeks who were workers in the garment industries. I recall the Yiddish sweatshop song I printed at the head of my article:

> I work, work, work without end,
> Why and for whom I know not,
> I care not, I ask not.
> I am a machine.

"These people," I wrote, "were cast into the turmoil of the let-alone civilization of America; no one paid any attention to them, or cared what happened to them—with the result that many of them were literally worked to death."

I can never forget my first visits to these workshops, the crowded homes in slum tenements, the swarming, half-fed children—and the sweat, the noise, the obscene poverty. It took hold powerfully upon my sympathy and my imagination. I wanted to write an entire book on what I found; I wanted it filled with pictures, both photographs and the finest available drawings, of what I had seen. But there was no room—and no time—although the magazine did give me generous space and used many good pictures. It also printed an introductory paragraph that greatly helped the circulation of the article:

"The extraordinary story here given of labor warfare in New York City interprets, perhaps better than any amount of purely academic discussion, the real significance to the American people of the 'closed shop' with its antithesis, the 'open shop'—the most vital industrial question of the day."

What thrilled me most of all was the extraordinary idealism and patience with which these poor men and women came to their own help. They had to suffer everything, not only the loss of their jobs, but literally hunger and cold, in forming any organization at all. They kept at it for years, they struck again and again, and when they were discharged, and left homeless, other workers re-formed their lines and finally succeeded in organizing and re-creating the entire industry. The reform had come finally, as all really great reforms must come, from within, from the men themselves. It seemed to me at times that this was the most remarkable exemplification of a true American and democratic approach to the solution of problems I had ever known. It seemed also an exemplification of the magic of the American system in lifting men into new freedom, new independence, and a new attitude toward life. All of these things I put into my article.

CHAPTER XX

Popular Reception of the "Exposure" Articles

WHAT I REMEMBER best about the earlier "exposure" articles—my own as well as those of Ida Tarbell, Lincoln Steffens and others—was the extraordinary reception they had in every part of the country. Reading them again after forty years, the disclosures they make, so sensational then, seem now more or less commonplace; for the facts they contain are no longer *news*. They impress me as being swift-moving, hard-hitting narratives, but some of them seem now to be far too long. I have a feeling that they ought to have been "reader digested"—but don't see quite how that could have been done, since facts, facts piled up to the point of dry certitude, was what the American people then needed and wanted.

The articles do give an impression of sincerity and authenticity. They have much in them of what Ida Tarbell used to call "righteous indignation"—and I realize now, even more keenly than I did then, how much of that they had; for we were ourselves personally astonished, personally ashamed, personally indignant at what we found, and we wrote earnestly, even hotly. My own articles are marked here and there with a kind of hortatory fervor that I should now omit: nevertheless they express what I felt, strongly, at the time. One other point impresses me sadly, that while there have been superficial improvements in forty years in the conditions we reported, the deeper-seated injustices remain, still unpurged. We are still far from the democracy of our vision.

I think I can understand now why these exposure articles took such a hold upon the American people. It was because the country, for years, had been swept by the agitation of soap-box orators, prophets crying in the wilderness, and political campaigns based upon charges of corruption and privilege which everyone believed or suspected had some basis of truth, but which were largely unsubstantiated.

Coxey's Army had been a flaming example of unrest. It was only more concretely sensational than the earlier campaigns of the Greenbackers, the Populists, the early Socialists and even the sober Single Taxers. Bryan's campaign in 1896 and those that followed were vigorous, if blind, expressions of the same unrest.

There had also been a confusing "scapegoat era," when the uncertain and ill-informed public felt that if only they could fasten their sins upon some scalawag leader and drive him into the wilderness, all would be well again. Even Theodore Roosevelt, in the earlier days, was looking for "the devil in the mess." So it was that Coxey and Browne had been punished for walking on the grass of the Capitol lawn, and Debs locked up in prison where he became an even more intense revolutionary radical. But the punishment of individuals never accomplished anything; the conditions remained unchanged: the agitators only became more and more vocal. One or two able writers—Henry Demarest Lloyd, for example—and at least one earnest magazine of small circulation, the *Arena*, were appealing to thoughtful people, but had awakened no widespread popular interest. Certain sensational newspapers, Hearst's and others, only added to the confusion and unrest by the more or less extravagant reporting of the various disorders, with declamatory editorials, usually proposing political changes that led nowhere. They increased the unrest and indignation of the public without providing the soundly based and truthful information necessary for effective action under a democratic system.

What the early "exposers" did was to look at their world, *really* look at it. They reported honestly, fully, and above all interestingly what they found. And the public, now anxious and indignant, eagerly read the long and sometimes complicated and serious articles we wrote. Month after month they would swallow dissertations of ten or twelve thousand words without even blinking—and ask for more.

We at *McClure's* immediately felt the response—hundreds of editorials and quotations in the newspapers, a deluge of letters, commendations or attacks in political speeches, even references in sermons. We published pages of them in the magazine and in our announcements.

We were often sold out at the newsstands, and our subscription list, as the business manager used to say, was "gaining fast on the up-grade."

Each of us had his own group or groups that were especially interested—Miss Tarbell the business men, Steffens the politicians, and I labor leaders and employers—and the letters we received, the brick-bats as well as the bouquets, seemed highly encouraging to anyone who believed in the democratic method. They showed that ordinary men were not only willing but eager to know the truth.

We also began to receive enthusiastic responses from leaders in American public life, especially students of social, economic or political conditions—to say nothing of argumentative letters from agitators and reformers who criticized us unmercifully for not accepting their particular brands of reform, at the same time that they eagerly appropriated the ammunition we were supplying to belabor other agitators and reformers with whom they did not agree. Occasionally a correspondent would ask indignantly why we ourselves remained so unmoved. I remember one letter from an angry reader, who asked how I could make such exposures without saying in plain terms that these men were thieves and traitors who ought to be in jail. What he wanted was "red-hot invective." I remember thinking considerably about this letter, finally suggesting to my critic that if I became angry, or showed it, he wouldn't. If I "blew off," wouldn't he feel relieved, even satisfied; wouldn't he be tempted to do nothing more about it? But with the ugly facts, the complete picture, the truth, vividly and dispassionately set forth, wouldn't he and other honest men be stirred to the point of doing something about it themselves?

As our campaign advanced it became clearer and clearer that we were by no means alone; that a large number of thoughtful Americans were growing increasingly anxious or indignant about the lawless conditions existing in so many walks of our life. We had strong responses from stimulating and thoughtful leaders in the country. I recall a delightful letter from Carl Schurz, whom I had long admired at a distance, inviting me to come to see him. He had been a notable figure in the state of Wisconsin where I grew up. He was one of the many able Germans who had fled their native land after the revolution of 1848, and had thrown themselves eagerly, even passionately, into the democratic life of America. Schurz had been a general in the Northern army during the Civil War, American minister to Spain, United States Senator from Missouri, Secretary of the Interior in the Cabinet of President Hayes. In his earlier days in Germany he had known Mazzini and Kossuth, and naturally became a warm friend and supporter of Lincoln and a veritable bulwark of strength in the anti-slavery movement. His whole life had been a struggle against corruption and inefficiency in public life.

I found him in his book-walled study uptown in New York; a tall, gaunt, gray man, then about seventy-five years old. He wore a long dressing gown and looked at me eagerly, smilingly, through his thick glasses. I wish I had made complete notes of the enlightening conversation we had, since it went to the very heart of the fundamental problems in which we were both interested: how men could better learn to govern themselves in a restless, crowded, and more-or-less lawless world. His experience had been so varied and his knowledge of both America and Europe so comprehensive, that I sat willingly at his feet, and came away with a sense of humility and of gratitude, inspired to go forward with the work I had been doing.

There was a quality of the prophet—the philosopher in action—in Carl Schurz that I was not to discover again in any such measure until I came, some years later, to know Louis D. Brandeis. Both of these men had an incorruptable objectivity of mind combined with a sound common sense in public affairs rare in this country or in any other, at any time. I had quite a different attitude toward Theodore Roosevelt with whom, beginning in 1903, I was to have a voluminous correspondence and many lively meetings and conversations.

President Roosevelt was greatly interested in my early labor articles. He wrote me as follows regarding my account of the New York situation and Sam Parks, the labor boss:

I am immensely impressed by your article. While I had known in rather a vague way that there was such a condition as you describe, I had not known its extent, and as far as I am aware the facts have never before been brought before the public in such striking fashion. How emphatically this revelation emphasizes the need of drawing the line on *conduct*, among labor unions, among corporations, among politicians, and among private individuals, alike! The organs of the Wall Street men of a certain type are bitter in their denunciations of the labor unions, and have not a word to say against the corporations. The labor leaders of a certain type howl against the corporations but do not admit that there is any wrong ever perpetrated by labor men. . . .

I believe in corporations; I believe in trade unions. Both have come to stay, and are necessities in our present industrial system. But where, in either the one or the other, there develops corruption or mere brutal indifference to the rights of others, and short-sighted refusal to look beyond the moment's gain, then the offender, whether union or corporation, must be fought, and if the public sentiment is calloused to the iniquity of either, by just so much the whole public is damaged.

Can you not come on here and see me some time at your convenience?

I was naturally greatly pleased that he should be impressed by my articles and that I had been able to contribute to his own knowledge of conditions, for he occupied the place of pre-eminent power in the United States, with a field of action and publicity far exceeding that of men like Carl Schurz. What he said echoed across the country, reaching people in every little hamlet and crossroad. What a thing it was, I thought, to have a President who was genuinely interested in these ugly aspects of our common life, and who was not afraid to attack them wherever they might be found. I became for a time his ardent and more or less uncritical follower.

But as the years passed Roosevelt's typical reaction, that of balancing the blame, without going to the root of the matter, and of seeking the "devil in the mess," satisfied me less and less. His actions often seemed to me to be based not upon principles well thought out, but upon moral judgments which were, or seemed to me to be, too hasty. His notion of a square deal was to cuff the radical on one ear and the conservative on the other, without enlightening either. He had no "single track mind"! He ran full-speed on all the tracks at once. Too often he rode down opposition without understanding what it meant, or talked it down with a torrent of phrases. But what energy and gusto he had, what wholesome enthusiasms, what common human goodnesses and courtesies!

I recall my astonishment at receiving an invitation to lecture at Harvard University. Next to the President's invitation to luncheon at Oyster Bay nothing could have awed me more. It had begun with appreciative letters from John Graham Brooks, Professor W. Z. Ripley, Professor F. W. Taussig and others—whom I had thought of as living in a rarefied academic atmosphere far removed from the rough and tough, sweaty, ill-smelling quarrels of coal heavers, rivet drivers, and sweatshop workers. I recall with keen pleasure the dinner with Professor Taussig and a number of other Harvard teachers, the penetrating questions they asked, and the lively discussion that followed. It seemed to me I had never met a group of men more genuinely alive than they, more deeply interested in the real problems that confronted America. I was not only vastly encouraged then, I think of it still as a fine and generous gesture made by those distinguished scholars to an inquirer venturing in a field, their field, where angels might well fear to tread. With one of them I made a friendship of casual meetings and intermittent correspondence that lasted for forty years.

What had worried me most regarding that Harvard lecture was the knowledge that I was not an easy or fluent speaker, and I feared I might not meet the expectations of the fine men who had invited me. I remember trying to reassure myself by quoting from Mr. Dooley that "when a man has something to say an' don't know how to say it, he says it pretty well."

I was full of my subject. As I wrote my father regarding the lecture, I believed that we were on the "verge of a new political struggle in which monopoly of capital, on the one hand, and of labor on the other, will be the chief issues. I am not theorizing: I am dealing with concrete facts. Theories never get under a man's skin: facts do. I shouldn't wonder if some of the things I say tomorrow night may shock the academic mind—which is always about ten years behind the living age."

As a matter of fact I did not shock these men at all: they were not ten years behind the living age—not more than five anyway!—and, after I got started and forgot myself, I think I really interested them and the audience of students who came to hear me.

The early response to the exposure articles was thus encouraging in every way. It seemed for a time that the walls of corrupt Jericho, shaken by the blasts of our trumpets, were already trembling toward complete demolition. I had much still to learn about Jericho.

It was not long before the invitations to speak here and there, to join organizations, to reply to innumerable letters and meet men, some of them really worth while, became a burden and an interruption. I was often glad that I lived seven hundred miles away in Michigan, even though it did involve commuting to New York once or twice every month.

CHAPTER XXI

I Try to Serve Theodore Roosevelt

It became clearer every day that we must go on with our "exposure" articles. The popular response had been unmistakable. They were not only profoundly interesting to write—like explorations in an unknown land—but they were plainly helpful. And I was eager for more dragons to slay!

Next after the struggle between capital and labor upon which I had been working, I wanted most of all to understand the railroad problem. It was then one of the leading subjects of discussion in Congress, with proposals to regulate railroad rates and increase public control through the Interstate Commerce Commission, and it was being bitterly agitated by able young political leaders, like LaFollette, in the West.

I began to read everything on the subject that I could get hold of. There really wasn't much to be had in those early days, the dry reports of Congressional committees, a few pamphlets, and a book or two by early agitators like Governor Larrabee of Iowa. There were two or three studies by scholars: *Railroad Transportation; Its History and Its Laws*, by Arthur T. Hadley, afterward president of Yale University; *State Railroad Control*, by Professor Frank H. Dixon; and the book I found best of them all, *The Railroad Problem*, by A. B. Stickney, who had himself been a western railroad president. I studied the discoveries that LaFollette was making in Wisconsin and got the advice of some of the foremost experts in the country, such as Professor W. Z. Ripley of Harvard, Dr. Carroll D. Wright, who had been United States Commissioner of Labor, and John Graham Brooks, then President of the American Social Science Association. I talked with members of Congress who were interested in the pending bills.

More encouraging than anything else was the enthusiasm expressed by Theodore Roosevelt. He was attacking the problem, then as dangerous as any in the entire political field, with what seemed to me to be real sincerity, real determination. Could there be a finer thing to do than to help him by building up popular understanding behind him?

I may say that up to this time I had little or no interest in Roosevelt as a political leader—or, indeed, in political issues generally. My only concern was to learn about the railroad problem—and if it led into the White House I intended, if possible, to follow it there.

In my earliest personal acquaintance with the "redoubtable Teddy," as he himself liked to be called, he was a soldier, not a poltical leader. This was in 1898, upon his return from the Spanish War in Cuba. I went down with him to Montauk Point where the Rough Riders were in camp, and wrote one of the first, if not the first, extended biographical articles about him, published in *McClure's Magazine*, November, 1898.

It was the personality of the man that chiefly attracted me. I remember how deeply I had been impressed by a call I made upon him when he was Commissioner of Police in New York City. When I entered the huge room that was his office he was dismissing his last visitor and I saw him turn quickly in his swivel chair to an open book on the draw-shelf. In the few seconds that I took to reach his desk he was absorbed in that book—a book, he told me later, on Sioux Indian culture.

"It is surprising," he said, "how much reading a man can do in time usually wasted."

I thought I had never before come across such concentration of purpose. He seemed never to waste a moment of time. In later years, as I came to know him better, I had further illustrations of this characteristic. I was sometimes asked to meet him while he was being shaved in the little anteroom that adjoined his office. This process had its anxieties and alarms, for the President could not talk without gesticulating. I was usually unable to get in a word of what I wanted to say until the barber reached his chin. I often wished he had a double one!

His energy, his ubiquity, his versatility were astonishing. I recall cutting out a bit of verse from the British *St. James Gazette,* thus characterizing him:

> Smack of Lord Cromer, Jeff Davis a touch of him,
> Little of Lincoln, but not very much of him,
> Kitchener, Bismarck, and Germany's Will,
> Jupiter, Chamberlain, Buffalo Bill.

During 1904 I recollect having had one or two talks with the President on the railroad problem which was then rising ominously on the political horizon. In one very long letter to me in August, 1904, he had set forth his attitude regarding this and other dangerous issues. It seemed to me to be too vague and general, not firmly nailed down with documented facts.

On January 2, 1905, I received this letter:

MY DEAR MR. BAKER:

When are you coming down again? I think your last article in *McClure's* is far and away the best discussion of lynching that I have seen anywhere. You know how much I admire your treatment of labor matters; but upon my word I think this is even superior. I am anxious to see you. Come down some time when you can take lunch with me.

Sincerely yours,

(Signed) THEODORE ROOSEVELT.

I was in Washington on January 28 and lunched with the President at the White House. It was a charmingly informal meal, the only guest besides myself being Mrs. Henry Cabot Lodge. I find this account in my notebook:

"The President is fond of laughing out in a big, hearty way and of joking with his boys. He chaffed Archie upon spilling his gravy, setting the table to laughing by inquiring, 'Am I the father of swine?' and planned, with all the zest of a boy, an afternoon horseback ride with Ted. After the meal the President drew me aside where we continued to talk, chiefly on the subject of railroad legislation.

"His chief trouble was with the Senate.

" 'The reformers complain because I will not go to the absurdity of refusing to deal with machine Senators, but I must work with the material that the states send me. Senator Platt came in this morning and asked me to do six things. Five of them I granted, because they were reasonable and just: the sixth I refused because it was not just. Senator Platt went away satisfied and will help me.' "

The President was especially impatient with the radical reformers:

"One must proceed in this railroad legislation by evolutionary methods, not by revolution."

Speaking of his own difficulties, he said he thought no President save Washington and Lincoln were confronted by more difficult questions.

"I am no genius," he said, "but I am working hard to do the right thing all the time."

The President said he had sent my article on labor conditions in the mines of Colorado to Colonel Carroll D. Wright, Commissioner of Labor, who had made an independent investigation and reported that my report was "accurate and fair." At the same time he criticized an article I had written on "Lawless Finance," on the ground that it laid all the blame on the business interests of the country, and declared that bribery was due quite as much to the blackmailing demands of legislators.

"But Mr. President," I tried to argue, "my job is not to assess blame on anyone: I am trying to get at the facts and report them as truthfully as I can."

A few days later, at a formal luncheon given to honor Carroll D. Wright, where there were many distinguished guests, the President inveighed with characteristic vigor against the "pinhead opposition in the Senate" and then came out roundly: "I want to be specific—such pinheads as [Senators] Morgan and Bacon."

In the October (1905) number of *McClure's* appeared the announcement of my new series, called "The Railroads on Trial," and I well remember the editorial perspiration it caused in the making. We said in part:

Charges of the utmost seriousness have been, for a long time, and are now being preferred against the men who control and operate the railroads of the country. They are at this moment upon trial, not merely because President Roosevelt has called a special session of Congress to decide whether these men have properly conducted the large interests intrusted to their care, but they are on trial before the higher court of public opinion . . .

The chief purpose of Mr. Baker, in the present work, is to make just such an investigation as every citizen himself would make if he could command the time. And he has brought to the investigation exactly the interest of any reader of *McClure's Magazine*—that of the American voter, who is deeply concerned in the welfare of his country.

The warm approval of my first articles by the editors of *McClure's*, both S. S. McClure and John S. Phillips, encouraged me to ask President Roosevelt if he would like to see the proofs of it. He responded on September 8 as follows:

MY DEAR MR. BAKER:

Yes, I should greatly like to see the proof of your November article, and that not because of any good I can do you, but because I have learned to look to your articles for real help. You have impressed me with your earnest desire to be fair, with your freedom from hysteria, and with your anxiety to tell the truth rather than to write something that will be sensational, that will appeal to shallow and ignorant people, and that will make your articles widely read and admired for the moment by crude theorists. I shall look forward to seeing the proof.

With regard,
Sincerely yours,
(Signed) THEODORE ROOSEVELT.

So I sent him the proof, I need not say with what fear and trembling, for his approval might be the measure of the usefulness of the entire series I had planned. He could command the incomparable sounding board of the White House. I was greatly relieved to have his letter of September 13:

MY DEAR MR. BAKER:

I haven't a criticism to suggest about the article. You have given me two or three thoughts for my own message. It seems to me that one of the lessons you teach is that these railroad men are not to be treated as exceptional villains but merely as ordinary Americans, who under given conditions are by the mere force of events forced into doing much of which we complain. I want so far as I can, to free the movement for their control from all rancor and hatred.

Sincerely yours,
(Signed) THEODORE ROOSEVELT.

I began to hear from people all over the country, including some of the ablest experts in that field. A member of the Interstate Commerce Commission wrote that the article on rebates was "certain to influence public sentiment deeply. You are doing splendid work: go ahead." Professor Ripley of Harvard wrote me that the "last article" was "extremely good and promises everything for the future." While such letters as these gave me assurances that I was on the firm ground of fact and could defend myself there, the messages that came to the magazine from the little men of the West—cattle growers and fruit growers and small business men—and there were a great many of them—pleased me far more.

I endeavored in all these articles, even more than I had in writing on the labor problem, to bring out the facts, the truth, with no "final solution" to present, no pet remedy to recommend. As I wrote my father from Wichita, Kansas, where I had found the problems unusually complex:

"The further I get the less sure I become as to remedies, the further I am from recommending any fine-spun theory which is to cure all the evils. I have lots of letters from socialists and other extremists scolding me because I do not draw the conclusions they think I should and recommending their particular brands of salvation."

I had, for example, a good-humored letter from Upton Sinclair, who was an enthusiastic socialist, in which he said that he had read my last instalment, and remarked that "you can beat even the rest of the folks on *McClure's* for getting together facts minus conclusions."

This ironical comment I regarded as high praise.

For I doubted then, and I have doubted ever since, short-cuts and wholesale solutions. Changes in institutions are indeed necessary, but as John Stuart Mill said long ago in his autobiography, they are attended with "less benefit" than ardent spirits expect. It seems to be a failing peculiarly American to begin dosing before the diagnosis is complete; we dislike to be quiet and slow; we hate to think things through. We believe in formulas and slogans, we like "drives." We have a pathetic faith in legal enactments such as the 18th Amendment, and changes in the "system" such as the initiative and referendum. There may be considerable education of individual minds in the process of campaigning for such reforms, but it is astonishing how little, how very little, they change actual conditions.

I am not even sure of democracy as a universal cure—that is, if it means what it seems to mean to many people. But I am strong for democracy as a way of life—if it means what I think it ought to mean.

Ignorance is the real enemy.

The fireworks following the publication of my articles were not slow in beginning. My articles were not to be left unanswered. The railroads had a powerful and well-financed organization to reach, and influence, the public opinion to which I was appealing so hopefully. I had found nothing like it in my studies of the labor problem, or indeed, in the investigations for my earlier articles on certain aspects of "lawless finance." Here, I saw at once, I was getting down into and coming to understand the heart of the matter—*where the truth really hurt.*

The President, who was at work on his address to Congress, was also making the same discovery, considerably, I think, to his surprise. He wrote asking if I knew anything about a man named Rathom, and what he was doing. It was a great satisfaction to be able to inform him immediately that I knew Mr. John R. Rathom and his pamphlet "The Farmer and His Friends," and that he was employed by a powerful publicity agency which represented the railroads. No money was spared in putting the railroad's interests before the people, in such a way as not to seem to come from the railroads. I said in part:

"As for John Rathom, I believe what he tells me, that he spends no corrupt money; and I am fair enough to wish that the railroad side may be fully and honestly presented to the people—as I told him. But they do *not* present their case frankly as the railroad case: they conceal their identity, issue cunningly prepared statistics and plausible pamphlets which *assume* to present the problem fairly. In John Rathom's address—the foundation of the pamphlet you send me—Rathom appears as the farmer's friend, not the hired railroad agent which he really is. His letterheads declare him to be a lecturer. Thus by deceit these publicity agents not only seek to influence public opinion, but they employ all the *great leverage of the power of the railroads, their advertising, their passes, their political influence.* And when worse comes to worse, as it did last year in Wisconsin, they will buy newspapers outright. It is anything to muffle the truth!

"To meet such conditions, the quality of truth-telling must be peculiarly bold and vigorous, else it does not strike home. It warms a man's soul to see the facts about the railroads and life insurance coming out. If once the truth can be got out and spread abroad, there is something fine in the way the people act upon it."

Just about this time I began to see innocent looking little articles in various newsapers, some of which I cut out and pasted in my note-books. Here is one:

"An influential senator, one of the leaders of the upper branch, says President Roosevelt is already tired of his venture into the railway regulation field and wishes he had kept out of it. 'He is in a hole in this matter,' said the senator in question, 'and he is now looking to us to help him out. If we adopt his recommendation and pass the legislation he asks for we shall throw the country into a panic and he will have to take the responsibility for it—he and the Republican party together. We shall do no such thing. We will save the President from that blunder.' Mr. Roosevelt took up this agitation without having given the subject proper study. . . . Now he is weary of the whole thing and his active mind is turning to new toys. He is a man who must have a new plaything in the line of national policies about once in so many days. He springs a scheme and because he can't get it through in five minutes he grows tired of it and takes up a new hobby. That is the way it has been with this railway rate business . . ."

There were many variations in this insidious form of attack. I was suspicious to the point of certainty as to where it came from.

On October 16, I was surprised to receive from the President the galley proofs of his proposed message to Congress, accompanied by the following notation:

"Now I send you herewith the first proof of my message, dealing with corporations—that is, the first seven galleys. Of course I must ask you to keep it strictly confidential; but will you give me any comments which your experiences teach you ought to be made thereon?"

I need scarcely comment upon the deep joy and satisfaction I felt at being thus consulted by the President—or the seriousness of the responsibility I felt. I knew perfectly well how little I really knew about the complicated problems involved in the new legislation, but then, who was there at that time who did? I also knew that my chances to help would be greatly enhanced by keeping the confidence and co-operation of the man in the White House, who could so wonderfully reach all the people of the country.

I confess that I was much disappointed with the message upon the first reading of it. It was too general, there was too much of the President's favorite balancing of good and evil—the good corporation against the bad corporation—and what seemed to me the lack of sureness in striking at the "guts" of the evil, as he himself had called it. I was terribly afraid that he was plumping for a solution that, while it might help a little, and look good politically, would fail to reach the heart of the matter.

I knew that my only course, so far as the President's message was concerned, was to tell him the truth as I saw it. Why shouldn't I? I had no party allegiances, and I wanted no office. So I centered specifically and directly upon what seemed to me the most important defect in his recommendations—writing him on November 11, 1905:

The chief recommendation in the message is that the Commission be given power to fix a *maximum* rate. I have just been in the West studying the relations of the Beef Trust and the railroads. The tap-root of Armour's power, as you know, is railroad favoritism, and I have asked myself over and over, trying to see the question on every side, whether the power to fix a maximum rate, which you suggest, will touch this specific case of injustice. Armour's evil power arises in part from his ability to force the railroads to give him a lower rate on dressed beef than they give the unorganized cattle-growers on their cattle.

The danger in this case lies not in the fact that any rate is too high, indeed both cattle and beef rates are probably too low. The danger is thus *not* a maximum rate but a minimum rate. Armour does not care what the rate is, high or low, so long as he gets his differential, so long as he can force the railroad to make a lower rate on meat than it does on cattle.

Similar conditions prevail in most cases of competition between commodities and between localities. Therefore, Mr. President, it seems inevitable, if we are really to control the rate and to prevent further fattening of trusts upon railroad favoritism, that an impartial governmental tribunal must fix a *definite* rate. . . .

In making this comment I seemed to have touched the sore spot in the message. The President responded immediately:

MY DEAR MR. BAKER:

Many thanks for your letter of the 11th instant. I am inclined to think that it would be better if the Commission had the power to fix a definite instead of a maximum rate; but the Attorney General in his opinion, which of course you have seen, expresses the opinion that the maximum rate is certainly constitutional, whereas it is not certain by any means that the definite rate would be constitutional. The Supreme Court's attitude is more than doubtful on it. Now, the one thing I do not want is to have a law passed and then declared unconstitutional. The maximum rate might not reach cases like you quote . . . but it will do a good deal. . . .

Sincerely yours,
(Signed) THEODORE ROOSEVELT.

Senator Knox is inclined to the exact view Moody * takes.

There followed a long and rather heated correspondence on the point. In a letter on November 17th I suggested a remedy that had taken shape after several conferences I had had with able students of the question—that is, to "empower the commission, not to fix a rate, but to *condemn* a rate, whether too high or too low, leaving to the railroad itself the power of making the changes. . . . Administered by a commission of high-class intelligence, such power could be exercised to the utmost advantage of abused shippers, and it would also enable the railroads themselves to cast off such an old man of the sea as the Beef Trust. . . ."

I also said in my letter:

I do not think this power to condemn would reach the seat of the difficulty with such certainty as the power to fix a definite rate, but it would, in my opinion, be far more efficacious than the power to fix a maximum rate. . . .

The President responded with a four-page typewritten letter beginning with the statement, "I think you are entirely mistaken in your depreciation of what is accomplished by fixing a maximum rate" and defending the original remedy he had proposed. His attitude in the correspondence which followed was so characteristically

* Attorney General William Henry Moody.

emphatic that I believed my suggestion would come to nothing. What was my surprise, when I read the message in its final form as delivered to Congress, to find that the President had inserted a paragraph, almost in my own words, regarding the regulation of minimum rates. While it was what I had hoped, it was so hedged about and weakened with limitations that its usefulness seemed doubtful. But it was *something*: and there are the best of evidences that it helped in the passage of the Hepburn Act.

CHAPTER XXII

The President Attacks the "Muckrakers"

I DEVELOPED my relationships with Theodore Roosevelt somewhat more fully in the last chapter than was perhaps necessary, in order to explain what soon followed—the attack made by the President on the magazines and magazine writers for their campaigns of exposure of corruption in the business and political life of the United States. I remember one day that spring (1906) meeting a friend on the street.

"Hello, Muckraker," he bantered me.

I did not at first know what my friend meant, but I speedily found out. At a meeting of the famous Gridiron Club in Washington, an organization for encouraging candor in the relationships of public officials and newspaper correspondents, the President had charged the writers of "exposure articles" with extravagance and untruthfulness, likening them to the "Man with the muckrake" in Bunyan's *Pilgrim's Progress*. He had attached a name of odium to all the writers engaged in exposing corruption regardless of whether they deserved it or not.

The news of the attack spread like wildfire over the country. The President, always intoxicated by the discovery of a new catch-phrase, was apparently delighted with the response he had received, and since the speeches at the Gridiron Club were never reported, he announced that he would make the same address a few weeks later at the laying of the cornerstone of the office building of the House of Representatives, April 14, 1906.

It was difficult for me to understand this attack, considering all that had recently happened, all that the President owed to the investigations and reports of at least some of the magazine writers, the more than friendly relationships that had existed in my own case, the many letters of approval he had written regarding the work I had been doing.

I believed then, and have believed still more firmly since—it seems now to be the opinion of historians generally—that the work of the magazines in setting forth the evil conditions then existing had been of great service in arousing the public to support the President's efforts. John Chamberlain, in his excellent book, *Farewell to Reform,* remarks that the muckrakers did "an incalculable amount of good," and goes on to quote William Archer, who wrote (in the British *Fortnightly Review* for May, 1910) that "the influence of the *McClure* type of magazine; . . . paved the way for President Roosevelt and potently furthered the movement with which his name will always be identified."

In this article Archer spoke of the *McClure* type of article as a "richly documented, soberly worded study in contemporary history." " 'Thorough' and 'understatement,' " he said, "were the two pre-eminent *McClure* words. And if *McClure's* turned up plenty of corruption, why, corruption was the dominant fact of American life at the time."

"Muckraking," he goes on to say, "provided the basis for the entire movement toward Social Democracy that came to its head in the first Wilson Administration."

The more I heard of the President's proposed address, the more anxious and indignant I became, the more fearful that such an attack might greatly injure the work which we were trying honestly to do. I finally decided to write him the following letter (April 7, 1906):

MY DEAR MR PRESIDENT:

I have been much disturbed at the report of your proposed address to the Army and Navy Union; and I am writing you now because you have so often expressed your willingness to hear from me at any time.

Admitting the criticism may in certain instances have gone too far and that at this moment too little emphasis may be laid upon the "good in the world," which I quite agree with you is predominant—or what would be the use of trying to arouse it to action?—it seems to me of the utmost importance that we maintain the right in this country of speaking the truth upon any subject whatsoever. As Lowell said: "Democracy in its best sense is merely the letting in of light and air." Now, the letting in of light and air in the matter of current business conditions, toward which you yourself have contributed more than any other man, and for which your administration will, I sincerely believe, be chiefly remembered, is neither pleasant nor profitable for the rascals upon whom the light is turned. Even admitting that some of the so-called "exposures" have been extreme, have they not, as a whole, been honest and useful? and would not a speech, backed by all of your great authority, attacking the magazines, tend to give aid and comfort to these very rascals, besides making it more difficult in the future not only to get the truth told but to have it listened to? And the first to stop the work of letting in the light and air will be those who have been trying honestly to tell the whole truth, good and bad, and leave the field to the outright ranters and inciters. Already there exists an indiscriminating attack upon the so-called exposures which may prevent the careful study of modern conditions and the presentation of the facts in a popular form.

Very sincerely yours,

(Signed) RAY STANNARD BAKER.

I had an immediate response from the President as follows:

April 9, 1906.

MY DEAR MR BAKER:

I am in receipt of your letter of the 7th instant. One reason I want to make that address is because people so persistently misunderstand what I said, that I want to have it reported in full. For instance, you misunderstand it. I want to "let in light and air," but I do not want to let in sewer gas. If a room is fetid and the windows are bolted I am perfectly contented to knock out the windows; but I would not knock a hole into the drain pipe. In other words, I feel that the man who in a yellow newspaper or in a yellow magazine (I do not think it worth while to say publicly what I will say to you privately, that Hearst's papers and magazines are those I have in mind at the moment, as well as, say the New York *Herald* and similar publications, daily and monthly) makes a ferocious attack on good men or even attacks bad men with exaggeration or for things they have not done, is a potent enemy of those of us who are really striving in good faith to expose bad men and drive them from power. I disapprove of the whitewash brush quite as much as of mud slinging, and it seems to me that the disapproval of one in no shape or way implies approval of the other. This I shall try to make clear.

I shall carefully read what you say about the railroads.

Sincerely yours,

(Signed) THEODORE ROOSEVELT.

When I read his speech, which he delivered on April 14, I found that he had made no such distinctions in it as he had made in his letter to me. There was indeed the familiar balance of approval and disapproval, whitewashing against mudslinging, but he did not "think it worth while" to acknowledge the service of those men who had been striving to tell the truth, honestly and completely, whose work he had repeatedly approved, and for whose help he had again and again expressed his appreciation. There had recently, indeed, been an outbreak of highly sensational publications—like Lawson's *Frenzied Finance*, and Phillips' *Treason of the Senate*, although even these contained much truth that the public was entitled to have. But the President, unmindful of his own motto, "the square deal," classed all of us together. He certainly knew, even before he received my letter, the interpretation that would be placed upon his attack. The Chicago *Tribune*, on the next day, listed the names of the writers, whether sensational or not, all together, as being cast into outer darkness.

I met the President many times afterward and there were numerous exchanges of letters, but while I could wonder at his remarkable versatility of mind, and admire his many robust human qualities, I could never again give him my full confidence, nor follow his leadership.

Two other personal experiences that I had with Theodore Roosevelt should be related here, I think, because of their bearing upon his later career. The first was a conversation I had with him in the late summer of 1908, after William Howard Taft had been nominated at the Republican convention—largely under Roosevelt's pressure. The President, for the first time in my experience with him, seemed tired. He said several times:

"I want to get away so that when the new administration comes in my opinion will not be asked, nor my advice sought. If I talk, people will say that I am interfering where I have no right to interfere. If I refuse to talk, they will say that my silence is disapproval. The best thing I can do is to go entirely away for a year or more—out of reach of everything here; and that is what I am going to do."

He had decided to go to the wilds of Africa, a thing he had long wanted to do, and to hunt big game. He would sail as soon after March 4 as possible. I suggested that the people might not be through with him, that four years hence they might be clamoring for him more insistently than they were then.

"No," he said, with a curious finality, a kind of sadness, a note which I never before heard him strike, "revolutions don't go backwards. New issues are coming up. I see them. People are going to discuss economic questions more and more: the tariff, currency, banks. They are hard questions, and I am not deeply interested in them; my problems are moral problems, and my teaching has been plain morality." *

I believed at that time, that he had put aside a third-term nomination, which he could have had at the turn of his hand, from the highest conception of his moral obligations. I knew, from a former talk with him, that he had been tempted almost to the point of yielding, that the pressure had been tremendous, but that he had asked himself simply, "What is right in this matter?"—and the thing he thought right, he had done.

The second experience illustrates his instinct for occupying the center of the picture—for stealing the show.

It was in December, 1917, at a critical moment of the World War. Germany was preparing a terrific blow in France. Russia was in anarchy. Our own home situation, with shortages of food and coal and transportation, was growing constantly worse. But the theater where Fred Stone's *Jack o' Lantern* was playing was crowded to the doors.

At the end of the first act the audience arose, and the orchestra began playing the "Marseillaise." Wild cheering followed. In a moment I saw what the reason was. In one of the stage boxes sat Sarah Bernhardt—the "Divine Sarah"—that most extraordinary of French women, old, worn, crippled, and yet with an inextinguishable spirit, courage, zest of life. She wore a huge hat and youthful clothes and seemed—that great artist—to be enjoying the nonsense of the play, the bright lights, the familiar applause of the audience.

A moment later the crowd had discovered there in the middle of the orchestra seats another celebrity. Who but Theodore Roosevelt!

The Colonel was quite in his element. He was evidently enjoying himself hugely, waving salutes to his friends, and presently standing up and bowing right and left. Momentarily we forgot all about the

* I published the essence of this conversation in an unsigned editorial in *The American Magazine*, September, 1908.

Divine Sarah, until the Colonel turned and made a low bow to her across the orchestra. A moment later he and his sister, Mrs. Robinson, turned into the aisle and marched—marched—around through the foyer to greet the great Sarah. What a drama—what cheering—and the Colonel at the heart of it! The house was full of young officers in their bright new uniforms and by the time the Colonel marched back again scores of these men had crowded into the foyer to salute and shake hands. The Colonel beamed upon them, and roared out:

"I've got three sons in it myself."

That was one of the real Roosevelts!

I have always thought that if there had been a foreign war during his administration Theodore Roosevelt would have been "perfectly delighted." He would have conducted it well, if not greatly, and his own historical importance and that of his administration would have moved upwards among the records of notable American administrations. As it is, the years of his presidency present few remembered greatnesses, save his own astonishing personality. He left little of vision or of creative statesmanship to his successors. Young men are not likely to look back to him, save possibly as an apostle of the strenuous life; they will not look back to him for inspiration as to Thomas Jefferson, Abraham Lincoln, Woodrow Wilson.

Roosevelt's "muckrake" speech, timed by one of the ablest politicians ever to occupy the White House, marked the apex of the "muckrake" movement. He was aware that the tide was turning. The great success of *McClure's* in interesting and influencing the American public and in the financial prosperity it was achieving, had drawn many other writers and magazines into the field. There had been sensationalism; and there were now evidences that the "literature of exposure" was being overdone. Public interest had begun to be satiated.

The President's address may or may not have had anything to do with the strong effort that began about that time to strangle the "muckrakers" once and for all; but the assault, which had started earlier in the year, became more and more evident. In February, I had had a letter from S. S. McClure which said:

"I learned to-day that there is a very strong probability of J. Ogden Armour suing us for some of our statements in the January number. It shows these fellows are touched. That makes me feel like going on stronger and deeper and taking up matters more thoroughly in regard to the Beef Trust. . . ."

Some time later a libel suit was actually begun against *McClure's* for statements made in one of my articles by an owner of a private car line who lived in Milwaukee. He was then also attacking LaFollette, who was pressing his campaign for railroad regulation in Wisconsin. This suit, as I shall show later, was pressed to the bitter end—with what anxiety, what weariness, what loss of money, what waste of precious time. It often seemed that the suit was merely a part of a general and well-organized plan to confuse and delay the effort to abolish the evils now so clearly evident.

The Armour Company did not go forward with a libel suit. It had means perhaps more effective. We heard that they were threatening to cancel their advertising in *McClure's* and that other important advertising contracts might be affected. While I believe they did not actually cancel their contracts, the threat was alarming enough, since advertising was the very lifeblood of the low-priced magazines. This kind of boycotting, if carried through, might prove a far more serious business than a suit in the courts.

There were other developments in the same general campaign. The meat packers, evidently determined to meet publicity with publicity, began a series of articles, signed by J. Ogden Armour himself, in which he set forth the case of the packers and scoffed at my statements in *McClure's*. They were published in the *Saturday Evening Post* where they would reach the widest possible reading.

It seemed to me that this furnished me with the opportunity, which S. S. McClure had suggested, for an article on the Beef Trust, and I went at it with the determination to answer the charges that the packers had been misrepresented by agitators and magazine writers, who had "worked up a misinformed and prejudiced public opinion against them."

I made my article as strong and sound and unsensational as I could. I had been charged with seeing only one side of the case, but I had not failed to consult the Armour people while I was making my preliminary inquiry, and I now went to see them again. In fact, Mr. Armour himself invited me to come. I had several long talks with him and with Mr. Meeker, one of the directors of Armour & Company; Mr. Robbins, President of the Armour Car Line; and with Mr. Urion, attorney for Armour & Company.

In writing my railroad articles I had scarcely given any thought to Mr. Armour personally. His name was little more than an abstraction which had come to express a huge industrial and commercial machine which, in some of its operations, seemed to me to be inimical to the public good. I imagine that to most people of that period the names of Armour, Swift or even Rockefeller and Morgan were more or less abstractions.

When I first talked with Mr. Armour's associates, they said to me:

"If you had known Mr. Armour personally, you would not have written as you have."

No, I should not—quite. I should have seen more clearly the human side of the problems. In discussing cold economic questions, or in condemning what seems socially wrong, it is disturbing to feel that the man who represents the things which we look upon as evil will go home at night to his children, that he has friends who love him, that he is not an abstract force, but a mere man like the rest of us. In our judgments we constantly forget this personal equation unless we know the man, and then we are likely to overemphasize it.

What happened there in that Chicago office was that Mr. Armour came alive to me as a human being. I was surprised to find him so engagingly direct.

"I can tell you frankly," he said, "that I never really wanted this place. My older brother had been trained by my father to succeed to the control of the Armour Company. When he died there was no one else to step in and take charge of its affairs, or to protect the interests of many other people, including members of my own family."

I found that Armour had reasons enough for his course. To Armour, Armour was perfectly logical. I thought that if he could get down among us—but he couldn't and that was the pity of it—we should all like him. I did.

I looked at him newly and with keen interest. He was still a young man, simple in his manner, and retiring in his disposition. I found that his likes and dislikes were about the same as those of most Americans. He sat at the same desk in the same little office where his father sat; and he was not a rich idler, wasting his patrimony. The first Armour was accustomed to surprise his clerks by coming down at half past seven in the morning, ahead of the janitors and office boys. The second generation Armour might at least have enjoyed an eight-hour day but he didn't. The great machine in which he was a cog, albeit an important one, drove him as he would never have dared to drive his own workmen. He, too, I thought, was a sort of slave to industry, with no union to protect him. In short, there he was, held in his place on the wheel as firmly as any Polish butcher who knifed hogs in the Armour packing house.

On the walls of the little office I saw portraits of his father, of his older brother who had died, of a class in Armour Institute, founded and supported by Armour's money. Another portrait, which occupied a prominent place, was that of the lion-headed Dr. Lorenz of Vienna. It was only two or three years before this that the sympathy of the entire country had been enlisted in the effort of Dr. Lorenz to cure Mr. Armour's little daughter, Lolita, of hip disease. Afterward the famous surgeon came to this country upon Mr. Armour's invitation and at his expense, and operated upon scores of crippled children who would otherwise have been unable to secure such treatment.

Mr. Armour had succeeded to the large responsibilities of the business only five years before. He had inherited great wealth and power: he had added materially to both. I suppose that at that time he could have been numbered among the richest men in America.

I recall thinking how curious Mr. Armour's position was. On the one hand he commended competition as the only fair regulator of industry, asserting that the law of supply and demand was the only law that could operate successfully in controlling the cattle, beef, and fruit business. On the other hand, he was himself, so far as I could learn, secretly doing his best to prevent competition and build up monopoly in every business with which he was concerned. In other words, he wanted free competion for the people who dealt with him;

and he wanted unrestricted power to do away with competition when he dealt with them.

Well, I liked Mr. Armour, but it seemed clear to me that his likableness had little to do with the hard problems of social injustice we were studying. One of his strange defenses of his situation, in which there seemed an implied admission of the evils of the system under which he was thriving, was that even if he should step aside the man who took his place would be forced to play the game just as he did. He would still have to meet the competitive practices of other packers. It made me believe even less than ever I did before that the mere scotching of the "devil in the mess" would change anything.

I put all of these things into my article, but I also reiterated and strengthened the well-authenticated facts regarding what was happening to the little men of the West—the little business men, and the farmers and the fruit-growers, how they were suffering because of Armour's methods.

I was proud of that article. I felt that I had presented all phases of the situation more clearly than ever before. It ought to help the leaders, the reformers, including Mr. Roosevelt, who were trying to forge remedies.

My editors liked it, or told me they liked it, and yet I felt their reluctance to publish it. They were not critical: they were unusually gentle with me. There was, indeed, a new uncertainty in the editorial atmosphere. Wasn't the public becoming satiated with these subjects? Were articles of the kind as timely as they had been?

Well, time passed: *the article was never published.* No other editor seemed willing to take on a study so "completely controversial." I didn't blame anyone: there it was: the Man on the Wheel in journalism also had his necessities and constraints. One of the most painful, certainly, of all his trials is to be loaded to the muzzle with ammunition which he is not permitted to fire off. That hurts!

Other things were also hurting. I recall vividly, as we recall moments of strong emotion, the sickness of heart I felt coming back to my desk and reading the many letters from readers who had been reassured and encouraged by our articles, whether those of Ida Tarbell, Steffens or myself. I had not at all minded the stinging editorial attacks on the "muckrakers," the lampoons in comic papers and the like that followed Roosevelt's attack, for they were in some measure counterbalanced by an equally strong defense in liberal newspapers and magazines, but I hated to think of hundreds of men whose chance of any real hearing before the court of public opinion would be destroyed.

There was another startling and, to me, wholly unexpected development. It appeared that *McClure's Magazine* itself was in the process of inner disintegration. I happened to be absent from New York when I heard the first, rather malicious, rumor that a "break-up" was coming, and that it was due to a "vital disagreement" regarding the publication of further "muckraking" articles. I felt that the very earth was dropping out from under me.

I found upon my return to New York that the revolt was a real one: but while the criticism of muckraking which had burst out after the President's attack may have been an irritant, the real break rested upon deeper and more personal reasons with which I had long been familiar. It had been growing more and more difficult, on the part of members of the staff, to work with S. S. McClure. While he possessed real editorial genius, there existed many of the difficulties of temperament which go with genius.

All this time the libel suit of the Milwaukee man dragged its weary way along. The complaint was based upon statements in my article on the private car industry.

I had made, as usual, every possible effort to found my reports upon thoroughly authenticated documents, and in this case, my statements were based largely upon an official report made by Railroad Commissioner Thomas, of Wisconsin, to Governor LaFollette. I was supplied by Mr. Thomas with a list of the vouchers and the amount of the commissions actually paid. These facts and figures were used in a public speech delivered by Governor LaFollette at Milwaukee on November 4, 1904. They were subsequently published in the newspapers, and were not publicly controverted at that time.

Upon the appearance of my article certain of these statements were denied, although I had followed accurately the official report—with the assertion *that the report itself was inaccurate.* Indeed, the Railroad Commission of Wisconsin was induced to re-examine the books of the Milwaukee Railroad and issue a revised report.

I did my best to explain the matter in an editorial in *McClure's Magazine* for April, 1906, which was headed, "Some of the Difficulties Encountered in Investigating the Railroad Problems—The Unreliability of Official Documents."

The case was tried finally in New York City by a judge who had once been a railroad lawyer, before a jury of city business men. I had no hope from the beginning of a favorable decision. I had sat for weary days and weeks in the trial room of Eugene Debs at Chicago in 1894—and had seen him convicted, not upon the real questions involved, but for contempt of court. In this case of ours there were bewildering discussions of complex business arrangements—wheels within wheels—to unutterable confusion, often sending half the jurors off to sleep. I came away, day after day, with only one comfort—the knowledge that what I said was essentially true, even if it was found technically illegal to say it.

We lost the case. Damages of $15,000 were assessed against *McClure's*—besides the large legal and other expenses of the trial itself—to me staggering sums of money, which were paid without one word of recrimination for the part I had played. I have always considered this an evidence of true sportsmanship, a tribute to the quality of my associates at *McClure's*.

CHAPTER XXIII

Home in the Country

IT WAS TRULY a fortunate circumstance, when the winds blew, and the floods came, and all my little world came tumbling down, that I had a safe haven to which I could retire.

In the space of a few months I had seen the work I had been so hopefully doing as a "maker of understanding"—as I liked privately to think of it—suddenly interrupted. Had not the President of the United States himself denounced us all as "muckrakers"? Was I not being dragged through a miserable suit in the courts—insufferably depressing, time-consuming, costly, without hope that the real issues would ever be intelligently or helpfully discussed?

At the same time, the institution that had seemed to me as permanent as anything could be in a transitory world—I mean *McClure's Magazine*—seemed to be crumbling under my feet. I was left with no certainty, at the moment anyway, of continuing to do the work to which I was most deeply devoted; I was lost in a fog of contention and antagonism. In the afterlook these ills seem trivial enough: at that time they were all but catastrophic.

It was fortunate, perhaps beyond anything else I ever did, that I had set up a home in the country. It was only a small house with a bit of land, but it was my own. I had paid for it; I held it in fee simple; it seemed to me in those days an extraordinarily beautiful place.

I went home utterly beaten down with weariness, worn out physically and mentally. I had a warm welcome there, and many interesting and simple things to do.

When I began writing this autobiography, I thought I ought to leave out any mention of the little inconsequential, unimportant commonplace things I did during this period of my life. I knew well enough how much they had meant to me, but would anyone else be interested in them? The more I thought of it, however, the clearer it seemed that I *must* put them in—or some of them—for I know now how much of the satisfaction, yes, the happiness, of my future life rested upon these simple country experiences; not only the things I did but the men and women I came to know and the part I played in what might seem the trivial affairs of a country neighborhood. This was indeed the beginning of my "David Grayson" years and all that came out of them in surprised satisfaction. No, they must go in!

"Yesterday," as I wrote to my father one November day, "Jessie and I mucked away in our garden with Alice and the two boys—and the baby nearby helping or unhelping. I have taken to hard physical work for two or three hours every day. Within the last week or two I've split eight cords of wood and got it into the cellar, and I've mulched the fruit trees, spaded around the shrubbery, tinkered with hammer and nails and generally made myself useful, besides tramping all over our immediate creation. Within a mile of our back door in the Chandler marsh country I can find stretches of wilderness not surpassed in the Rocky Mountains, though of a different sort."

How I envied in after years the explorer I was in those days! I liked almost every man I met in the roads I tramped in, I enjoyed stopping at likely looking farmhouses—with the excuse of inquiring for directions—just for the chance of meeting and talking with the people who lived there. I found that almost any house in our country had a story connected with it.

On these excursions my troubles began to fly away and the earth became a place of enchantment—full of amusing, even exciting, adventures. From every excursion I came home to put down in my inner journal some of the things I had seen or felt or liked.

The human adventures pleased me most of all, but I also became interested as never before in the natural beauties of our neighborhood. Sometimes I went to walk with Dr. Barrows, the bird enthusiast at the college, who knew, I think, every bird in that country and where they nested, what their songs were, when they migrated and when they returned, almost to the day. I was often out with my old teacher, my wife's father, Dr. Beal, who was not only the college botanist but one of the keenest and surest observers I have ever known. He would never be satisfied with an implication or a supposition: he had to know. One fall, I remember, he read an article on the phyllotaxis of cones—that is, the arrangement of the scales upon the cone—in which the writer asserted, pontifically, that this arrangement followed a rigid mathematical order. Dr. Beal wanted to see whether Nature had been sufficiently consulted in the matter: and he picked every cone from a large Norway spruce and examined and tabulated the arrangement of the scales upon each specimen—a considerable task. And he found that Nature was as beautiful in her exceptions as she was in her rules.

Nature, he said, was not finished, nature was developing and changing—and that was what made it so fascinating to him even to the last year of his life, when he was ninety-one.

"You can never tell," he said, "what Nature will be doing."

He worked throughout his whole life in the service of science, always without haste, without waste, without rest.

I found, a little to my own surprise, that I got real enjoyment out of watching a sparrow taking a bath, after a summer rain, in the water collected in a cabbage leaf in my garden, or listening to the myrtle warbler who made her nest in the nearby thicket. After I began to keep bees, I was fascinated in studying them, both as I saw them in their hives and as written about in many old English books. I liked to observe the wonderful competence of their social organization and to learn the well-guarded art, in which mistakes were instantly and sharply punished, of handling them properly, so that I might increase my product of honey. It was these things that interested me most; they became a great part of my life.

I also found out how much more satisfactory my home life in the country and my neighborhood interests and friendships came to be, than anything I had known in the city. When I was at home I really lived there. I did not make evening visits, as in the city, and rush away in the morning before the children were up. I was a genuine part of the life of the family and of the neighborhood. I came really to know my children—we had two boys and two girls, Alice, Stannard, Roger and Rachel—for I could see them in their daily life, watch what they were doing in school, and above all play with them. Remembering my own rich boyhood and the part my father had in it, I tried to imitate it as far as I could. We went on many tramps, especially on Sunday, we had picnics in the beech woods, we swam at Pine Lake, and waded and boated in the Cedar River. As the boys grew older I took them on long and hard camping and fishing trips, so that we could become thoroughly acquainted. I told them innumerable stories, not so good as my father's but at least I could hold my audience spellbound, especially with the stories that made them "shiver."

We were very much in the country. It was a straggling, unorganized village, where we could know personally all or nearly all of our neighbors. At first there was no schoolhouse, no church, not even a post office. We all had to take hold and help: I did not know at the time how important this was. I was elected a school director, one of three, and we spent unnumbered hours planning and building the first schoolhouse in the town. I learned much from this experience about how people work together in a democracy, all the more understandable because on so minute a scale.

I remember also the evening visit of one of my neighbors who said to me:

"We've got a schoolhouse started. Now, we need a church."

I was not a member of any church but I attended the meeting that was called to discuss this subject. I was brought up a Presbyterian, but of all religious services I think I liked best that of the Quakers, at least in their silences: when the talk began I was not usually so certain; I found myself descending from the high places. I liked best of all what I had seen of their way of life, the genuineness of it.

Baptists, Congregationalists, Methodists, Presbyterians, Unitarians, and others attended our meeting and of those present all seemed satisfied upon one point: that the town was too small for a church for each denomination. We must all get together on a community church: a kind of old-fashioned meetinghouse, with emphasis upon its social aspects. Some of us even hoped that the matter of creeds and practices could be made less diversive—and found others who did not at all agree with us. But we knew that we would all have to give up something to get something better.

Fortunately we had very little money: there were no rich people in the neighborhood. What could we do but unite? We finally agreed upon a People's Church. I found an enthusiastic young architect in New York who liked the ideas we had and agreed to make plans, at very low cost, for the kind of building we wanted. It was not to look much like the ordinary church. Assembly rooms of various sizes open seven days a week were to occupy the first floor, providing for every sort of gathering: women's clubs, political meetings, Sunday school, children's playrooms, a kitchen for community suppers—everything. The church auditorium, usually occupied only once a week, was to be upstairs—a small, comfortable, quiet place for worship.

When I brought the architect's drawings back from New York the people threw up their hands. It was an interesting plan, but how raise money in such a small community for such a building? After much discussion, and much quiet inquiry as to the amount of money that could be raised locally, I took the plans and the promises back with me to New York. It had been suggested that some church-building society, many of which we understood in our innocence had large endowment funds, would help us.

"Don't you believe it," a hard-headed old fellow in the town had declared. "If you go to the Presbyterians, the church will have to be Presbyterian: and if to the Methodists the church will have to be Methodist. The divisions go too deep. You'll find that out."

Just as an experiment in human relationships I went up to see the secretary of the Congregational Church Building Society who promised to put the matter before his committee.

Time passed. I made several other visits to see various committee members—always carrying the plans and the promises with me—and just as I was about to give up hope, the miracle happened. These men not only had the root of the matter in them, they had imagination. We got the money—twenty-five hundred dollars, as I remember—on the same comfortable long-term arrangements that any carefully named Congregational Church would have had.

The church was built, and from the beginning it demonstrated its usefulness. Beginning too large, it was soon too small. The little village became the active and prosperous city of East Lansing with some six thousand people not counting six thousand students in the nearby college. A beautiful new building that cost $490,000 now occupies a commanding site in the center of the community. It is still called the People's Church, and it is still, and genuinely, just that.

I also learned much by trying to play some minutely small part in the politics of the town and the state. I considered myself an independent in politics, but our community, being overwhelmingly Republican, I went with Charles Collingwood and A. M. Brown to attend the Republican party meetings and caucuses. I began to understand, at first hand, some of the fundamentals of American political method—and how and why they were inadequate or corrupt. I found here everything in little that existed, big, in Chicago and St. Louis and everywhere else. Both Collingwood and Brown were honest and intelligent men and they did their best to get their neighbors—like me—to attend the meetings, discuss the issues, and help to get good men nominated, not only for the little local "jobs" but for the legislature, for Governor, for President. But they could rarely get more than a handful of men to "run the show" as Collingwood used to say. I recall one meeting of some importance when there were only five men present, besides Collingwood, Brown and myself. *Someone* had to turn the wheels of the democratic machine. And if good men would not take the time and do the work for nothing, there were plenty of small, mean, corrupt men who would do it, and take their pay where and when and how they could get it. So many Americans wanted good government without being willing to contribute anything whatsoever, either in time or thought; they wanted something for nothing.

I do not need to enlarge further upon these experiences. They were immensely valuable to me. If *understanding* was what I wished most to achieve, where could I find a better laboratory than I had in my own small community? Or how better discover the "art of living in a crowded world"? One thing I came to believe more firmly than ever before was that the primary need in curing the ills of our body politic was not new mechanisms or a new system of government, however inciting they appeared to sanguine reformers, but more knowledge, more understanding, more sense of obligation on the part of all the people, more willingness to sacrifice immediate profit for future welfare.

Of one thing I was certain, that I got satisfaction, I got health, more than anything else I got enlargement, out of these intervals in the country. While I wrote of my experiences in my notebooks, which was pleasure enough in itself, I did not consider for a long time making any literary use of what I was seeing and feeling. Moreover, affairs in New York were looking up: we had organized a new magazine called *The American,* in which I was beginning to be deeply interested.

But I had glimpses of the possibilities and the satisfactions that might arise if I could really go free there in the country and do the kind of work I liked best to do. I recall one rather ridiculous incident: the positive thrill of joy I felt one spring day upon breaking my leg. It was a serious fracture, but after the first few days of pain, I sat by my quiet eastern window, my splinted leg on a chair, and my mind gloriously free to go where it would and do what it pleased. I wrote a number of little poems I had long had in mind and while I had real pleasure in working on them I never even tried them on the publishers. The trouble with me was that I could never satisfy myself when I tried to put the poetry I had in me into verse: nor the stories I had in me into novels.

I drew up out of the dark hiding places of my mind the fragmentary gatherings I had made while in Arizona on the subject of thirst in the desert. I had been greatly interested in it and had talked with several cowboys and sheep-herders, and, best of all, with a wind-bitten old miner, about their desert experiences. I had stored away what I found, intending to use certain of the incidents in my Arizona novel. I now got them all out and fitted them together in a story. Just as I was completing it I saw an announcement in *Collier's Weekly* of large cash prizes for the best short story. I knew perfectly well, having served for enough years in editorial offices, that there was little or no chance of winning the prize for a story like mine—it was no wonder of a story anyway—but it amused me to send it in under a *nom de plume* and see what it would do. To my great surprise it took one of the lesser prizes, more than enough to pay all my doctor's bills and leave me a surplus to buy two new chairs which my wife had long wanted for our living room.

I enjoyed this experience so much that I considered breaking my other leg.

CHAPTER XXIV

We Take Over the American Magazine

IN THE SPRING OF 1906 a group of us, editors and writers, after many difficult negotiations, and in my case much depression of spirit, left *McClure's Magazine* and bought *The American Magazine*. We took possession on July 1, and set up an office at 141 Fifth Avenue, in New York City.

By "a group of us" I mean most of the staff of *McClure's Magazine*—John S. Phillips, always the thoughtful and far-sighted critic; Albert A. Boyden, our hard-driving manager editor whom we loved even when he chastened us; John M. Siddall with his extraordinary editorial perception of those qualities of human interest and timeliness which are the lifeblood of the popular magazine; and three writers who had long been associated with *McClure's*—Miss Tarbell, Lincoln Steffens, and myself. To this group we had the good fortune to add, as "editorial associates" a long time friend and contributor, William Allen White, and Finley Peter Dunne, whose "Mr. Dooley" had become, by virtue of the sanity and humor of his comments upon American life, a kind of unattached elder statesman. Both of these men, we knew, would add greatly to the good name of our new venture.

When I think of Ida Tarbell I recall a remark of Finley P. Dunne, speaking for "Mr. Dooley,"

"Iderem's a lady but she has the punch!"

She did have the "punch" and she still had it at the age of eighty-four.* No one could have been more exacting than she was as a studious inquirer, or more devoted to the truth of the matter, letting the chips fall where they might. And no one was ever more determined as a fighter for the things she believed in, and lived for. She was steady and sound, never sensational in the manner of her writing

* Ida Tarbell lived to be eighty-six years old. She died January 6, 1944.

or in the way she lived, and yet few series of articles in any American journal have ever been more fundamentally sensational than her history of the Standard Oil Company and the doings of John D. Rockefeller and his associates. Truth is always sensational, cutting like a keen fresh wind through the fog of pretense and secrecy, and the slime of corruption. Well, Ida Tarbell was the best of us; I have kept in my notebook, under her portrait, her statement of "the chief essentials for promoting the general welfare." They are today, as they were then, marked by solid common sense:

1. Health.
2. Enough food, shelter, and clothing for every man, woman, and child, with a little fun thrown in.
3. Freedom to go out and find something to do, and along with it freedom to express our opinions.
4. An end to force—at home and abroad, in government and industry—as a method of settling our difficulties; the substitution of co-operation, negotiation, decent consideration for each other's opinion. Such a program is vitally necessary to the continued existence and growth of our aims as citizens.

She saw with clear eyes the evil in the world, and yet she believed in men; she believed in the "upward spiral of human progress."

And there was Lincoln Steffens! He comes back to me as I write with astonishing vividness, turn of speech, glance of eye, feel of hand, many little incidents of no consequence but of the essence of our intimacy. The common likings, familiar divergencies, chance meetings, confidences given and withheld, letters written and received—all that make up the texture of a long friendship.

I think we might never have been irresistibly drawn together, never have instinctively sought each other out, if we had not become associates in the same enterprise, eagerly engaged in similar tasks, meeting familiarly every day, discussing ideas and projects that we considered GREAT. I soon came to like and admire him. I have run across many references to him in my notes, like this one November, 1904:

"I have seen a good deal of Steffens this trip and the more I see of him the more I like him. He is the genuine thing, with real weight and breadth of manhood."

I often loved him for the gifts of sympathy he had and the moments of generous courtesy, although they were sometimes barbed with ironic counterpoises.

I enjoyed especially the sudden, amusing, paradoxical quality of his mind. I shall not forget a parable he made for me one day when we were out on an after-luncheon stroll:

"Satan and I," said Steffens, "were walking down Fifth Avenue together when we saw a man stop suddenly and pick a piece of Truth out of the air—right out of the air—a piece of Living Truth."

" 'Did you see that?' I asked Satan.

" 'Yes,' said Satan.

" 'Doesn't it worry you? Don't you know that it is enough to destroy you?'

" 'Yes, but I am not worried. I'll tell you why. It is a beautiful living thing now, but the man will first name it, then he will organize it, and by that time it will be dead. If he would let it live, and live it, it would destroy me. I'm not worried.' "

Stef lived for a number of years in a delightful house on the shore at Cos Cob, Connecticut. He had a small sailing boat which he called "The Cob of Cos Cob"—and several times when I went up to spend Sunday, we sailed down the river mouth into the blue waters of the Sound. And one of these excursions was near to being the last for both of us.

It was a hot summer day with so little wind that the Cob scarcely made headway, the sail swinging emptily back and forth. The heat was stifling.

"Baker, what do you say to a plunge?" Stef said to me.

He tied the boat to an oyster pole, remarking that there was no wind to make trouble, and we stripped off our clothes and plunged into the water. We were both good swimmers, and struck out boldly into the Sound. It was glorious. Presently we turned back and swam lazily toward our boat.

"Stef," I said, "that Cob of yours seems to be drifting."

"No, it's tied."

We continued to swim lazily.

"Stef, that boat certainly *is* moving," I said.

It appeared later that the boat had pulled up the oyster pole and was drifting in with the tide.

We began swimming hard. For a time it seemed that the boat was moving faster than we were. We looked at each other, said nothing, and began swimming for our lives. I thought I should never be able to make the last few yards. I remember getting one arm over the gunwale, half conscious, but hanging on. It was some time before either of us recovered the strength to climb into the boat.

"Baker," Stef remarked, "those grafters we've been after came near getting a break, didn't they!"

In the earlier years I thought of Stef as a kind of Socratic skeptic, asking deceptively simple questions; later in his life he sometimes seemed to me to have a kind of messianic complex. I always thought he was at his best, doing his greatest work—in the sense of complete self-fulfillment—in the days when he was still the eager, observant, thirsty reporter, striving first of all to understand. When the conscious reformer stepped in and took him over the less effective he seemed—to me—to be. I thought that he began to lose something of his objectivity, humility, even humor. He seemed no longer the avid searcher for truth: he knew what the truth was. I could not help remembering sometimes his own parable regarding the truth!

I had from the beginning a strong feeling of affection for Will White. He came from the Middle West, just as I did, and knew the "folks" out there. Moreover, he was determined to stay where he was, living his life as he most wanted to live it, editing a good newspaper in a country town. He never yielded to the temptation, which has been the bane of many an able young writer, of deserting the country and the people he knew best and joining the struggling literary colony in New York. He came to the city when he wanted to come (bringing Mrs. White to take care of him), stayed as long as he wanted to stay, gave us no end of good suggestions fresh from the soil, worked out plans for new articles and stories, and then went back to Kansas where he belonged. He had the reputation of being a humorist. He was that and much more, for his pictures of life were full of affection and understanding. One article he wrote for *The American,* "The Partnership of Society," was in reality a sermon of great sincerity and power informed by a tender concern for the sorrows and troubles of all mankind. We called attention in our introduction to the need of "such discourses from sane minds . . . when conservatism is a wallow of selfishness and radicalism a riot of hate." I recall also an exuberantly delightful article comparing the town of Emporia, where he lived, with New York, which he occasionally visited, and—you have guessed!—exhibited the vast superiority of Emporia.

"We are all fairly close to the throne in Kansas," he wrote. "The high priests of politics do not impress us. Two United States Senators were in Emporia last fall, and both went wagging across the town to the depot, carrying their own valises. We refuse to get out the Second Regiment Band for anything less than a Cabinet officer. We are 'gentlemen unafraid' and a few years ago, when a vice-president came through the town, making speeches at the end of a railroad train, he pumped in vain for applause by mentioning two of the town's dignitaries. He couldn't fool us; we knew them both. The town gave one a beautiful funeral, and would be happy to do the same service for the other at any time reasonably soon. For, although we live among elm trees, on wide, velvet lawns, in paved streets, and although we have three free public libraries in town, although we have one four-story skyscraper, the gentlemen who fifty years ago debated the slavery question through the brush of eastern Kansas, with Colt's Ready Reckoner as their parliamentary guide, are still able to bring in a considerable minority report."

Love of life, high spirits, balanced with good hard common sense were of the texture of the man. I saved his comments in the Kansas City *Star* on being sixty-five years old, which contain a fine bit of humorous self-revelation:

"Lady Luck has been good to me. I fancy she is good to everyone. Only some people are dour and when she gives them the come hither with her eyes, they look down and turn away and lift an eyebrow. But me, I give her the wing and away we go. . . .

"So here I stand in my middle 60's thumbing my nose at the future and throwing kisses at the past, challenging fate to do her worst, for I have beaten her at her own game, I have come three score years and five and have won—being lucky—more than my share of the tricks."

I knew Will White * for about forty years; he was a dear friend.

* William Allen White died on January 29, 1944, at the age of seventy-six.

I recall many interesting meetings and talks we had, the visits I made at Emporia and the visit he made at Amherst. I remember how we fought and bled and died together at the Paris Peace Conference, how we sometimes differed quite sharply in opinion without in any way shaking our friendship. When I think of Will White I do not think first of the books he wrote or even of the good causes to which he was devoted. I think of the man himself, earnestly and honestly and with humor trying to live his life greatly and truly.

Peter Dunne was one of the most penetrating social satirists we have known in America; he was also a good companion and associate. He loved to talk—if the company was right: he loved so much to talk that he was likely to talk away all he had to say and it was with difficulty and infinite procrastination that he got anything down on paper. He had a little closet of an office just opposite mine. He would hurry in about noon, close his door with determination and sit down at his desk. All would be quiet for ten or fifteen minutes and then I was likely to hear his voice over the partition:

"Baker, what do you think T. R. has up his sleeve in that Aldrich business?"

He was off, and I too! And when he left for luncheon, a little later, there would be three or four, or more, pages of yellow copy paper each with an opening sentence or two of the essay which Boyden wanted by Thursday *without fail.* I doubt whether he ever got a manuscript ready on time. He would open his letters and leave them on his desk usually unanswered.

"Any letter left for two weeks," he said, "answers itself."

I am sure he liked us, as we liked him: I think we also amused him. Everything amused him! We were youthful and dead in earnest—and he was wise. Chance was sure, change was slow. And yet I think he was at heart as deeply earnest as any of us—and as much a "liberal" or "radical"—when it was not too much trouble. He hated shams and pretentiousness and stupidity—and laughed at them with "Mr. Dooley."

One of the early articles published in *The American* after we took it over was a "Dooley" "On the Power of the Press"—a good one too; but he had begun to be tired of Dooley and wanted, as he said, to write English for awhile. He could do it, too, as he proved in a department which Phillips instituted called "In the Interpreter's House." But he soon tired also of that: he could give it no such satiric edge as he gave the Dooley sketches, and it lacked the widespread popular appeal.

Peter Dunne was my friend; not intimate, not in all things; but working side by side in the same fine enterprise we came into understanding and sympathy upon several aspects of life. These we discussed often and eagerly, and I, at least, felt that in these matters, we knew each other where we really lived. There were ranges of his life I never touched, that I somehow did not care to touch. There were still wider ranges in my life he never knew, I never opened to him, knowing instinctively that he would not care for them.

We met thus upon a few rather narrow facets of our lives, and I, at least, deeply prized the intimacy. It seems to me as I think of it as good an example as any in my life of friendship as an *art,* an art because it was selective, as all art must be, and perfect within its own limitations. So many friendships are wrecked upon the rocks of indiscriminate intimacy.

It was a rare group we had there at the beginning of *The American Magazine*: men genuinely absorbed in life, genuinely in earnest in their attitude toward it, and yet with humor, and yet with sympathy, and yet with tolerance, far more eager to understand and make sure than to dream of utopias. We really believed in human beings: we really believed in democratic relationships. We "muckraked" not because we hated our world but because we loved it. We were not hopeless, we were not cynical, we were not bitter.

Two hateful world wars will leave little, I am afraid, of the spirit we knew in those days. The other day I re-read the earliest announcement of our new magazine venture with a kind of nostalgic surprise. It couldn't have been true—it was too naive. But there it is in black and white, with the names of a dozen derring-do editors and authors signed to it.

"We shall not only make this new *American Magazine* interesting and important in a public way, but we shall make it the most stirring and delightful monthly book of fiction, humor, sentiment, and joyous reading that is anywhere published. It will reflect a happy, struggling, fighting world, in which, as we believe, good people are coming out on top. There is no field of human activity in which we are not interested. Our magazine will be wholesome, hopeful, stimulating, uplifting, and above all, it will have a human interest on every page, whether expressed in fiction or articles or comment or editorials."

CHAPTER XXV

Enter David Grayson

In those early days of *The American Magazine* I went to New York once or twice a month and returned to my home in the country with my head on fire with new ideas, new undertakings. What visions we had, what plans we made!

All of us had plunged into the enterprise with astonishingly little regard to the future. No one of us had much money: we put into the common fund all we had and more. When we could not convince hard-headed investors that our enterprise had any great chance of succeeding, we dragooned our dearest friends to help us, and we were still in debt when the purchase of the new magazine was completed. More than this, each of us agreed to cut down on his or her salary (Miss Tarbell was one of the most dauntless of the adventurers) until we could "get going."

I think there is nothing in this world so dizzily stimulating, so glamorous with faith and hope, as such an enterprise as ours; resting in complete confidence upon one's friends, devoted to what one considers high purposes, each sacrificing to the limit for the common cause. Any man who has had even one such experience, and risen to it, has known one of the finest things that life has to offer. Whatever had happened before, whatever the difficulties and disappointments, whatever might happen afterward of disillusionment or of failure, nothing can dim the memories of such an experience.

At one of our early meetings in New York—I think it was in Ida Tarbell's book-lined study with the comfortable little tea table in front of the fireplace—John Phillips, our editor, urged each of us to look into his literary cupboard, not only for new ideas, but for written or half-written articles or stories or novels, whatever we might have, finish them off and get them down at once to Boyden and Siddall. We must make every effort to start the new magazine with a bang. It must be worthy of the announcements we were making.

Although promising nothing for myself, I took that appeal to heart. I considered the two partly written novels I had in hand—all I had to show for months, yes years, of laborious thought. Well, they would not do. I could not finish them in time and, worse still, I had begun to doubt, even if I could command all my time, that I could ever satisfy myself with them. I got them out as soon as I reached home—they were still largely in the form of memoranda and detached chapters and paragraphs—and read them over with a cold eye and despairing spirit. I knew then, at last, that I could never finish them even with forced labor. I saw that they were not for me—not my free and natural method of expression. I spent several days thinking about them and one morning with a kind of anger, I tore them up to the last page and went for a long tramp, up and along the Cedar River.

What a sense of relief and joy I felt that day. When the half gods go, the gods arrive! All that day remains vivid in my memory. When I reached home again, I began to turn over the notebooks in which I had been for years putting down all the little things that had never found a place in my finished articles and stories—incidents I considered too intimate, thoughts neither fully digested nor adequately expressed, groping inquiry into what the world, including my own life, might mean, with innumerable quotations from books I was reading, which had somehow helped me. Above all, there were the fragmentary and often careless pages in which I tried to express the joy I had, and the sense of beauty and of peace, in country life and country ways: incidents in the village I lived in or on the long tramps I made in country roads.

It was on that day or the next that I re-read the advice of crusty old Cobbett, in his book *Rural Rides*, on the way to write. I had turned to that book a hundred times in the past, not because I considered it infallible but because it often "spoke to my condition" as the Quakers say.

"Sit down to write what you have thought, and not to think what you shall write. Use the first words that occur to you, and never attempt to alter a thought; for that which has come of itself into your mind is likely to pass into that of another more readily and with more effect than anything which you can, by reflection, invent. . . .

"Thoughts come much faster than we can put them upon paper. They produce one another; and this order of their coming is in almost every case the best possible order that they can have on paper; . . ."

I think it was that very evening that I began to write, and all so easily and so freely, just as the words came to me. I did not consider any title or introduction, nor care in the least whether I was embarking on a short story or an essay or a novel. All I wanted was to get down, right away, some of the things I had boiling in my mind. I cannot be quite sure of the earliest paragraphs I wrote, but I think these were the ones, since they express the strong feeling of release and joy I had felt so sharply during the tramp that very day in the country:

"I cannot well describe it, save by the analogy of an opening door somewhere within the house of my consciousness. I had been in the dark: I seemed to emerge. I had been bound down: I seemed to leap up—and with a marvellous sudden sense of freedom and joy.

"I stopped there in the field and looked up. And it was as if I had never looked up before. I discovered another world. It had been there before, for long and long, but I had never seen nor felt it. All discoveries are made in that way: a man finds the new thing, not in nature but in himself. . . .

"I forgot myself, or where I was. I stood a long time motionless. My dominant feeling, if I can at all express it, was of a strange new friendliness, a warmth, as though these hills, this field about me, the woods, had suddenly spoken to me and caressed me. It was as though I had been accepted in membership, as though I was now recognized, after long trial, as belonging here."

I never wrote more easily or freely, or with greater delight. I used the first words that came to me and never attempted to alter a thought. After several days of steady writing I began to think of organizing the more or less detached incidents, stories, bits of observation, philosophical asides, that were piling up on my desk. I looked them over more or less critically, considering also many similar passages in my notebooks. I could see that they were all expressions, in one way or another, of my own experiences in the country, and of the joy I had in country people, in tramping in country roads, and in country gatherings, farm auctions, political caucuses, meetings in churches and schoolhouses. Everything I knew about country life poured into my mind, my boyhood in the wilds of Wisconsin, my winters teaching school in farming communities in Michigan, bits and strays from my years in an agricultural college, and most vivid of all, the experiences of recent years in our own home in the village of East Lansing. I found myself also writing about the interest and beauty of the natural scene—fields and hills, rivers and forests, everything in nature that stirs a man's soul.

This then was inevitably the material I had, what I and no one else was thinking and feeling and living. I saw right away, however, that it would be difficult for me to write such a highly intimate and personal narrative and use the names of all the people I knew or met, all the places I visited. This would, I knew, circumscribe the full expression of my thoughts, and sadly limit my characterizations of people and places. I decided to invent a fictional framework, a farm in the country, with all the characters true to life as I knew them, but with names and identifiable incidents somewhat concealed. I was to find later that I had not made all the disguises as impenetrable as I thought—to my occasional and not always amusing embarrassment.

My material began to fit itself into this fictional pattern with an ease that fascinated and surprised me. I even started the first chapter without the fumbling delays I had often to encounter. I headed it with a quotation from Walt Whitman:

"I think I could stop here myself and do miracles."

"I came here eight years ago as the renter of this farm, of which soon afterward I became the owner. The time before that I like to forget. The chief impression it left upon my memory, now happily growing indistinct, is of being hurried faster than I could well travel. From the moment, as a boy of seventeen, I first began to pay my own way, my days were ordered by an inscrutable power which drove me hourly to my task. I was rarely allowed to look up or down, but always forward, toward that vague Success which we Americans love to glorify."

When I finished that chapter a title literally flew into my mind and I wrote it down at the top of the first page: "The Burden of the Valley of Vision." I did not then know where it came from; I found it later in the Book of the Prophet Isaiah. It had probably been hidden for years in my subconscious memory, deposited there by my father reading some Sunday morning from the old red-bound family Bible to his six tousle-headed, dreaming boys; or perhaps it came from the Scotch Preacher there in his high pulpit in the country church we went to.

In about three weeks, even though I could not devote my whole time to the delightful pastime of that task, I had written six chapters, possible instalments for the magazine, and had given them these titles:

The Burden of the Valley of Vision
I Buy a Farm
The Joy of Possession
I Entertain an Agent Unawares
The Axe Helve
The Marsh Ditch

It was not until I had the completed manuscript in my hand that the spell broke. I had utterly let myself go, given everything I had, shamelessly disclosed all my thoughts and feelings—and my critical sense now suddenly awakened. I saw, literally saw, that infinitely precious manuscript of mine being passed around among the readers and editors in our office in New York—a process familiar to me from long experience. I knew the very men who were there to pass upon it—one in particular who had a way of casting aside, wearily, wearily, the "lifeblood of a man there written down"; and the very words I had heard him use: "Ho hum, another mistake."

I found myself suddenly and completely turned editor—looking at my manuscript with a hard cold eye. Who would read it? Whom would it interest? Would it make us new friends? What good would it do the magazine in terms of increased popularity? Would it, in short, increase our circulation? In all honesty, looking at my manuscript that dull morning, with the devastating eye of sober practicality, I could not but admit that it had no chance whatever. It was indeed a kind of story, but it had no plot—and would, therefore, fail to hold the reader. Worse still, it had no "love interest," no mystery, no suspense; no one was murdered in it. How build up a magazine on any such foundations?

I have rarely in my life been lower in my mind than I was during the next few days. It seemed to me, after all the glory of the last few weeks, that I had failed utterly. I even decided not to submit it to the editors at all. I had plenty of other work to do, good work too; why take any chances with such a venture? Even if the editors finally decided to use some part of it in the magazine, what effect would it have, being so utterly different from anything I had written before, upon the serious studies I had been publishing? I felt that I should do nothing to lessen the effect of the "muckraking" articles which had been highly useful, I believed, in helping to make people understand the problems that were facing America. At that very time I was beginning work on a new series regarding the Negro question in the South, the most impressive example I could anywhere find of the difficulties we Americans were having in practicing the art of living together in a crowded world. If I could understand and make other people understand all the aspects of such a perplexing problem, what a thing that would be! Would not such an unrelated narrative as I had now written confuse readers and weaken the impact of the facts I intended to set forth? I may have taken myself and my work far too seriously—but I am trying here to present what I felt and thought at the time.

It presently occurred to me that I might submit my manuscript under a pen name. I had done it many times before: and once had three articles in one number of the magazine, one under my own name, one under a *nom de plume* and one unsigned. I could thus submit it under pledge of secrecy to John Phillips, who was my loyal friend. I could count upon his telling me honestly what he thought of my sketches, and he would send them back to me, as painlessly as possible if he did not like them.

So I signed the manuscript with a name I had long been rolling under my tongue, "David Grayson," and sent it off to New York. In the letter I wrote to John Phillips I said that I wanted to preserve a complete anonymity, that I did not want even the men in the office to know of the series, and I wound up with the entreaty:

"Take care of my child."

It is difficult for me in later years to realize the intensity of feeling that went into this venture, the overwhelming passion of interest and hope I had, and the despair that went with it, but there it was. I had moments when I *knew* it was not good enough—that I myself was not good enough.

"It's all I've got to give," I cold-comforted myself in my notes, "and I've given it. I'd like to be more than I am: but cannot. If people, even a few people, like what I have written I shall be well rewarded; if they don't, I cannot help it."

All this may seem ridiculous. I was no novice as a writer: I had been contributing to newspapers and magazines and even publishing books, for many years. I had received, and given, many hard editorial knocks. But this seemed to me something entirely different, not the best I had dreamed of doing, but the best I could do—*being what I was.* It had a devastating finality about it. I tramped the country roads and awaited word from New York.

That word came sooner than I anticipated—a telegram from John Phillips:

"Manuscript a delight. Bully boy. Send more chapters. Best wishes."

My first difficulty was the choice of a title for my essays. My editor, like all good editors since the world began, having found a bright new penny insisted upon spending it at once. He'd have my first chapter illustrated and rush it into October, or November at the latest. It was imperative around Christmas time, wasn't it, to "knock their eyes out," as the youngest and most ferocious of our editors used to remark. Certainly it was imperative—but where is the title for your opus?

Now titles had been a kind of secret obsession of mine for many years. I caught them up on sunny days out of the thin air: I had them out of books and plays: I pilfered them from Shakespeare and the Bible and *Romany Rye* and *Alice in Wonderland* and *Tom Sawyer* and no end of other writings. There was safety in having plenty of good titles handy for any novel or story I might suddenly write. Good titles, like the mustard seed which the man took and cast into his garden, might even breed great trees of books with the fowls of the air lodged in their branches. Every writer knows that it is sometimes easier to find a story to fit a title than a title to fit a story.

My trouble was not a dearth of titles but a plethora. They were scattered all through my notebooks: I had put down scores of them, and the appetite growing with what it fed upon, I included in my collection titles that I knew I could never, by any possibility, write a story to fit. I liked the very look of them—to say nothing of the taste and the smell. Two of the plums of my collection I found, of all places, in the *Meditations of Marcus Aurelius*: "A Stranger's Sojourn" and "Smoke and Ash and a Tale." I knew well enough that I should never be heavy-browed enough to write even a little essay with such grim intimations of mortality. For the great and gloomy Emperor's comment that calls out the first is this:

"What belongs to the soul is a dream and vapour, and life is a warfare and *a stranger's sojourn,* and after fame is oblivion."

And the other is this:

". . . bring to thy recollection those who have complained greatly about anything, those who have been most conspicuous by the greatest fame or misfortunes or enmities or fortunes of any kind: then think where are they all now? *Smoke and ash and a tale* . . ."

Once, when I was in the mood, I spent most of one grisly night rolling about in my bed, furiously constructing a mighty novel based upon the thesis that life was indeed a dream and a vapor and that after fame was oblivion; but in the morning I found cheerfulness breaking through and concluded that while I had invented a very fine novel I could not write it.

Another prize in my collection I had from Omar Khayyam, one of the earlier editions:

"Oh the brave music of a *distant* drum."

For that I even got to the point of writing a meditative, but not too mournful, essay which I called "The Brave Music of a Distant Drum."

I had also long been hiving up titles for my autobiography. One of them that took a strong hold upon me at one time I rejected because my readers might not know what it meant: they might not realize how many autobiographies I could turn out if I really put my hand to it! The title was "The Seventy Last" but I considered it would not be clear without the context written by the old Jewish prophet (II Esdras):

"The first that thou hast written publish openly, that the worthy and the unworthy may read it: but keep the seventy last that thou mayst deliver them *only* to such as be wise among the people, for in them is wisdom and the stream of knowledge."

Similarly I had innumerable titles in mind for the essays that I had now written. There were such sober, roast-beef titles as these:

"Annals of a Countryman."
"Long Days and Quiet Thoughts."
"A Little Town I Know."

There were several titles that intrigued me, but seemed too metaphorical, so that I resisted the temptation to use them:

"Brother Dust."
"Pleasant Bread."

The latter, somewhat extended, "A Day of Pleasant Bread," I used for a chapter in my book. The publishers, considering that it could make its perilous way alone, later brought it out in a separate edition, beautifully bound and illustrated.

I was all on fire for a time with a title I found in one of Cowper's poems, since it seemed so perfectly descriptive of some of the things I was trying to express: "Loop-holes of Retreat."

These were the lines I found it in:

'Tis pleasant, through the loop-holes of retreat
To peep at such a world—to see the stir
Of the great Babel, and not feel the crowd.

Although I liked these lines very much, I found after tasting them a thousand times that they somehow lost their savor. For I did not really like peep-holes: I wanted to be out with the folks. I wanted to know the busy world and live it deeply. So I chose my title, and for fear that if I delayed any longer, the youngest editor of them all might drop dead of apoplexy, I telegraphed it to New York.

Adventures in Contentment.

I have been a writer now for more than half a century, devoting my whole time to that art or profession and, what is more surprising, making my living at it. But I have never in all that time been able to escape the inevitable reactions that accompany the production of even a short essay or story, to say nothing of a book. When I get into a piece of writing that really interests me, I begin to think it positively the best thing I have ever done. It begins to write itself. I work on it day and night. I enjoy it prodigiously.

When I have put the period to the last word of the last paragraph, the crystal ball into which I have been gazing suddenly shatters. I begin to be critical and doubtful. I wonder whether anyone in the world, except the poor slave of a proofreader, will ever read what I have written. I even look with indulgent skepticism upon the very words in which the editors, and above all the advertisers, express their approval. About the time that the first installment of my *Adventures* was published, in November, 1906, all stories, novels, and even articles were "stunning" or they were not "stunning." If they were "stunning" they were likely, if you were excitable, to "knock your eye out," or else they were so "breathlessly absorbing" that you "could not lay them down": or you were compelled to "sit up half the night"—never the whole one—to read them.

I could not possibly see how my quiet country sketches as they were printed from month to month could qualify under any of these categories. They would certainly stun nobody and, I hoped, destroy no one's eyesight. I knew well enough that I didn't want to see them again, or read them—at least for many, many years. The only great book was always the one I had not yet written. I could put into it all the beauty, the humor, the pathos, the understanding, I had missed in those I had written before.

Well, I am still, in my seventy-fifth year, looking forward to the great unwritten book.

Of course I was pleased that Phillips and the other editors liked my sketches well enough to publish them. I had responded to his request that all of us turn out our literary cupboards to fill the yawning emptiness of the first numbers of the new magazine. I was no longer worrying about them: since my contributions were being published under a *nom de plume*, I should not be blamed for writing them. In the meantime I could go on with the "great series" on the Negro question in the South to which I was now turning my whole attention. In September of that year (1906) there had been at Atlanta, Georgia, one of the worst race riots ever known in the United States. What better field could there be for working at my self-appointed task—much thought about, all too little tried—as a "maker of understandings"? How were whites and Negroes to live together peacefully in a crowded world? My early articles on the subject were widely advertised and soon became a "real success" from the editorial point of view.*

It seems ridiculous in the afterlook, but I even looked incredulously upon the efforts of my editors to give the early installments of my new essays a truly delightful presentation. Tom Fogarty, then a relatively unknown artist, was to do the illustrations. I had never met him nor he me. I was dubious about some of his earlier work that I had seen: but I had to acknowledge that the sketches he made were really charming. I could not have believed that anyone could so interpret and express the inner spirit of what I had written. I soon found that he had long spent his summers in the country of northern New York and was a true lover of all the fine things he saw there. The sketches he made for that first installment, a hayfield at haying time, a plowman plowing, Charles Baxter's carpenter shop, and above all the portraits of Harriet and Horace, seemed perfect to me. He and David Grayson worked together for many years after that; with the growing understanding and mutual regard which writers and illustrators do not always feel for each other.

On the whole, however, I was gloomy about the whole project: but I was heartened by a letter I soon received. I carried it for some time in the breast pocket of my coat. It was written by Lincoln Steffens, who, as an editor and as a friend, had been early let into the secret of the authorship. It was certainly one of the finest appreciations that ever I received in my life. I am abashed to print it here, but how can I leave it out?—it was then, and has remained, one of those creative documents in a man's life which give him courage to go on:

* The series began publication in April, 1907, and continued in 1908. It was afterwards published in a book called *Following the Color Line,* Doubleday Page and Co., 1908.

LITTLE POINT
RIVERSIDE, CONNECTICUT

July 25, 1906.

MY DEAR BAKER:

Your David Grayson . . . is beautiful. I had just written a paragraph about you, telling how you were a reporter. I showed how much that meant of straight vision and intellectual integrity, but when I sent off my "sketch" and then picked up the "Farmer Unlimited" I was ashamed. And I was ashamed because I never had realized that there was in you such a sense of beauty, so much fine, philosophic wisdom and, most wonderful of all,—serenity.

It's a real creative art, Baker, far above and beyond reporting. I respect reporting. I have great ideas of what can be done by telling the facts and the stories of life about us. I would have *The American* report and report and report, till men had to see what a state of servitude they are in, and fight for very shame. But what I'd have men stirred up for would be only to raise them to a state of mind into which you put them without effort in these articles.

David Grayson is a great man. I can see now, rather late, that he has some of your traits. I can see now that you might naturally rise to his heights, but—I'm late. You said you had some things you had done, like this, for pleasure. I'd like to look through them. You have been practising a sort of fraud on your friends or, rather, you have let them defraud themselves . . .

And, Baker, fine as it all is in the big way, it is fine in detail, too. At every crisis, every time a clumsy hand would have gone wrong, you were just right, exactly right. It's an extraordinary thing. It did me good; it reminded me of art and right living and the love of man for man. These are things I am writing about in my article on Lindsey, but, just the same, you recalled the conception of them intimately used as if from afar. I'm afraid to tell you what I think you should do hereafter.

I can say in all honesty that I was vastly surprised at the response that followed the publication, month by month, of my *Adventures.* In those early days of the popular magazine, "fan letters" had not become an accepted prodigy as they have since then, and they were welcomed by both publishers and authors as veritable signs in the skies. I could not understand the response then, and I am not sure I have ever understood it since. I had sometimes prided myself on the "reader-response" to my articles on the labor problem, on the lawless control of the railroads, on the Negro question, and the like; they gave me the feeling of being really useful to hapless human beings—but it was nothing like this.

Many of the letters were written to me personally in care of the publishers; far more were written to the editors of the magazine—and since I was then preserving a strict anonymity, they were for the most part acknowledged by Albert Boyden. Sometimes he sent me "budgets" containing extracts from the comments. I have just been re-reading a few of them that I find still among my papers. They give me much the same feeling as they did in those long-ago days, a kind of mystified astonishment, they were so wholly unexpected.

I could have expected a few letters from genuine lovers of country living or of nature, but here were letters from all kinds of people and from all parts of the country. One of the earliest was from Richard Harding Davis, then one of the best-known story writers in the country, who wrote to congratulate an "unknown author".

Quite a number of letters came from book publishers who were apparently willing to gamble on the book after reading the first installment. Knowing something from experience with canny publishers, this surprised me most of all.

These letters have now been coming in a steady stream for thirty-eight years. Sometimes the outpour was reduced to a trickle, but a new series of the sketches—now published in nine books—would start it going strong again. There have been scores of reprintings and new editions in this country and in England, and several translations in foreign languages. The circulation in England and the English dominions—Australia, Canada, South Africa—has been almost as great as in America. One of the books has had forty-five printings in England. A great many thousands in cheap editions have been published, and in all, according to the labor-of-love calculations of my daughter Rachel, there have been some two million copies of the books sold.

CHAPTER XXVI

Living under a *Nom de Plume*

My adventures with David Grayson have always been more or less inexplicable to me. They have been my life, rather than my work. I have always had in hand articles and books devoted to serious subjects. I spent twenty-one years of hard labor in writing *Woodrow Wilson: Life and Letters; Woodrow Wilson and World Settlement*, and other related books. I wrote or edited eighteen volumes on that subject. I do not now regret the experience; it yielded some of the richest incidental rewards a man can know. But I was often under heavy pressure—"Where is that manuscript you promised for last Wednesday?"—so that I did not know which way to turn, for weariness. I was sometimes ill and often discouraged.

It is no light thing to say, but I honestly believe I could never have come through with the tasks I had to do, even as haltingly as I did come through, if I had not had a home in the country that I could return to, that I deeply loved, and that I could write about. I have quoted many times the line out of the Roman Horace, who also knew the weariness of cities.

"How gladly I return to my woodlands and my little farm that restore me to myself."

I never did the Grayson writing under pressure—except once and that was more or less of a failure. I wrote when I was ready to write, and what it pleased me to write—never, at the moment anyway, thinking of publication. It was all more or less left-hand work, the product of moments of real living snatched from tasks I thought more important.

I have never been able to explain why it was—perhaps it is not necessary to explain it—but when I was working on my land, or tramping country roads, or climbing the perfect hills, I became a new person, harmonious with a different life. Even the closest of my highly perceptive editors found nothing in the style of the *Adventures* to remind them of the articles or even the casual stories and editorials I wrote. One night I went out to dinner with a member of our staff who had a beautiful home in New Jersey. Somewhat to my amusement and alarm, the company began discussing the new "country sketches." My good friend said he knew who wrote them.

"Who?" someone asked.

"They are not letting out the secret," he said, "but it is J. S. Phillips. They're just like him."

The discussion became fast and furious. My friend's wife suddenly turned to me.

"Now, perhaps Mr. Baker wrote them."

Before I could think of just what response to make, my host said emphatically,

"Oh no, Baker couldn't have done it. It's entirely out of his line."

It was not only a different literary style, but so strongly did this personality finally fasten upon me that several times in my garden or on the roads, when I was suddenly addressed, I caught myself responding in a voice strange to me—to my great embarrassment.

And yet the style I wrote in seemed as native to me as the usual style of my articles. I never thought of it any more than I thought of describing David Grayson's personal appearance, or my own.

Part of the time, I can see now, I was the reporter, perhaps the too serious reporter; and part of the time the true liver, the enjoyer. We usually got along fairly well together, except when Grayson, coming in full of exciting adventures, tried to pilfer Baker's writing time. Grayson had sometimes to be put in his place, reminded that there was great and serious work to be done if people were really to learn the art of living together in a crowded world. Sometimes Grayson's conscience seemed really troubled—but not often. What a sad spectacle—this degeneration from duty into enjoyment! Not long ago I ran across a paragraph in my notes in which Grayson bemoans his situation:

"Who was ever so afflicted as I am? Fated to enjoy intensely a wicked and unreasonable world! How change human beings who are palpably unjust or unreasonable, to say nothing of iniquitous, when they interest me so much, when I like so many of them just as they are? If I could utterly reform the world I am not sure I should like it half as well as I do now—

"Woe is me!"

If David Grayson was only a "mood," as one commentator long ago called it, it was a mood that was life-giving and life-saving for me. When the world seemed wholly out of joint, it was a rebound into the deep, quiet places of the spirit.

It was amusing to me at times, amusing and absurd, how envious of Grayson Baker sometimes became. Baker would write a tremendous article, over which he had labored and sweat for weeks. It would be published in the same issue with one of the little spontaneously written Grayson sketches. Baker would receive a number of commendatory or critical letters, a few editorial comments, some hostile, and would himself sometimes begin to doubt the thoroughness of his observation (so much he had not had time to see) and especially his own hesitant conclusions. But the little Grayson sketch would bring a veritable downpour of grateful and appreciative letters, the burden of which was that Grayson had helped make people understand and enjoy their lives a little more deeply and fully. Strange: what I did so earnestly, even passionately, strongly moved by what Miss Tarbell used to call "righteous indignation," never seemed to satisfy anyone, not even myself. As a "muckraker," hating the want of humanity in our common life, I tried to expose, arouse, drive people to better social relationships: I liked to think in later years that David Grayson was working for the same thing, more or less blindly, in another way. For he was presenting the beauty of neighborliness, the richness of the quiet life, the charm of common things. Each in its way was a spontaneous expression of what I thought and felt.

I had no idea when I began writing these *Adventures* of the effect they might have or what people would get out of them. So many of the letters I received seemed to imply that the *design* of the books was to give courage and hope; could I have been more effective if I had really had some such design? It was not, honestly, there. I am afraid I was writing because I liked to write and because it helped me to live as I wanted to live. This, as precisely as I can put it down, is the unvarnished truth of the matter.

"You have sublimated the *real* but commonplace experiences of life that we all enjoy," wrote one correspondent, "but never take the time or have the talent to write about."

I thought this remark touched one of the secrets; for is it not true that an overwhelming proportion of every man's life is made up of little things, little common everyday events, scenes, duties? If a man has not learned to live with them comfortably, to enjoy them, he simply has not learned to live. He has no technique of joy. He must rush to other places, seek noise, confusion, sensation. He must dull his mind instead of sharpening it. He must get out of books at second hand what he cannot find in his own dooryard. His life soon becomes thin, weak, superficial: he has been feeding upon the husks of a far country when there were boundless riches at home.

Especially in the last few years a great many of the letters I have received have come out of the heart of sadness, doubt, weariness, which now afflict the nation and the world. So many people, as Thoreau said, lead lives of quiet desperation. Recently I had a letter from a woman in New York state who told me her story: "a mother of six, ranging from six months to twenty years of age." So much to do! She had to "stop between every three words to straighten a wobbly baby in her pillows on the floor." "Your books," says she, "give me courage and comfort and help me to take things as they come, minute by minute."

She puts her finger, it seems to me, on one of the fundamental longings of the human heart—"the hunger that I feel *for some acknowledgment that all my weariness and effort pays.*"

About many of these letters that have been coming to me during the last quarter century I have felt completely helpless. *They want more than I have got.* I have put the best I had in my books: they long for more: for the appetite for sympathy and understanding in human nature is insatiable. In cases that I have found particularly moving, I have replied as heartily and generously as I knew how, and often precipitated an avalanche of new letters, which I could not answer as they deserved and still find time to do my own necessary work. When people seem to want more of me than my books give them, I sometimes quote a remark that I found in one of Walt Whitman's letters to Anne Gilchrist:

"My book is my best letter, my response, my truest explanation of all."

So many of these correspondents and many of those who have come to see me have sent or brought little gifts, never anything expensive: often precious garden seeds, rare plants and shrubs, unnumbered books. Many have sent me pictures of their homes and of their children. One proud father has presented me nearly every birthday with a picture of a son christened David Grayson; the latest, which came only a few months ago, was that of a fine young soldier in uniform. Many have sent good things to eat, a cake of honey to compare with my own, wild rice gathered by hand in the north country, piñon nuts from Arizona, and innumerable other things.

When I look into the *Adventures* themselves after all these years —I shrink! How much I could now improve them, or think I could. How much would better have been left out. And yet, what use? If people like what I have written, if it amuses them, or helps them, or comforts them, or instructs them—as the writing amused and comforted and instructed me—they will imperturbably go on with the reading of the books, demanding new editions when the old ones run out—and so on, and on, until they no longer find anything in me to interest them. Then they will quietly drop me and the "iniquity of oblivion" will scatter over me her merciful poppies, and I shall be remembered no more.

A great many people who have written me or come to see me down through the years appear to think that they can find peace of mind by moving from the town into the country. They think that there is some magic in living on the land. A man came here not long ago who thought that it was my home in the country, my hills, my orchard, and my bees that made me happy. He thought he might buy him a house nearby and be happy too. There have been times when I have thought of writing to some of those who think mere living in the country can make them happy in the words of Charles Lamb in one of his letters to the ever-moving, never contented Coleridge:

"Is it a farm that you have got? and what does your worship know about farming?"

And yet I firmly believe that if everyone could get his feet, somewhere, somehow, down upon the soil, he could live a richer and a more interesting life. Not field-farming necessarily, but at least a little plot of ground, a garden, an apple tree or two, bees, flowers—a pot of tulips in the window! It is not a panacea, it will not of itself make men happy—but it will help, it will provide the soil in which contentment may easily grow. For it somehow links the soul of man with the creative spirit.

In two of the books I wrote under the name of David Grayson, *The Countryman's Year* and *Under My Elm*, I have especially related some of my own daily adventures as a "part-time farmer" at Amherst, and set forth the reasons for my enjoyment of the country way of life. I believe firmly that the time will come, in an age of motor cars and flying machines, when many more city people will find it possible to live on the land, to their own better health and keener satisfaction. I don't mean that life in the country is without its difficulties and hardships—I know what they are—but if the man is a worker, and both man and wife are contented with simple living, with *living* more than with money-making, it offers real and deep satisfaction. It is for many a return to reality, getting back to honest dealings with nature. You can't cheat an acre of land! As Goethe said, I think in Eckermann's *Conversations*:

"Agriculture is a very fine thing, because you get such an unmistakable answer as to whether you're making a fool of yourself or hitting the mark."

So many things in the country I love well—it is difficult to make comparisons. One thing I know of a certainty: I like to see things grow, especially things I have myself planted, or bred, or tended. I like to go out of an evening after the day's work is over and I am tired, and walk about my garden and orchard, or down into my field. I like to see the young corn pushing up through the brown earth and the grassland coming green with clover and red-top. I like to watch the young bees playing in front of the hives, and the blossoms coming thick on the apple trees. Nothing, I think, gives a man more solid satisfaction than to climb up into a fruit tree, which he himself with his own hands set out, a frail sapling, a few years ago. To have watched a tree grow through the years, to prune it, spray it, and finally to reap the fruit of it is to know the peculiar joy of creation.

One of the reasons I like to see things grow is that I feel that I myself have a part in the process: something fine I am helping to make. I like the quiet generosity of the response: the growth that goes on when I am asleep, or tired, or ill—if I am not ill too long. I don't know just how to express it, but I feel a kind of gratitude for that. Even the risks and the failures add zest to one's devotion; for if things go wrong, I can go to the rescue. I can feed or fertilize, I can cultivate or irrigate, I can dip or spray or prune. And at the end of the season when the corn stands six or eight feet tall, like ranks of grenadiers in the fields, and the neighbors come to tell me what a crop I have, it gives a glow of satisfaction that comes, I think, in no other way. Yes, I like to see things grow.

I must speak of one other aspect of David Grayson's career that was sometimes irritating, sometimes amusing, always more or less incomprehensible. Soon after the essays and stories began to appear in book form, I heard of men who were traveling about the country calling themselves David Grayson, and writing, or giving readings, in one case even preaching, under my pseudonym. I received letters from people whom David Grayson was said to have visited; one in particular contained an unpaid board bill! A veritable storm presently broke out in Denver where one of these lively fellows was having quite a career. He was not only writing and lecturing under the name of Grayson, but was apparently doing it with such success that he had entranced a young woman, whom he was about to marry. We received anguished letters from the girl's friends, and telegrams of inquiry from Colorado and New Mexico. He was presently exposed with flaring headlines in the Denver *Post* and other papers. Under pressure from two newspaper men he admitted that he had not actually *written* the David Grayson stories, but argued that he had sent so many letters to the man who was writing them that he felt he "had a share in them."

A month or two later I had a distressful letter from the bride confessing that she had married him under the impression that he was the David Grayson who was writing for *The American Magazine.*

One imposter who traveled in Tennessee and North Carolina gave author's readings of my essays. He copied them out of my books, changed the titles, and afterward presented them as original manuscripts to friends he had made.

I have always had the curiosity to meet one of these fellows face to face. From what I have heard, they possess gifts I have always envied; for example, that of standing up before a company and reading my own writings without feeling that my legs are wobbling. But I shall probably never have this privilege.

I thought at first that these impostures were due to the fact that my identity was not known. Other absurd problems had also arisen to make me rue the day when I had ventured to write under a *nom de plume.* In 1915, after the secret had been kept—more or less kept—for ten years, I yielded to the often repeated suggestions of the editor of the Bookman that I "confess and seek absolution". I sent him a highly impressionistic scrawl showing me with both hands up. To this he gave the caption "Both hands up. Grayson surrenders his anonymity," and published it with the article he wrote.

The skies did not fall, nor the impostors cease their imposing. They have been at it here and there ever since; some use the Grayson, some the Baker name, some both.

CHAPTER XXVII

Rise of the Insurgents—Taft as President

Toward the end of Theodore Roosevelt's administration I attended a little dinner at the City Club in New York at which a group of us, who called ourselves Progressives or Independents in politics, discussed what we should do, whom we should support in the coming election. Among those present were Louis D. Brandeis, Norman Hapgood, then editor of *Collier's Weekly*, and Lincoln Steffens. It was not a mere question as to whom we should vote for in 1908, whether Taft the Republican or Bryan the Democrat, but how to strengthen the non-partisan liberal movement in which we were deeply interested and which we saw, or thought we saw, rapidly developing. Where was understanding leadership for this movement to come from?

In the earlier days I had had no interest at all in politics. I thought it about the worst possible means of securing an honest and thorough examination of the difficult economic and social problems, let alone reaching reasonable solutions of them. I disliked intensely the petty juggling for power and for offices that went by the name of politics. I disliked catchwords and slogans.

But it was inevitable sooner or later under our democratic system that all these problems should be carried over into politics. Politics could not be abolished nor even adjourned, as indignant good people sometimes advocated: it was in its essence the method by which communities worked out their common problems. It was one of the principal arts of living peacefully in a crowded world. And politics demanded organization, and organization, leadership. While there must be men with gifts to see and set forth the conditions and problems to be met—whether as scientists, or writers, or preachers—there must also be men with the genius to organize and lead the people.

I had learned by sad experience that I was neither an organizer nor a leader. I was so disturbed by existing conditions that I tried to institute a reform movement in Michigan where I was living in 1908: but I got nowhere, except in discovering, after a sound trouncing or so, that I had no capacity in this field, that my genuine function was, after all, that of the writer, trying to see and understand what was going on, and reporting what I found to the people.

I comforted myself with the thought that good followers were just as necessary in a democracy as good leaders, perhaps more necessary. There could even be great followers, as well as great leaders; the difficulty was to find strong, wise and honest leaders to follow.

Theodore Roosevelt was the first leader in whom I became deeply interested. He had become the hope of the young liberals, the "insurgents" and progressives of that period. In the beginning we had great faith in him.

While the redoubtable "Teddy" continued to dominate his party and to hold the warm allegiance of his trusted personal friends and followers—such good and able men as Gifford Pinchot, James A. Garfield, and William Allen White—not a few younger men, of whom I was one, began toward the end of his administration, to question not only his objectives but also his method as a progressive leader. Was it enough to dispense moral judgments? Or balance these judgments between, say, the "good" trust and the "bad" trust? It began to seem a little like Bryan's comment that the financial problems of the country could be easily solved if "our hearts were in the right place."

Would people who were suffering under inequitable tariff laws, unjust railroad rates, and the overbearing power of great monopolistic organizations accept any such easy avoidance?

Roosevelt himself had confessed that he was not primarily interested in the great economic and social questions that were confronting the nation. He had even said that so far as the tariff question was concerned he was an "agnostic," in short, he had neither strong principles, nor any real program for meeting the most troublesome issues then facing the people.

I can't remember what, if any, conclusions we reached at that dinner. The little conferences in those days, which I look back to with keen pleasure, were far more valuable for the pointed questions that were raised, the information exchanged, the lively controversies we had, than for any decisions we reached.

It was in these gatherings that I came first to know Mr. Brandeis, and to value every word he had to say. I thought then, and continued in all the later years to think, that his was one of the clearest minds in American public life. He had a positive genius for picking apart the snarls into which public discussion so easily degenerated, and at the last leaving in the minds of those who heard him, not sweeping conclusions, not easy remedies to propose, but clarifications on which to build in the future. He was one of the rare public men who did not "view with alarm," nor stoop to personal abuse, nor waste time mourning over the past mistakes of public men: he was always looking ahead, trying to create something good and sound out of materials that were ready at hand. For instance, he built a new system of non-profit life insurance based upon those fine old co-operative institutions, the savings banks of Massachusetts, a system that did not succeed by hectic advertising, but by winning the confidence and saving the money of common people. It has had a great success in Massachusetts, and is now spreading to other states.

When it came to the election of 1908 I voted for Taft with hope rather than with confidence. The plain fact was that the country knew next to nothing at all about the real Mr. Taft until after his election. He was a large, dim, charming personality of whom his friend Theodore Roosevelt, who was choosing him as his successor, had painted an heroic portrait.

"To a flaming hatred of injustice, to a scorn of all that is base and mean, to a hearty sympathy with the oppressed, he [Mr. Taft] unites entire disinterestedness, courage both moral and physical of the very highest type, and a kindly generosity of nature which makes him feel that all his fellow countrymen are in very truth his friends and brothers."

There was a great deal of truth, so far as Taft, personally, was concerned, in this beneficent portrait, but it gave no inkling, as Roosevelt himself must have realized a few years later when he and his friend fell out, of what Taft, the leader, really believed, or would do when he was safely seated in the White House.

Taft was a lawyer whose ambition it was to sit on the Supreme Court. His approach to public questions from the first was that of the legalist. He seemed to believe that Roosevelt and the reformers had gone far enough: it was time to "complete and perfect the machinery . . . by which lawbreakers may be promptly restrained and punished," as he said in a campaign address in Cincinnati, July 28, 1908.

This was just the program that the "stand-patters" wanted; they too thought the reformers had gone far enough. At a dinner on April 30, only a few weeks after Taft's inauguration, Joseph H. Choate, the most notable lawyer of his time, spoke with fine sarcasm of the legal activities of the Roosevelt administration.

"Corporation lawyers," he said, "were universally condemned only about twelve months ago. It is time they had their inning."

But the Progressives believed that only a start had been made during Roosevelt's administration; that the real battle was yet to come, and it was soon evident that their efforts to understand and solve the important problems of the railroads, water power, trusts, the tariff, and the like, were to find small encouragement at Washington. The familiar visitors at the White House were no longer the liberals of Congress, or the nation, but such so-called "stand-patters" as Senator Aldrich of Rhode Island, and Speaker Cannon of the House of Representatives.

The next year or two was to see a tremendous outbreak of political revolt, and the appearance of an Insurgent Movement without precedent in the country.* It was, significantly, most strongly evident in Taft's own supposedly conservative party. The National Progressive Republican League soon had among its signers eight United States senators, among them such powerful leaders and campaigners

* A list of the non-officeholders of the National Progressive Republican League may serve to give an idea of how widely the movement was spread throughout the country. Alfred L. Baker, Illinois; Ray Stannard Baker, Massachusetts; Albert J. Beveridge, Ex-U. S. Senator, Indiana; Charles R. Crane, Illinois; Louis D. Brandeis, Massachusetts; Frank L. Dingley, Maine; James R. Garfield, Ohio; Hugh T. Halbert, Minnesota; Francis J. Heney, California; Fred C. Howe, New York; E. Clarence Jones, New York; Geo. S. Loftus, Minnesota; Fremont Older, California; Gifford Pinchot and Amos Pinchot, of Pennsylvania; James A. Peterson, Minnesota; George L. Record, New Jersey; Gilbert E. Roe, New York; W. S. U'Ren, Oregon; Merle D. Vincent, Colorado; William Allen White, Kansas.

as LaFollette of Wisconsin, Bristow of Kansas, Norris of Nebraska and Cummins and Dolliver of Iowa. Besides these senators, the list included sixteen members of the House of Representatives, six governors of states, and nineteen other active public men, including several well-known writers.

A similar insurgency was rapidly developing in the Democratic party. Woodrow Wilson was overturning the powerful New Jersey machine, and a vigorous young man named Franklin D. Roosevelt, then a state senator, was organizing the insurgent Democrats in the New York legislature. Judge Lindsey in Colorado and Brand Whitlock in Ohio were vigorous supporters of the new movement.

"An insurgent," remarked Theodore Roosevelt, who viewed the movement with some anxiety, "is a Progressive who is exceeding the speed limit."

What made the movement especially alarming to the conservatives was that there was little or no difference in their objectives between the insurgents of the two old parties. Governor Woodrow Wilson said in a public speech:

"If somebody could draw together the liberal elements of both parties in this country he could build up a party which could not be beaten in a generation, for the very reason that we would all join it."

The movement was not socialist; although the Socialists were then stronger in the country, probably, than ever before. In an article I wrote at the time I tried to define and contrast the two movements. "The emphasis of the Insurgent Movement," I wrote, "was upon the development first of strong and honest political machinery; that of the Socialists, upon immediate economic reforms.

"The Insurgent believes," I went on to say, "that once the people get the power they can be trusted to use it properly. If the people wish then to adopt any part or all of the Socialist economic program, well and good. If, on the other hand, the people turn out to be economically more conservative than some of the extreme radicals desire, also well and good. It is a people's government, and this is the democratic spirit."

In seeking better political machinery, the Insurgents advocated various new devices of democratic control: direct nominations, the initiative and referendum, simpler forms of controlling city governments, direct election of United States Senators, and stringent new laws to prevent corrupt political practices.

But the Insurgents, even if they often differed among themselves, also had a program of economic reform calling for lower tariffs, conservation of natural resources, a parcel-post system, a national income tax, pure-food legislation, a Federal Reserve system, and stringent governmental control of all public utilities.

As I write this list I am impressed by the fact that so many of the objectives of those truculent revolters of 1909–1911 have already been realized in whole or in part: and I exult in the thought that these changes, now generally accepted, are the work of our own deeply entrenched, soundly native, often bumbling and inefficient, democratic system.

It was sad to many a man like myself, who had voted for Taft and who really liked him personally and hoped that he would measure up to the tremendous responsibilities and opportunities that he faced in 1909, to find that he was rapidly losing the confidence of the country. I knew what a hard fight he had ahead of him, and I wanted to help him, in my own small way, if I could, with my pen. I had met him several times and heard him speak not only to great general audiences but more intimately to groups at dinner; but he was not the kind of man who eagerly welcomed writers, as Roosevelt had done, nor had he the gift of enlisting most of them in his own personal army. One talk I had with him something more than a year after he came into the Presidency, I shall never forget. I have it fully reported in my notes. The tariff bill was then under hot discussion in Congress, and the President had already been somewhat widely criticized for his attitude toward Mr. Aldrich and Mr. Cannon. And the so-called "Ballinger case" was just rising above the popular horizon.

"A great number of people were waiting for him in the cabinet room," I wrote, "including several senators and congressmen. Nearly an hour late he came out of his private office; a great, breezy, active, boyish, good-humored personality. I had liked him on previous occasions when I had met him and I liked him now, from what I saw of him in action, better than ever. He had a frank, free, whole-hearted way of greeting his visitors, giving one that impression of joy of living which is one of the most beguiling of human traits. Once or twice he threw one of his great arms over the shoulder of a congressman and led him off into a corner to talk over some especially private matter.

"He asked me to remain to the last and I went with him into his private office. In Roosevelt's time this little office, opening out upon the White House park, had the air of a quiet study, with the surroundings of a man of general culture—flowers on the table, a riding crop and a tennis racket in the corner, a few books of history, or fiction, or even poetry, on the corner of the table. Now the office had become, and not without significance, a law-office. On all sides of the room were cases filled with law-books, nothing but law-books.

"The extraordinary frankness of Mr. Roosevelt as a talker has often been commented upon. But Mr. Taft impressed me at once with a candor that was even more remarkable than that of his predecessor. He talked with perfect freedom of Congress, of the post-office department, of promotions in the army, and of his likes and dislikes of certain high officers. I had hesitated at first about asking concerning questions so intimately before him at that moment as the tariff—but I had no need to hesitate. He outlined his position with a degree of frankness and earnestness that left in my mind no doubt of his essential sincerity. I had entered his office full of the doubts which were then beginning to creep into the popular mind regarding the ability of Mr. Taft to get tariff revision which would satisfy the country, but he swept them all aside with a sort of easy optimism, which is one of his most evident characteristics. Don't worry; everything will be all right!

"He looks one in the eye with an engaging frankness and good-humor, he smiles, he has a common, direct, democratic way with him, and when all is said he is a fine figure of a man; big, strong, handsome of face, clear of countenance, winning of manner; the sort of man one would like as a personal friend."

I came away from the White House that day fully convinced that Mr. Taft not only would do what he said he would, regarding the tariff, but that he *could* do it. "Wait," I said to those I met who criticized him; "when the time comes he will put his big hand down. He will get what he wants."

I remember well the intense personal disappointment and discouragement I felt in watching the crumbling of Taft's administration. I had been devoting most of my time for a number of years to the campaign of the so-called "muckrakers," helping to awaken the people to the evil conditions that existed, and I had seen vigorous support arising on all sides, expressing itself in Congress, state legislatures, and even in the most corruption-ridden of cities. And here in Washington, at the very heart of the American system, the old forces were resurgent, the old leaders seemingly again in full control. There were again the familiar scandals in the public lands department, which led to the Ballinger inquiries; the tariff-lobbyists seemed stronger than ever; and legislative campaigns to cure the evils connected with the railroads and the trusts were apparently forgotten. The men in control at Washington were complacently reading the Progressives and Insurgents from the West out of the Republican party.

"A mirage," said Secretary Ballinger of the Interior Department, referring in his speech at St. Paul to the uprising.

"Hypocrisy," said the President himself, referring in his speech at Newark to the criticism of his administration.

"Treason," said Attorney-General Wickersham, at the Hamilton Club.

I may have been too impatient in feeling the situation so strongly; I had not yet learned that great popular movements are always slow, that there are often pauses and reactions while they regather their strength, and that one cannot judge deep-seated popular trends of opinion by what he finds in Washington. On one of my trips westward I stopped over to call on some friends at Rochester, New York. In the course of that visit I met a remarkable man, a professor in the Rochester Theological Seminary who seemed to me, after a long and interesting conversation, to be a true prophet of the times. His name was Walter Rauschenbusch. He said that he had been writing some prayers for the new age.

"Read me some of them," I said.

The very first he called "a prayer for all public officers." It made a strong impression upon me: it appealed to God in concrete terms regarding the problems then facing the country.

When he had finished reading, I said to him: "I hope that prayer not only gets to God, but to the American people. They need it."

It struck me all at once that I could, perhaps, help in getting it to the people. I asked Professor Rauschenbusch to let me take it with me. We put it on the back of the first page, frontispiece, of the February (1910) issue of *The American Magazine*. Here is a copy of it:

O God, thou great governor of all the world, we pray thee for all who hold public office and power, for the life, the welfare, and the virtue of the people, are in their hands to make or to mar. We remember with shame that in the past the mighty have preyed on the labors of the poor; that they have laid nations in the dust by their oppression and have thwarted the love and the prayers of thy servants. We bless thee that the new spirit of democracy has touched even the kings of the earth. We rejoice that by the free institutions of our country the tyrannous instincts of the strong may be curbed and turned to the patient service of the commonwealth. Strengthen the sense of duty in our political life. Grant that the servants of the State may feel ever more deeply that any diversion of their public powers for private gain or ambition is a tampering with a sacred trust and a betrayal of their country. Purge our cities and states and nation of the deep causes of corruption which have so often made sin profitable and uprightness hard. Raise up a new generation of public men, who will have the faith and daring of the Kingdom of God in their hearts, and who will enlist for life in a holy warfare for the freedom and rights of the people. Bring to an end the stale days of party cunning. Give our leaders a new vision of the possible future of our country and set their hearts on fire with large resolves. Breathe a new spirit into all our nation, and let us rise from the dust and mire of the past to gird ourselves for a new day's work.

We began at once to have letters from all parts of the country, from readers who liked what one of them called a "really modern prayer for a really modern cause." We followed it up for many months with prayers by Professor Rauschenbusch "for all lawyers" "for all doctors" "for all employers" and so on.

I became so much interested in what I found going on in Rochester that I went back there several times. I learned that a remarkable reform movement was under way, backed not only by the religious leaders but by organized business men, the Chamber of Commerce, the Civic Clubs, and organized labor. Their motto was "Do It for Rochester"—and they were really doing it! To the astonishment of everyone, and to the alarm of the powerfully organized politicians of New York, they turned out one of the most strongly entrenched Republican bosses of the State, George W. Aldridge, and broke up his "machine." It was all such a glorious story of success, showing what the people could do when they really set their minds to it, that I wrote an article about it, heading it "Do It for Rochester" and it was published in September, 1910. It was a vast encouragement to find that such movements as this were going on quietly, unheralded, in many towns and cities of the country. "The campaign in Rochester," I said in my introduction to the articles, "shows that the political unrest in America is no mere superficial disturbance, but a great, steady, long-continued movement of the public mind."

But the new movement seemed to be hopelessly bogged down so far as Washington was concerned. Taft's near friends could only keep saying, "Wait, wait"—always with a fainter and fainter voice. By the middle of 1910 the President had almost completely lost his hold on the liberal forces of the country. I wrote an article for the July, 1910, number of *The American Magazine* in which I tried to explain the man and his record. It was called "The Measure of Taft" and I put at the head of it this quotation from Bacon's essay, "Of Great Place":

"A place sheweth the man. And it sheweth some to the better, and some to the worse. 'If he had not been emperor, all would have pronounced him fit for empire,' saith Tacitus of Galba."

I might well have called my article "The Tragedy of a Misplaced Man."

"All through his life," I wrote, "men have liked Mr. Taft, and have pushed him forward. It is singular, indeed, to what a degree his advancement has been due to personal friends rather than to the people. Up to the time he was president he had never held but one elective office . . . At every turn there was a loyal friend of "Old Bill" Taft to suggest his name and commend his qualities . . . From the earliest years he was the select member of his family . . . No money and no effort were too great to be given by the Taft brothers when Bill was to be benefited and pushed forward . . . His friend, Governor Foraker, appointed him judge . . . He was appointed solicitor-general by his friend President Harrison; he was appointed by his good friend McKinley to the presidency of the Philippine commission and afterward as civil governor . . . His sturdy admirer, Roosevelt, appointed him Secretary of War, and then the same powerful friend . . . pushed him into the presidency . . .

"Thus he was advanced, not by the rough impact of powerful convictions impressed upon an eager people, but easily and serenely by virtue of the charm of his personality and his loyal friendships with those high in public life . . .

"And there will be few, today, who know the facts, who will assert that Mr. Taft is not doing what he believes to be right, as far as any misplaced man could possibly do it. He *intends* to do right.

"Mr. Taft found himself, as Roosevelt's successor, in the midst of a vast and chaotic, but profoundly fundamental, outburst of moral enthusiasm. It was more like a great religious revival than anything seen in this country in many years.

"Now, mere moral enthusiasm never of itself gets anywhere. It must be boiled down to its insoluble residue of hard, cold, clear intellectual propositions. New definitions must be struck out; the leader, with a sort of divine carelessness, must announce his course and play his part. Lincoln laid down the law, and uttered the clarion note of leadership in words that cut like a sword through the confused but none the less passionate popular emotion on the slavery question, when he said: 'This nation cannot exist half slave and half free,' and when he said to the Southern disunionists, 'We won't go out of the Union, and you shan't.'

"But we have heard nothing clear, nothing sure, nothing strong, from Mr. Taft,—and the country drifting, drifting toward a crisis.

"When at his famous speech at Cooper Union in February, 1908, a man in the audience put to him the most poignant question of this age, 'What is a man going to do who is out of work and starving?' Mr. Taft replied: 'God knows, I don't.'

"And this is Mr. Taft: a leader without an answer for his times. 'God knows,' or Roosevelt knows or the Supreme Court knows—I don't."

So it was that Taft alienated the most virile, clear-thinking, and courageous group of men then active in our political life: Cummins,

Pinchot, LaFollette, Dolliver, Beveridge, Bristow, Garfield, Cooper, Clapp, Lenroot, Madison, Murdock, Norris—and many other able men. He himself was more or less responsible for the growth of the revolt that was sweeping the country, that toward the end of his administration became the outstanding political force in the nation. It was the opposition to Taft that led up to the organization of the Bull Moose party and the nomination of Theodore Roosevelt in 1912. It was largely responsible for the astonishing victory of the Democratic party of that year and the election of Woodrow Wilson.

I found myself profoundly interested in all these developments. When I gave up hope in Taft and his administration I turned eagerly to the Insurgents—trying to understand what they stood for, and what they proposed to do. Above all I was searching for a new leader who could be trusted with the aspirations of an honestly progressive, and truly democratic, movement.

CHAPTER XXVIII

Bob LaFollette of Wisconsin

THE FAILURE OF TAFT to follow Theodore Roosevelt in the leadership of the liberal forces in America, discouraging as it seemed at the time, really served to increase the determination and widen the influence of the Insurgent Movement. LaFollette of Wisconsin became more and more the representative leader—the man to whom the Progressives of the country, especially those of the West, began to turn with confidence.

My own discovery of LaFollette was a great satisfaction to me. Wisconsin had been my home state and I knew that it was dominated by a powerful political machine backed by the great railroad and lumbering interests. I had heard of LaFollette from my uncle, who was a lawyer of Hudson, Wisconsin, and then a partner of United States Senator Spooner who considered LaFollette a "firebrand" and a "wild-eyed radical." Spooner and his friends at that time were doing their best to put out that firebrand!

After being well warned one day of the danger of any association with LaFollette, I left the little old-fashioned country law office at Hudson all ablaze with curiosity to know what a real political "firebrand" was like: I wanted to meet and know a "wild-eyed radical."

It was not long before I had the opportunity. "He impressed me strongly," I wrote in my notes. "A short, thick, active man with a big head, red face and hair standing in a stiff pompadour."

I learned that as a young man fresh out of Wisconsin University, he had become a starveling lawyer, and later a crusading district attorney at Madison, the state capital. When he began really to enforce the law, he found himself in conflict with the political bosses and the "interests" behind them. Up to this point he had followed the pattern of many other ambitious young Americans who wanted to get into politics. Some of them, with the wisdom of the serpent, knew that if they stirred up enough of a row, really threatened the citadel, the bosses would crowd grudgingly over and let them in, and they could, or hoped they could, live happily ever after. But LaFollette's eyes had been opened to what bossism in America meant. Through one cyclonic campaign after another he found his way into the governorship of his state, and in 1906 he had reached the United States Senate against the fierce and continuous opposition of the old leaders. While this accomplishment was remarkable enough in itself, it did not seem to me as significant as the method he had used in doing it. The more closely I looked into his Wisconsin campaigns the clearer it seemed that he had developed a new technique in practical politics.

One of the most urgent problems then before the state was that of unjust railroad rates and rebates, and the impotence of the people in securing any changes. Some ardent young reformers would have entered the fray flying banners with the usual slogans recommending that the crooks be clapped into jail, or that the railroads be "taken over by the state"; but without the ammunition of facts and figures which would prove their case. Roosevelt would have denounced the evil doings of the "bad" railroad owners and commended the work of the "good" ones. Taft would have proposed more laws to punish the men who had broken former laws.

LaFollette began first of all to find out what the facts really were. What rebates did the railroads pay and to whom; what was the cost of the service rendered; what were the true profits; who owned the railroads and what was their capitalization in comparison with their valuation? Since the taxation of railroads was well known to be fixed by the men who controlled them, how much was the state being defrauded?

He went at it as a scientist would have done. At that time no outsider could get access to the records of the railroad companies; they were almost as secret as a man's own private account book. He had to interview shippers, farmers, small manufacturers, many of whom, although suffering from the inequitable practices, were so dependent upon favors from the railroads that they dared not give their names. It was a costly process and he had no money and, at first, almost no support. He finally secured state laws enabling state officials to get at the books of the companies. He was fought at every turn by the best legal talent the railroads could employ. He labored prodigiously. I have never known any other public man who worked year after year with more dogged determination than he. At the same time that he was collecting this ammunition he had, perforce, to carry on his political campaigns, and keep his supporters behind him.

In his early campaigns he had acquired convincing oratorical powers: he could make fascinating dramas even out of railroad rates.

In 1908 we got him to come to East Lansing, Michigan, to speak in the great auditorium of the Michigan State College. Every seat was filled. It was in no sense a political speech: he was not a candidate for any office, he was making no partisan appeal. He did not base his appeal upon generalities, he had no familiar moral bombast to offer. It was a fact story he was telling, and he knew well the secret of the power of the specific incident—which also contributed largely to the success of the early "muckraking" articles. He told the stories of the little Ole Olsons of Wisconsin, showed how their very livelihood depended upon railroad transportation, described the injustices they suffered, traced his own efforts to get to the companies' books, and what he finally found there. He showed clearly what it was necessary to do to remedy the disease. He offered no easy cure-alls, but laws based upon a complete knowledge of the facts.

I recall, on the occasion of that address, how quietly he worked up to his climaxes, until he had every eye in that audience fixed upon him. When the interest was at its sharpest, we heard a curious little jangling noise. LaFollette stopped and picked up the watch he had placed on the table.

"Mrs. LaFollette," said he, "thinks I talk too long: and has ordered me to put this alarm-watch on the table and stop when it goes off. I have now talked an hour and a half . . ."

A great laugh went up from the audience and vociferous cries, "Go on, go on!" So the speaker went on, for at least another hour. Not a single person, so far as we could see, left the auditorium: and there was the kind of cheering at the end which one does not hear too often—the deep sympathy that goes with complete understanding. When Mrs. Baker and I stood up, a bronzed old farmer with a white beard who had been sitting in front of us turned slowly around and said,

"I know now how the Apostle Paul must have preached."

It was speeches like this, buttressed with facts and set forth with impressive sincerity, that won LaFollette his victories. And be it noted here, that having been elected to high place he did not forget his campaign plans and promises. He spent a good part of the remainder of his life working for better railroad control.

LaFollette's method seemed to me then, and still seems, to have been founded firmly upon scientific principles. It was the method not of an adolescent but of a mature democracy. It was based first of all upon a thorough-going exploration of the facts by honest leaders, whether statesmen, scholars, or writers, and was followed by the educational process of informing the people regarding those facts. The process was difficult, the way was long; it took courage and faith to carry it through, especially if one's own career and livelihood was dependent upon it, as was that of LaFollette.

One of LaFollette's devices for spreading the "good news" was a little magazine which circulated widely throughout Wisconsin and neighboring states. He edited it, and lost money on it, for many years. On a banner line across the top of the first page he placed the motto he loved best:

"Ye shall know the truth and the truth shall make you free."

He believed in that motto; he believed that if the people were told the truth they would, sooner or later, act wisely upon it, and it would, given time, help to make them free—which is the essence of the democratic faith.

When he first went to Washington as the senator from his state, LaFollette found himself again a lone fighter. If the odds of money and power were against him in Wisconsin, they were now doubly against him in Washington. In that "Millionaires Club," as the United States Senate was sometimes called, he was at first practically the only man who stood for popular rights. Every device was used to cajole or flatter or coerce him—all to no avail. They used against him the almost irresistible force of social ostracism. When he arose to speak, many of his colleagues would seek the lobbies and leave him talking to empty seats. Who that heard it will ever forget the occasion in April, 1906, on which he spoke on the railroad bill? The galleries were crowded, but the seats of many of his colleagues were empty. Finally Senator LaFollette burst out with these prophetic words, uttered in a voice charged with emotion:

"Mr. President, I pause in my remarks to say this. I cannot be wholly indifferent to the fact that Senators by their absence at this time indicate their want of interest in what I may have to say about this subject. The public is interested. Unless this important question is rightly settled seats now temporarily vacant may be permanently vacated by those who have the right to occupy them at this time." (Applause in the galleries.)

That prophecy became almost literally true. Many of the "old guard" vanished utterly before that puff of applause in the people's gallery. Five years later LaFollette had become the most formidable leader in the Senate.

I felt so strongly about the fundamental soundness of LaFollette's method that I urged my associates in *The American Magazine* to publish a series of biographical articles setting forth the facts as to his leadership in Wisconsin; and I spent part of the broiling-hot Washington summer of 1911 working upon them with the Senator in his office, often going home afterwards to dinner with him.

The LaFollettes' was one of those hospitable, old-fashioned homes, which reminded me often of my own early home in Wisconsin. There was the long table filled with the family, young and old, and often guests dropping in, and much good talk and laughter. Mrs. LaFollette, whom I came greatly to admire, was the heart and soul of it. She liked sometimes to go to the Rock Creek Cemetery and worship in the leafy cloister near Washington's greatest work of art, Saint-Gaudens' "Memorial." After one such visit she wrote:

"One day it came to me quite suddenly, that after all there was no mystery in this great work of art, that like all fundamental truth it was simple. It is not grief, nor resignation, nor peace, nor satisfaction. It is all of life, not a phase. It is experience—life's composite. One has lived all and felt all, has known happiness and has suffered so much that there is nothing more to fear; yet is not bowed down, but is strengthened—a soul prepared to live, ready for eternity."

Belle Case had been a fellow student of Bob's—the Senator liked to be called Bob by his friends—at Wisconsin University. After they were married, indeed, after her first child was born, she attended the law-school and was graduated in 1885. She was the Senator's closest friend and adviser; he never made any decision down through the years without consulting her. There were four children born to them; Fola, the oldest; Bob Junior, then a steady-headed boy of sixteen who was to follow his father as United States Senator from Wisconsin; Phil, the mercurial, who was to become Governor of Wisconsin; and the youngest of all, "little Mary."

Sometimes after dinner the Senator or some guest would read aloud, usually stories or poetry as far removed from politics as possible. The Senator had always been a lover of Shakespeare's plays, had lectured on *Hamlet* and *Iago* and at one time had thought of being an actor. He liked to read aloud from *King Lear, Othello, The Taming of the Shrew.* He loved Robert Burns and could give his poems a Scotch turn that was inimitable. I shall never forget several evenings devoted to a series of amusing Irish folk tales, called "Darby Gill and the Good People."

In the writing of LaFollette's autobiography, my own contribution was relatively unimportant. I helped at the start, I think, with suggestions as to the most effective arrangement of the material for magazine publication and, by asking innumerable questions, brought out some of the facts that I thought would interest readers not so familiar with Wisconsin affairs as the Senator was. But the narrative after the first few chapters was the Senator's own: he had told the stories scores of times on the platform and, once started, poured them out resistlessly. We collaborated with the greatest personal enthusiasm in the revisions that followed.

The American began publishing the articles that fall, at a time when LaFollette was a probable nominee for the presidency. Afterwards they made a good book, *LaFollette's Autobiography*, valuable to this day to any student of American political development.*

At the beginning of the campaign of 1912, LaFollette was an outstanding candidate for nomination to the presidency. He had won

*Fola LaFollette, the Senator's daughter, has in preparation a thoroughgoing biography begun by Belle Case LaFollette, which is soon to appear. It will be especially helpful in its account of the later years of the Senator's life.

the complete confidence of the great majority of the people of his own state and had become the soul of the genuine national progressive movement to which I have referred. He had attracted a group of ardent young men, of whom I was one, who had been disappointed and disillusioned by the administration of William Howard Taft.

Many of the ablest political leaders of the West, including a strong group of his associates in the United States Senate, were among his supporters. A group of young liberals who had been devoted supporters of Theodore Roosevelt during his administration—Gifford Pinchot, James R. Garfield and others—had joined the movement. It became clear in 1911 that LaFollette was the only truly progressive leader to whom the country could turn with any hope of success.

As I shall presently relate, I had come to know Woodrow Wilson in 1910 and had been strongly attracted by his remarkable preparation for high statesmanship, his gift of oratory, and the courage of his struggle for more democracy as President of Princeton University. But he had seemed to me, for lack of political experience, and the want of any organization to back him, to be unavailable as a candidate in the oncoming campaign of 1912. LaFollette was, for many of us, the most hopeful candidate then in the field.

But no one then thought of Theodore Roosevelt, who had been absent from the country killing beasts in Africa, as re-entering the political picture. No one remembered his genius for stealing the show! Upon his return he had seemed to favor LaFollette as the national leader of the Progressives, even indicating that he would support him, but after months of backing and filling, he finally seized control of the Progressive movement, organized the new Bull Moose party, and entered the arena as its candidate.

LaFollette continued his struggle to the last; the climax came at the never-to-be-forgotten, intensely dramatic, publishers' dinner at Philadelphia on February 2, 1912. LaFollette came late to the dinner. He was worn-out with labor and anxiety, one of his daughters being dangerously ill at a hospital in Washington. He broke down there in the midst of what was to have been the greatest speech of his career—the speech with which he hoped to win the East.*

* See my account of these fateful incidents in Volume III *Woodrow Wilson: Life and Letters*, p. 270.

To those of us who were there and who were LaFollette's friends it was a tragedy beyond tears. It has been much written about: I need not go into it here. What I like to remember best was the glimpse I had two days later into the soul of that indomitable man. He had suffered as few men have ever been called upon to suffer: he showed it in his face: but he did not offer either explanations or excuses. He sat in his chair white-faced and perfectly still while Mrs. LaFollette and one or two other friends tried to keep up a cheerful conversation. When he did begin to talk, it was of a struggle then going on in the Senate. He was going back to fight the old battle in behalf of the people, just as in the past.

He continued to have a strong progressive following; and even though I became an ardent follower of Wilson in 1912, thinking him by all odds the best of the three candidates in the field, I still believed in LaFollette's genuine democracy. I find a letter I wrote to him on August 2, 1912—during the campaign:

> I have been following the events in the Senate with the keenest interest, I can assure you. I was afraid the Progressive group was hopelessly split—but all that was needed was the strong leadership which you are giving them. I believe you are stronger today in the country than you ever were. The old *Springfield Republican* chortles daily over your fight on T. R. We are all for Wilson up here.

I had long believed in a Third Party movement which would draw the liberals of the country together. I even thought that the new Bull Moose party had a sound platform and the support of many sincere men. I wrote to LaFollette on September 9, 1912:

> If Roosevelt were not leading the new party, I should be with it heart and soul; as it is, I shall vote for Wilson, though I have no confidence at all in the old Democratic party, and believe that Wilson's election will only mean a split in his party with very little accomplishment for the next four years. As for Roosevelt, I think there is not the slightest chance of his election, and the big fight will come later, to shake his grip on the party.

In crowding LaFollette ruthlessly out of the race, Roosevelt not only failed to win the election himself—and incidentally defeated another old friend, Mr. Taft, the Republican nominee—but he elected Woodrow Wilson, whom he disliked even more bitterly than either LaFollette or Taft.

No man of my time in public life equaled LaFollette as a fighter, none was more fundamentally a democrat. There was much of the old Puritan spirit in the man—fierce, incorruptible, independent. He always seemed at his best as the governor of his state or its representative in Washington where, in his thorough-going way, he could know all the "folks" and count upon them for support. But western insurgency, of which he was the foremost representative—however true its diagnosis, however real its charges—was less than national in its appeal, and LaFollette's powers of leadership seemed to fail him when the unit was the nation, still more when the issues became international.

While I never lost the strong affection and admiration I felt for Bob LaFollette I could not follow him, a few years later, in his attitude during the first World War. I had at first been a pacifist myself, eager to find a way by which the country could avoid being drawn into the war but, in common with a vast number of other Americans, events gradually convinced me. The climax in my case came with the publication of the Zimmermann notes revealing the treacherous negotiations of Germany with Mexico and Japan to seize parts of our own Southwestern states. When the decisions, one after another, had to be made, I found that I must support Wilson, not LaFollette. I could not understand how LaFollette and the little group of Insurgents whom Wilson called "wilful men" could, with all the facts in hand, take the position they did. They apparently had no alternative constructive program; not even their own long-time followers were behind them with such unanimity as to warrant the desperate fight they were making.

But there were not a few Americans who felt as I did that the storm of execration and vilification that broke upon LaFollette at that time was a kind of popular madness. I knew he must be going through the fires of hell in those days. It is painful enough seeing a true friend suffering for his convictions when you think him right, harder still seeing him suffer when you think him wrong. In the first case your support may ease his burden, in the second your opposition or your disapproval adds to it. I find in my notes of March 16, 1916, these words:

"Ever since those last days of Congress I have been thinking of LaFollette and trying to write him."

I drafted a letter, beginning it thus:

MY DEAR SENATOR: I have been on the point of writing you these many days, but have held back fearing, as a real friend ought never to fear, lest my letter be misunderstood. While I do not fully comprehend the doings of those last days of the old Congress: and while I cannot see any way out now, for the country, save the firm support of the President, yet I have for so long felt a deep affection for you (and I think there are few outside your family who have had better occasion to know you for what you are than I)—and I have so long trusted the fundamental honesty and rightness and democracy of your views (as I still do) that I wanted to, and must, drop you this word of confidence and high regard.

But try as I would, I could not say anything that I felt might not add to his suffering, and I did not finally post the letter. I wish now I had.

Bob LaFollette died on June 18, 1925, Belle LaFollette six years later in 1931. In a letter I wrote to "Young Bob," then his father's successor in the Senate, I tried to express my admiration for Belle LaFollette in these words:

I have just seen the news of your mother's death. It came as a real shock; she gave such a sense of vitality, of overflowing life, that I could not even think of her as growing old.

I had a deep admiration for your mother. She was one of the few really great women I have ever known: great in her own right, great without any need of formal office or honor, great in intellect as well as in human sympathy. I remember, so often in the old days in Washington, when I used to see so much of all of you, how wise she seemed in her counsel. If your father knew *how* to fight, she knew *when*. I have always known why you and Philip have gone forward so brilliantly in politics, for I remember so well many little incidents that seemed, at the time, to be pointing the way.

I could not help writing you, not merely in sympathy—that you will understand—but with congratulation that you had such a mother, and could, for so many years, have enjoyed her friendship and profited by her counsel.

CHAPTER XXIX

I Meet Woodrow Wilson

In a sound and enduring democracy, it is not the leaders who pick their followers, but the followers who pick their leaders. It is therefore necessary that followers should have strong convictions and be willing to fight for them.

With the downfall of the LaFollette movement in 1912, the so-called Progressives and Insurgents found it necessary to look for another leader. Some of them turned back to Theodore Roosevelt, who had staged his "return from Elba" in April, 1910, and had been eagerly watching for an opportunity to take over the command of the "Grand Army." Others were beginning to look hopefully to a new leader who was making an extraordinary fight in New Jersey—Woodrow Wilson.

I saw and heard Woodrow Wilson for the first time at a dinner given on January 21, 1910, by a group of political progressives. The great ballroom of the Hotel Astor in New York City was crowded. At that time I knew nothing about him except that he was President of Princeton University, but I had in my pocket an extract torn from a newspaper of a speech he had delivered on the hundredth anniversary of the birth of Robert E. Lee. This was it:

> I wish there were some great orator who could go about and make men drunk with this spirit of self-sacrifice. I wish there were some man whose tongue might every day carry abroad the golden accents of that creative age in which we were born a nation; accents which would ring like tones of reassurance around the whole circle of the globe, so that America might again have the distinction of showing men the way, the certain way, of achievement and of confident hope.

I thought I should like to know a man who could express such aspirations as these, and indeed, the meeting proved to be, for me, not only an unforgettable, but a truly determinative experience. No other speaker I had ever heard made an impression quite so vivid and clear-cut as he. I felt that here was the kind of thinking statesman the country needed and could trust.

During the next day or two I began to hear of a speech Wilson had made only a week before at a bankers' dinner at the Waldorf-Astoria. It was supposed to be a try-out by the great financial interests of New York of George Harvey's candidate for the presidency. Would Woodrow Wilson please them: or would they please him? The veritable kings of the American earth were there. J. Pierpont Morgan was in the place of distinction at the head table. The Secretary of the Treasury, Franklin MacVeagh, was the guest of honor; and scores of men were present whose word was law in the financial world—George F. Baker, A. Barton Hepburn, George M. Reynolds of Chicago, and others. Frank A. Vanderlip was toastmaster. Wilson, in his brief address, which was badly reported, had told these powerful men exactly what he believed.

"Banking is founded on a moral basis and not on a financial basis. The trouble today is that you bankers are too narrow-minded. You don't know the country or what is going on in it and the country doesn't trust you. You are not interested in the development of the country, but in what has been developed. You take no interest in the small borrower and the small enterprise which affect the future of the country, but you give every attention to the big borrower and the rich enterprise which has already arrived."

Morgan, who sat next to Wilson, was deeply offended by the speech. He was seen by a reporter to "look glum and puff his cigar energetically." When Wilson sat down, Morgan let him know that he considered the remarks personal. Wilson responded instantly that he had no idea of making any personal application, he was speaking of principles.

All this interested me intensely. Here, it seemed, was the magical touch of great leadership: the touch of courage. I could not be content until I had met the man himself. Was he after all really available as a national leader? I was just then preparing a series of magazine articles which I hoped might serve to clarify a highly confused political situation. I intended also to characterize the men who were likely to come to the front during the campaign of 1912.

So I went down, upon Mr. Wilson's invitation, to call at Princeton. I met the first Mrs. Wilson and the three daughters who were in the library at Prospect House when I arrived, and who withdrew after a few minutes of animated conversation. The hours that followed remain memorable to me. In Mr. Wilson's frank and free discussion of the questions of the hour I was conscious again of the extraordinary sense of sincerity and conviction I had felt at the Astor dinner. Here were clear, practical, well-reasoned suggestions for remedies, based upon a breadth of understanding of American institutions that I had found nowhere else. I did not know at that time that most of his life had been devoted to studying and writing about the American tradition and the American democratic system.

Another thing impressed me. He seemed to have little or no interest in politics, as such. Every other leader I had met recently had gone into problems of the political balance of power—what the industrial North demanded, what the restless West must have, where the South stood. How to carry New York and Indiana!

He felt that what was needed, above everything, was clear thinking. He made one suggestion that seemed quite the most extraordinary I had ever heard from a political leader. He proposed that Americans who had the great public questions at heart should correspond quietly with one another as did the leaders in the days of the American Revolution. What he wanted was thorough inquiry and careful thought before going to the people with proposals for changes. His fundamental method resembled that of LaFollette.

I left Princeton convinced that I had met the finest mind in the field of statesmanship to be found in American public life. And yet, in an article I wrote afterward—I confess sadly—while I referred with regretful enthusiasm to Woodrow Wilson's unequaled qualifications, I concluded that he was politically impossible. Was he not wholly without practical experience? He had not known until recently even the leaders of his own party in New Jersey, he could not name the head of the Democratic organization in his own town. He had never been in the state capitol building. Above all, he was practically unknown to the mass of voters throughout the nation. How was it possible in two years' time to train a man then fifty-four years old to win a national election to the presidency against well-organized and seasoned opponents who knew every trick of the game? I think there were reasons for my conclusion that he was politically unavailable; I did not believe in miracles.

But the miracle happened: it really happened! It was one of the most astonishing in our political history. It has always seemed to me an excellent demonstration of what an awkward, fumbling democracy can sometimes do, in spite of everything, in getting the best-qualified man into the most important place at the time when he is most needed.

If he had been in any sense, the "ordinary political leader" there would never have been any miracle. But he was not, and this must be recognized first of all, in trying to understand his career. He had indeed high gifts of leadership, but he never fitted easily into the traditional political world of personalities, aimless party conferences, and the sordid struggle for patronage. A thinking leader is never easily understood; he is not popular with politicians, or with those men whose idea of the best government is the one that most easily yields them special favors.

I watched eagerly Wilson's meteoric career in New Jersey, his election as governor, his defeat of the powerful Smith-Nugent machine, and his swift success in getting from an astonished and doubtful legislature a group of reforms that, a year or so earlier, would have seemed fantastic. But much as I desired it, I could not believe that his nomination for the presidency at Baltimore was even a remote possibility. His campaign had been carried on by an organization hardly worth the name, amateurs with scanty financial support. If certain well-tested traditions of Democratic conventions had not been broken, and all the little but potentially important accidents had not favored his chances, he could not have succeeded.

I was overjoyed by the result—even though the hopeful and really earnest group of Progressives and Insurgents who had been supporting LaFollette was immediately shattered. Most of them—Gifford Pinchot, James R. Garfield, William Allen White and others who had formerly been Republicans—sang "Onward, Christian Soldiers" at the Bull Moose convention in Chicago and campaigned for Theodore Roosevelt. Some of us who considered ourselves Independents—Louis D. Brandeis, Charles R. Crane, Norman Hapgood and others—turned to Woodrow Wilson.

It was the most interesting and exciting campaign I have ever known. There was less political buncombe, less appeal to ancient party slogans, and far more vital discussion of the issues of the time. Wilson was largely responsible for this: he was as free a candidate as any ever known in an American presidential election. He had no long background of political attachments and obligations, he had made no promises to anyone: he was interested above all in ideas, and in making clear actual conditions as he saw them. He said that he would gladly head such a "committee of correspondence" as he had early proposed in his conversation with me.

I helped in my narrow field in every way I could. I wrote articles, I helped organize Wilson Clubs, I even dared to make speeches! And nothing else that ever happened in American politics pleased me as much as the election returns of 1912.

"Now," I wrote an old friend, "we shall really get something done."

"No president in the memory of living men," I exulted, "will enter the White House under more favorable conditions, or with greater opportunities for achievement than Wilson. He has a clear field: he can be as great as he can be.

"But the storm is sure to break later; as soon as he begins to act, as soon as he begins to take sides on great questions—at that moment the struggle begins. If he is truly progressive, as he says he is, then he will have arrayed against him the most powerful material forces in our life—the great financiers, the great business interests with their engines of publicity and their power of influencing the prosperity of the Nation."

I watched his progress closely. My "ifs"—"if Wilson is truly progressive," "if Wilson can stand the strain"—began gradually to disappear from my notes. Six months after he came into office, I wrote:

"President Wilson's note on the Mexican situation this morning is a real inspiration. Here is a man who would have the Nation rely upon moral principles and the power of justice rather than upon force. No bluster, no blow—but kindness. Wilson is making a great success so far."

Although I was sometimes anxious, seeing the power of organized lobbies in Washington, the progress that the new President was making often seemed to me magical. On January 14, 1914, I wrote:

"Washington is truly seeing a people's government. Progress is really being made. The great thing in the new currency law (a weak measure in many ways) is that it establishes finally the principle of governmental control of our national currency and banking system. The new trust bill provides for an industrial commission which will establish the principle of government regulation of commerce and industry: a great step. This—added to the drastic revision of the tariff, the parcel-post system, the proposed government development of Alaska—certainly makes a record . . ."

I had been going to Washington and writing about Washington for a number of years, and the "New Spirit in Washington," which was the title of one of my articles, seemed all but astonishing. I found a wholly different type of men going to the White House from those of Roosevelt's and Taft's time. Thoughtful men, thorough-going, studious men. Both Brandeis and LaFollette were giving Wilson the best they had of information and of advice.

"I come back from Washington feeling intensely that what the country needs now most of all are *thinkers*. The mass of people are right in their general instincts and desires: but when it comes to the application of those desires to the complicated affairs of the day it requires a high quality of thoughtfulness and a real passion for public service. We have worshipped action so long in America that we scarcely feel the need of thinkers, but it is the thinker only who can guide us now."

So I wrote an article under the title "A Thinker in the White House" for the May number (1914) of *The American*.

I had met Mr. Wilson a number of times during the campaign and his first year in the White House, but I had never had a real talk with him, such as I often had with Roosevelt and even with Taft, until September, 1914, about a month after the outbreak of the Great War. There was at that time much complaint of the difficulty of getting to Wilson: he was "cloistered," he "would not confer." Some of Wilson's loyal friends—and I think the President himself—were conscious of this criticism and wished to meet it by frankly explaining to the public at large the policies and purposes of the administration.

"On September 7," I wrote in my notes, "I went to see President Wilson and talked with him until one o'clock. He looked very well, clear-eyed, confident, cheerful. A neat gray suit looking as though it were just from the tailor: a black band on his left arm: * a dark red tie with a gold ornament. His desk very neat, with a bouquet of roses near him. He was affable and frank. I used to think that T. R. was often dangerously open in his conversation—but W. W. when he really gives his confidence is fully as free. Said that his greatest difficulty at the moment was to keep the peace advocates from rocking the boat. Felt that he had nearly reached the end of his economic program as outlined in the campaign and in the Democratic platform. Some social reforms still to achieve but he thought most of them should be the work of the states. Next two things to be done were:

"1. Improve our machinery of commerce. Shipping to be built up.

"2. Develop further conservation policy. 'Conservation for *use*.'

"Said he believed in the appropriation of $30,000,000 to buy merchant ships for the government. Not for a permanent government merchant marine, but to bridge the difficult problems produced by the war. The government could stand a temporary loss of money on the project—the private shipowners could not. The government would go out of the business when private shipping had mastered it."

His emphasis in his talk was nearly all upon domestic issues: neither he nor the country had as yet awakened to the dread possibilities of the war in Europe.

I was pleased not only with the President's clear exposition of his policies, but more than ever before with the man himself—his forthrightness, the sense of inner discipline he gave, the kind of self-confidence in the leader that convinces and inspires his followers. The article I wrote following this visit, entitled "Wilson—after Twenty Months," was perhaps too enthusiastic to be objective. At any rate, I find this expression in my notebook of the doubt I felt regarding all politicians:

"I have not perhaps been discriminating enough in my criticism of Wilson (as in the coming December article)—I have perhaps accepted him too completely. It is dangerous to accept any leader, especially a political leader, without reserve. He cannot be wholly right."

* Mrs. Wilson had died on August 6, 1914.

Many of Wilson's closest friends—all along during the months of 1915 and 1916 when he was trying to understand the immeasurably difficult international problems incident to the great war, and to formulate policies for meeting them—did not understand the consequences of having a thinker in the White House, one with whom thorough preparation was absolutely imperative as the basis of action. What a hullabaloo the critics made!

"I hear on all sides the same story," I commented in my notes on July 17, 1915, "of the inability to reach the President. Mr. Wilson is not seeing even his closest friends or the members of his cabinet, but, as Norman Hapgood says, 'He remains at Cornish communing with God.' Hapgood says that the only man who has talked with him recently is Colonel House—and he not since the last German note. Miss Jane Addams was here the other day, but could not reach him. She has just returned from Europe where she visited all the belligerent countries; she not only has facts, but she has vision. The danger is that Mr. Wilson will make his decisions upon too little knowledge. It is a very ticklish situation: the country wants Mr. Wilson to be firm and yet almost no one wants war. How both these desires can be satisfied it is difficult to see. But the people so far have great confidence in Mr. Wilson: and are waiting for real leadership. He can do almost anything within reason and be supported. He is the head of the nation to which the world is now turning for leadership—and the people are with him. What a time to make dreams come true! Will he rise to it? Is he big enough? The proof of his monkish method is the success of it."

The President's methods infuriated Theodore Roosevelt: "mollycoddle," "sissie": he could not in the least understand Woodrow Wilson. I tried to analyze and compare the two men.

"Wilson works with ideas, T. R. directly with men. Wilson starts the processes of reason and of thought: he is the kind of democrat who wishes men to govern themselves by their own inner processes. It is distasteful to him, as to any high-minded man, to drive his fellow-men by appeals to their fear or their cupidity or other emotions, to do what they ought to do upon reason and right. T. R. has no such 'mollycoddle' compunctions; having seen what he wants he goes straight for it with any implement that may be at hand. The temptation of Wilson is to think and reason too much, that of T. R. to act too much. In my judgment the future lies with the Wilsons."

I watched Wilson eagerly and sometimes doubtfully, all through the year 1916. He was under steady and ferocious attacks to which he made no response. Unfounded scandal stories began to be whispered about by anonymous cowards—a certain Mrs. Hulbert.*

"When there is no longer any way of attacking a man," I wrote, "they begin to spread personal scandals which cannot be publicly met or denied."

Also he was "obstinate," he "would not take advice," he was a "dictator." He "wasn't big enough for the job."

"In this vast conflagration," I wrote, "what we want are immaculate giants—and there aren't any."

But in spite of all the furor of attack and criticism, I noted that most of the really thoughtful men I knew were withholding comment, were patient as the President himself was patient, with such enormous and complicated problems. It seemed to me also that the masses of the people were content, for the time being at least, to go on following the President. I was supported in this view by a talk I had (April 5, 1916) with Mr. Grasty and Mr. Wiley of the New York *Times*, who told me that the *Times* intended to support Wilson for re-election that fall.

In those days I was thinking a great deal about the function of followers in a democracy—since I was one myself. A follower must watch himself lest he be carried away by the charm, the magnetism, the glittering self-confidence of his leader—as I had been, for a time, by Theodore Roosevelt. I once heard as good a follower as William Allen White say of his allegiance to the Bull Moose party in 1912: "Roosevelt bit me and I went mad." A follower must consult his own inner mentor: he must keep himself free to criticize. He fails to serve his leader faithfully if he remains blind to his mistakes.

While I had formed a high regard for Woodrow Wilson, and had recognized that his task in such a time must be largely that of a thinker, I knew that a real leader must also act. He must lead his

* Better known as Mrs. Peck. She was first the wife of Allen Hulbert. After his death she married Thomas B. Peck. After her divorce from Mr. Peck in 1912, she took back the name of her first husband and was thereafter known as Mrs. Mary A. Hulbert.

followers. In the spring of 1916, I found myself beginning to share the wide-spread criticism of the President. Why didn't he *do* something? So I went down to Washington to attend the Jefferson Day banquet at the New Willard Hotel on April 13, where the President was scheduled to speak.

As I entered the hotel I could hear the newsboys crying extras—our soldiers were being mobbed at Parral in Mexico. Even more serious was the German situation. The President was being sharply criticized within his own cabinet. I had talked with Secretary Lane that afternoon, and had found that he did not at all agree with the President: he wanted war with Mexico straightaway, and he wanted it even with Germany.

As usual, the President began to speak quietly, and wholly without gesticulation. There was the definite heightening of his color I had noticed before upon such occasions. "The President," I wrote in my notes, "has a singularly *living* face, alert, full of keen power."

After the first sentence or two he seemed to have his audience absolutely in hand. He had not made a real public speech in some time. Great events had been taking place: there was a sense of intense expectancy, even of anxiety, in the air. He had the usual perfect command of himself, the usual rare felicity of expression, the usual lift of aspiration at the close.

A moment of dead silence followed his final words: and the cheering, while hearty, was not as hearty as I had expected or hoped. I did not myself cheer at all, as I recalled afterwards. There was something about the speech I could not quite understand. It was either very great, or not great enough.

My nearest neighbor at the table, an old acquaintance, turned to me and said:

"I like his spirit, but what is he going to *do*?"

I recognized this instantly as a part of my own reaction.

"What is needed," I wrote in my notebook immediately after I left the dinner, "is a concrete and constructive leadership: if Wilson does not furnish it for higher ends, Roosevelt is on hand to furnish it for lower ends. Wilson can get the country if only he will *lead*."

Four days later he acted vigorously, powerfully; he read his ultimatum to Germany at the Capitol—the first step in the process that led us finally into that dreadful war.

I had afterward a strange personal experience with that Jefferson Day speech. It was weighty and it was eloquent, and I might well have dilated upon the oratorical lift of that moment and of how the audience was thrilled and inspired. But it was exactly as I have said: quiet, even solemn, not too greatly applauded, with the people getting up weary near midnight from the littered tables, and moving through the heavy air reeking with tobacco smoke, eager to be out, wondering what they themselves thought of the speech, demanding a sign to stir their sluggish faith. The interest had also been somewhat diverted by the entrance, just before the speaking began, of the new Mrs. Wilson and the ladies of the cabinet. It was the first time many of those present had seen the dark, handsome woman who had so recently become the President's wife.

But I found that I could not get the President's words out of my mind; the speech was being discussed everywhere I went. It occurred to me suddenly that in certain of its passages he was doubting *us*, who were his followers: he was asking us if we had the courage to meet the perplexities and dangers he saw so clearly. They were grave words he had spoken to us:

"Are you ready for the test. . . .

"Have you the courage to go in? Have you the courage to come out according as the balance is distributed or readjusted for the interest of humanity?"

The address and indeed the entire incident became suddenly dramatic in my mind. It had been a very great occasion—with the gloomy background of the World War, heightened by our own impending crisis in Mexico, and there had stood up to speak the most powerful man, momentarily, in the world. He knew well his responsibility: he had spoken not to inflame emotion but to make men think. He knew that what he said might bring a great and peace-loving nation into the war, the thought of which he hated, with historical consequences beyond fathoming. He wanted these facts, as he saw them, solemnly considered.

"Are you ready for the test?"

I wondered afterwards if most really great moments are not like this, and come dramatic, come thrilling, come beautiful, only in the after-look, through the atmosphere of distance and the perspective of time.

CHAPTER XXX

The President "Opens His Mind Completely"

After President Wilson's address at the Jefferson Day banquet—one of his greatest in setting forth the problems that he was facing and the conclusions he himself was reluctantly reaching—he was evidently anxious to secure as much publicity as possible. At any rate, a few days later I had an invitation to call at the White House. The conversation I had with Mr. Wilson on that occasion seems to me so important and so highly interpretive of the man and of his views that I am including here the account of it from my diary.

"Friday, May 12, 1916.

"I had a wonderful talk with Mr. Wilson, two hours long, from eight to ten in the evening in his library upstairs in the White House. I want to set it down fully before the impression begins to be distorted by reflection or perspective, or influenced by discussion with other people; and this even though much of it cannot possibly now be used in public.

"I was shown into the study a few minutes before the President arrived and had a moment to look about. Two very large paintings hung on the wall: one a fine copy of Watts' Love and Life, with a poem of the same title on the bookcase at one side; the other a representation of the signing of the treaty with Spain in the McKinley administration. McKinley is standing at the end of the table: a fine figure, and Hay and the Spanish ambassador are represented as sitting and signing the treaty. Genthe's striking portrait photograph of the new Mrs. Wilson has a prominent place on a nearby bookcase. A book by Earl Grey, *Fly-Fishing*, lay on the corner of the table—although I feel sure Wilson never cast a fly in his life. His desk is a great litter of books and papers; a filing cabinet behind it; his own typewriter desk in the corner. It is the quiet retreat where he does all his serious work.

"The President came in stepping quickly and lightly. 'How are you, Baker?' The rise and fall of his intellectual interest and enthusiasm express themselves wonderfully in his eyes. Two or three times when I told him some fact that interested him a look as of keen appetite came into his face. He pounces upon things half said and consumes them before they are well out of one's mind. And his pounce is sure, accurate, complete. He instantly adds what you give him, whether fact or opinion, to his own view of the situation: so that to an extraordinary degree you go along with him and arrive at that meeting of the minds which is so rare a thing in discussion. One may pass a whole evening with some men and find them still lumbering along on their track and you on yours, and though much talk has passed, you have never really met.

"One of the first things he said was this: 'I am delighted with your namesake in the Cabinet [Newton D. Baker, the new War Secretary]. It is a comfort to have him with me.' He said that Baker had a trained administrative mind and that his experience as Mayor of Cleveland made him especially useful.

" 'He is a very different type from Mr. Garrison,' I said.

" 'Entirely different. Garrison is an intensely argumentative man. He wore me out with argument. When he met a fact, instead of accepting it as facts must be accepted, as inevitable, he wanted to argue about it indefinitely. Baker accepts it, makes room for it, and goes ahead.'

"This led to a consideration of Mr. Bryan. He said that, different as they were in character and temperament, Bryan and Garrison were somewhat alike in their mental processes. Bryan was also an argumentative man to whom facts, when they conflicted with his logical processes, were not acceptable. He told me how he had labored to show Bryan what were the *conditions* they had to meet: and that Bryan, after listening, would immediately slip back into the smooth channel of his theories and begin to argue along the old lines. Bryan had not the scientific mind. But the President gave him great credit for the one-year delay treaties. This was his own idea, Wilson said, and some such delay-method must be one of the cornerstones of future international relationships, if peace was to come to the world.

"I asked him if he was less a party man now than when he came into the White House, recalling that he had told me in a former talk that he believed strongly in party government. His recent experiences with the dull tools in Congress might, I thought, have changed him. But he is still a strong party man. Told me the story of a barber who once shaved him in New York, during the Seth Low-Van Wyck mayoralty contest. The barber said he was going to vote for Van Wyck.

" 'Isn't he less able than Mr. Low?' Mr. Wilson asked.

" 'That may all be,' said the barber, 'but if we elect Low and he doesn't make good there will be no one left to punish.'

" 'Low had no party behind him,' observed Wilson, 'only a dissolving committee, while Van Wyck had a powerful organization which could be held responsible.'

"He said he regretted personally the fact that he as the president was said to be stronger than his party. It placed heavier responsibilities and obligations upon him. The best work was done when party and president were of equal regard. He reiterated his belief in 'responsible government' and a closer working together of congress and president. The president had an undue advantage now: what he said had universal publicity, while what congressmen said in reply did not reach the people in any such degree. He thought some modification of the English system would bring about better team work in public affairs. This was, indeed, the thesis of his first, perhaps his best, book, *Congressional Government.*

"He made many references to this nation as being intensely conservative—conservative-minded—and thought it due to our more or less rigid written constitution, our diverse population elements, and our instinctive fear of interfering with the cement of our national institutions. But the only way for a party to live, he said, was to be going somewhere, moving—in short, being progressive. One could only think ahead. He said that on that very day he had labored with a group of senators regarding the confirmation of Brandeis and Rublee, both Progressives.*

" 'But most of them never think ahead,' I remarked.

" 'Most of them never think at all,' he said.

* His appointments of Brandeis to the Supreme Court and Rublee to the Federal Trade Commission were being bitterly opposed for confirmation in the Senate.

"We then fell to talking about his program. He quoted Oliver's book on Hamilton, that passage which comments upon the power of the leader or party with a program as contrasted with the leader or party having none.

"His own success during the first sixteen months of his administration has been due, he thinks, to having a definite program, approved by the people and set forth in the party platform.

"Most interesting of all to me was his explanation of his attitude toward the war. He referred to the chapter in his book on the Constitution in which he showed that in times of peace when domestic problems are uppermost, congress comes to the front, but when foreign affairs intrude the people look to the president. His foreign affairs policy must then be his own.*

"His chief reason for making the preparedness campaign in the West was to test public opinion. He does not, he told me, read newspapers, though he glances over headlines and reads certain editorials like those in the *Springfield Republican*. Says Tumulty, his personal secretary, reads everything and reports what he finds. Has certain close friends who are ears for him. Spoke warmly of Colonel House and of his disinterested service. House goes about meeting and seeing people and reports to him. He had sent House twice to Europe even though Bryan didn't like it. Bryan himself wanted to go—actually!

"We talked much of the qualifications of leadership. Wilson's mind wholly different from T. R.'s. I remember some such conversations with T. R. in which it could be seen that when T. R. defined a leader he described himself: but Wilson's mind divides and classifies leaders and places himself where he thinks he belongs. The first need of a leader was *enthusiasm*. He must believe something strongly. Therefore he must have a program and be going somewhere. He must understand his people and stir them to response, either emotional or intellectual. He said that the leader must be able to judge swiftly as to whether men were telling him the truth or not. It was possible to winnow the truth regarding a matter by talking with a sufficient number of liars, as in the Mexican matter. Said that the lying about Mexico was prodigious. What all the liars agreed upon was probably true, what they all differed upon was probably lies.

* *Constitutional Government in the United States,* Chapter III.

"He said his Mexican policy was based upon two of the most deeply seated convictions of his life: first, his shame as an American over the first Mexican war and his resolution that while he was president there should be no such predatory war. Second, upon his belief in the Virginia bill of rights: that a people had the right 'to do what they damned pleased with their own affairs' (he used the word 'damned'). He wanted to give the Mexicans a chance to form a strong government of their own. Moreover, he did not want one hand tied behind him at the very moment the nation might need all its forces to meet the German situation.

"He is thinking more than almost anything else, he said, just now, about what this nation may be called upon to do toward helping to bring about peace. Not a word of this was, of course, now to be breathed abroad. When was the time to offer our good offices? Should he outline tentatively some of his plans or ideas at the dinner of the League to Enforce Peace which is to meet the latter part of the month? He asked my advice and I told him I thought the time had not arrived to offer good offices or call a peace conference, but that I thought he could help prepare opinion by guarded statements in his coming speech.*

"I asked him also regarding the proposal to call a conference of neutral nations, which I have long thought to be a good one, but he said he thought it would at this stage hamper rather than help us to be associated with a group of little nations. In any event we should have to bear the brunt of the conflict, and that responsibility was better not divided. He talked at length and with great enthusiasm of the new Pan-American treaties which are to make us partners with South and Central America, rather than guardians. He thought it a great step in advance. This is not public yet, and will make a great stir when announced. He thinks some such idea as this must be applied to the world situation.

"He spoke of the proposed tariff commission: did not believe in it when he came to the White House, but the facts were now plain. Must be prepared for stormy conditions and quick action at the close of war. Need an expert commission. Tariff should never be taken wholly from politics, because tariff is a form of taxation.

* This meeting was held at Washington on May 27, 1916.

"I asked him squarely which he would rather meet in the coming election (1916), Roosevelt or Hughes.

" 'It matters very little,' he said. 'We have definite things to do, constructive things, and we shall go ahead and do them. Roosevelt deals in personalities and does not argue upon facts and conditions. One does not need to meet him at all. Hughes is of a different type. If he is nominated he will have to be met.'

"He commended many Congressmen highly and said Congress was underrated. Spoke of the ability of Mr. Glass of Virginia—'a man we shall hear from.'

"Said he was convinced that the people of the country—the mass —wanted peace, not war, but also that if war came after every effort had been made to avoid it, they would go into it sadly but vigorously.

"Just as we were parting he said that his talk with me was not an interview but a conversation, the purpose of which was to enable me to found soundly and truly whatever I might write about him and his policies.

" 'I've tried to open my mind completely to you and to show you just what I am thinking upon these questions,' he said. I think he did."

CHAPTER XXXI

Five Happy Years

ANY MAN WHO is rash enough to think of himself as happy should first define what he means by happiness—and then not be too sure.

Once, a long time ago, I collected a number of definitions of happiness and think the best of them was from the wise man of *Religio Medici.*

"For every man truly lives so long as he acts his nature, or some way makes good the faculties of himself."

Few men are ever really happy who do not know how to act their natures, or truly make good the faculties of themselves, and that never for long at a time.

Looking back along my years I can think of no period I enjoyed more deeply, none when I felt that I was more truly living, than the years from about 1910 to about 1915; and none that seemed unhappier than the years from 1915 to the end of 1917.

In 1910 we moved from our home in Michigan to Amherst, Massachusetts. I had been growing more interested every year in the country way of life. It seemed to me—to all of us—that we could live more naturally and freely in or near a small village than in the city. I had found that such a life was far better adapted to my particular kind of work; but I wanted more land to work with, and our growing family needed a larger house. Dr. Beal, now a widower, had retired from his professor's life and we wanted him to come and live with us. My dream was of a few acres with hills not far off, a field or pasture, an orchard, a possible cow, a pig or two, chickens and turkeys. I did not think of bee-keeping, which gave me finally so much satisfaction, until several years later. I wanted a place where I could work with my own hands and yet keep on with my profession.

I knew well enough from my experience in Michigan that any such experiment in true living must represent all sorts of compromises—what life is not a compromise?—but it was what I had dreamed about and what I longed for. Our land had to be near a town where there were good schools for our children. Our home had not only to meet the requirements of a large family, it must also be the home and workshop for a busy writer as well as a "part time" farmer.

I had already fallen in love with New England. I had made numerous visits there. My own people had come from Vermont and Massachusetts and Connecticut; my boyhood had been full of the stories of the Green Mountain Boys and of the beauties of Lake George and Lake Champlain, of maple-sugaring in spring, and the trees hanging full in the autumn with apples and walnuts and chestnuts, of which we in the cold northwest knew nothing.

One perfect October week-end, with sunshine and clear cool air, the best New England knows, I visited an old and dear college friend of mine, Kenyon L. Butterfield, who then lived in Amherst, Massachusetts, and was President of the Massachusetts State College. On Saturday afternoon we climbed to the top of Mount Lincoln. The leaves were in their full autumn coloring, the chestnut burrs were opening and the nuts were falling. Men in the little fields were beginning to husk their corn. We saw a wild deer in a steep trail near Orient Brook. We flushed a covey of partridges. I thought I had never seen finer wooded hills, or clearer streams, or more comfortable old tree-shaded farmhouses with grassy lanes leading up to them from the country roads.

I fell hopelessly in love with the town and everything in it: and the next spring we moved there, all of us, with all of our belongings. We bought the back end of the old Smith farm, a field of about ten acres that had been in cultivation for a hundred years. At that time no road led into it or past it. Save for one magnificent elm near the top of the hill and a fine maple in the lower pasture, it was bare of any planting.

Here Dr. Beal realized *his* dream, that of building a home for his daughter and her family, big enough for all of us to live in. In one corner of it I was to have my first comfortable study with enough shelves for my books and a toby closet and drawers for my papers. And Dr. Beal was to spend a benign old age—he lived to be ninety-one—in his study at the other corner among his precious botanical specimens, with the portrait of his greatest hero, Louis Agassiz, hanging above his fireplace.

We have lived in this home ever since. Every tree, every shrub, every berry bush around the house and in the garden we planted with our own hands. We have lived with them through many summers and winters; we have cared for them; pruned and cultivated and fed them. We know them personally and intimately: all their little individual excellences and beauties; all their waywardnesses—and we love them.

Some of the trees that we set out as saplings dug from a near-by hillside, have grown so tall that we can sit in the shade of them on hot summer days and they fend off the chilly blasts of winter. Our grandchildren now build secret tree-houses high among their leafy fastnesses and swing from their branches. What a miracle—all in thirty years!

I got acquainted with my near neighbors, many of them Polish farmers. I experimented with raising the usual crops grown in our valley: corn, potatoes, and even onions, always doing as much as I could with my own hands. It was an experience full of interest to me, full also of many other rewards—though not much money. I not only enjoyed the work but my health improved, and I found I could do more and better writing in a week in Amherst than I could in two weeks in New York.

I will admit that I sometimes found it difficult, especially during the first warm days of spring with so much going on out of doors, to keep sternly down for the required time to my writing. Often on pleasant summer mornings I was up at dawn or earlier. I had a table on the wide west porch where I could, whenever I lifted my eyes, look off across the valley to the hills. I made good progress with my writing for an hour or so, and then the country began to come alive around me. The sun rose higher, the grass put on its spangles of morning dew, and all at once the countryside seemed to awaken gloriously—the birds were singing, the dogs exchanging morning greetings across the fields, and the cows lowing, eager to be milked and turned out to pasture.

For some time, by sheer determination, I could keep my pen

going—even though I might feel like whistling or singing with the best of them.

One temptation I could never resist. I sat where I could look out over my beehives, and when, sometimes in the warm forenoon, I heard the roar of a swarm rising in the sunny air, I stopped even in the middle of a sentence and ran down to see which colony it was coming from. After that, of course, I had to look up often to make sure where it was lighting, in what apple tree or on what currant bush, and presently, with what a rush of pleasure, I threw my pen aside and went out with my hive tools and with veil and gloves to cut down the great brown swarm and rehive it.

All these things, of course, interrupted me. I failed always to do as much writing as I had intended or hoped—I could never satisfy the voracious editors—and yet I never came back to my work on the porch, or in my study, without a fresh sense of the wonder and the beauty of life—a new appreciation that I was a humble part of it all, and new realization that it was infinitely desirable. I never spent such a morning as this without resolving never again to be dogmatic about anything in this world; I began to learn that life, after all, was first, and writing second.*

I often felt guilty that I should dare to enjoy anything as much as I did my experience on this bit of Connecticut Valley earth. There was something positively immoral about it, wasn't there? Didn't I deserve the fearsome epithet of being an "escapist"? Going off and enjoying myself when the world was positively crumbling into ruin and desolation with the ills it suffered? Well, I blamed most of it on David Grayson who loved nature and the quiet life, and since I was trying to make good the faculties of myself, I went on doing what I wanted most to do, and writing what I liked best to write.

I suppose "every man judges the Fair as his own wares have gone in it." My wares in those years were going well. My books were selling; they were even beginning to be published in London and I was hearing from them in Australia, New Zealand, South Africa, and elsewhere. For the first time in my life I was beginning to feel really secure—or thought I was. I did not have to groan every month when

*I have told much more about these Amherst experiences in two books by David Grayson, *The Countryman's Year* and *Under My Elm.*

I made up my accounts, thinking where the money for the next few months was coming from. *The American Magazine*, which we owned as a group—John Phillips, Ida Tarbell, Bert Boyden, John Siddall and I, with several others—was for the time being going strong—that is, if we did not think too intently about the money we still owed upon the purchase price.

To be busy with what one likes best to do is in itself one of the top-rounds of happiness. But it is by no means the highest round. To be *free* to do what one wants to do *most* is certainly another round or so upward. I had always enjoyed writing—almost any kind of writing—but until the years of which I speak I was never quite free to go, to feel, to do, to experiment, even to play, just when and where I wanted. I used sometimes to gloat over the fact that I was being well paid for work I should have been glad to do for nothing.

My greatest enjoyment certainly came from the Grayson writings. What keen pleasure I had knitting together on a thread of fiction the impressions of my many tramps in a freshly discovered New England—a book called *The Friendly Road*. But these essays represented only a small part of my production as a writer. Since they were the products of actual experiences in the country and with country people—and real experience is not hastily or casually plucked from any wayside—I had to wait until I had warmed them in my mind, and most important of all, put them down in my notebooks. They were my unhurried left-hand work. During all the years in which I was writing them, I was expending far more time and energy on articles and books that I thought of as more "serious"; but enjoying much the same freedom in doing them. I cannot look back upon that period without amazement, especially when I consider the years I have since devoted to a kind of slave-labor, even though it was self-imposed. Was it possible that I could ever have been so free to act my own nature?

When, for example, I became interested in the new canal at Panama and began to think of it as a significant manifestation of the American way of doing great things, I had only to pack my bag and be off. What a trip that was, my first in southern seas, my first glimpse of the tropics. I spent a couple of weeks with General Goethals traveling up and down, or riding in a little private car, along the vast ditch into which the water had not yet been turned. I watched with admiration that fine engineer and administrator at his work. I saw how cleverly we were outwitting the jungles, killing the mosquitoes, conquering the diseases that had defeated the French when they had tried to dig the canal. I made a visit of several days up the Chagres River into the tropical jungle. Two stout natives poled or paddled the dug-out canoe I hired. I saw innumerable alligators on the beaches, slithering away into the water as we approached. I saw several iguanas, a great lizard-like animal that the natives considered a delicacy to feast upon. I had been told that monkeys were plentiful: I saw only one. I slept in a palm-thatched cabin high up above the river, and I was awakened in the night by the whippoorwills just as I had often been when camping as a boy in the northern wilderness of Wisconsin.

I wrote articles for our magazine on Goethals and his work. As an American I felt proud of the canal; I considered it a kind of symbol of the American gift of imagination, American inventiveness, American willingness to gamble on such vast and costly enterprises. I thought it might fire the interest and ambitions of the rising generation.

For the same reasons I made a wonderful trip—wonderful to me—to the Hawaiian Islands. I visited many of the plantations in both Oahu and Hawaii. I talked with the feudal barons who owned them. I looked into the lives of the Filipinos, the Japanese, the Porto Ricans who labored for them—I had many rich and interesting experiences about which I wrote several articles for our magazine.

I was always finding men who interested me; usually men who were devoting their lives to some great work, or men who might have in them capacities for leadership to be discovered. They usually belonged to the classes I admired most—the artists (the doers and creators), the scientists (the discoverers and inventors) and the saints (who lost themselves in serving others). I liked to go to see such men and I liked to write short articles about them. It did not matter to me whether they were important, or rich, or famous—if I thought they were living great lives or doing great work. We had a tinker at Amherst named Thompson, who could have laid claim to an old verse-motto known in our town:

If I were a cobbler, it should be my pride
The best of all cobblers to be;
If I were a tinker, no tinker beside
Should mend an old kettle like me.

He not only mended old kettles but everything else in our town, including the precious instruments used in the college laboratories of physics and astronomy. There was nothing he could not make or mend: he had become a real scientist and mathematician; his fame spread across the countryside. I rejoiced on that commencement day at Amherst College when I saw old Tinker Thompson, gray-headed and stooped, stepping up to the platform along with famous scholars and statesmen, to receive a Master's degree. That was what he really was—a Master. I thought it a fine imaginative recognition of real worth in a democracy.

Well, I wrote about Thompson the tinker. I wrote about Brother Dutton, saint, who lived among the lepers of Molokai. He was an American, a Vermonter, and he went to Hawaii to succeed Father Damien, who was made famous by Robert Louis Stevenson. When Damien's leprous hands could no longer hold the crucifix, the leadership passed on to Brother Dutton. Only once in twenty-five years did he climb the mountain back of the prison-like settlement of the lepers, look far out to sea, and return to his place. I wrote about Major Moton, the Negro leader, who followed Booker T. Washington as the head of Tuskegee. I wrote of my friend "Bill" Kent, Congressman from California, a rich man who became a great public servant—and many other good men.

I went out to call on "Uncle Henry" Wallace of Iowa. I had been hearing and reading about him for several years. He was the founder and owner of *Wallace's Farmer*, a real guide and leader of the western farmers' movement—a notable personality. He took me with him on a visit through the southern counties of Iowa where he knew almost every man, woman and child. It offered me a fine experience in human relationships. I came to know and like his son Henry Wallace, then editor of *Wallace's Farmer*, who was to become Secretary of Agriculture in Harding's cabinet. And I shall not forget coming into the office with Uncle Henry after our return from southern Iowa and of having him stop me in the hallway and point to a young man sitting in a little cubby of an office.

"That," said Uncle Henry with pride in his voice, "is the best of all the Wallaces. I want you to meet him."

His name also was Henry Wallace, and he was just then out of college. He had unruly red hair and an awkward look of embarrassment. I presume he knew what his grandfather had been saying about him. He is now Vice-President of the United States.

There was much I saw and enjoyed, and much I learned on all these trips. I had come to like even better than I had in the earlier years to write about men who were doing great and good things. But such articles, short or long, never seemed to awaken the public interest or stir people to action like the so-called "muckraking" exposures I had written a few years before. For goodness, even greatness, is rarely sensational.

But the thing that gave me the soundest satisfaction of all in those happy years, that made me most confident of the future, was the remarkable wave of reform then sweeping the country. I had been more interested for years in this uprising than in anything else. I had been helping with my pen in every way I could. I may have been too sanguine—it's a fault I have—but it seemed to me that a good and great revolution was under way in America. It seemed a genuine and sincere awakening to the social and economic and political ills that had so long afflicted the country. Many of the best men in the nation were coming into leadership, the old bosses and political rings were being overturned, corruption rooted out, and constructive new laws, in the states and the nation, were being enacted.

Woodrow Wilson was in the White House and was making a gallant and successful campaign to correct deep-seated evils. It was a keen pleasure to me to go to see him from time to time and to write about what he was doing. Washington was a very different place from what it had been a dozen or fifteen years before when I began to know it well. I wrote an article, published in *The American* in June, 1914, which I called "The New Spirit at Work in Washington."

"It seems like a new world," I said. "Today there is a spirit of service, of earnest endeavor, a desire for full publicity which was largely wanting then. The Government is more closely responsive to the people than ever before."

I tried to give a picture of the Washington I had first known—"a little principality in itself, very jealous of its secrets, and largely impervious as to what was actually going on." I spoke of the "diplomatic corps" of Big Business which then dominated everything.

"I recall the Steel Ambassador from Pennsylvania," I wrote, "and the Oil Ambassador from New Jersey, and the noble Woolen Ambassador from New England, upon whose shield was emblazoned a lamb, quartered, with the wool drawn over its eyes. These distinguished men, when they visited the Halls of Congress, were not consigned to the gallery where they could hear themselves maligned, as at present, and take no part, but were welcomed as peers in the lobbies, and even sat comfortably, with hands clasped across their roomy persons, on the floors of the Houses. Ah! the good old days!

"Since then, what a change there has been. A change in the whole attitude of Washington and of Congress toward the people. At present, under Wilson, all the executive departments of the Government are stirring with new life."

The President seemed to me to be making a very great record, but I tried to see him objectively, never disregarding the background of agitation and preparation which led up to his successes. For neither Mr. Wilson nor his party alone originated these reforms. They were the outgrowth of years of agitation, muckraking, popular education, insurgency. Bryan, Roosevelt, LaFollette and other radical and progressive leaders had a part in it. The Socialists had a part in it. Even the writers had a part in it. It was a great, slow-growing, public movement which, resting through Mr. Taft's administration, had now come to fruition under Woodrow Wilson.

Looking back, since then, I can be even more sweeping in my comments on the domestic achievements of Woodrow Wilson than I was then. I believe no former administration ever put upon the statute books a greater body of constructive laws dealing with social and economic problems.

I tried more or less clumsily in those articles to determine Wilson's "central and controlling idea." I quoted various things he had been saying that I thought interpretative.

"The business of Government is to organize the common interest."

"My thought is of America. America is greater than any party."

"There is one lesson that some men never seem to learn," he said, "and that is that whenever they try to serve themselves, and make it obvious that they are trying to serve themselves, the thing they least succeed in doing is serving themselves; and that the only way in which you can connect yourself with the forces of success is by connecting yourself with the forces of society, because every man will be as little as himself if his thought is centered upon himself."

What he was demanding of those who could understand was *more democracy, real democracy,* applied in all the aspects of the "common interest." We shall understand more clearly as the years pass that this was the keynote, the great central idea that Woodrow Wilson brought to America and to the world. Democracy was his word: it had long been a more or less meaningless political slogan. He gave it new meaning and force. It was this democracy that I believed in.

CHAPTER XXXII

Three Unhappy Years

THEN THE WAR came—August, 1914.

To millions of Americans, of whom I was one, it was not at first a reality. We went on being happy! I was living contentedly in the country, feeling free to write what I wanted most of all to write, watching with satisfaction the efforts on all sides to make America a finer place to live in.

And then suddenly, if imperceptibly, my world, the world of a majority of Americans, began to break up. We had been living in a relatively sheltered paradise, busy with our own peaceful progress, maintaining our "standard of living," increasing our riches, oblivious to the fact that the world we lived in was becoming over-crowded and that we could no longer live to ourselves alone. Few of us knew or cared about "international relationships," still fewer knew how the other peoples lived.

These facts did not become clear at once—not even to the President of the United States. We described what we had in our own souls by the slogans we repeated: "America first," let Europe "stew in its own juice." We closed our eyes to what was going on in the world, and blindly demanded, as in the campaign of 1916, to be kept out of the war.

It seemed to me as we drifted steadily toward war that everything I had been interested in was threatened. All quiet inquiry, all the processes of reason, all sympathy of understanding, all the courtesies of co-operation in a peaceful world—all gone. I had considered, however naively, that I had a calling as a student of the art of living in a crowded world. I liked to think of myself as a "maker of understandings." I remember a talk I gave in which I tried to emphasize, in that time of the gathering world storm, the especial need of such understanding. It was at the twentieth anniversary of the Hudson Guild of

New York. The Hudson Guild was a notable social settlement founded by John Lovejoy Elliott, who was a true lover of his fellowmen. I had been greatly interested in his work, and I called my talk "Makers of Understanding."

Here are some of the things I said:

"In the last year or so, especially since the beginning of the Great War, I have been fond of trying to imagine what sort of a person the typically necessary leader of the present time, in this world, should be: what qualities he should possess, what he should do, what he should say.

"I cannot possibly think of him, under my definition, as a soldier. Nor can I think of him as a politician serving the narrow and immediate interests of a party, nor as a minister or priest, devoted to the upbuilding of a church or the inculcation of a creed. I cannot even think of him as a prophet, though there was never a time when a true prophet was so needed in the world as he is today . . .

"Here we all are in this city, in this country, and in the great world, torn apart into bitterly antagonistic groups, races, classes, nations: having little understanding of one another and few common sympathies. This ignorant and selfish condition lies at the root of problems here on Manhattan Island: and it is the fundamental cause of the great war in Europe. What we need then, in our leadership, are great mediators, great producers of common understandings—men of deep human sympathies who know both sides and can make each side see and feel the position of the other. To this type of leader I like to give the name of Introducer . . .

"I like to think of the Introducer sitting in a Half-Way House something like this, not urging men to join political parties or churches, or to cleave to their own nation whether right or wrong, but using every energy to produce social understanding and a wider human sympathy. There is nothing more needed in the world today: nothing requiring a higher type of leadership.

"I have liked to think of Dr. Elliott ever since I first met him, as of the true type of the Introducer, a representative of the new leadership. Here he is in his Half-Way House in one of the most conglomerate and complex neighborhoods in all the world, engaged in trying to bring about that mutual understanding and mutual confidence which must lie deep down—the very foundation stones—beneath the structure of democracy.

"I think it must be a matter of sadness to most thoughtful men and women that up to the present time there has arisen in connection with the world war, either in belligerent or neutral countries, so little of supreme or constructive leadership: leadership imbued with the new enthusiasm I have endeavored to describe, and big and broad enough and strong enough to fill the high place of Introducer among the nations. But I think we may be certain that when he does come, whether he be nominally a statesman, a priest or a prophet, he will be filled with this faith and this purpose and no other. He will be supremely a Maker of Understandings."

Several friends of the Hudson Guild movement and of its genius, Dr. Elliott, liked my informal talk and brought it out in pamphlet form. It was distributed among New Yorkers and others in the country who were interested in public affairs. One of the copies was read by Theodore Roosevelt, then retired to Oyster Bay and bitterly critical of the attitude of the Wilson administration regarding the war in Europe. He wrote me the following letter about what I had said:

SAGAMORE HILL

January 11, 1916

DEAR MR. BAKER,

Do you think that in Belgium it makes much difference now whether its people do or not believe in the Hudson Guild spirit? It will make just as little difference here in the end, unless we *do* think of the "typically necessary man" for the U. S. at the present time as a soldier, of the type of Washington and of the men who gave Lincoln his strength. If we can't defend ourselves, it will be of no more consequence what we think of the Hudson Guild than what the Chinese think. But if we do, as our first duty, fit ourselves for self-defense, then it will be necessary in addition to work for precisely the Hudson Guild idea, as an anti-scorbutic to the Altgeld—LaFollette—demagogue theory and practice on one side, and the equally base and anti-social plutocratic-reactionary theory and practice on the other side.

Yours very truly,

(Signed) THEODORE ROOSEVELT.

Theodore Roosevelt's letter was representative of other criticism of my little talk. Yes, there were times and places when the soldier became the necessary leader of the state—and there was war, and destruction, and hunger, and sorrow. The soldier appeared because the makers of understandings, the introducers, had failed. There had not been enough of them, they had not believed enough in themselves, nor been able and persuasive enough—and the world had reverted again to the old and brutal method of meeting, but never settling, the problems of living together. While I was more convinced than ever by Mr. Roosevelt's letter of the necessity—if civilization was to develop, let alone endure—for makers of understanding to continue their labors with even more boldness and imagination, I could not help feeling that I was now facing a world in which men of my kind had no place, no useful service to perform. The kind of work I had done through many years seemed no longer wanted. How make sense out of the vast conflict in Europe? How develop a constructive program in such a time of passion?

If the country went to war, would not all the hopeful advances that had been made in recent years go by the board? Even Woodrow Wilson himself said, in that last bitter struggle with doubt, on the eve of his demand for the declaration of war:

"Every reform we have won will be lost if we go into this war. We have been making a fight on special privilege. We have got new tariff and currency and trust legislation. We don't know yet how they will work. War means autocracy. The people we have unhorsed will inevitably come into the control of the country, for we shall be dependent upon the steel, oil and financial magnates. They will run the nation." *

I began anxiously to watch Wilson's attempt to deal with the submarine sinkings and the many other problems connected with our neutrality. I should probably have qualified as an "appeaser" if that name had then been invented. So, I think, would have the masses of the American people. So, in reality, would have the President of the United States.

"If there is any alternative [to war] for God's sake, let's take it." he said in his anguish.

Few men then realized that this was no mere civil war in Europe: it was a world revolution.

* See *Woodrow Wilson: Life and Letters,* Vol. VI, page 506.

Everything also began to go wrong with me personally. *The American Magazine,* which had seemed to be unusually prosperous, and to have a really promising future, began to slip. My own life as well as most of my savings were wrapped up in it. I saw the control which had seemed to be firmly in our group of friends sold to a publishing company far more strongly financed than we were or could ever hope to be. I could see that *The American* would soon become a very different kind of magazine from the one we had tried to make—undoubtedly with a much more popular appeal. I could see, or thought I could see, that our old freedom of complete expression as writers could not be maintained. I resigned at once.

I had at first no doubt that I could easily make a living as a free lance. I continued to write what I most wanted to write, including my opinions which were strongly pacifist, of what America should do in the crisis that confronted us, but for the first time in many years I could not find a publisher for some of the articles I cherished most deeply. If it had not been for two things, my life in the country where I could get my feet down into the faithful earth, and the writings of David Grayson which went on, war or no war, I should have been in hard luck indeed. Several proposals were made to me to go to Europe as a correspondent, or to study this or that particular situation, all of which I refused, since I felt at that time that I could contribute little or nothing of any value. I turned back as many a writer has done in times of emergency to the novels I had had had in mind for so many years. I hired a dingy back room in New York City where I could have access to certain material I needed, and I wrote and wrote. When Harry W. Garfield's coal-order, in the coldest winter New York had ever known, cut off the heat in my rooming-house, I wrote with my overcoat on and all the bedclothes wrapped around my knees. I attended peace meetings, I signed appeals and resolutions, I even made speeches. It was an unhappy time.

I did not see President Wilson often during most of this hard period, but I continued to watch closely everything he did, and I was often sharply critical. I tried as never before to understand something, at least, of the real backgrounds of the European war and our relationship to it. The more I looked into each of Wilson's decisions and studied his notes, the more I felt that, under the circumstances, he could scarcely have done anything else. Since then, I have often thought that if the warlike Theodore Roosevelt had been president at that time he might easily, by demanding immediate war on Germany, have split the country wide open. Wilson's patient dealing with crisis after crisis, his reluctant conversion to preparedness and finally to war, truly expressed the awakening and slowly changing convictions of the people. When he finally closed his war message to Congress with the words of Martin Luther "God helping her she can do no other," the majority of the Nation was with him, as I was, fervently.

As the war progressed and the issues grew clearer I became more and more sincerely convinced of the necessity, if there was to be even a relatively free world to live in, that the Germans and all they stood for be defeated. Even though I disliked slogans, it was, after all, a war to "make the world safe for democracy"; and it began to be clear that a great new system of co-operation among the nations was a distinct possibility. I seized upon the idea of a League of Nations with warm approval. It seemed a sensible and necessary development of the art of living in a crowded world.

With this new perception of the issues of the war, came an intense desire to help the good cause along, without knowing where I could take hold or what I was fitted to do. I joined a group of writers that called itself The Vigilantes, and made a trip through the Middle West, the states I knew best, where strong opposition to the war still persisted. In Wisconsin, Minnesota, and Missouri especially, a large population of German and Scandinavian origin remained unconvinced. I wrote a series of short articles, asking no pay for my work, that was syndicated in many newspapers. I tried honestly to get at the cause of the disaffection and to set down the situation as it existed. I called no names, I abused no racial or national groups; I offered no remedies. I tried to make people understand.

I don't think my articles pleased the Vigilantes, which soon became, as a body, essentially and even bitterly propagandist. One of the members chided me because I declined to take along for distribution a package of pamphlets dealing with German atrocities, which seemed to me inexcusably violent and essentially unauthentic. I did not see how I could look for truth with such a blunderbuss in one hand. This body of Vigilantes, like earlier ones in our history, seemed to want to shoot first and inquire afterward.

I was somewhat comforted, however, by hearing that President Wilson had asked to have my articles sent to him. They also had the approval of Colonel House, Congressman Kent of California, and many others who wanted to know what the facts really were.

I believe it was this series of reports that opened the way to new opportunities wherein it seemed to me I could again do the kind of work for which I considered myself best fitted.

CHAPTER XXXIII

My Mission to Europe

DURING THE EARLY WINTER of 1917–18 many disturbing rumors were reaching President Wilson and the State Department concerning the growing unrest that existed in the Allied countries. Norman Hapgood, for example, who was a clear-headed observer, came back from Europe with confidential reports of the growing power of the "peace-by-negotiation" movement in England, the increasing opposition to the Government in power, especially Lloyd George, and the restlessness of labor in all the Allied countries of Europe.

These reports were not surprising. It was the fourth winter of a gigantic and exhausting struggle. Food was short in England—scarcely a three-week supply, with roving submarines in the Atlantic threatening to cut it still lower—hospitals were full of sick and wounded men, stored capital was rapidly crumbling away in tax levies, and there was widespread anxiety over the rumored strength of the spring offensive which the Germans were preparing.

Little news of these dangerous conditions found its way into the press, either in Europe or in America—the censors took good care of that—and worse still the American Embassies in Europe seemed hesitant about reporting fully upon these developments. The very suppression, no doubt, magnified the unreliable "inside stories" that did get through—the anxious reports of returning correspondents and diplomats, and the word-of-mouth rumors that began to circulate widely.

As the winter of 1917–18 deepened, rumors and reports of the unrest grew more widespread and specific. President Wilson felt that he was not being properly informed as to the actual conditions; and he wanted really to know.

Early in February, 1918, I was asked by the State Department to go to Europe and make inquiries regarding these restless elements, and report confidentially what I found. On February 10, Counselor Polk gave me a letter of authorization to Ambassador Page:

I will appreciate it if you will send forward any letters he may wish to write me and forward any telegrams to me in the Embassy code that he brings in.

I had long talks with Secretary Lansing, Counselor Polk, and Colonel House, the essence of which I set down in my notes (on February 19):

"I am to report fully for the information of the President and the State Department on the state of radical opinion and organization, especially the attitude of labor in England, and later, possibly in France and Italy. I am to have confidential introductions to various leaders over there, and am to send my letters in the Embassy pouch and cable my special reports in secret code."

I called one evening on Justice Brandeis, whom I regarded as one of the wisest men in Washington, a friend who had often in the past helped me greatly. He talked like some old Hebrew prophet on the moral aspects of the war. Germany was an evil force to be utterly put down. There could be no compromise. "But," said he, "you can help a hard-driven President most, not by arguing these self-evident facts, but by reporting the truth exactly as you find it. The truth is what he wants and needs; he can make his own deductions."

These were precious words, confirming what I had already determined upon, and I treasured them.

Colonel House and others suggested that in certain quarters in Europe I might secure franker and more complete information if I was not known as an agent of the government, and accordingly I made arrangements with Herbert Croly to represent *The New Republic*; I was also accredited as a correspondent by the New York *World*, although I never found the time to send any despatches to either of them.

I sailed for Liverpool on "ship No. 529," which proved to be the comfortable old *St. Louis*. At the last, I found it hard to break away, hard to leave my family, hard to give up my usual work—not harder, probably, than it was those days for hundreds of thousands of other

Americans who had been summoned to serve in Europe. On the day before I sailed, I went out into my snowy garden and worked for a few hours at the pruning of my grapevines. It was stolen time, but I could not go away without a parting salutation. I knew how I should miss my garden, my orchard, my bee colonies.

On the very first night at the Savoy Hotel in London, I was aroused from sound sleep by the terrific booming of guns, deep and ominous. Going to the window over which the curtains had been closely drawn and looking upward, I saw the Great Dipper there in the clear dark sky. An instant later a flash of light leaped like a drawn blade above the tops of the buildings and began thrusting and probing among the stars. It found light fleecy clouds not visible to the eye without that penetrating gleam. A moment later another shaft appeared and then another and another, like restless fingers probing the heavens, following each rift of cloud, then darting swiftly forward and pouncing upon some other suspicious spot in the sky. There could be no doubt that we were in the midst of an air raid. Straightway there were other bursts of the anti-aircraft guns, nearer and more terrific; and far in the sky, as the searchlights crossed them, I could see the star-like bursting of the shells. I heard running and talking in the halls outside, and quickly dressing myself, I went downstairs. An Englishman in the lift remarked: "Fritzy is at it again!"

In the rooms below, the late diners were pouring out, but without excitement. Taxicabs were huddled under the arches outside and the Strand in front was as deserted as a road in Arizona. A lone policeman at the corner told me it was the first raid they had had in two or three weeks. Evidently staged for my first night in London!

The morning papers, which I eagerly awaited, had nothing whatever to say except that an air raid was in progress, and the evening papers gave only the bare facts of the ugly business, without mentioning any definite localities. It seems that several of the airplanes had reached London and that eleven persons were killed and forty-six injured. The German report of the raid published in the London papers read as follows:

During the night, from March 7th–8th, London, Margate and Sheerness were attacked with bombs by several airplanes. Good effects were observed.

This was my introduction to England.

In planning my campaign of inquiry I decided to talk first with several liberal-minded Englishmen whom I already knew or to whom I had letters of introduction, men upon whose breadth of view and whose devotion to the truth of the matter I knew I could count. I wanted to understand the backgrounds of the situation before I met the leaders of the restless groups in whom I was chiefly interested.

But I had first to overcome the inevitable difficulties that confront a traveler in a country at war. I had to register with the Police in Bow Street, I had to find a quiet apartment to live in—comfortable rooms at 68 Curzon Street, W. I wasted no end of time at the Food Control Offices. While I was there a woman was loudly protesting that she could get no sugar—had babies, must have sugar. She had filed her application long ago, but no sugar.

"Sorry, but I cannot help you. You will simply have to trust in Providence."

"That," said she instantly, "is what I've been doin' all me life, and never got nothin' by it."

The first Englishman I went to see, even before I talked with Ambassador Page, was Professor Gilbert Murray of Oxford. While we were at lunch, army flying machines from a near-by training field were whirring noisily overhead, but no one took the slightest notice of them; a symbol of an acceptance of the facts of war even in a little quiet town, which we were far from having reached in America.

Murray's view of the current situation was gloomy enough. The war, as it affected England, was at the lowest ebb. Russian conditions were desperate; the coming German offensive in the west promised to be the greatest of the war. The shipbuilding situation was admittedly bad, food was short—"not three weeks' supply in hand."

Before I left the United States there had been a report, apparently well substantiated, that Lloyd George might have to resign. Professor Murray told me that the crisis had temporarily passed and that while the Government was under fierce attack (the *Saturday Review* had asked that very week, "Is there a Government?") there seemed no likelihood of an early overturn. We in America also know how bitterly an administration can be attacked and yet go on functioning with a fair degree of success. Both of our democracies have learned to ask, "Well, what is the alternative?"

Professor Murray told me that the Asquith liberals were genuinely accepting Wilson's leadership and his program of action, and in this they were supported by nearly all of the labor groups, including the Labor Party.

The next Englishman I went to see, on March 13, was Professor Graham Wallas. I took a long walk with him in Highgate Village where he lived, and stopped for tea. He was the author of *The Great Society*, which had attracted so much attention in America a few years before. He had lectured at Harvard, the distinguished Lowell Lectures. A thoughtful scholar, he had all the simplicity that goes with spiritual distinction, but I found him a down-hearted philosopher in his outlook upon the war. He said the people were beginning as never before to ask what it was all about—why these terrible sacrifices in life and property were still necessary.

"I have lost not only relatives but a good part of the best of my students."

He said he was for Wilson's program, that Wilson was the only real leader the war had produced. Nevertheless, how long would people continue to fight for ideals, however high? If the war went on much longer, where would be the forces for reconstruction? Would there be vitality enough left to rebuild the world on a democratic basis? The most hopeful movement in sight was the League of Nations—a fine idea, necessary of realization if ever the world was to live decently after the war, but so far it had been subjected to no hard thinking or skeptical inquiry. No one had tried really to solve the enormously difficult concrete problems which confronted the world; such as the control of the tropics, the regulation of migration between nations, as Japanese into America, the use of natural resources in backward countries, and most of all the problem of Asia.

Wallas said that the Lloyd George Government was undoubtedly unpopular in many circles, conservative as well as radical, but would a change of Government indicate to the world that we were weary of the war?

I was curious to see how much of British opinion this highly intelligent point of view of Professor Wallas represented. Was it merely the pessimistic questioning of an idealistic philosopher?

The next day I went to a dinner at the Criterion to hear an address by Lord Bryce, whom I had met in America some years before. He had grown old and shaggy, with bristling white hair, a frosty moustache and a scraggy beard—a little, likable, kindly old man. His address was graceful, smooth, brief and purposely hopeful, as it was intended to be, but not penetrating or really informing.

During the next few days, I met a number of men who helped me greatly in getting a clearer general view of the British situation. Among them were A. E. Zimmern, a member of the Round Table group who had written a fine book, *The Greek Commonwealth,* and Lord Charnwood, the author of an excellent new life of Lincoln.

I had tea at the Brooks Club with Lord Charnwood, and talked for two hours or more, and later we went out through the dark streets to the Bath Club in Dover Street and talked until midnight. I found Lord Charnwood most interestingly contradictory: a real worshiper of Lincoln, a defender of the House of Lords, and a strong believer in democracy—for America. He did not trust Lloyd George and yet supported the Government and was strong for the war.

I did not see Ambassador Page until March 16. On that day I went to dinner with him and Mrs. Page at 6 Grosvenor Square. It was a quiet home dinner. Mrs. Page, as in old times, was all cordiality. It seemed odd to find these simple American people whom I had known so long, surrounded by tall English servants.

I knew well that such a mission as mine—how much more the visits and inquiries of Colonel House—must irritate the Ambassador. I had been advised in Washington to tell him as little or as much as I considered necessary about what I was instructed to do. I had made up my mind at once. As a member of the firm of Doubleday Page & Co. he had not only been my publisher for many years, but a good friend whom I liked and trusted. I told him exactly and fully what my plans were; I told him I needed his help. I am glad to say I got it, generously.

The Ambassador had had heavy work since he came to London, and showed it. He was more nervous, less easily charming than of old, but he was friendliness itself. He pounced on me at once to find out whom I had seen. He thought I ought not to see the radicals! What was the use? They represented nothing. He seemed relieved when he heard I had talked with such men as Lord Charnwood and Gilbert Murray. I told him I wanted to see everybody, for how understand radical opinion without seeing radicals? We did not get to the subject of Wilson at all—or avoided it. I found that he was much dissatisfied with the whole American position and with Wilson's leadership. He seemed to have no sympathy with the great underlying liberal forces of England, for he feared that they might weaken the spirit of the people in the war.

I was to have one more highly instructive glimpse of British opinion before I began to see much of the dissenters; a glimpse of the confident strength of the Government, the "hard-working majority opinion" of the House of Commons, as one Englishman expressed it in talking with me. This was important; for how understand the strength of dissenting opinions without knowing something of the strength of the forces, the majority, that the Government could command?

On March 19, I sat through the debate in the House of Commons on secret diplomacy, led by Trevelyan and Ponsonby, both left-wing leaders, who were of the opposition. They demanded a committee of the House to keep in touch with foreign affairs, and thus prevent the evils incident to the making of secret treaties. They brought forward especially the secret arrangements of England with Russia for the control of Constantinople, and the treaty offering Italy the Trentino if she would come in with the Allies. Mr. Balfour occupied the ministerial bench. A tall, thin, droopy man, he sat most of the time on the small of his back, sometimes with one foot part way up on the desk opposite, sprawling and lounging and occasionally making a note on a pad. When he came to make his answer, the House immediately began to fill and he to dominate it. His bearing was marked by distinction, his speech hesitant but impressive. As a figure he loomed above any other man who appeared. His speech was that of the defender of old methods—old and undemocratic—his manner that of the tired ironist. He bantered, turned satirical and paradoxical, and said that "when this committee is established, it is quite certain I shall not be Foreign Minister." That is, he would step out rather than work with such a committee. While speakers on the other side were in dead earnest, it was evident that, in the House of Commons at least, they were hopelessly in the minority.

CHAPTER XXXIV

I Meet the British Labor Leaders

I FOUND MYSELF deeply interested in meeting the leaders of British labor—Arthur Henderson, Ramsay MacDonald, Philip Snowden, W. C. Anderson, F. W. Jowett, and many others. I was helped in approaching these men by my acquaintance in former years with many of our ablest American labor leaders, both those of the right wing, like Gompers, and those of the left wing like Debs, Heywood, and Andrew Furuseth. I had sometimes heard the British leaders called "better" or "abler" than ours, but the more thoroughly I became acquainted, the less I liked these adjectives. The difference was not in ability, but in experience. The British labor movement was much older than ours, the workers had advanced beyond the period of restless organization and were attacking the larger political and social aspects of their place in society. No leader in America at that time had such problems to face as had Ramsay MacDonald or Arthur Henderson—to say nothing of Sidney Webb.

British labor already had a political organization—the Labor Party—with forty members in Parliament, and one member, Arthur Henderson, in the Cabinet. They had their own influential publications. At their conventions which I attended, political problems, the issues of the war, and peace aims occupied far more time and provoked more vigorous and highly intelligent discussion than the primary problems of corresponding American unions—such as the right to organize, the closed shop, the minutiae of negotiations with employers, and so on.

After the war began, the Labor Party had split into two factions. The socialist group was led by Ramsay MacDonald, Philip Snowden, W. C. Anderson, F. W. Jowett, and others, who wanted to keep out of the war. They were the loudly vocal group; but the rank and file of labor, however opposed to conscription, had been pro-war. Arthur Henderson had been the leader of this large group. In the reorganization of the Labor Party, he took a foremost part, siding neither with the extreme socialist or pacifist group nor with the extreme "patriotic" group. The platform he stood on, I found, was almost exactly that of President Wilson. The Memorandum of War Aims, adopted not long before I arrived in London by the Inter-Allied Labor and Socialist Conference (largely the work of Sidney Webb), was essentially the Wilson program, indeed quoting Wilson's four proposals as bedrock principles. This action had resulted in unifying to quite a remarkable degree the labor and liberal forces of Great Britain; and Henderson had become the undisputed leader. A square-shouldered, square-headed, blue-eyed, ruddy-faced Scotchman, Henderson was trained as an iron moulder and had become a lay Methodist preacher. He was a "tee-totaler." His face, at first sight, was singularly impassive, and he seemed heavy and slow. While he was a natural born politician, he had a touch of self-consciousness which is lacking in the born leader in England. Henderson used the brains of Sidney Webb and Ramsay MacDonald, and supplied the gift of forthright leadership.

Henderson spoke of Wilson as the great leader of democratic opinion in the world and said that little could be hoped for while Lloyd George was dominating the British Government. He divided England in regard to war into three groups.

1. The pacifists, who were willing to make peace on almost any terms. A very small number. Among these he included the group of Tories who would be willing to make a "business peace"—that is, a peace by arrangement and trading of territory.

2. The "bitter-enders," a strong body of the population, led at present by the Government and Lloyd George.

3. The labor and "sanely liberal group," supporting the war but anxious to seize every opportunity of supplementing military effort with moral, political and diplomatic efforts.

While this general division was corroborated by a number of members of the House of Commons, they all agreed that there was a large body of doubtful opinion in England, that might easily be thrown one way or another by a sharp turn in events. England was under very great strain, anxiety permeated every home in a way that we could not yet realize, and a great German victory in France, with the prospect of an interminable continuation of the war, might plump a large body of opinion in favor of a negotiated peace that would give Germany her way in the East, restore France and Belgium—"that's all we really went to war for"—and give England more colonies in Africa, and new rights in Mesopotamia and Palestine.

But one thing I learned during those late days in March and early April, 1918, never afterward to forget, was that whatever opposition might exist, however bitter the criticism of its leadership, when the supreme crises came the English people stood united in a grim, unbending determination to fight to the end. One felt it in the very air of their streets; one came to a new understanding of British character and British civilization.

In my second letter to the State Department, I felt sure enough to say that the great mass of labor distrusted Lloyd George thoroughly but that I had found almost no one who wanted to turn him out, at least at that critical moment.

"No party," I wrote, "would want to venture the huge responsibilities of the coming summer, the crisis of the war, and take over Lloyd George's burdens and mistakes—and then have to fight a possible general election in the fall."

The long-expected German offensive on the Western Front fifty miles long, with 800,000 men, began on March 21. With it came, finally, a sensation of relief: waiting had become intolerably anxious; and at once irritating home problems, war aims, post-bellum arrangements, were forgotten.

On March 24 I made this notation in my journal:

"No one thinks or talks of anything else but the great battle in France. Special editions of the newspapers were on the streets all day and the headlines are most alarming—as these from the *London Times:*

BACK TO THE SOMME

BRITISH ARMIES ON THE DEFENSIVE

PERONNE AND HAM LOST

PARIS BOMBARDED

The war: 4th Year; 234th Day

One afternoon I went around to tea at the Pages' and was fortunate in finding Secretary Baker there. He called out when he saw me,

"Hello there, Ray Stannard Baker!"

"He is just over from Belgium with his staff," I wrote in my notebook, "most of which was with him at the Ambassador's, and is going back tomorrow after seeing Lord Derby and Mr. Lloyd George. Referring to the battle in France he said earnestly:

" 'The British are going to hold them.' "

But later one of the secretaries came in with the telephone news that the Germans had Peronne and that more American troops had been thrown into the battle.

Secretary Baker was the same light-footed, active man as ever, all wires and energy, his eyes very black and his face full of wrinkles, some of which were assuredly war wrinkles—a kindly, smiling, eager, able man.

In the afternoon, there being a feel of spring in the air, I got on top of a bus and rode into the East End along the old Roman road to Old Ford and back. It was a poor substitute for the tramps I made in New England or for the spring work on my own land, but it was the best I could do—all I had time for.

"London displays few flags," I wrote in my notebook. "They are not flag worshipers as we are, they are such thorough patriots that they do not need to talk about it. There were not even many soldiers on the streets of those outlying districts. One notices everywhere the absence of young men and the notable number of women workers. Here and there sandbags have been piled high in the entrances to tunnels and tubes, and there are occasional air raid shelter signs. At one church in the poorest section I saw a kind of shrine and beneath it a list of soldiers of that neighborhood who had been killed—a very long list. In front of this were pathetic offerings in old cracked vases of crocuses, tulips, and jonquils."

One evening I went to Barrie's play *Dear Brutus* at the Windham, with Du Maurier in the leading part—a charmer. The theater was crowded in spite of the nightly fear of air raids. The program carried this presumably comforting reassurance:

The whole of the auditorium is covered by a main roof which consists of steel girders supported by two feet of concrete surmounted by asphalt.

I had been wanting to look into conditions in the working-class districts and was greatly pleased to visit Mr. Grinling, who lived in Woolwich in the midst of a vast forgotten population of more or less depressed workingmen. He inherited a considerable fortune, went to Oxford, was associated at the very earliest in the Toynbee Hall movement, and had been in Woolwich for thirty years—where he lived with the severity and simplicity of a monk, freely serving every kind of democratic cause. There was a quaint little garden behind the house with rock-fringed beds, an old cedar tree, and vines along the wall. He had portraits of the great democrats of the world around him: Mazzini, Whitman, Tolstoy, Ibsen, Edward Carpenter, William Morris, and Prince Kropotkin and a striking portrait of Dante. Kropotkin he knew well: Keir Hardie he loved. He had toiled all the years to inspire the "first principles," the "faith" of democracy, in the great crowded districts around him. He told me at length of the labor situation in England and of the democratic revolt from the old, hard, red-tape trade-unionism. He increased one's hope for the common man.

I went with him to a neighborhood meeting of workingmen. Solid, sober, slow men these were, smoking their pipes; working hard all day, not getting quite enough food to eat, nor clothes to wear, but keeping quiet about it. What a sense of reality they gave as they sat there all through the long evening, discussing their small affairs and practicing the infinitely difficult art of living together—*practicing* self-government. One had lost a son, one a brother, and so on; but there was not one there who did not believe that the war must go on to the end because it was *right*.

I had further evidence as to this attitude from another man who could assuredly qualify as an expert. This was Thomas Burke, with whom I went to lunch, the odd, slim, slight, dry little author of *Limehouse Nights,* a penetrating if gruesome book on the dregs of East London life. He came up in an orphan asylum, worked as an errand boy and clerk, got into a second-hand bookstore and discovered Stephen Crane.

"Everything I am," said he, "I owe to Stephen Crane."

He gave me direct testimony regarding the reaction toward the war of the great silent lower masses of London. A conservative people, these—with the conservatism of poverty—driven about upon the surface by a diversity of newspaper voices; but tough underneath and possessed with the obstinate belief that the British would not be beaten, never had been, never could be. They didn't like the war, hated it, had suffered by it, but had no notion of stopping until the Germans were beaten.

About this time, I saw another moving demonstration of the way the British people were meeting this fearful crisis. On Good Friday, March 29, I attended one of the most extraordinary religious services I have ever known. It was called a "Great Prayer of the People" for help in winning the battle. It was held in Hyde Park. I wrote in my diary:

"A great multitude of people was gathered on the Green, many soldiers of all services, wounded men on crutches, rich and poor, adults and children. On a raised platform were a number of churchmen and free churchmen of all denominations, headed by the Bishop of London. No church lines are drawn at a time like this when the destiny of civilization hangs in the balance. They prayed mightily to God for victory. I stood there also, praying deeply in spirit, but also wondering! I suppose many Germans are also praying today to God to help *them* to win the battle, and probably with as sincere a belief in their rightness as we have in ours. Is God confused? I say 'many Germans,' but from such revelations as those in the Lichnowsky memorandum, now just published, there must be doubts creeping in."

CHAPTER XXXV

Studying the Peace-by-Negotiation Movement—The Lord Mayor's Dinner

IT WAS SOME TIME before I was able to get a real understanding of the so-called peace-by-negotiation movement in England, in which the President was especially interested, and of which the State Department could, apparently, learn little.

Mr. F. W. Hirst, editor of *Common Sense*, the mouthpiece of the movement, had invited me to call on him. I found my way with some difficulty through the dark city streets to his home, where I met Lord Buckmaster and had a talk lasting until after midnight.

I found them both much excited about the Czernin "peace-feeler" which had been published in full on April 4. The *Times* and other conservative papers had criticized it as being hypocritical and untrustworthy but the liberal *Manchester Guardian* and the *Daily News* were hopeful that it might furnish a possible opening toward peace. Mr. Hirst thought that this fact ought to be cabled to America for the influence it might have on Mr. Wilson, who was to make a much-expected speech at Baltimore within a day or two.

I found that Hirst, and most of the men interested in the movement, reduced most of the questions at issue to cost. He believed in a League of Nations, but was not enthusiastic; he said that all wars had been finally settled by compromise and that this one must also be. He presented many facts to show that Germany was still enormously strong, could not be beaten. He would seize the first opportunity of negotiation: and would let the Germans have their way in the East if they would evacuate Belgium and leave the other questions to the peace conference.

" 'How about the restoration of Belgium?' I asked.

" 'That's no great matter,' he said. 'Stop the war a couple of weeks earlier and the saving in the cost of military operations by the belligerents would restore Belgium.' "

I set down his opinions in my notes quite fully because he represented a considerable number of powerful and high-class business and professional men in England, who were actively supporting his journal, *Common Sense*. In England any man who does not conform is likely to start an organization of his own and, if he can get the money and sometimes when he can't, he begins publishing a weekly paper—evidences certainly of the vitality of the democratic method in that country. Some of these small groups are exceedingly vocal. There is a determination in the expression of divergent opinion in England which we do not have in America, and to the inquirer the difficulty lies not so much in discovering all these groups of opinion as in measuring quantitatively how much they represent.

Allied with these big business men in the "stop-the-war" movement were the Lansdowne group of conservative lords. I found that fundamentally their reasons were very much like those of the business group represented by Mr. Hirst. Old solid institutions were threatened: civilization was rushing madly into unknown dangers: everything they knew as strong in the Empire was being threatened. Lord Lansdowne was an old man, a distinguished old man, who had lost a son in the war, but it was not necessary to charge, as H. G. Wells had done, that he was fearful of his own skin or even the skin of his class: it went deeper than that: the solid foundations of England and the Empire, as Lansdowne knew them, and had helped to build them, were being shaken. His two chief supporters, Lord Buckmaster and Lord Parmoor, were champions of the two oldest and most respectable institutions of England.

Lord Buckmaster was an attractive and scholarly man: one of the great lawyers of England. He had had a brilliant career: not yet past middle age he had been Lord Chancellor of England (under Asquith). He had a profound sense of the sacredness of English law, and the power and beauty of orderly judicial procedure. The war had shaken his world and all its hereditaments. All law, all guarantees, were being swept overboard: the constitution was set at naught: the government was an autocracy. He quoted Franklin's phrase: "There was never a good war nor a bad peace." He was apparently willing to give Germany what she wanted in the East, urging that it would be foolishness for the Allies to attempt to restore Russia when Russia, by her own treaty with Germany, had settled the problems of her Western provinces: and besides, these provinces were not really Russian anyway! He would stop the war now, and save everything possible. He was much stronger for the League of Nations than Mr. Hirst. He evidently found in it a promise of vital new legal sanctions and controls, and an appeal to orderly judicial methods.

Lord Parmoor I did not meet: but he was said to be the most distinguished ecclesiastical lawyer in England: knew all the traditions and sanctions of that ancient institution, the Church of England, and had defended them. He saw the war threatening even that mighty and beautiful edifice that rears itself upon the soil of England like the perfect towers of Westminster Abbey. The war must be stopped lest this ancient institution be injured.

It was not, it seemed to me, mere personal selfishness with many of these men, it was really a fierce, narrow patriotism. And it seemed certain, if a great "break-up" should come, that they would command a respectable and distinguished following. They were willing to work with, even praise and cultivate (as Mr. Hirst was doing that week in *Common Sense*), such extreme Socialists as the Snowdens, who were as far from them in every essential belief as heaven is from hades. They would join hands with anybody to overturn the wild Lloyd George and stop the war!

The morning following my conversation with Mr. Hirst and Lord Buckmaster I called on Mr. Massingham, the editor of the *Nation*, whose work had long interested me. He had been one of the steadiest and bitterest of the critics of the Lloyd George administration and one of the supporters of the demand for early peace negotiations. So critical was the *Nation* at one time that it was barred from the foreign mails. Massingham was a brilliant writer and a determined fighter in the cause.

While I duly reported to Washington what all these leaders of the "peace-by-negotiation movement" had told me, together with what their critics said about them, it did not seem to me, in spite of the great wealth and position of many of its proponents, that it played any really important part in influencing British opinion. For I had been seeing the steadiness with which the great mass of the British people were resolved to go forward with the war and who believed that the English must and would win.

On the first anniversary of America's entrance into the war, April 6, 1918, I had an invitation to the Lord Mayor's dinner at the Mansion House to celebrate the occasion. It was a grand affair.

Mr. Balfour made a speech, but he did not excel supremely on such an occasion as he did in the kind of bantering and ironic discourse which I had heard in the House of Commons. Nevertheless, it was a good speech, and Ambassador Page's in reply was even better. Mr. Page was greatly cheered. He was liked in England and he succeeded, as always before, by a genuine quality of friendliness and helpfulness. People *liked* him.

I was placed next to a colonel serving in the Ministry of Information—a fine fellow, a Canadian by origin, but a bitter and extreme Tory. When I told him, in answer to his question, that I was trying to understand the liberal and the labor movements in England, he said I must be sure to see the right people—*not* Arthur Henderson. He actually thought Henderson a radical!

I was amused when I tried to tell my colonel of one extreme of Toryism which I thought we would both agree was rather absurd. It concerned a cotton manufacturer of Lancaster, whom I met on the ship coming over. He was rich, had mills in Liverpool, cotton plantations in America, shooting preserves in Scotland, and he was, upon occasion, a lay church reader—all Tory! When I asked him about the labor leaders and their agitation in England, he responded hotly:

"Do you know what I would do with them? I would put them up against a wall and shoot them to a man. We have got to win this war."

I supposed this would evoke deprecation from my colonel friend, but he took it in dead seriousness and began to argue that if the Government had shown the courage at the start to handle a few of the agitators in this way, very different conditions might have resulted.

One man I chanced to meet at the dinner impressed me greatly. After paying my respects to the Lord Mayor, who gave me two fingers out of a lace cuff, I was cast up near a man who stood at the moment gazing absently into the dim arches above us with a kind of musing, reflective look. He fascinated me at once.

"Remarkable face," I thought, "remarkable eyes."

A moment later he "came to," and we had quite a conversation, but without my finding out who he was. When I got into the dinner and looked at the place list, I discovered that I had been talking with the Archbishop of Canterbury.

In his speech Mr. Balfour expressed the view plainly held by the great majority of those present when he said that there was ". . . not room for the ideal cherished by the German military party and the ideals cherished by the great free democracies of the world. One or the other must prevail . . ." And he was loudly cheered when he referred to President Wilson as having crystallized these democratic ideals "in words which have gone the circuit of the earth, and have found an answering echo in every man who knows what freedom means . . . He has stated them with a perfection of form and a force of language which few, if any, living public men can rival . . ."

On the day after the Lord Mayor's dinner Mr. Wilson's Baltimore address was published. It was his famous "force, force to the uttermost" speech which attracted unusually wide comment, and varied approval. I wrote of it in my notes, "It will not at all please Lord Lansdowne or Lord Buckmaster and others of the peace-by-negotiation group whom I have been seeing. The Tory press, of course, emphasizes the last paragraph with its 'force, force to the uttermost, force without stint or limit.' On the other hand, the extreme pacifists wished that Mr. Wilson had seen an opening in Czernin's last speech to encourage negotiation, but they are all glad of the very tone which the conservatives lament, 'Thank God, he doesn't descend to calling the Germans names!' The speech has evidently quite wonderfully expressed the great solid middle conviction of England, although it aims, probably, at higher and clearer moral objectives than most of the British now think it possible to attain."

I summed up my view of the whole situation in my notebook:

"The American ideal as expressed by Mr. Wilson, the essential thing that America is fighting for, is not at all the ideal of the Lloyd-George Government—if it has any ideals at all beyond beating the

Germans. The real support of Mr. Wilson, as it has been all along, is found among the labor and liberal groups here, which understand what he wants. It is plain also that in France, in the Government now in control, our American help is looked upon not as a means of reconstructing the world, but as a means of driving the Germans out of France and restoring Alsace-Lorraine. Clemenceau rejects the idea of a real League of Nations and says nothing about future disarmament. The leaders are all 'realists' except Mr. Wilson, and it is doubtful, if the allies were to win now with the present Governments in control, whether there would not be an old-fashioned trading peace, with scant effort to realize any of Mr. Wilson's ideals. Military victory is really all they are after, but the labor and liberal groups here feel that Mr. Wilson is fighting for something beyond and above that—for a peace built upon new and sound guarantees."

On April 9, Parliament sat and Lloyd George introduced his new man-power bill with the dangerous provision for the application of conscription laws to Ireland. While he was speaking at Westminster, a new offensive of the Germans was beginning on the French front. Conditions were recognized as being most serious. If they had not been, Lloyd George would never have dared bring in so drastic a measure; everyone knew the Irish would make trouble.

I lunched the next day with Ambassador Page in the Embassy lunchroom. There was much talk of the new offensive north of Arras which was apparently breaking through the British lines. Pessimism was admittedly increasing. Our own Admiral Sims was there. He was the best representative of the tough old sea-dog we had in our navy. He didn't so much look it, he said it! He would decapitate all the Irish, thought that Irish conscription could be enforced with "trifling losses." He would hang certain members of Parliament, and as for the pacifists and labor leaders, why, they should quite simply be shot. As for the war in France, let the British and American armies withdraw and fight the Germans on the sea for twenty years if necessary. The navy would do it! British generals were a poor lot, and Americans not much better, but Foch was a thinker. He criticized sarcastically the large cavalry force which Haig, with his traditional enthusiasm as a cavalry officer, was maintaining on the French front.

Several hundred thousand of them, so he said. He suggested that the best use to which the horses could be put, since people were beginning to get hungry, would be to butcher and eat them. Yet the Admiral was doing good work there, had one hundred and seventy-five American warcraft under his command, and was co-operating perfectly with the British. He was an efficient man, I should say, but think of a world ruled by men of that type!

Although the danger in France was becoming formidable, and the anxiety great, Lloyd George's "reckless proposal" met a far wider and more determined opposition than any other Government measure of the time. It was attacked mildly by Mr. Asquith, vigorously by such papers as the *Daily News,* which was always in opposition, reasonably and with far greater influence by the *Manchester Guardian,* which had gained force because of its tendency to support Lloyd George in all real crises, and finally by the *Chronicle,* whose editor had formerly been regarded as one of Lloyd George's "pet pressmen." Of course the whole Irish nationalist and radical group was in wild revolt, threatening actual rebellion.

Mr. Page was as pronounced a "bitter ender" as any Englishman I met—said all Germans were liars and the path to peace was an overwhelming military victory. He spoke of imagination as one of the chief necessities of statesmanship and said that Lloyd George, in his judgment, had a better equipment of it than any other British leader. It was the best thing I had yet heard said of Lloyd George.

While the news from France was bad—could scarcely have been worse—the life of London went rolling on. All the streets were crowded, the stores were full of purchasers, restaurants busy, taxicabs a-plenty, and an enormous amount of love-making and marrying and dying were going on. Courts were in session, schools keeping, reformers spouting on the Green. New books were being published and sold, and professors were lecturing upon such subjects as these:

"The Ceylon Expedition of 1803" at the Royal Historical Society.

"The Present Day Application of Experimental Psychology."

"Timber—Its Identification and Mechanical Properties."

The very morning that hundreds of dying British soldiers were being brought into London, collectors were trading as usual at "Messrs. Puttick and Simpson's" where "a Chinese Famille Noir vase, finely enamelled with prunus trees, K'ang-tsi period" was sold for two thousand guineas!

Verily, the everyday habits of life are stronger even than a thundering great war not a hundred miles away.

One evening I went to a reception given for Bertrand Russell by Mrs. Hamilton at her apartment near the Thames Embankment, which, in the dark and deserted streets, I had the deuce of a time finding. It was a crowd of "intellectuals," nearly all pacifists. Bertrand Russell was the hero of the occasion because he was under arrest and would shortly be tried for sedition. He expected to be locked up and set to sewing mail bags—this distinguished scholar and philosopher, coming from one of the most notable families in England. I had opportunity for only a few minutes' conversation with him in that buzzing group, but he invited me to come to see him.

I was somewhat surprised at Professor Russell's appearance, for I had anticipated some signs of pugnacity. He was a man of slight frame, not tall, with a rather small head, iron-gray hair, a red face and a receding chin. He had a quiet, almost diffident, manner. He referred frankly but ironically to his coming trial. He seemed to enjoy the prospect of martyrdom.

I met one or two people at the reception who wanted to stop short off, anywhere: any peace was better than war. Among these was Sir Hugh Bell, the great steel man. Scotchy, gray-bearded, blue-eyed, and extremely contentious. Before we had been talking two minutes he sprang upon me with the proposition that Wilson was a "jingo," and that it was a great misfortune that America came into the war at all, for the carnage was thus indefinitely prolonged. Finally, when I got a chance, I asked him bluntly if he would stop fighting now in the midst of the battle.

"If you have hold of a pig by the ears, and he is after you, you can't let go, can you?" he replied.

These detached intellectuals! Afterward, I walked home through the wet, dark streets of London—thousands upon thousands of more or less stupid human beings, all bearing the terrible anxieties of the war, but going steadily straight forward: enduring and fighting. The great masses of people in this England were certainly behind the war to the very end.

CHAPTER XXXVI

I Meet Several Lords, a Former Prime Minister, and a Labor Leader

I LEARNED THAT Lord Lansdowne was to speak in the House of Lords, where the new Irish conscription bill was to have its first reading. Lord Charnwood invited me to attend. Just as we were entering he pointed out to me an odd-looking chap who was hobbling down the corridor ahead of us.

"That," he said, "is our half-witted member. In an hereditary body like this, it must occasionally happen that some degenerate scion of the old stock has a seat, and of course he always presents himself on important occasions."

I related this incident afterward to a member of the House of Commons.

"Never mind," he said, laughing, "he became quite indistinguishable as soon as he took his seat."

The House of Lords was a beautiful and dignified old room, with fine wood carving, comfortable spaces, and subdued colors that blessed the eye—withal, a wonderful simplicity. The speaker wore an enormous and rather ridiculous wig and the secretaries had smart little curls, like fresh pine shavings, all over their heads. About a hundred peers of the realm were present, looking as a group not unlike our Senate, although there were, I think, fewer young men. I had heard it called a dying institution, but like an old, old man, with much experience of life, it had a kind of impartial wisdom—to which no one paid much attention. The speech by Lord Lansdowne, balancing all the issues presented and spoken without the remotest passion or even energy, seemed to me one of the wisest monologues upon a burning question I ever heard, but it came to no effective decision whatever. It was wise with the neutrality of great age. Lord Peel presented the bill in a quiet speech and it was supported by Lord Salisbury, a terrific Tory bitterly opposed to Irish Home Rule. Lord Londonderry and Lord Buckmaster and others made speeches—all probably counting for nothing much, since Lloyd George, the fiery little Welsh commoner, had ordered the passage of the bill and these poor lords were merely maintaining their right to pat or poke it on its way through. Afterward it would be passed onward, with immense solemnity, to the King, who, so far as vital legislation was concerned, was also maintaining an empty prerogative. What a huge fabric of seemingly useless ceremony clings around this British government!

All were in reality dancing to the tune of the little Welshman. One could not but admire his audacity, his willingess to stake his political life upon whatever measures he had at heart at the moment, and the helplessness of his innumerable enemies to stop him. Gentlemen, aristocrats, commoners, or "bounders"—he worked with them all. No one seemed to dare to touch him. I wondered if I should not wind up by admiring him.

Lord Charnwood took me out to his country seat at Lichfield, north of Birmingham—two or three hours' ride in a crowded train. It was a fine old place, a fine old town, a notable cathedral. Stowe House was mentioned in Samuel Johnson's letters, since he was a frequent visitor there. The house had been occupied by Maria Edgeworth's father, and later by the Thomas Day who wrote that impossible boys' book, *Sandford and Merton,* wry memories of which I had from my childhood. The place was not large but the surroundings, the garden, the distant view across Stowe water to the Cathedral, were exquisite. Lady Charnwood's mother, Mrs. Thorpe, a lively, cultivated old lady, lived with them, and there were several children: an older boy in Eton, a daughter with a Burne-Jones face, and a little chap of seven or eight, very solemn, who, when I asked him if he liked jam, replied, "Yes, do you?" In the evening we went to the vesper service at the Cathedral, which I enjoyed.

I found here, for contrast with the misery of working-class conditions which I had been seeing, glimpses of upper-class English country life, the leisurely comfort of it—which will probably never be again. I was taken care of by a manservant who looked a little like a United States senator: my bag unpacked, my clothes brushed and folded, my bath prepared, a hot-water bottle put in my wondrously comfortable bed, and tea and biscuits brought upon my awakening—all in a way unknown with us in the United States.

These people saw plainly the vast revolution the war portended, with Demos arising out of the flames of the conflagration, and felt that nothing again would be the same. This charming, comfortable, refined life of the few, living upon unearned income, would all be swept away, and with it many amenities and beauties of life, and yet they did not shrink from going forward. And the Master of the House leisurely read American history and wrote a really excellent life of Lincoln.

I dined with Lord Eustace Percy, the son of the Duke of Northumberland, at the Cavendish Club. He had just returned from America where he had been attached to the British Embassy—a charming and likable young man. He had been at Oxford and before the war was one of a group of young Tories interested in social reforms. He was for a time resident in an East End settlement. In America, he was in sympathy with the Bull Moose party. It was amusing to find Englishmen so strong for democratic movements in America and so doubtful about them at home. We talked until nearly midnight, deeply to my enjoyment.

It was plain that the young lord was eager to take the democratic view of life, but one had only to scratch him a little here and there with comments on British conditions to find how deeply the Tory tradition was ingrained. His opinions on the state, the church, the British navy, his sense of *noblesse oblige* toward dependent people (which is a very different thing from the democratic relationship), the suspicion of popular education, the want of downright trust in human beings, were all apparent as one got through the superimposed intellectual sympathies.

The first instinct of so many of the Englishmen I met was to treat me politely as an American—and America just then was a tremendously important factor in the war, especially economically. But once I began to express myself about British conditions, perhaps more strongly than I felt, I was rewarded (and sometimes well beaten as in some of my talks with the redoubtable Lord Percy) by the good stout give-and-take of honest argument—which was what I wanted.

Lord Percy was a member of the Round Table group which sat in close around Mr. Lloyd George. Josiah Wedgwood said that the struggle in the future for the leadership in world affairs would be between the Round Table and President Wilson, and that the Round Table would win. It was really a Tory group headed by Lord Milner, who was a kind of Bismarckian socialist. It was both imperialistic and federalistic. Oliver, the talented biographer of Alexander Hamilton, was one of the group.

"The Round Table," I wrote in my notebook, "represents an admirable, honest, and patriotic group of men, but their interests are:

"1. Primarily, in building up a British Commonwealth on a federal basis.

"2. Secondarily, in arranging a world-dominating Anglo-Saxon alliance of English-speaking people.

"3. Failing both, in a League of Nations.

"They might be ever so effective in the first two and not accomplish what seems to some of us the great purpose of the war. It is only by some form of a league of free nations that wars can be prevented in the future. Leadership in the larger, constructive measures for a league of nations must rest with Wilson and America."

Through the kindness of Professor Gilbert Murray, I was able to meet Mr. Asquith. He lived in a solidly respectable old house, three stories and mansard, buff stuccoed, facing on Cavendish Square. I expected to find a tall man, slight in frame, but he was a robustly built, erect old gentleman with white hair brushed back from his ruddy forehead. He had a large, full face with a prominent nose, and a chin which, in profile, was set down broadly into a full-fleshed throat. His eyes had the variegated and broken pupils of age. He was alert in his motions, and while talking stood with his back to the fire, or paced up and down the room. He wore a wrinkled blue lounge suit.

His study, in the front of the house, was that of the scholar, altogether a place of fine dignity with book-lined walls and engravings of famous Englishmen—and Napoleon over the mantel. He was a scholar, a lover of neatly turned phrases and the worthy expression of sound ideas. His book of mild addresses, then just published, was that of the cultivated gentleman, loyal to his government even though it was led by his personal enemies; chivalrous to opponents; strong in preserving traditional coolness of discussion and decision even in the heat of war; anxious to lead, but not to force public opinion; in all ways quite the reverse of Mr. Lloyd George, Lord Northcliffe, and all that ruthless group of fighters then in power in British politics.

He was the kind of Englishman who had tended in times past to look upon politics—and war too—as a kind of high-grade sport, a gentlemanly game. So many of the fine younger men who held this view were slaughtered at Mons.

When Lord Northcliffe returned from America, he had made this comparison of Asquith and Wilson.

"Both of them," he said, touching his forehead, "are strong up here, but Wilson is also strong down here"—touching his chin—"and I will lay my wager in this war on the man who is strong down here"—again touching his chin.

In talking of Mr. Wilson, it seemed significant, or at least interesting, that Mr. Asquith's first comment should be:

"You have a President who can use the English language."

He asked me if Mr. Wilson had great power as an orator. I said I thought he appealed more powerfully to small groups of thoughtful people than to huge popular audiences.

"Roosevelt is probably stronger there," he said, "but what turgid floods of commonplace!"

Speaking of the League of Nations, Mr. Asquith said that he had been one of the earliest to suggest it, but that the idea had been given a great impetus by Mr. Wilson. He believed in it thoroughly, but thought it would require careful consideration and could not be hastily developed. It was difficult to get for it any proper consideration while everyone was absorbed by war. He felt that American liberalism was essentially in agreement with British liberalism, of which the present British Government was non-representative. He thought that Irish conscription was "more than a mistake—it was a tragedy."

He spoke of the need of national unity at such a time and said that no man should consider mere political advantage. He was not afraid of the task of forming a new Government if it were presented to him, but he must be sure of a mandate from the country.

About this time also I was seeing some of the ablest radical leaders in England, who interested me greatly. One of them was George Lansbury, so different in type from any labor leader I had known in America. He was the editor of *The Herald*, the Labor paper having the largest circulation in England. He invited me to lunch with him and his staff of able young radicals.

Lansbury was a burly Englishman with a cropped beard, ardent blue eyes, and a mellow and emotional voice—a cockney in his speech. And a Christian—really a Christian! He had the love of men and of God in his heart. He was not at all a thinker, rather an evangelist, strong and happy in a creed that satisfied him. There was no logic in him, except the incontrovertible logic of good will. He hated war and believed in Utopia but argued that there could not be any real solution of the vexing problems of the day without a change in the spirit of men. War was wrong: peace was right. It was as simple as that! He was for a League of Nations but would make peace, if he could, without getting it. He wanted democracy, but would negotiate with the Germans in the faith that if peace could be secured, the democratic forces in Germany would operate to overturn the Hohenzollern tyranny. And curiously, while he discarded military force as a method, he would eagerly adopt economic force for compelling the Germans to do this or that. He spoke of the "economic weapon"—to starve human beings with "economic weapons" seemed somehow better to him than to puncture them with bayonets.

I was told by a good friend that I should see Philip Snowden, "one of the clearest headed radical leaders in England." I found that he was campaigning in a by-election in Northern England, but Mrs. Snowden, also an ardent socialist, invited me to luncheon at a curious little radical club in Soho. I found her to be a vivid, able, clear-speaking woman. Although opposed to the Government and seeking the earliest possible peace by negotiation, she said that the I. L. P. group (the Independent Labor Party) was not by any means for "peace at any price," and that no one wanted to stop in the midst of the battle then going on.

The leadership of the I. L. P. was mostly "intellectual" or "middle-class" but the mass was Labor, and seemed to be growing. While it constituted the left wing of the new Labor party, there were extremists still beyond—like the extremists of the British Socialist party.

The chief demands of the I. L. P. were these:

1. That the Allied Governments declare their exact war aims, renounce all secret treaties, and make it clear that they had no selfish purpose of aggrandizement.

2. That they take their stand with President Wilson upon the principles of self-determination of nationalities.

3. That they declare for a real League of Nations with extensive powers.

"If we get ourselves right," said Mrs. Snowden, "and take our stand firmly upon a disinterested policy, we stand a better chance of winning the confidence of the German democrats. They do not trust Lloyd George or Clemenceau any more than we do. If we show that we are not fighting in any way for aggrandizement and the Germans do not then come around, we can go on fighting with a free conscience."

One of my pleasures during all this period, a pleasure that was also a great opportunity, was the many conversations I had with Ambassador and Mrs. Page. I recall one of them especially. They had gone to Sandwich, on the English Channel, for a brief vacation; the Ambassador was not only worn out, he was ill. I was invited for a week-end.

It was a most beautiful trip through the rolling fields and hills of Kent, and, the day being perfect, I enjoyed it keenly. Major Astor had loaned them his beautiful shore house, almost the only one in all that region that had not been turned over to the coast defense. The hotel, not far off, was used as army headquarters. Anti-aircraft guns were everywhere scattered along the hillside and on the golf links; there were trenches and wire entanglements near the shore. One anti-aircraft gun was nearly in front of the house, and during the raid on the Sunday night I was there it kept up a hot barrage fire. One would think it the last place in the world for a vacation: but the

Pages seemed not to mind it in the least. The name of the Astor estate was "Rest Harrow." "Harrowed Rest" would have been better.

"The Ambassador," I wrote in my diary, "is a delightful companion, as is Mrs. Page: a man essentially sound and sweet, and his years of experience here in London have not in the least changed him. I have never known anyone, I think, with such graces of tactful humor.

"I had long talks with the Pages—full of the most interesting narratives of their experiences in London. They have been everywhere and seen everyone, including, of course, royalty. Mr. Page has started an autobiography for his children, the opening chapter of which he read to me. If only he would write indiscreetly—but can any Ambassador ever do that?"

At noon three members of the Embassy Staff appeared in an automobile, having driven down from London, and I went back with them, whirling through the beautiful country roads, flashing past quaint villages, and with one stop of half an hour at Canterbury, reached London in less than three hours. But it was a sin to rush through such perfect country and see so little of it.

CHAPTER XXXVII

A Rebellious Ireland and My Report of What I Saw

LLOYD GEORGE'S DEMAND for Irish conscription had swiftly developed a nation-wide crisis; threatening repercussions in Ireland and bitter new attacks upon the Lloyd George Government. On April 29 I had a cablegram from the State Department asking me to look into the problems of Irish conscription.

I had already had several conversations with Sir Horace Plunkett, who seemed to me one of the soundest men I had seen—wise, brave, and quiet. No man in the Empire had done more than he in recent years for the economic and social reconstruction of Ireland, chiefly through the development of agricultural co-operation. He invited me to go with him to Dublin. His man met us at Kingstown on the morning of May 1 and took us out to his beautiful estate, called Kitteragh, at Fox Rock—which was afterward burned down by a rebellious mob. The crisis was imminent. The British Government was sending in troops, artillery, flying machines and the like, in part to prevent revolutionary disorders, in part to be prepared for a conceivable German attack on the west coast of the island. We heard that a German submarine had recently landed ammunition in one of the wild coves well-known to revolutionary Irishmen.

In Dublin that day, I had a long talk with one of Sir Horace's principal associates, the Irish poet and editor, George W. Russell, "A. E.," who was a leading Irish nationalist. A great, shaggy-headed man with a ruddy face, crisp beard, and spectacles, he was sitting crouched over a little coal fire where a pot of potatoes kept wildly boiling over. The walls of his study were covered with painted frescoes of his own doing. I found him in a rebellious and pessimistic mood. His friends had told me that since he resigned in disgust from the Irish convention ("it gagged me to sit with them any longer") and especially during the last few weeks since the British Government had enacted the Irish conscription law, he had grown more radical and more hopeless. He could see little chance now of curing the difficulty without bloodshed. He hated war, he said, and could not see that the Allies were fighting for anything more than the old selfish ends.

"We come to resemble that which we fight, as your Emerson said, and before this war is over we—and you, too, in America—will be as autocratic and militaristic as Germany."

He thought it was pure hypocrisy for the British to talk of fighting for the rights of small nations and continue to treat Ireland in the manner she had. Civilization as we knew it, he said, was being destroyed—possibly a good riddance—and it was not improbable that the world was about to enter a dark age: a long period of hopeless anarchy. He spoke with the utmost passion, like some modern Jeremiah, upon the sorrows of the new Jerusalem.

Later, I heard the most revolutionary talk from labor leaders whom I went to see. They hated the British so passionately that they even wanted to see them beaten.

"If England wins, Ireland is doomed to many years more of English rule. Germany has never done us any wrong, but we are not pro-German: we are anti-English: we are pro-Irish."

I found everywhere, even among steady-headed men, the conviction that the Irish would fight desperately before submitting to conscription.

A few days later, at the invitation of John Dillon, who was then the leading Irish nationalist member of Parliament, I traveled across Ireland to County Mayo. I saw British soldiers everywhere: guarding bridges and railroad stations as though this were a hostile country. Signs of great prosperity were abundant: cattle and sheep in the green fields, the land newly dug and the spring crops starting, cottages freshly thatched and white-washed, and the peasantry well-clad and comfortable looking. Ireland had suffered not at all from the war, except for the slight losses of volunteer soldiers. I saw more young men of stout military age not in uniform than I had seen in all England. Food was plenty: when we came in to dinner that night at Mr. Dillon's home in Ballaghaderreen there was a huge roast of beef at one end of the table and a huge leg of mutton at the other; and white bread. They had had no rationing system as yet and had been short only of sugar.

The next morning, Sunday, there was a tremendous meeting in the central square of the town. "No conscription" posters had everywhere been posted over the government recruiting notices. The revolutionary leader of Sinn Fein, De Valera, was there, escorted down the main street like a conquering hero—a tall, rather fine-looking, dark man, wearing a plush hat and black leather leggings, and carrying a little stick—the man of the hour. Thousands of men came marching into town, part Nationalist and part Sinn Fein—old opponents temporarily united. Fifteen bands! Hundreds of flags bearing the legends, "No blood tax," "No conscription." It was a wholly orderly meeting with good addresses by Dillon, De Valera, and a priest named Flanagan.

The speakers were on a platform set upon beer kegs and as the crowd increased everyone tried to climb up on it, so that the speakers were nearly crowded off. First the boards broke through, then the railings, and finally some of the beer kegs tipped over and began to roll down the hill—taking the crowd with them. Symbol of revolution—everyone wants a place on the platform; and everyone presently slides off.

It required no microscopic eye to discover the hatred of England. Even a cry of "God save the Kaiser" elicited cheering. It made one feel the terrible gravity of the situation. The priests plainly were behind the movement: at mass that morning the people put down over £700 ($3500) on a little table in front of the church as a defense fund. I saw one peasant contribute a one-pound note.

Several days later I went to Belfast and Northern Ireland, the heart of the opposition to Irish home-rule. No tougher, less-yielding human beings, I think, ever lived on this green earth than these Scotch-Irishmen. The extreme Ulsterman, it seemed to me, was exactly matched by the extreme Sinn Feiner, both for themselves alone. There seemed to be no spirit of give and take: no desire anywhere for what Mr. Wilson called "accommodation."

I lunched at the Ulster Club with some of the great business men of Northern Ireland. They were all rich and powerful, vigorous and efficient, and because they were prosperous and contented under present conditions, resented any change. They believed that Britain would never dare coerce them because their production of ships, rope, motors, linen and the like was necessary to the conduct of the war.

"British soldiers will not fire on us while we are holding up the imperial flag."

I shall not soon forget the force with which one of these men brought his great hairy fist down upon the table, closing, forthwith, any further discussion of Home Rule.

"We won't have ut."

It seemed to me a kind of symbol of the character of these northern Irish: obstinate, dour, strong. They may be broken: they do not bend.

I had visits and long talks with many other Irish leaders, both South and North: and cabled what I found to the State Department. I concluded my report with this remark:

> I have often thought, since I have been over here this time, that the Englishman at his best is about the finest product of civilization now to be found on earth, but when one sees what he has done, collectively, in Ireland, one is tempted to think him the stupidest. I was at dinner the other night with a group of delightful English people and the manner in which they discussed the Irish question—"a little blood-letting will do no harm"—was positively terrifying, and made one feel that if ever the British Empire went to smash it would be upon that green island west of the Irish sea. . . .

On June 13 I lunched, on the invitation of Granville Barker, the British playwright, with Mr. and Mrs. Sidney Webb. There were two really notable intellectual groups in England—the Round Table group, and the Webbites (the Fabian Society). Both pulled strings behind the political screen. The Round Table group supported the Government, the Webbites the new Labor party. One was pre-eminently interested in foreign imperial affairs, and included Lionel Curtis, Philip Kerr, A. E. Zimmern, Lord Eustace Percy, F. S. Oliver, Colonel Amery—with Lord Milner, the tutelar saint.

The other, less well integrated group was profoundly interested in domestic affairs and included the most thoughtful of the radicals—

the Webbs, Bernard Shaw, G. D. H. Cole, and others, though they often did not agree among themselves. Webb had written the program of social reconstruction for the Labor party which was so widely heralded in England and in America. He was the real intellectual force behind Henderson and the Labor party.

I had somehow imagined Webb, whose books and pamphlets on labor subjects I had been reading for many years, as a big, slow, hairy man. He was hairy, but small, alert, quick-minded, with a rather dogmatic professorial air. He had bushy hair and eyebrows not very gray, and a full beard and moustache, much yellowed with tobacco. He had a prominent nose and a full red face, and wore glasses with black rubber rims anchored by a cord somewhere below so that when they fell off they could be quickly retrieved. He had remarkably small, well-formed, white hands and wore a noticeable ring. His dress was careless. Beatrice Webb was taller than her husband, and had a face of fine dignity and serenity. I liked her on the spot. She had thoughtful dark eyes, dressed all in black, and smoked her cigarette with easy grace. To sit between the Webbs—"between the lion and the unicorn," as Barker expressed it—and be instructed in the laws of economic affairs, was surely one of the great experiences of life. Everything was documented with immense knowledge. The fields were all clearly laid out, and neatly surrounded by hedges. Each laborer was assigned his proper place, and his value exactly estimated, so that the chance visitor in these vineyards (like myself) might have no misconceptions. One felt not only that he was learning about the labor problem in England but that he was actually in the presence of it.

I found the Webbs great admirers of President Wilson, and anxious for a better understanding between the democratic groups of England and the United States.

It appeared clear to me in those days when the fighting in France was so near and so bitter, with the outcome still hanging in the balance, that Wilson's prestige was growing more rapidly than ever before.

The *Manchester Guardian* on June 11 said of Wilson's leadership:

Perhaps the greatest and commonest mistake which men make is to regard idealism as a sort of sentimental weakness, all very well for the cloister or the academy, but quite unsuited for the rough work of life and useless to the practical man. On the contrary, it is ideals which dominate the world, and nothing great is accomplished without them. The Americans are a fairly hard-headed and business-like people, yet they are more than almost any people open to the appeal of what is often derisively called sentiment. . . .

Mr. Scott, recognized as one of the great editors of England, who was undoubtedly the writer of this editorial, then propounded a question which seemed to me to need asking and answering again and again:

. . . What is idealism? It is the appeal of the higher emotions—to pity, to justice, to generosity, to devotion, to sacrifice; and anyone who knows anything of the springs of human conduct in at least the higher races knows that the emotions represented by these terms are by far the strongest by which men can be swayed. Even now it is a misdirected idealism, devotion to perverted yet strictly impersonal ends, which is the strength of the German nation, and it can be defeated only by an idealism truer and higher than its own . . .

I recognized, of course, that this strong English approval came chiefly from liberal and labor sources. The more conservative groups, if skeptical regarding the substance of Wilson's idealism, kept quiet about it and bowed down eagerly enough before the unanswerable argument of armed men that America was then sending into France.

On that same day A. G. Gardiner also said in his comments in the *Daily News*:

When the history of the war comes to be written the speeches of President Wilson will shine out like beacon lights in the darkness. . . .

"If it were not for Wilson's leadership during this crisis," I wrote in my notebook, "the world of thoughtful men would be a dark place indeed. I have moments of being proud of my country."

Another powerful supporter of Wilson's ideals had appeared just at that time. This was Viscount Grey, who had come out with a pamphlet on "The League of Nations" in which he took his stand strongly with the President. I learned that he had done this only after consulting with many of his friends and supporters, so that the publication represented the considered movement of quite a group of leading Liberals. This pamphlet carried great weight, for Grey was looked upon as one of the most trusted leaders in England. I found that he had even been suggested as a successor to Lloyd George, but when the matter was put before him formally he responded by telling the story of a certain old Chinese philosopher who had retired from public life to a desert place. Affairs became so complicated that the Emperor sent messengers to invite him to come back. He listened to them patiently and then went away and washed his ears. This was the only comment Grey had to make upon the suggestion that he return to public life.

At the same time that I was seeing much of liberal and labor leaders, I was also meeting various members of the Round Table group. I had a long talk with Philip Kerr * at 10 Downing Street. We had tea together. He had been with Lord Milner in South Africa, and was then Mr. Lloyd George's secretary, and one of his closest advisers. He came from a distinguished old family, went to Oxford, and represented the highest type of British character and culture. An unusually handsome man personally, of the intellectual type, with characteristic English blue eyes, a high-bridged nose, and broad forehead, he was one of the most attractive and charming men I met in England.

It was plain that these Round Table men were more interested in British imperial reorganization than in the League of Nations. They believed in the League, but as something rather distant. The war must first be won. They were anxious to have the League explained before they came out for it. Their knowledge of foreign affairs and their realization of the complications which any international arrangement would involve, made them hesitant and skeptical.

I also called on Colonel Buchan † who was most cordial. We talked chiefly of Lord Milner, the leader of the Round Table group, and I found that Buchan had been his private secretary in India and had the highest admiration for him. Buchan said Lord Milner had played a far greater part in the conduct of the war than most people

* Philip Kerr, afterward Lord Lothian, Ambassador to the United States.
† Colonel Buchan, afterward Lord Tweedsmuir, Governor General of Canada.

realized, that he had been the chief instrument in bringing about unified military command in the person of General Foch, and that he was the most unselfish and devoted of men with no idea but to serve the Empire and bring about a better world commonwealth. Colonel Buchan invited me to dinner to meet him.

The very next day I had quite a contrary view of Lord Milner, probably closer to the popular opinion in England. This came from A. G. Gardiner, editor of the *Daily News*. He said that the liberals generally regarded Milner as a dangerous man: a Prussian in his ultimate beliefs. He cited his record in South Africa as an imperialistic organizer, his efforts to bring in coolie labor, his land-policy of colonizing British people among the Boers, thus doing in South Africa just what Germany was trying to do in Poland. That he had seized upon the imagination of enthusiastic young men of the Kerr, Curtis type, made him all the more dangerous.

I tried to summarize my findings briefly in my letters to the State Department, some of which, I was told afterward, were sent immediately to the President.

CHAPTER XXXVIII

"The Greatest Conference the Labor Party Ever Held in England"

SIDNEY WEBB HAD URGED ME, especially, to attend the Conference of the British Labor party, called for the last of June. He gave me a platform ticket so that I could hear and see everything that went on.

"It will be the greatest ever held in England," he said. "You ought to attend it straight through."

I attended every day for a week, and found it quite the most revealing exhibit of British opinion I had yet had.

Vigorous attempts had been made by Northcliffe and the conservative press to prove that a split in the ranks of Labor was impending, and that, after all, the Labor party did not really represent the rank and file of the working class. I found that our Labor delegates, Gompers and others, well instructed while they were in England, were spreading the same doubts in America.

It was plain from the very beginning of the Conference that violent extremes did exist in the movement, but it was also plain that the forces of determined cohesion were far stronger than those of disruption. Labor knew well that if they were to secure their objectives they must sternly put down their differences. All of the ablest leaders, from the conservative Mr. Barnes of the War Cabinet to the Radical pacifist Mr. Snowden, were there—and all were striving to maintain Labor unity, and to prepare for the coming elections with a strong social program.

The vital problem of the Conference—as anticipated—was the attitude of Labor toward the Lloyd George Government.

They were well aware of the power they had. Vernon Hartshorn, head of the Welsh miners—as hard as nails and as practical as mackerel for breakfast—told me that the Welsh miners could, if they desired, stop the war in a few weeks. They could strike. With the German offensive the French coal supply had been further depleted and South Wales had to make up the deficit.

"But," said Hartshorn, "it is a question with us how to use our power to the best advantage in securing democratic aims."

It was an extraordinarily well conducted conference, and greatly increased my admiration for the genius in self-government of the British people. One of the incidents of the Conference provided "the most dramatic surprise that ever happened at a Labor gathering."

"In the midst of the absorbing debate," I wrote in my notes that night, "I saw, from where I sat on the platform, a dark, foreign-looking young man coming up the steps. He was so strikingly different in appearance from the average stocky, ruddy Englishman and Scotchman, so tall, with such a pale, set face, red-lidded eyes and powerful jaws, that he at once attracted attention. No one on the stage or in the audience of a thousand or more delegates seemed to know who he was. When he had advanced several steps down the platform Arthur Henderson turned to greet him as though he were just another Labor leader, and quite the funniest thing of all happened. The visitor stooped over and kissed Henderson on his broad red cheek—a resounding smack—so evidently unexpected that the Englishman blushed like a schoolgirl. Not many people except those close by on the platform, perhaps fortunately for the decorum of the occasion, saw the episode. Henderson turned quickly to the delegates and introduced the stranger as Kerensky, the Russian leader who, only a few months ago, held all revolutionary Russia in his powerful hands.

"For a moment there was dead silence, for the Russian leader had been conjured to the platform like a rabbit out of a box. No one even knew that he was in London: there had not been a line in any newspaper. He had suddenly disappeared from his great place in Russia, and for months no one had heard of him—and here he was standing before the delegates of the Labor Convention, being introduced in the most matter-of-fact way by the presiding officer. It was so utterly undramatic that it was intensely dramatic.

"The true Englishman abominates having his phlegmatism tampered with. I sat where I could look into the faces of the delegates and I have rarely seen quite such an expression of mass embarrassment—and then angry wonder, and outraged skepticism. The uproar, which was by no means wholly complimentary, came later.

"Kerensky delivered an impassioned address in Russian, harsh, strong, challenging, which was poorly translated into English by a companion. It was an eloquent appeal for stricken Russia.

"No one seems to know just why Henderson should have staged such a drama, or introduced such a player, unless it was to emphasize, in the midst of the engrossing discussion of domestic problems, the international aspects of the labor movement."

I append here a few paragraphs from my report to the State Department, sent on July 8, since they express certain conclusions I had been coming to.

In my letter the other day I referred to the new Labor party as the most precious and vital force in British life today. There is no doubt of the growing power of the party. The successful conference . . . with the exhibition it gave of essential political unity, added greatly to its prestige. It is today the best organized party in England, with the clearest policy and the greatest sense of real power behind it . . .

But it should not be forgotten for a moment that while the Labor movement generally is in sympathy with Mr. Wilson's democratic policies, and indeed incorporated them in its statement of War Aims, there is a strong element that now begins to fear that the war spirit will run entirely away with America. They feel that America, coming freshly and enthusiastically into the war, will become so intent on a "knock-out blow" that it will fail to seize upon opportunities that may arise to secure a democratic peace by diplomatic means. It must not be forgotten that a large proportion of the Labor party here is socialist with a profound distrust of "capitalistic" and "imperialistic" governments. They have a deep-seated belief that even if the Allies should crush Germany, these imperialistic and capitalistic forces in England and France would be so strong that there would be no assurance that they would seek a really democratic peace; and they also believe in an international conference of working-class parties when the time is ripe for it. No one could attend the recent conference without being convinced of the strength of this feeling. . . .

One other comment should be made in this connection, and that is the great influence Mr. Wilson's speeches have had, all along, upon the labor and liberal groups in England. Several Labor party leaders showed me with satisfaction their pocket copies of the President's "four-point" address at Mt. Vernon, reported in full on July 5 in many British papers.

The *Manchester Guardian* said of it in an editorial:

"President Wilson's speech at the tomb of Washington will take rank with the best of Lincoln's speeches in the Civil War. It is a vindication of the high democratic ideals of the United States in entering the war, which will live in history as long as the vindication of Athens in the speech of Pericles reported in the second book of Thucydides. . . . America is now convinced that the fortune of democracy, not in Europe alone but all over the world, depends on defeat of the German rulers in this war."

It was remarkable how all the Tory papers (and the Northcliffe Press) emphasized the "no compromise" part of this speech: and the liberal press emphasized the idealistic parts, especially those which referred to the organization of a League of Nations. The way in which Wilson gets both the fighters and the reconstructors is marvelous.

About the middle of July, I received a letter from Frank L. Polk, Counselor of the State Department, expressing appreciation of the reports I had been sending and asking me to go to France and Italy in order to report on conditions there. There was a postscript which interested me:

P.S. I should like to suggest that each weekly report be in two sections. One section similar in every respect to the reports you have heretofore made, and the other section to be very brief and to contain simply the summarized conclusions to be drawn from your remarks in the first section.

It is my purpose to send the second section to the President for his information.

I went immediately to France. I had already learned of the restless French labor situation from talks in London with Frenchmen who had come over to confer with the British leaders. But I wished first to see something, for background and balance, of what the war had meant to the people of France—not Paris alone, but the lesser cities and the country villages—and also to see other than labor leaders, and try, as I had done in England, to understand their point of view. It is futile to study any opposition whatsoever without being fully aware of what it is that is being opposed, and how much of reason and of power there is in that opposing position. I traveled the entire length of our American line of communication across the country from St. Nazaire to the front in the Vosges Mountains—Apernez, Nantes, Tours, Chaumont, Neuf Chateau, and

Baccarat. Then Paris again, then the vast battlefield above Chateau Thierry—from Meaux to the shell-torn front—Epieds, Courpoil, and Picardie Farm, where General Edwards had his headquarters and where I slept in a barn with a hole in the roof made a few days before by a cannon shot. I was at Belleau Wood and Vaux, where I was glad to find my brother, Roland, a soldier of our First Division, just out of the terrible ordeal of that bloody battle and still alive. Then Paris again, and long talks with many interesting people.

I wish I had here the space and time to tell of some of the things I saw at the various fronts I visited, the stark realities of war; yet I find that I do not now care to recall most of the things I saw and heard, the sheer bloody horror of them. Besides, we are now in an even bloodier war than the one I saw, and the details of my experience have been overshadowed by this new tragedy.

One incident I can never forget. I saw one of our soldiers die in a miserable cobble-paved courtyard, back of our lines where a temporary hospital had been established. It was near Epieds. He was a fine-looking young fellow, scarcely more than a boy; and his legs had been nearly shot off with machine-gun bullets. He looked around at me once—wistfully. Then he was dead. I asked where he came from and the orderly said, "Rockford, Illinois." Even with the roar of the great battle going on a mile away, I could not get the sight or the thought of that boy out of my mind, indeed out of my very soul. I could not help thinking of that family at home in Rockford, Illinois, waiting, hoping. I knew well those Middle Western towns, I knew well the kind of people who lived in them.

A few things I remember pleasantly, especially the remarks I heard in France regarding our men, that they were "tall," "lean," "stern," and indeed when I saw them, those splendid fellows from Iowa and Nebraska, marching in endless lines toward the battle front in the Forest of Fere, I knew what the Frenchmen meant. Whitman had the right word for it—"aplomb."

I find in my notes this paragraph regarding them—a paragraph I could write then, but not now:

"Endlessly, all one long evening, all the officers on foot with the men, silently, swiftly marching. Youth afoot. Youth, with no back look, no preconception of a narrow and selfish old world. Youth, going forward to fight and die for a better world. And it came to me with such a sense of relief and uplift as I cannot describe, that we older ones with our doubts and fears would not even be consulted. They are the autocrats of the future, these lads, dusty with the dirt of Vaux and Belleau Wood, and muddy now with the clay of the Forest of Fere. They will pass through fire and come to know themselves in a way our untried generation never could have done, and will return with high and stern ideas of what the future must be like. These boys are the voters, the legislators, the builders, the presidents of the future. The world is theirs, not ours. The impressions that they gain, these bold young second lieutenants, suddenly steadied by great responsibility, the impressions of needful discipline, the conviction that many comforts are not essential to human life, the ability they get to judge men by the great simple tests of courage, endurance, decision—the hates, loves and loyalties they acquire under frightful stress—the lesson of the presence of death—these men with no soft schooling in books and dogmas, these men, not the old tired Hindenburgs and Clemenceaus and Curzons, will rule the future."

Later in my trip I went to Belgium, with passes difficult for any civilian to obtain secured for me by my old friend Brand Whitlock, who was the American Minister there. I saw ruined Nieuport, and the bitterly defended front line trenches along the Iser Canal where soldiers of both German and Belgian armies had been spending years of their lives in mud and dust, among ruined towns, to the point, in some cases, of insanity. I remained two nights in La Panne, the last foothold of the Allies in Belgium, where the King made his headquarters, and where bombs were dropped by the Germans on both nights I was there—they hoped to get the King.

But the important part of my visit to Belgium was the long talks I had with Whitlock, who was at that time one of the best-informed Americans on the continent of Europe. I found him the gifted observer I had known, with a rare equipment of direct experience to draw upon. His approach was that of the tested liberal; indeed, the last time I met him before the outbreak of the war, I had considered him an out-and-out pacifist. He gave me a survey of the situation in bloody Europe which I could, perhaps, have secured in no other way. He knew personally most of the leaders in both France and England and many in Germany, and his judgments of them seemed to me soundly informative. He was able also to speak with confidential knowledge of the Americans who were coming over—of the excellence of some of them, and the blundering deficiencies of others—all most helpful to me.

The American Ministry, driven out of Belgium, had taken refuge on the cliffs above Le Havre in France. I came down from La Panne, a Homeric ride two hundred miles or more, along the coast of France. I left at three o'clock in the morning in a motor car driven by a Belgian courier—such a ride, often over roads that had been bombed, as I hoped never again to have to make.

Whitlock had grown gray since I last saw him, and no wonder. What sensitive man could have gone through the German invasion of Belgium—the destruction of ancient cities and the incalculable tragedy of the loss of human life, tens of thousands of innocent women and children killed, wounded or homeless, and the flower of the youth of Belgium destroyed—and not been shaken to the roots of his being?

Whitlock quoted the passage in the Bible from which Kipling took the title of one of his books, *Many Inventions*.

"Lo, this only have I found, that God hath made man upright; but they have sought out many inventions."

I thought of all this as I saw the sky at La Panne full of flying machines; saw the poison gas rising in noxious yellow fumes beyond the horizon on the battlefield of Chateau-Thierry; heard the clanking advance of the huge steel leviathans, the armed tanks; and grew cold with the shock of the explosion of mighty guns in the low valley of the Marne.

Whitlock gave me, as always, the feeling of great understanding, sympathy, charm. But like so many thoughtful men of fine instincts, who before the war were pacifist and humanitarian, he sorrowfully admitted that he was now hopelessly confused in his outlook. Fine natures suffer under the lash of such events. As regards the Germans he had formed stern judgments; all the more impressive for their low-voiced finality.

"When I see what they have done," he said, "it seems sometimes as though, before we get through with it, we shall have to destroy a large part of the race."

"That sounds hard from a pacifist," interrupted Mrs. Whitlock, "but you don't know what it means to live for four years in such an atmosphere of violence and cruelty."

In a report to the State Department on July 27, I set forth my first, more or less hasty, conclusions as follows:

One is strongly impressed, here as in England, that the sincerest support of American war aims as voiced by President Wilson is found among the radical and Labor groups. Here as in England one often has the uncomfortable feeling that the Government leaders support Wilson more or less with their tongues in their cheeks, as a matter of policy. They want our powerful armies and our vast money resources, but they really think our war aims, as expressed by Mr. Wilson, a kind of moonshine. More and more as our power increases, as our achievements give us the right to take a stronger stand, must we furnish the constructive and unifying leadership. There has got to be greater unity all along the line and a clearer agreement upon war aims. It is appropriate that military unification should be in French control. They are closely in contact with the war: it is on their own soil: but one cannot look to the French (or even to the British) for the greater moral and political leadership. They are too close to the actual fighting; men cannot think with guns going off in their front yards. They are even less interested here than in England in the League of Nations, or in any constructive policy. All thought here is centered upon rooting the Germans out of France: getting them away from Paris so that Big Bertha will not be shooting into churches, and killing orphans. One sometimes actually feels like a kind of fool theorist to introduce here the subject of the League of Nations. No, great constructive leadership has got to come from America.

CHAPTER XXXIX

I Report to Washington on the Threat to American Objectives

I HAD A MESSAGE at Paris from Mr. Polk suggesting that I prepare, as soon as I could, a summary of my findings regarding the situation in England. Accordingly, I returned immediately to London, coming to Southampton by the mailpacket which was guarded by three destroyers. London, again in fog and rain. It was like getting home; the very *smell* of London was good in my nostrils.

That afternoon when I went out, the boys were shouting on the streets,

"Splendid victory! Americans win great victory! Splendid victory!"

The paper I bought contained the headlines,

HUNS DRIVEN IN CONFUSION ACROSS THE VESLE

AMERICANS CAPTURE 8,400 PRISONERS AND 133 GUNS

These were the very Americans I had seen so recently marching to the front: they had crushed the Soissons-Rheims salient.

As I went about I was conscious of a profound change that had been going on in England during the few weeks that I had been away. War weariness, it was plain, was rapidly increasing; and at the same time the more favorable turn of the war in France was bringing to the front the unsettled problems of the coming peace. These changing conditions found expression at both extremes of the social scale: the spread of the peace-by-negotiation movement among the rich, and the drift to the left of the radical groups. Both sides had suddenly become anxious as to what the peace might bring, how it would affect the interests of each.

Lord Inchcape, for example, made a speech in the House of Lords lamenting the declining income of the aristocracy. The newspaper account of this was headed "Poverty of Peers."

> . . . What with taxation and the depreciation of the sovereign, said his lordship, a peer's income was now only worth something like £1,800 a year. Assuming the war would end by March 1919, our net national debt would be £6,000,000,000, and our annual expenditure £700,000,000. We were living in a fool's paradise so far as popular notions of prosperity were concerned. It would take the best part of a generation to get back to the position of August 1914 even with the strictest economy. . . .

Other lords joined in the lament. The war was ruining them and it must be stopped immediately.

At the other extreme, I heard when I called at the new Labor party headquarters in Eccleston Square, many evidences of the drift of the whole labor movement in England, as in France, toward the left. There was a deepening irritation with the Lloyd George Government; the leaders felt that Labor was being controlled without consultation or consent. The Government was dominated, they said, by Northcliffe, Beaverbrook, and Hughes of Australia, a group of strident, unthinking reactionaries.

It also seemed to me that Wilson was losing something of his extraordinary hold on the democratic groups of England. It was clear, in all the liberal journals, that doubt was beginning to supplant the former enthusiastic support. The *Manchester Guardian* was questioning his Russian policy. The *Labor Herald* (articles by Brailsford) said his hand had been forced by France. The *Nation* said that the new pronouncements of the Government regarding the tariff destroyed the idea of a League of Nations. The Allied Governments were apparently going ahead with the declaration of an economic policy which threatened everything that America was fighting for.

Were we really fighting for the "commercial and industrial domination of the world"? President Wilson had said we were fighting for a disinterested peace. Was he really being crowded out of his position? Would his policies be twisted out of all semblance to their original meaning? What were we going to get out of our investment of blood and treasure in this war? Mere national safety for France? The interest on Russian bonds owned by the French? Preferential tariffs and more colonies for the British Empire? What was it that we were going to get for ourselves if we desired, as Wilson had said, no material return?

I confess I was greatly cast down by what I found in England. I may have been overly pessimistic—I was certainly worn out, physically and emotionally. I wrote in my diary:

"I am bound to put these facts down honestly as I see them. I admire Wilson profoundly, but at present these are the facts . . . Between the forces of greed and revenge at one end of the scale, and the forces of doubt, weariness, and fear at the other, where now is the trumpet voice of great statesmanship? We must fight on, but we must not let either of these extremes run away with us. The situation seems to have reached the point where mere speeches by Mr. Wilson are not enough: there must be agreement and clear understandings between the Allies. We have got to be as implacable, as exacting, in our purposes as the French or the British are in theirs. We are now in a powerful position to demand what we want; we shall lose that advantage when victory comes."

I had these feelings strong in my mind when I wrote the summaries of the situation in England (and in France as I had been seeing it) which the State Department had requested. I never tried harder to put what I believed to be the truth into a report.

> I confess, coming back from the battlefields and looking about me here in England and France, and indeed hearing some of the echoes from America, I have moments of fear lest our sacrifices go for nothing. It came to me freshly, seeing again the familiar political, diplomatic, and economic forces at work, how difficult it will be to snatch any worthy democratic result from a victory over Germany if the present forces in control in England and France have their way. We do not realize in America even yet how strong these traditional European ambitions and jealousies really are. . . .
>
> The men who are in control both in France and England today are men who, while they eagerly welcome our troops, our supplies and our money, and are earnestly set upon winning the war (just as we are), have for the most part little or no sympathy for our war aims as expressed by Mr. Wilson. . . . They distrust the whole idea of a true League of Nations, they are far more interested in trade preferences and enlarged territory after the war; they believe in disarmament for other nations but not for themselves; what they really want is a new world

domination with themselves and ourselves dominating; what they decidedly do not want is a democratic peace. I am conscious in making these rather sweeping statements that I am perhaps doing injustice to the view of certain members of the Government, but the main indictment is absolutely sound. . . . Here is an editorial from the *London Globe*:

". . . The stakes are the commercial and industrial domination of the world. They are worth playing for and the enemy knows that we hold the trump cards. . . ."

Now, the *Globe* is an extreme reactionary paper, but it expresses only more boldly and clearly what a large number of the most potential leaders in England really believe. Hughes of Australia is now one of the most vociferous spokesmen of England, warmly commended by the Northcliffe press, and his speeches have much the same ring. Northcliffe himself, who is one of the most powerful single individuals in England, has no more real sympathy with Mr. Wilson's war aims on their constructive side than has this writer in the *Globe*. Lord Beaverbrook, who is controlling the vast organ of British propaganda, is not, certainly, working for a democratic peace, and neither are Earl Curzon or Lord Milner. As for Mr. Lloyd George, he is for anything that is uppermost at the moment. He rides exuberantly upon the crest of every wave. He has no yesterday and no tomorrow. Clemenceau, while probably a more dangerous leader so far as our war aims are concerned, is preferable to Mr. Lloyd George, for one knows exactly where he stands and what he will do. . . .

All these things tend to increase Labor unrest. . . . The workers assert that while the government asks them to make unlimited sacrifices of the dearly won fruits of organization, draw on their man power to the limit for war service, accept dilutions of unskilled men, and forego vacations, they allow the manufacturers and capitalists who own the plants to engage in the most ruthless profiteering. Working people point to the enormous dividends of the munitions manufacturers which have been distributed even after taxes upon excess profits have been deducted. . . . I enclose clippings relating to these disclosures . . .

Mr. Wilson's voice during the last year has been the only really unifying and moralizing voice so far heard during the war. To a degree which astonishes every American who comes over here (or goes to France), his leadership has elicited the support of all the best forces of the Allied Nations. He has given them a vision of something really worth enduring and suffering for. *But of late there has been a tendency to question and doubt among the democratic groups which have given him in the past his only honest and sincere support . . .*

Mr. Wilson can never hope for whole-hearted support upon the reconstructive side of his program from those at the moment in power either here or in France . . . I believe that we shall find that we shall have to be as implacable and exacting in securing *our* disinterested purposes—if we are to get anything at all out of our investment of blood and treasure—as these interests in seeking their purposes. The great source of Mr. Wilson's strength is that while each government group over here can command a part of its own people, Mr. Wilson, insofar as his policy is disinterested and democratic, can command large and powerful groups in all the nations. They never can get real unity, because each has a separate and selfish policy, while he can. Therefore we must never let these democrtaic forces in England and France get away from us, which they threaten to do. Mr. Wilson's later speeches have been so balanced that they have had support from both factions here, as I have several times pointed out in these letters, each adopting and interpreting to its own ends the part that it approved. To an extent the *positive* influence of Mr. Wilson has thus been neutralized . . . A unified political leadership is more important at this moment than a unified military leadership.

I had the best of evidence, though it came long afterward, that this letter was placed at once in Mr. Wilson's hands. He himself referred only once, in conversation with me, to my inquiries in Europe in 1918. He was a man always sparing in his spoken approval—far more in his praise—of the work of his associates. If men did their duty why should they be praised for it? It was perhaps a virtue too stern, too cold, but how Woodrow Wilson's friends responded when he did approve! One day after his retirement from the Presidency—he was then living in the S Street home, a broken old man—I was talking with him about the political backgrounds of the Peace Conference and spoke of what I had found in England and France in 1918. After a pause he said quietly:

"Your letters at that time helped me."

Indeed, in his speech in September, soon after he received my summary report—from which I quote above—he made just the points I urged in order to strengthen the democratic forces in England and France in taking a firm stand for our idealistic program. I don't know, of course, that my letters were directly responsible for this action: I like to believe that they helped.

In an autobiography a man perhaps is committed to the explanation of his reactions as well as his actions, even though they may do him no credit. I confess that at the end of six months in war-torn England and France, I had become profoundly disheartened. Mr. Wilson had touched the imagination of the nations as no other leader had done. And it began to seem, now that Allied victory was assured, that everything he stood for, everything that America was fighting for, was endangered, if not already lost. I argued with myself that this might well be a mere personal reaction, I was tired, I had been working too hard—I wanted to go home. But there it was, a reality. War sooner or later gets into a man's soul. All the evidence of universal suffering and cruelty that I had seen in France, that dripped daily from the front into England, suffering I could not relieve, sorrow I could not ease—all these things left me bleak and empty. It was fortunate for me at that time that I had long before discovered a remedy that often in years past had cured my distempers. I had learned to take to the country and the hills.

I find many entries in my notes describing these life-saving excursions. There is no more beautiful land in the world—unless it be New England—than the English and Scotch countryside. I wish I had space here to tell of some of these David-Grayson-like adventures which have been so much a part of my life. I must content myself with one of them: a tramp in the early morning near Bridgend in South Wales, where I had gone to look into a new project in agricultural co-operation.

"I set out in the early morning. A southern mist, not quite rain, upon the distant green hills softened all the landscape into a mysterious and half-wild beauty that was as indescribable as it was charming—for it was like an emotion of nature. The hedges were full of wild sweet roses and along the fields the foxgloves were in bloom: the grass was a wilderness of yellow buttercups and daisies and paintbrush. I found a number of beautiful ancient stiles in the stone fences of which I made sketches, thinking that I could someday —when peace comes—copy one of them at Amherst. The meadows are poor and weedy and look unproductive, but the grain fields, where the old soil has been plowed and put into cultivation, are thrifty enough. Even with all the pressure of war necessity I understand that it is difficult to get these farmers to break up their old fallows.

"The country seemed almost deserted. I saw hardly anyone on a tramp of six miles—even in the romantic old thatched villages, such as Merthyrmawr, which I passed through. I did meet upon the roadside a queer wild-looking old woman—thin, light, shabbily clad, with stringy white hair. She was resting by the roadside and I stopped to ask her the way to Ogmore Castle. She answered in excellent English and with quick wit, baring a mouthful of browned and broken teeth. She asked if I would help her with her load and I saw by the roadside an enormous gunny-bag of faggots that she had been gleaning in the forest. She wanted it lifted to her head. I don't think she herself could have weighed above eighty pounds and the bag was literally as large as she was. It was all I could do to lift it to her head. She staggered a little at first under the weight but soon balanced it, and smiling broadly, exhibiting her brown fangs, she thanked me and then, to cap the climax, walked over to the hedge and picked up a large dry limb which she balanced under her arm and set off down the road—the huge bag of faggots with the little thin old body under it.

"I tramped through Merthyrmawr village and on across a wire-swung bridge and so through the fields to the ruins of the ancient castle of Ogmore—very picturesque in its mantle of ivy. All about were the calm fields, a thatched cottage slept in the valley below, there were sheep and cattle quietly feeding in the upland meadows, and a brown-clad fisherman, pipe in mouth, was whipping the sparkling stream just above the old castle where the current curled out of a placid pond full of rushes. I crossed by a row of ancient and worn stepping stones, walked around the old embattlements, crossed the choked moat and so penetrated to the interior of the castle, now grown up to thick grass, vines and young trees. How I wished then that some power I had could have rolled back the years, over 900 of them—over 500 before Shakespeare—to the days in this wild and beautiful valley when horsemen in bright armor were riding in across the drawbridge where now there is only a ridge of turf, gathering in this resounding stone court, welcomed perhaps by their ladies leaning from the embrasured windows.

"I remained there for a long time in the slumbrous June silence. I forgot all my weariness and all my doubts. A skylark rose singing to the skies, I heard the distant bleating of sheep and there were rooks holding undisturbed dialogue somewhere beyond the walls. So I came back across the stepping stones, lingered to take in anew the picture of the ruined walls against the green hill-lines, and walked back through the fields, stopping awhile to talk with a slow, strong, girl farmer in smock and boots, and a boy riding a great farm horse, and thus with great enjoyment came swinging back into Bridgend with such an appetite for dinner as would make a tenth century knight curl up with envy. I have fallen completely in love with this beautiful land . . ."

Such stolen hours as these, such perfect excursions, gave me releasement: I don't believe I could have endured the strain of my work in England if I could not have had them.

CHAPTER XL

The Last Days of the Great War

I SPENT THE LAST two months of the World War in France and Italy, trying, as I had in England, to understand the underlying currents of public opinion and reporting what I found to the State Department. It was a rich experience, the notes of which would make a book in themselves. What I learned was invaluable to me a little latter as a background of understanding when I became a part of the Peace Conference at Paris.

I visited Milan, Turin, Genoa, Rome, Florence, Venice and other Italian cities; I saw both conservative and liberal leaders; I talked with many editors and students, and I can say truthfully that the commanding interest in Italy at that time was centered upon what Woodrow Wilson was saying, and what the Americans proposed to do in the coming peace conference. In after years I found it difficult to credit this all-but-mystical ardor, even though I was there and saw and felt it. In the cities many walls were placarded with the words of Woodrow Wilson, headed: "Parole Scultore di Wilson" setting forth extracts from his recent speeches. His portrait appeared in innumerable shop windows. I collected a large number of post cards with his picture and many with quotations from his addresses. An Italian editor I knew told me that he had actually seen candles burning underneath Wilson's picture in home windows. I should doubt whether there was ever before in any country such a demonstration of faith in the leader of another nation.

Nor was this devotion confined entirely to the working classes. I found not a few leaders who seemed to have a similar confidence in Wilson and America. I went to call on one of the distinguished scholars of Italy, Luigi Luzzati, once foreign minister of Italy, who had negotiated directly with Bismarck the first commercial treaty of Italy and Germany. He had been the champion of many reforms. He was a dark-skinned, hooked-nosed, burning-eyed old man who wore a black skull cap drawn down until it bent over the tops of his ears, with one flap sticking up like a horn. He read me a statement regarding the war on which he had been working, the paper held about two inches from his eyes. He spoke excellent English but his voice was like thick gruel. He said he respected England, admired France, loved and admired America, and admired and hated Germany. He told of a conversation he had with Bismarck in which Bismarck said:

"The German people fear only God."

To which he had replied, "Your excellency, the Italian people love God and so do not fear him."

In referring to Wilson, he said: "He is a great man; a very great man."

He told me about a series of lectures he was preparing to give at the University of Rome, called, "The Contribution of the United States to the Progress of Constitutional Law in the World." He wished to emphasize the new sense of power, unity, imagination, that America gave to the world under Wilson's leadership.

"The British constitution," this remarkable old Jew said to me, "affords liberty for British citizens, but the United States constitution declares freedom for all men. The English have not known until recently complete religious freedom; the French have declared for religious freedom, but do not practice it; in your unique and admirable country, the principle of religious freedom has not only been adopted, but applied and acted upon."

Luzzati said he had often criticized and attacked the American protective tariff system and disapproved of the speculative character of American business, but that American action since coming into the war had absolved us of all sin.

It became clearer to me as I traveled in Italy and France, as it had in England, that Wilson's real support came from the masses of the people. His words had awakened the passionate faith and understanding of the middle and working classes, who longed for more democracy, more freedom. The old Jew Luzzati spoke truly the feeling of the people, that the United States "declares freedom for all men," and they believed that Woodrow Wilson was the Messiah coming to Europe to bring it to them. They were prepared to give him—

and did give him when he arrived—the greatest and most genuine popular reception ever given any man in modern Italy; but some of us who stood by watching these vast demonstrations of peoples who were expecting, immediately, the coming of the millennium, began to wonder and to doubt.

As the days passed and the excitement and rejoicing increased, both in Italy and in France there were still more disturbing evidences that the new heaven and the new earth would not prove so easily and swiftly attainable. From the middle of October on to the armistice on November 11, each day seemed to bring nearer the miracle of peace in the world—not the terms of it, but the fact of it.

"October 14, 1918. The papers this morning," I wrote in my diary, "contain the announcement of Germany's acceptance of Wilson's terms. *The real trouble is now about to begin!*

"October 16. This morning comes news of the demand of Turkey for an immediate armistice and peace—as usual on Wilson's terms. The Italians have captured Durazzo and the Belgians, with British and French help, have driven forward again on their front, taken eight or ten thousand prisoners, and captured Roulers. Our Americans are advancing in the critical region north of Verdun. The Duchy of Luxembourg has appealed to Wilson for protection; the whole fabric of Prussianism is crumbling in disaster.

"All the papers are full of Wilson.

"November 1, Paris. Such a whirl of events, the very world on fire! Great battles in progress, dynasties crumbling, new nations being born, the statesmen of the world sitting at Versailles to decide the fate of the peoples.

"In America, the Republicans under Roosevelt and Lodge are making a strong fight to return a Congress at the election next week unfavorable to Wilson. American attacks upon him are being given much prominence here in the conservative press. Will Hays, chairman of the Republican National Committee, is reported in the London *Times* as charging that Wilson's 'real purpose' is to reconstruct the world 'in unimpeded conformity with whatever Socialistic doctrines, whatever unlimited Government-ownership notions, whatever hazy whims may happen to possess him at the time . . .'

"The reactionaries in all the Allied countries will read this with glee; and it will help to make the American program for the peace more difficult of realization.

"November 4. This morning we have news of the surrender of Turkey and the opening of the Dardanelles and Bosphorus. Revolutions are breaking out in Vienna and Budapest; the downfall in Austria is complete and Germany cannot, it seems, last much longer.

"November 5. Austria capitulated yesterday at three o'clock. We hear that the British are soon to land in Constantinople. Our Americans are driving north along the Meuse where they have already cut the main line of retreat of the German army by way of Sedan and Metz. We hear that American losses in this fighting are heavy.

"Today also occur the important American elections. The attack of the opponents upon the administration has been unremitting.

"It is a great pity that Americans cannot see what Wilson has done for Europe and how he is regarded here. Our people are in an unthinking mood of warlike fury. They want to 'kill the Kaiser,' and have not yet stopped to look ahead. It is easy, four thousand miles off in America, to talk about 'marching to Berlin.' They haven't seen the mud, nor felt the cold rain of the Argonne. I have talked with many private soldiers and have seen recently a good many men —officers and Y.M.C.A. and Red Cross men who have been closely in contact with the soldiers—and they *don't like war*. They hate it, and want to get home as soon as ever they can.

"November 7. Still wonderful news. Wilson's final transmission of the Allied terms to Germany was made yesterday and they are stiff indeed. It is a fine thing to have full-blown approval of the Wilson program (except that part relating to sea power) set down by the Allies in black and white.

"We heard this morning that the Germans are already sending their white-flag delegation to Foch.

"November 8. Great news this morning. The German representatives are meeting General Foch to ask for armistice terms. The war is practically certain to be over this week. At the last it has come swiftly. The Americans have taken Sedan and have cut the all-important railroad which the Germans might use in their retreat, and the British are close upon the fortress of Maubeuge. Still more threatening for the Germans are the wide disturbances at home. Their fleet is in mutiny and there are strikes at Darmstadt, and other places. Their situation is plainly hopeless.

"News comes from America that the Republicans have carried the House of Representatives and perhaps the Senate. A tragic decision! It will weaken Mr. Wilson, although the new Congress does not sit until next year.

"November 9. The Germans have seventy-two hours from yesterday morning to accept or reject the armistice terms. They must accept, for the whole country is apparently ablaze behind them.

"Paris is now filling up with all sorts of people from all the little corners of the earth, leaders of ambitious new nations, awaiting the coming Peace Conference. About every second man of this type one meets fishes out of his pocket a copy of a cablegram that he or his committee has just sent to President Wilson. It is marvelous indeed how all the world is turning to the President. The people believe he means what he says, and that he is a just man set upon securing a sound peace.

"November 10. The Kaiser has abdicated and there is a full-blown revolution in Germany. News of it was on the streets last night, and at the restaurant where Boyden and I had dinner, girls came in waving the Tri-Color and the Stars and Stripes, and then we all began singing quite spontaneously the 'Marseillaise,' following it by 'Marching through Georgia.' Everyone is awaiting news of the signing of the Armistice.

"November 11. Well, the war is over!"

Even before the Armistice was signed believers in a democratic peace along the lines laid down by Woodrow Wilson had begun to be anxious, if not actually discouraged, by the many new difficulties that began to arise. I find notes in my diary referring to these doubts:

"When one sees the ugly forces that exist in the various nations, the greedy, half-acknowledged territorial ambitions, the desire to reap commercial benefit from the war, the secret hostility among the victorious nations, one dreads the future, and wonders if peace can be had without the Allies flying at one another's throats."

I thought, also, a great deal about Wilson's own problems, and of his destiny.

"Wilson has yet to prove his greatness," I wrote in my notes some days before the Armistice. "The fate of a drama lies in its last act, and Wilson is now coming to that. Can he dominate this seething mass of suspicion and disbelief? No European statesman, I am firmly convinced, believes in his inner soul that Wilson's program is anything but a wild dream, very pretty, but quite outside the realm of practical politics. Can he 'put it over'? The leaders in Europe are secretly irritated by the preponderance of Wilson in diplomacy, by the way in which the Germans talk over their heads to the man in the White House, and the way in which, with that audacity which is the gift of great leadership, he takes the responsibility upon himself as the arbiter of the world's destiny. They don't like it, but they cannot help it.

"The English and the Italians will stand closer behind us at the time of the settlement than the French. The Peace Conference ought to be conducted in the English language, not in French, and it ought not to be in Paris. Brussels would be better.

"Another problem presents itself sharply: when it comes to the crucial point, can we Americans trust ourselves? *Do we really believe what Wilson preaches?* Are we willing to make real sacrifices and take on responsibilities to bring about the new heaven and the new earth?"

I venture to put down still another extract from my notes written during those chaotic days:

"Occasionally in Wilson I see a likeness to those rare moralists and idealists who from time to time have appeared upon the earth and for a moment, and in a burst of strange power, have temporarily lifted erring mankind to a higher pitch of comportment than it was quite equal to. I mean such leaders as Calvin, Savonarola, and Cromwell. . . . We will reform the old world, bring permanent peace, give all peoples freedom, make all men equal politically, and women the equal of men. We will stop intemperance by legislation, and destroy vice by advertising. I wonder—I wonder—and recall the old Norse fable of the God Thor, when he was the guest of the ancient Earth Giants, drinking out of the sea. Well, the old myth says that

Thor lowered the sea. And Cromwell changed England—a little—and Calvin the Swiss—for a time. Nothing, I think, is ever accomplished without an *excess* of faith, an *excess* of energy, an *excess* of passion. Wilson will do much. America will do much. We may even realize the League of Nations of the prophet's dream. But as I sit here today and look out over the roofs of old Rome, where in the distance rise the ruined baths of Diocletian, and the Colosseum with the weathered marbles of triumphant age, it seems to me I see the Earth Giants smile furtively, indulgently, as one smiles at youth. I cannot look upon it without a kind of love, for I, too, am a part of it; I am for the ultimate fling of this glorious excess. There is too little passion upon this earth, too little glorious and unrepentant living, too little faith in that which is beautifully impossible. It is a gorgeous age we live in, one that will never be forgotten. I thank God I am a part of it, that I, too, am taking a long breath and drinking out of the sea."

A little later as the hour of complete victory approached I wrote these words:

"The new lines of the struggle, after today, more clearly present themselves. Wilson has been accepted as a leader by elements which do not believe in him. The division is now coming. There were high and true words in his speech of September 27 which struck a chill to the very souls of the imperialists of England, France and Italy. Both liberals and conservatives have found comfort in Wilson's speeches in the past. But the conservatives have never believed that he really meant what he said. They have thought he was merely making rhetorical passes as they themselves have long been accustomed to do—to fool the people. They are beginning to fear that this is a stern, just man, who really means to do what he says. And he has such power as few ever had before in this world. From now on the division is coming. Men will instinctively take sides. For the first time, the new order has a leader of genius."

In my summary reports to the State Department of that period, all of which I understand were forwarded to the President, I laid all possible emphasis upon these conditions.

I soon began to see more clearly the dilemma that faced the President. *How could he work with the old imperialistic governments which were bitterly opposed if not actually hated by the masses, and attain the democratic objectives which he and the liberal forces were passionately demanding?*

Strong reasons were advanced in America, even by his friends, why Wilson should not go to Europe for the Peace Conference. They said he should remain in his high place and speak to the world. He should not make himself common. He should be the far-off sounding-board for great ideas. Even Colonel House, who was one of the President's closest friends, at first advised him not to go—and only changed his mind when he learned that Wilson was unalterably determined.

It had been perfectly clear, and I had so reported in my messages to the State Department, what the division of opinion upon this problem would be. The "people," recognizing Wilson as a leader who voiced their own highest aspirations, were vociferous in their demands that he come. The "ruling class," in Europe as in America, did not want him to come. For they knew he would make trouble for them: disturb their plans for making peace according to the old diplomacy.

Wilson knew instinctively that he could not remain on the heights. His genius as a leader taught him that. He must go through with it to the end. And the decision, any way one looked at it, was tragical. Recalling what I had seen in Italy, and in less degree in France and England, the utter faith he had awakened, the confidence that the dreams of a new world of justice and democracy were now, miraculously, to be realized, I wrote in my diary on December 6:

"I have, curiously, a feeling of doom in the coming to Europe of Wilson. He occupies a pinnacle too high; the earth forces are too strong. He is now approaching the supreme test of his triumph and his popularity. They are dizzy heights he stands upon; no man has long breathed such a rarefied atmosphere and lived. All the old, ugly depths—hating change, hating light—will suck him down.

"For all people are cruel with their heroes. They will pull them apart to see whether they have good, hard, heroic material all the way through. Does he talk well; does he sit nobly on his cloud? They are skeptical. Talk is cheap. They must see him act. It is not enough for him to declare in the words of Nehemiah, 'I am doing a great work so that I cannot come down.' They demand that he come down. Who cannot stand triumph? Let us see him in disgrace, with the crowd reviling him. They become impatient with his justness, fret at his idealism, chafe under his discipline, and finally, the last test having been passed, they will turn upon him and rend him. Will the memory of him live through all that? Then let it live. They will bow knee to him forever afterward."

CHAPTER XLI

I Am Unexpectedly Chosen to Play a Part in the Peace Conference

WHEN I ARRIVED in Paris from Italy some days before the Armistice in November I could scarcely believe it was the same city I had seen in July and August. It was a crowded, gay, busy Paris, all the stores ablaze, cabs swarming the streets, and in the Place de la Concorde, extending well up the Champs-Elysees, a great exhibition of captured German guns, flying machines, and tanks. Paris, with all the old, gay heedlessness of the mistress of the nations! Her lips were new rouged, her eyebrows penciled, and from the fringes of her dark raiment—for she was in mourning—hung glittering spangles of jet, promising a swift and forgetful return to her former gaiety. The American flag was everywhere—next to the French by far the most conspicuous.

On Armistice Day, the guns began booming and the bells ringing about eleven o'clock in the morning, and for the remainder of the day there was an unprecedented celebration. It was an exhibition of spontaneous popular joy of a kind I never saw before—perhaps no one ever saw. Entirely without police guidance of any kind—I did not see a single policeman during the day—it had an indescribable freedom, gaiety, and good humor, and yes, gentleness. It was, curiously, not victory that one heard celebrated, although there were cries of "Vive la Victoire"—it was "Vive le Paix." One heard everywhere, "The war is finished." This was the joyful news. The long struggle was past. The soldiers were coming home.

All the restaurants were so crowded that it was almost impossible to get anything to eat. Boyden and I—Charles Merz joined us also and occasionally other friends—saw it all from various parts of the Boulevards, the Place de la Concorde, and the Champs-Elysees. It lasted until late in the night. Pictures were flashed upon screens in various places in the evening, and Wilson's was always loudly cheered —next to Foch's. The French Chamber of Deputies resolved that "Citizen Woodrow Wilson, President of the great Republic of the United States, has deserved well of humanity."

In front of the Opera in the evening I was one of a vast concourse of people—fifteen or twenty thousand anyway. Singers on the brilliantly lighted balcony led with the "Marseillaise," and that song, bursting from the crowd, was enough to stir the spirits of the heroic dead. Such a thrill comes not once in a hundred years. They also sang "Tipperary" and other British and American songs.

The war now being over I considered that my task had been completed, that I could no longer be of any assistance, and I wanted above everything to return to my family and my home and my own hills in New England. I was tired and stale after many months of breathless work and excitement. I had my heart set upon spending Christmas at Amherst. I had already cabled my plans to the State Department, but as yet I had had no reply. So I went around to call on Colonel House in his study at the top of a curious old building on the left bank, to which one ascended by a circular staircase. I found him resting on a sofa, with a dressing gown over his knees—a little, light, deft, bright-eyed man, with a soft voice and winning manners. When I raised the question of going home, he was insistent in his advice that I remain. He praised highly the reports I had sent and said he had read them all.

"Stay on at least until the President arrives."

I accepted this plan with a heavy heart and went back to Italy to complete certain inquiries there. A month later when Ambassador Page * invited me to go with his party back to Paris in the private car furnished by the Italian government, I at once accepted.

We left Rome Sunday night, December 7.

In our party were Mr. and Mrs. Page and Signor Marconi, who was then, perhaps, the most distinguished citizen of Italy. I had long and interesting talks with him about the astonishing developments of wireless telegraphy and the adaptation of the principle of the Branly coherer in other branches of science and industry. We recalled our

* Thomas Nelson Page, then Ambassador to Italy.

former meetings, the first in Newfoundland in December, 1901, when I saw him receive the earliest messages sent by wireless across the Atlantic Ocean. He had aged greatly, and seemed highly nervous. We had a jolly dinner given by the Ambassador in the little hotel in the frontier town of Modane, and reached Paris Tuesday afternoon. We were met by army automobiles and driven to the Crillon Hotel which had been taken over by the American State Department for its Peace Commission. I was assigned to a fine room on the west side, from which I could see the little park at the foot of the Champs-Elysees. If I had known I was to remain right there in that hotel for six months, save for one brief absence, I should have been disheartened indeed.

I had come back from Italy much impressed and disturbed by the forces gathering in opposition to the President's plans of reconstruction. Colonel House, when I went to see him, was, as usual, strongly reassuring. He said that Mr. Wilson would stand firmly on his program and argued that both the Allies and Germany had accepted the Fourteen Points and could not go back on them. I could not believe then or later that he understood how strong were the forces against us.

The President arrived in Paris on December 14. Paris had a long history of well-staged celebrations: this for President Wilson was certainly one of its greatest. It was a mild, misty day with the people by thousands abroad in the streets since early morning. All the line of march was enclosed by soldiers and police, some of the soldiers mounted. At the corner outside the Crillon Hotel they had put up a huge banner reaching across the street, with the words "Vive Wilson" on it; and on the Champs-Elysees, a little way down I saw another banner: "Honor to Wilson the Just."

I made no effort to get any set place of observation, especially among the Americans, for I wished to be with the French crowd and to see how Wilson was received. I found a place in the middle of the Champs-Elysees where I could look a long way up toward the Arc de Triomphe. The broad avenue was clear, but the spaces on each side, the houses, the trees, the roofs, were all black with people. While we were waiting a professorial looking Frenchman near us climbed up on a box and began addressing the crowd on "Wilson's Ideals" and was greatly cheered. I had again the impression that the Armistice Day celebration had given me—of the French as a gentle people. From the talk all about us, I felt that they were genuinely and honestly sympathetic. There were many working men and women in the crowd, and innumerable children.

Just at ten o'clock a big gun near us began to boom, and soon afterward we saw the street under the Arc de Triomphe turn black, as the advance guard of cavalry appeared. Wilson, with the French President Poincare, was in the first carriage, bowing and smiling. His hair looked absolutely white, but his face was ruddy and vigorous. He was mightily cheered. Mrs. Wilson's carriage was so smothered in flowers that a girl who stood near me exclaimed that she couldn't see the President's wife at all. Neither could I. When the carriages passed I did not wait for the parade of French troops, but walked rapidly down to the Place de la Concorde where the carriages, which had been across the river, were again just arriving. Here also there were enormous crowds and much enthusiasm. I was told that the reception was in every way larger and more enthusiastic than that accorded to any of the kings and generals who had been there. The crowds were certainly as great as on the day of the Armistice celebration although there was not such an abandon of joy. Everywhere were American flags, even carried by groups of French students and soldiers, and everywhere the sound of cheering:

"Vive Wilson!" "Vive l'Amerique!"

There were no evidences of elaborate organization except during the actual procession of the carriages, and, of course, no disturbances of any kind. I was greatly affected by the sight of the weather-beaten regiments of French troops—mostly strong, bronzed men of thirty or forty years of age.

Everyone seemed to have a sense of the historic character of the event—an American President for the first time on foreign soil, and more than that, a man of commanding moral leadership, coming here to help decide the destiny of the world.

The French labor leaders had planned to bring about a great special demonstration, to put a million workmen on the streets, but Clemenceau had been unwilling. He avoided the issue by saying that they could have the demonstration if Wilson was agreeable, so they sent a wireless message asking Wilson to receive a delegation of workers' leaders, and suggested the street manifestation. Wilson replied, making an appointment to see the leaders at three-thirty on that afternoon (which he kept) but said that the manifestation was a matter for the French Government to decide. This made the workers angry with Clemenceau. While there was no organized demonstration, an enormous number of workmen, many of them socialists, were on the streets. The conservative parties said that the socialists were trying to use Wilson as a stick with which to beat Clemenceau and improve their own political situation. While this was probably true, they were the only group that really believed in Wilson.

A story going about Paris told of a remark made by cynical old Clemenceau:

"God Almighty gave mankind the Ten Commandments: and we rejected them. Now comes Wilson with his Fourteen Points—we shall see!"

Even before the President's arrival there were the plainest evidences on all sides that peace on the basis of Wilson's ideals had become more or less of a chimera, at least among the Governments. The *Manchester Guardian* expressed the situation exactly in the heading of its leading editorial on December 3:

THE SLUMP IN IDEALISM

The Paris *Figaro* said:

> . . . Here and there, one hears of people who still dream of a Wilson peace . . .

". . . Is it conceivable," asked the current number of the London *Daily News*, "that European statesmanship at this time of day can resurrect secret treaties and ask the commonsense of the world to honour them? . . ."

"It is," I wrote in my diary.

In spite of all evidences of reaction and opposition the President said in an address at the Sorbonne on December 21:

> . . . There is a great wind of moral force moving through the world, and every man who opposes himself to that wind will go down in disgrace. The task of those who are gathered here to make settlements of this peace

is greatly simplified by the fact that they are masters of no one; they are the servants of mankind, and if we do not heed the mandates of mankind we shall make ourselves the most conspicuous and deserved failures in the history of the world . . .

His reception in London and in all England was a triumph without precedent. He made a really exuberant speech at the Guildhall, evidently feeling sanguine regarding the results of the coming Peace Conference. At Manchester he said:

Interest does not bind men together. Interest separates men. . . . There is only one thing that can bind people together and that is a common devotion to right.

Woodrow Wilson had such power and such faith that even men who doubted began to think that something creative could and would be done at the Peace Conference. I had a letter at that time from A. J. Gardiner, editor of the London *Daily News*, in which he said:

I know how grave things are, but I rely on the stiff jaw of one great man.

Wilson returned to Paris in a blaze of glory, seemingly stronger than ever before. What a fighter the man was! His power in the world at the moment seemed irresistible. And yet I was writing in my diary on January 6, 1919, just before the Conference opened:

"With the results of the English elections fresh upon us, the support of reactionism in the French Chamber, the dominance of Sonnino in Italy, and the remembrance of the last election in America and the attitude of Lodge, Knox and Roosevelt, it looks momentarily pretty blue for a League of Nations, or any sort of constructive peace."

A day or so after the President's arrival I heard that he desired that I remain in Paris and help during the Peace Conference. I decided at once that I could not possibly accept any such appointment. I did not honestly feel myself equipped for it. "The first step toward failure," I wrote in my diary, "is the acceptance of a task beyond one's capabilities."

On December 18 I was shown a letter written by the President to each of the members of the American Commission:

Paris, 17 December, 1918.

MY DEAR HOUSE:

I have been thinking a great deal lately about the contact of the Commission with the public through the press and particularly about the way in which the Commission should deal with the newspaper men who have come over from the United States. I have come to the conclusion that much the best way to handle this matter is for you and the other Commissioners to hold a brief meeting each day and invite the representatives of the press to come in at each meeting for such interchange of information or suggestions as may be thought necessary. This I am sure is preferable to any formal plan or to any less definite arrangement.

I am also convinced that the preparation of all the press matter that is to be issued from the Commission is a task calling for a particular sort of experienced ability. I beg, therefore, that you and your fellow Commissioners will agree to the appointment of Mr. Ray Stannard Baker as your representative in the performance of this duty. Mr. Baker enjoys my confidence in a very high degree and I have no hesitation in commending him to you as a man of ability, vision and ideals. He has been over here for the better part of a year, has established relationships which will be of the highest value, and is particularly esteemed by the very class of persons to whom it will be most advantageous to us to be properly interpreted in the news that we have to issue. If you see no conclusive objections to this, I would suggest that you request Mr. Baker to do us the very great service of acting in this capacity.

I am writing in the same terms to the other members of the Commission.

Sincerely yours,

WOODROW WILSON.

I went to both Colonel House and Secretary Lansing and told them I could not possibly accept any such assignment, that it would involve executive and semi-political qualifications that I did not possess. I told them frankly, also, that having been away from my family for nearly a year I wanted to go home. Both said, "Go and see the President." This I did at once.

"Baker," he said, "we're over here to do one of the most difficult tasks ever entrusted to American leadership. I should like to have you remain: if it appears, after you try it for a few weeks, that you cannot make a go of it, I will let you off."

I accepted the task with many misgivings.

CHAPTER XLII

Organization of the Press Department at Paris

I BEGAN AT ONCE to organize the Press Department, having outlined the plans with Secretary Lansing. We were given offices at No. 4 Place de la Concorde only a few doors from the Crillon Hotel, the headquarters of the American Peace Commission, and I soon found an excellent assistant and secretarial help. With several score American newspaper correspondents accredited to our department, I knew well that I had plenty of trouble in store for me. I had been a newspaper man myself. I knew them well—their utter insatiability, and the impossibility of living with them at all unless they trusted you.

One thing I had determined to insist upon—I raised the subject with the President in my first talk with him—and that was that I should be admitted entirely and completely into the confidence of the Commission and know all that was going on inside. This was not because it was necessary to pass on all this information at once to the correspondents—that could be decided as the problems arose—but because I felt that I myself must *know* in order to be an intelligent servant. I regarded this as a reasonable demand, and made it a part of my agreement to try out the position. I was soon to learn how difficult it was in practice.

The entire delegation of American correspondents met in our office and formed an organization, similar to those in the Houses of Congress, with which throughout the Conference I did my best to co-operate. We had presently registered with us some one hundred and fifty correspondents representing various press organizations, individual newspapers, magazines and syndicates, and they were hungry and clamorous. In the early days before the Peace Commission really got down to work, real news was scarce and this made the problem still more difficult. Most of our men had in the beginning little knowledge of European affairs. The experienced British correspondents, when the events of the day were unimportant, could furnish their readers with the backgrounds of the various problems involved, speculate upon the solutions offered, comment on the leaders who were arriving at Paris. Not more than four or five of our correspondents were, in the beginning, equipped to do this. In order to assist them we drew heavily upon the information possessed by our American experts and issued a series of accurate statements regarding various highly complex situations. These were written, or the facts were furnished, by the best men we had—Professor Lord, Dean Haskins, Dr. Bowman, Professor Day, Professor Seymour, Professor Shotwell, Professor Young, Mr. Beer, and others—and in some cases they were worked out from masses of material gathered and digested by my assistant, Arthur Sweetser. I shall never cease to feel grateful to these able men for their generous co-operation. The statements thus issued proved to be invaluable and were eagerly used by many of the correspondents, sometimes being cabled over in full.

One of the most difficult problems I had to meet was that of arranging for press representation at the Plenary Sessions. Usually I was supplied by the Commission with only a few tickets for our Americans, since there were hundreds of correspondents representing many nations struggling desperately to get in. It may readily be imagined what room for explosive recriminations, charges of favoritism and the like, were inherent in such a position as mine. I knew well the skepticism—a skepticism too well justified in many cases—of "handouts" and prepared statements, and the dread felt by every really able writer—and we had some of the best from America—of being used by propagandists for their own ends. I had quite a number of devoted friends among the correspondents, who, I felt confident, trusted me. But there were also many I did not know, and several able men who represented powerful newspapers that were opposed to the President. I took an early occasion, therefore, to make a statement at one of the meetings of the correspondents pledging sincere co-operation. I add here one paragraph from the notes of that statement:

". . . Another thing I want to emphasize, I am not going to lie to you. If I am entrusted with information that I am required not to pass along I am going to say frankly that I cannot tell. If I don't know a thing I am going to say I don't know, and as far as possible I will make reports of facts I have to give uncolored by my own opinions or desires. This is my ideal. I don't know whether I can approach it or not. As every man here knows I have got a hard job—perhaps an impossible job—and I cannot do it at all without your co-operation." *

Throughout the Conference it seemed to be the policy of the French and the Italians to preserve as much secrecy as possible. The British had a more liberal policy, although it was plainly the intent of Mr. Lloyd George to use publicity, whenever possible, to forward British ends. Only the Americans, and here they generally but not always had the support of Mr. Wilson, endeavored to secure all the publicity possible. Publicity is indeed the test of democracy. But I wondered sometimes whether we Americans, if we had had the same fears and the same fierce and greedy traditional interests and necessities, would have done any better than the other nations. We were in fact ridiculously free from what Wilson called "material self-interest."

Those were hard, trying days, with a constant struggle that sometimes seemed overwhelming. The principal news in that early period came out of the meetings of the Council of Ten, and the League of Nations Commission. The meetings of the Council of Ten were held at the French Foreign Office in the Quai d'Orsay, sometimes two sessions daily, and while they were supposed to be absolutely secret, they leaked at every pore, at least to the French. I went over as the American representative and was present at the close of each one of these sessions; sometimes I attended the sessions themselves. I constantly urged franker disclosures, but usually to little purpose.

Those early weeks of the Conference were for me most difficult: one whirl of work, trying to meet all the requirements of an all-out-impossible task, often with the feeling that little or no real progress toward a "sound and lasting" peace was being made. So many of the discussions seemed to be mere jockeying for position among groups of clever diplomatic traders, and to have behind them no clearly held

* I have discussed some of these matter in chapters seven and eight, Volume I of my *Woodrow Wilson and World Settlement.*

principles or objectives, let alone any that were inspired, as had been President Wilson's recent addresses, by a passion for the general good of mankind.

Secretary of State Lansing was of course the head of the American Commission, next to the President. He was a rather cold, precise, timid man, with a thorough and useful knowledge of foreign affairs. He had never been the responsible American "foreign minister," for when Bryan resigned, the President himself had become, in reality, his own Secretary of State. But the President had all along consulted Lansing and relied upon him especially for advice on problems of precedent and procedure.

I think Lansing had an unhappy time of it at Paris. In common with the other Commissioners he had few real or great responsibilities. The Peace Conference soon resolved itself into a secret counsel of the heads of the great states, and they were too busy, or were unwilling, to take the other members of their Commissions fully into their confidence. This was true not only of the Americans but of the British, the French and the Italians. Clemenceau was the most dominating of the group. His foreign minister, M. Pichon, used to follow him around, carrying his brief case, like a nimble little secretary. Lloyd George apparently consulted Balfour and General Smuts more than Wilson consulted Lansing or House or Bliss, to say nothing of White, who was rarely consulted at all, but I heard many complaints from the British that even their Commissioners were not kept informed by Lloyd George.

When I went into Mr. Lansing's office I often found him sitting alone at the desk in his big room. Sometimes he had a block of paper under his hand on which he drew and shaded in elaborately grotesque figures or faces. Sometimes he was writing in his diary in a small neat hand. He and Colonel House were the incorrigible diarists of the Commission.

Secretary Lansing was often most helpful to me in explaining, with a patience that made me truly grateful, the backgrounds of some of the difficult problems the Conference had under discussion and the various solutions that might possibly be adopted. I asked him one day what his idea of a League of Nations was, and he replied:

"A method of organizing and expressing the will of the common people of the world."

I remember I thought this definition too vague and general at a time when the League of Nations Commission was wrestling mightily in an adjoining room with the all but insoluble details of a possible league. But it *did* get in the common people.

Colonel House was not only the busiest member of the Commission, but he also had the most influence, since he was supposed to be closer to the President than any of the others. He was also a member of what, from the American point of view, was the most important and active of the Commissions, that dealing with the organization of the League of Nations. He was indefatigable in trying to get the contentious ones together, smooth ruffled feelings, and encourage sensible discussion of impossible demands. Frequently qualities of mind are indicated by physical mannerisms. The Colonel had an odd way, when he was talking, of using his small, delicate hands and fingers as though he were picking things apart, or pulling them out to look at. This was one motion. The other was complementary. He patted and smoothed the imaginary object with his hands and fingers, his voice at the same time taking on an explanatory, reasonable, optimistic tone. He was full of smoothnesses.

He had clear eyes that shone brightly when he was interested, but could at times be cold and hard. At his morning newspaper correspondents' conference, which I often attended, he said very little—he had no power or presence on his feet—but it was noteworthy that of the four Commissioners the correspondents looked most to him. A rather exact gauge of the news importance of the four, as instantly recognized by the correspondents, was the size of the groups that gathered around each man. The chief center was Colonel House, next, Secretary Lansing, then General Bliss, and finally, fine old Henry White.

I was somewhat slow in making the acquaintance of General Bliss. In the early conferences with the Commissioners he had sat perfectly still, the very personification of the gruff, silent, honest soldier. I had, however, watched him closely. He was a strongly built man, not over-tall, and just a little stooping at the shoulders. Nature had intended him to be a hairy man, thick gray eyebrows, bristly gray moustaches, thick hair on his neck, and then changed its mind and made him bald, an extreme shiny baldness, except for a fringe of hair at the back and sides of his head. His deepset eyes—he wore no glasses—looked at first rather sleepy, but when he warmed up they opened wide and glowed with feeling. He was an intensely shy man, hating publicity above everything, and shrinking from meeting newspaper correspondents, unless he knew them, for fear of being quoted. He asked profanely why the ideas were not enough without having to tag them with a name—his name above all.

One morning I went in to see him for a few minutes' talk and remained nearly three hours—one of the most interesting and, to me, surprising talks I had had since I had been in Paris. I supposed that the General had been placed on the Commission for the value of his military knowledge, and no doubt that was in large part the case, and never was I more surprised than when I heard him express his full convictions regarding war. A great soldier, with deep knowledge of all that war implied, he was in reality a far-sighted pacifist, believing most strongly of all in Wilson's fourth point, the complete disarmament of the world.

I had already known something of him as a hard student. Years before, when I had met him on a voyage to Panama, he was engaged day after day in investigating experiments relating to army rationing and the transportation of quartermaster supplies. That morning at the Crillon I found him reading a series of papers on international law by Elihu Root. A day or so later when I went in to call I found him reading an old Latin book, which he had found in the Bibliotheque Nationale and I learned afterward that one of his intellectual hobbies was to find and read every line of the ancient Latin literature that has come down to us. No corrupt medieval Latin for him! *

He also had the practice of writing out his views and thoughts, for clearer definition, and his letters and reports, some of which he

* Several years after the close of the war I was calling on Secretary Baker at Cleveland. He told me that General Bliss had just been there. "He had heard of a bit of genuine old Latin in our Cleveland library and he came out here to look at it. I don't believe that anything else would have brought him."

read me, were the outright, sensible expressions of a man with an honest mind. They were more than that. Like his talk when he really warmed up in his conversation, they were full of metaphors, usually military metaphors. The stout and sane judgments of complex or difficult problems and situations were clarified by holding them up for comparison with common and well understood processes of life. Often his conversation had an almost poetical quality and the glimpses it gave of a fine democratic spirit—a man who was thinking fundamentally and constructively—were as charming as they were sound.

I had never heard anyone set forth more powerfully the argument for disarmament and the need for a league of unarmed nations, than this old soldier with the four stars on his collar. It was a kind of spiritual attitude in which a new organization of society, a new orientation, seemed as reasonable and necessary as it seemed unattainable, even absurd, to those who could not escape the old conceptions.

I came away from my talk with General Bliss, the first of many, feeling greatly encouraged. He would be a power in our Commission —if he were used.

As the Conference developed, General Bliss became more and more the pessimistic philosopher.

"Why deceive ourselves," he said to me one morning in his slow matter-of-fact way: "We are making no Peace here in Paris. What is there to make it out of?"

Another time he said: "We've really seen only five out of another thirty years war"—and once, with still deeper pessimism, "It looks sometimes as though we were drifting into another dark age."

Commissioner Henry White was the only Republican member of the Commission. I soon made his acquaintance and like to think of him always as a good friend. I find this account in my notes of my first meeting with him:

"Commissioner Henry White invited me this morning to go driving with him in the Bois de Boulogne. It was a misty, gray-blue morning, very beautiful along the Seine, among the bare trees. The Commissioner is a tall, powerfully built, fine-looking man, with thick white hair, and a full voice. He is slightly lame and uses his cane heavily. No member of our diplomatic corps has had a longer experience than he. In all the important foreign events since 1866 he has had a part. He has attended five international conferences—beginning with the International Sugar Bounty Congress in 1888—the present one being the greatest of all, of course. He is of the highest type of the old-fashioned diplomat, one who has played the game always with honor and probity, but nevertheless the old game of courts, kings and well-established traditions. He told with evident approval of what Lord Rosebery said to him regarding gossip—that he always had at least one charming young fellow, a titled sprig or an officer, in every capital, who would be invited about for his own sake, would listen to everyone, and each week write a letter to the Foreign Office giving the gossip of the dinner table, the clubs, and the court. This was an essential element of the old diplomacy.

"The Commissioner, while nominally a Republican—he told me he had been careful to keep out of all political partisanship—is loyal to the President, but regrets that he has not been willing to see more people and hear more of what is going on in foreign capitals.

"The charm of the Commissioner is in the very transparency, the naïveté of his position. Everything for him is clear and settled. He has grown sweet and mellow, full of human kindliness, with a widespread acquaintance among men who no longer count, and a wide familiarity with methods and forms which no longer move the world. He is a precedent holder, serving a great and original precedent smasher. He is like a fine old library, all bound in tooled leather, giving off that scent, dear to the archivist, of rich old books—full of knowledge which no one any longer needs to have.

"As we drove in the Bois, he told me of the changes he had himself seen in Paris, and spoke often, as fine old men do, of 'my time.' 'In my time this was so and so'—'in my time, there was here—' 'in my time there was there—'

"It being Sunday morning, we drove down finally to the beautiful American church, 'a sample of pure Gothic,' which the Commissioner himself had helped to build when he was at the Embassy here. He was one of the original committee, and he took me back to look up at the beauty of the nave and remarked upon the excellence of the stained glass of the high windows. We marched together down to the front seat, his commanding presence, his noble figure well noted there in the broad center aisle—like one of the Gothic columns, I thought, which support the church. We knelt with the others, the fine old man just a little behind. We stood with the others, he just a little late—and his voice boomed full and strong on all the prayers and responses. A little like the church itself, I thought him—full of wide spaces, solemnity, age. It was no surprise to find him there, for he is the upholder of all old institutions, old religion, old chivalry, old diplomacy—and one seeing him and hearing him during a forenoon's drive in the Bois, is so keenly beset with respect for the virtues of the old, that he is momentarily shaken in his devotion to the new.

"The peace will be made and he will sign it, but he will never know quite how it all came about, or what it means."

I had many other talks with the fine old Commissioner. He reminisced delightfully. In a world convulsed with mighty events, he told of seeing, one day in 1871, the Vendome column lying on the ground and observed, as though it were important news, that, though it appeared so tall, it did not reach to the Rue de la Paix.

I always stopped to watch him when he came into the Crillon from his little daily walk. His cheeks would be rosy like apples, and he wore a tall black hat with a broad black band around it, and carried a proper cane, looking quite the most distinguished man in the world.

I expressed my own conclusions as to the importance of the delegates at Paris in this notation in my diary made late in December:

"It grows clearer all the time that the only Peace Commissioner here is Wilson himself. They dare say nothing until he speaks: and no one can do anything until he is ready: and he will do nothing until he is *sure*."

CHAPTER XLIII

I Sail for America and Return with the President

IN FEBRUARY, THE PRESIDENT sailed for America on the *George Washington.* He had two chief reasons for going. One was to attend the closing session of the old Congress and sign any late legislation. The other, and perhaps the more important in his own mind, was to take home the first rough draft of the League of Nations Covenant. He wanted to weigh the opposition he might have to his proposals, and to encourage his supporters. The "Covenant," the work of the League of Nations Commission, had been one of the first fruits of the Conference; only a little had so far been accomplished in the settlement of the difficult questions of boundaries, economic reparations, disarmament, war guilt, and the like.

The President suggested that I accompany him to America, and the Peace Commission gave me a leave of absence.

We sailed from Brest on February 15. Save for the President's party there were only a few passengers, among them Congressmen White of Ohio, Helvering of Kansas, Norton of North Dakota, Ambassador Francis of Russia and Mrs. Francis, and Franklin D. Roosevelt. This young assistant secretary of the Navy had great charm of presence and of manner. He was enthusiastic and earnest, he was a mine of information regarding ships and the sea—but if anyone at that time had whispered in my ear that he was presently to become President of the United States, and direct its destinies through another and even more dreadful war than the one just concluded, how could I have believed it? Probably young Franklin Roosevelt could not have believed it himself.

We arrived in Boston on February 24, where there was a vast reception for the President.

I rode in the parade just behind him and could compare the crowds with those that had greeted him recently in Europe. There was better discipline and better policing in Boston than in any European city I had seen. One thing that impressed me freshly and strongly at the time was the keener look in the faces of the people—the average seemed more alive than the average in Europe. It was also a far better dressed crowd, more prosperous looking, than any I saw abroad, but this was no doubt due in part to the fact that the war had impoverished Europe to a degree that we could not realize. The President was loudly cheered all along the way, and stood up in his fur coat, lifting his hat, and smiling for the crowd.

He made a great speech at Mechanics Hall—one of his best. It far excelled the New York Metropolitan speeech which he delivered just before sailing again for France. On the latter occasion he was worn out with a terrific week's work.

I had five or six precious days at home in Amherst, never to be forgotten. In New York I saw many old friends and tried to get a clear idea of American feeling regarding the League of Nations and the Peace Conference. Among many such meetings, I had dinner one night and long hours of talk with Raymond Robins at Norman Hapgood's home, and heard his most interesting exposition of the Russian situation. I had a long talk with Dwight W. Morrow at J. P. Morgan's office. He was deeply interested in the League of Nations and seemed to me to have so many practical ideas regarding it, plainly the result of much thought, that I made a memorandum of them for the President.

We sailed from New York on the *George Washington* on Wednesday morning, March 5, at eight o'clock. The President's party took ship late Tuesday night after the great meeting at the Metropolitan Opera House with speeches by Mr. Wilson and Mr. Taft. I was on the platform so that I saw the wonderful audience; there was no question at all that the people were with the speakers and for the League of Nations.

Just at the conclusion of the speeches an Irish American Committee, headed by Judge Cohalan, appeared on the platform and demanded that the President declare himself for the independence of Ireland. The President told the Committee that he completely distrusted Judge Cohalan and refused to meet him. They withdrew and reappeared without Cohalan.

"They were so insistent," he told me afterwards, "that I had hard work keeping my temper."

He said that he believed that the Irish problem was a domestic affair of the British Empire and no foreign power had a right to interfere. However, he did believe that the Irish question, and others like it, might be taken up by the League of Nations—when established—as a probable cause of war.

On the return trip the President soon lost the worn, drawn look brought on by the heavy strain of work at Washington. Dr. Grayson, who watched him indefatigably during his entire administration, told me he had never known a man who could work longer and more intensely than Woodrow Wilson and rebound more quickly after a brief rest.

I had many and most interesting talks with Dr. Grayson during the voyage. He was one of the most charming, unselfish, and helpful of human beings: he was devoted to the President. He told me much of the physical limitations under which Wilson had lived and worked. He said that the President was partially blind in one eye, the result of a rupture of a blood vessel in his early years—the kind of a rupture which, if it had been in his brain, might have killed him. The plain fact was that the President had a high-powered intellect in a frail physical body. Grayson said he was almost the only man he had ever known who really overworked. Many people overate, overdrank, overplayed, overloafed—few ever really overworked.

I had a number of delightful talks with the President and Mrs. Wilson during this voyage. On such occasions he was full of good stories, witty and genial, but avoiding for the most part comments on affairs at Paris. It often seemed to me that the man himself, most of the time, lived the lonely life of the mind; that in order to meet the stupendous tasks that confronted him he reduced his private life to the utmost possible simplicity. One remark he made on that voyage seemed highly interpretative:

"A high degree of education tends, I think, to weaken a man's human sympathies."

In many instances, however, our conversations did reach down into the problems of Paris. I was eager to impress upon him the need of more and better publicity, for it had come to seem to me that this, beyond any other element, was a supreme requirement in defending and advancing the American demands. In the afterlook, such failure as Wilson suffered at Paris was largely a failure of intelligent and determined publicity. For publicity is the life blood of democracy.

In one talk in particular, as I have noted in my diary, I argued that what was needed now was not so much to convince the people of the necessity of *a* League, the great majority being already convinced, but to assure them that *the* League of the Paris Covenant was the best obtainable at that time. It was still more necessary to convince them that they could have it only by paying for it with self-sacrifice and service.

If the President was ever fearful of anything in his life, it was of publicity: he was afraid, I think, not so much of the facts themselves, but of the way they were presented. As a highly cultivated scholar he disliked exaggeration, distrusted sensationalism. And yet he recognized the need of publicity and often seemed irritated and offended if the clear stream of news was fouled at its sources or muddied with propaganda.

The most vehement and indignant comments I heard him make during that voyage concerned the control of the French press. He said to me that he had positive evidence of domination of many of the papers by the French Government: this in the form of an order issued through the Maison de la Presse (given to him personally by a French editor whose name, of course, could not be disclosed) in which were written instructions regarding three items of policy:

1. To emphasize the opposition to him (Mr. Wilson) in America by giving all the news possible of Republican and other opposition.

2. To emphasize the disorder and anarchy in Russia, thus provoking Allied intervention.

3. To publish articles showing the ability of Germany to pay a large indemnity.

He thought this system abominable; and if worst came to worst he said he could publish this evidence and suggest the removal of the Conference to Geneva.

I may possibly be excused for inserting here some reflections I find in my notes made during the last day or two of our voyage:

"I wonder sometimes if we take ourselves, now, too seriously. We think we are living at the heart of the most stupendous events, among the greatest men in the world. We compare this moment to that in which our forefathers were carving out the destinies of the American nation; this Covenant of the League to that Declaration, that Bill, that Constitution. It may be so. We do not know. Sometimes, as during the other evening when I talked with Raymond Robins about Russia, I find myself looking into a vast chasm of wonder, with the solid earth a-tremble under my feet. What if Lenin and those despised Bolsheviks had the creative secret of a new world, and we—we serious and important ones—were merely trying to patch the fragments of the old? I have moments—as last night in the black darkness of the belly of the great ship, with my bed stirring uneasily under me, and the living being of this strong machine breathing, straining, shaking, squeaking around me—I have moments when I wonder whether these ugly old shells of human organization are not too rotten to save, when I wonder if this Peace Conference is not after all, fooling itself, and us.

"I have had often, at Paris, and here on this voyage, where I have had moments to think, the terrible doubt as to whether the actual work of the Conference thus far is in any degree fulfilling the promise of Wilson's words. Wilson has phrased the hope of the world—the people come to power; he has spoken the great true word, but has he the genius to work it out? Has he the power? Above all, is the time ripe?

"How make peace when there is so little to make it of—so little of human understanding, human sympathy, above all so little willingness to sacrifice immediate advantage for the future well-being of civilization? How make any real peace in such an atmosphere of suspicion, fear, greed, hatred, as that which now pervades Paris?"

I wish I could set down an adequate impression of that voyage. It was quiet and simple: a small group and a friendly one. Coming out of strenuous days, controversies, and great meetings, the President rested. He showed in quiet and friendly relationships at his best—in a light in which I wish many Americans who thought him a cold, unamiable man, could have seen him. He and Mrs. Wilson were frequently on deck, once they played shuffle-board, and they came in quite regularly to listen to the excellent music of the ship's orchestra or to attend the moving picture exhibits. Sometimes after the evening entertainments, two or three of us would find the President and Mrs. Wilson at the bottom of the stairs near their cabin and have a good talk. We talked once, for example, of Lafayette, again of the French people and their peculiarities, again of golfing—with many stories and much laughter. On several days the President had various members of the party in to luncheon, starting simply with a quiet grace said in low tones, and the meal itself passing off with the friendly give-and-take of any American family meal.

The President and Mrs. Wilson quite won the hearts of the officers and crew of the ship. They had been passengers on the *George Washington* for three voyages—twenty-seven days aboard.

"It is getting to be a kind of house-boat," said Mrs. Wilson.

Mrs. Wilson read aloud to the President a good deal during the voyage. He enjoyed A. G. Gardiner's sketches of public men: *Prophets, Priests and Kings,* and *War Lords.* Admiral Grayson said that he had read to the President several essays by an author named David Grayson!

At the closing entertainment on Wednesday night, just as we were about to break up, a group of seamen in the back of the hall began to sing "God Be With You 'Til We Meet Again," continuing through all the verses. Then the whole company, including the President, who had a fine voice, sang together "Auld Lang Syne." I wondered among what other people in this world there could develop just such relationships or such a spirit.

We arrived at Brest at 8:30, March 14, and were met by the local celebrities and also by Colonel House. We went immediately to the waiting special train—and were soon speeding toward Paris.

CHAPTER XLIV

The President Throws a Bombshell

I DECIDED, during the return voyage to Paris, to make a strong effort to keep a more complete record in my notebooks of daily happenings at the Peace Conference. During the earlier period I had been driven as never before in my life. In addition to all my other duties I was subject to call, day and night, by restless and hungry newspaper correspondents; I was sometimes awakened from sound sleep by the ringing of the telephone at the head of my bed, often to deny some cock-and-bull rumor that had not the slightest basis in fact.

When I returned to Paris, the first thing I did was to abolish the tyrannical night telephone. I got up every morning at six o'clock, often earlier. I had a cup of coffee and a roll sent up to my room (after a fierce battle with the hotel management) and spent the next hour or so, until breakfast time, in blessed quietude. I wrote in my notebook, partly to get the confused events of the day into some sort of perspective, and partly because I thoroughly enjoyed it. I was able during this period of uninterrupted quietude to look into a few of the many reports and documents that came to my desk and I tried also, every morning, to read a little in some old, quiet, brave book with a wise man in it, to give me a sense of space and time and beauty that would somewhat temper the bedlam of crowded days wherein there was no space or time, little wisdom, and less beauty. I firmly believe that if it had not been for these moments of precious solitude every morning and the rare excursions I was able to make into the country, I should have found the later months at Paris intolerable.

I think I should also say, as well here as anywhere, that although I have often been tempted to make revisions and apologies based upon later knowledge and reflection, I have here put down what I actually did, what I really thought and felt at the time. I know well it is not the complete story: it is the record of one man who played a small part in great affairs. It is that one man's judgments at the moment of swiftly moving events. Possibly the chief value of autobiography lies in its indiscretions.

The President's real difficulties began when he returned to Paris. They had been in the making weeks before. It was perfectly plain, even in December that the French were doing their best to undermine the whole Wilson program. Both Clemenceau and Pichon, the foreign minister, were declaring the validity of their territorial claims and announcing their agreement with England in courses which would defeat the very principles to which, at the Armistice, they had already set their hands. One evening, early in January, I had dinner with Herbert Hoover, and a long talk. Hoover had been working longer with European problems (he had been feeding Belgium) than most of the Americans connected with the Peace Commission; and I came away newly impressed with the tremendous difficulties involved in the economic arrangements between the Allies. The struggle with Prussianism among ourselves might be as serious as that with Germany.

Many thoughtful Americans and Englishmen then in Paris—Norman Angell, Walter Lippmann, William Allen White, Ida M. Tarbell and others whom I was often seeing—were pessimistic. They saw little evidence in the President's speeches, that he realized the strength of the forces which were against him; and most of them were fearful that he would demand too little, be content with some super-Hague arrangement which would not stand the shock of economic rivalry.

When the President returned to Paris on March 14 after a month's absence, all these problems had grown immeasurably more difficult. Great unrest, uncertainty, irritated impatience, had spread all over Europe. There had been disquieting outbreaks, all but small wars, in various countries. Above all, the soldiers of the various armies wished to be demobilized and sent home.

Colonel House and Secretary Lansing had been left as heads of the American Commission with no clear instructions as to what they should or should not do. Discussion had of course continued in the minor Councils of Ten and Five, with one decision of enormous importance made without consulting the President. This was an agreement that there should be a speedy "preliminary" treaty of peace with Germany, settling the military and naval terms, establishing boundaries, fixing reparations—indeed almost all the issues *except* the organization of the League of Nations, which was to be left to later discussions.

The President heard of this decision before he left America: and had discussed it, acrimoniously, with Colonel House when he joined the Presidential party at Brest. It was, indeed, the beginning of the "break" between the two friends. The President—as well as many others—knew perfectly well what this stratagem meant. One of the first men I met in Paris—an able correspondent who was highly critical of the League—said to me:

"Well, your League is dead."

The news was all over Paris and it was highly pleasing to the French leaders. They were not really for the League at all; they wanted an armed alliance between America, Britain and France. They knew well enough that to delay the discussion of the League of Nations for four or five months would mean talking it to death.

On the morning after our arrival in Paris, about 11 o'clock, the President called me on the secret American telephone circuit and asked me to deny the report that there would be a separate preliminary treaty with Germany excluding the League of Nations.

"I want you to say that we stand exactly where we stood on January 25 when the Peace Conference adopted the resolution making the Covenant an integral part of the general treaty of peace."

It was clear enough that such a statement would fall like a bombshell in Paris: that it meant the overturning of the only important action that the delegates had ventured to take during his absence. It would be a reassertion of the President's unalterable determination, expressed in his speech at the Metropolitan Opera House in New York just before sailing, that the League of Nations was to be made an "integral part of the treaty." It might very possibly break up the Conference then and there.

After drawing up a statement in accordance with the President's request, it seemed of such vital importance that I submitted it to him after the noon conference. He approved it and we put it out at once.

It was one of the boldest and most radical assertions of leadership during the Peace Conference.

In this statement,* the President did not go out of his way to criticize what had been done while he was gone, or to attack anyone: he merely announced his purpose. It was an extraordinarily able stroke. By definitely recalling the previous action of the Conference, which had not been rescinded, he was in an impregnable position. He thus centered interest again upon the League of Nations. As to whether the treaty they were now making was called "preliminary" or "final" he did not in the least care, if he secured the reality which he was seeking: that the Covenant be made the basis of any "general" treaty of peace which contained territorial, economic, colonial, and other settlements.

While the President's statement aroused furious controversies, the high men at Paris perforce accepted it and began to work under pressure, as never before, to decide upon the terms of the treaty. Two days later the heads of state were conferring as though nothing had happened. But it was clear that there was still lightning in the clouds.

About that time the situation in Syria and Asiatic Turkey began to occupy the attention of the Big Four. There was hot discussion between the French and the British—the Italians breaking in—regarding their rights in Asia Minor and in Turkey under old (secret) treaties. Finally the President said, as he afterward told me:

"If the position in Syria is to be discussed only upon the basis of previous understandings between France, Great Britain, and Italy, then, of course, I have nothing to do with it, and can see no reason for taking any part in it. It is only upon the understanding that the whole problem is on the peace table without reference to old understandings, and with the clear purpose of not enforcing mandatories upon any of the people concerned without consulting their desires, that I can be of any assistance."

* See my *Woodrow Wilson and World Settlement*, Vol. I, p. 311, for the text of this statement.

This terminated the discussion immediately and it was decided to send an interAllied commission to Syria to make an investigation of the exact situation. The President asked me if I could suggest someone to go.

"I want the ablest American now in France who is not connected with the Peace Conference."

I suggested Henry Churchill King, President of Oberlin College, an able and honest man who had been in Europe in Y.M.C.A. work.

"Just the man," said the President. "I know him."

He was promptly appointed. The other member was Charles R. Crane. They made a most interesting and valuable report which was completely ignored at the time.

The Polish question came up for endless discussions. Other lesser problems consumed precious time. A great wave of criticism began to arise all over the world. Many began to doubt that Germany would sign the treaty when it was presented, and were asking, "What then?"

"While these men talk the world is falling apart." I wrote in my diary "great anxiety prevails here lest the peace be delayed until the whole world breaks down into anarchy. We have had news of the Hungarian revolution, with the accession to power of the Bolsheviks. Egypt is in rebellion. The British industrial situation is acute. Sharp criticism everywhere of the delay in the peace."

I told the President that most of the delays in coming to agreement were being attributed to him and that I thought a statement ought to be made explaining the exact truth. He said that the French were delaying and objecting at every point. The same report came from every committee: "The French are holding us back; the French are talking us to death."

The President told me that they would spend an hour getting Clemenceau around to a certain position and then find, the next time the subject was up, that his mind had reverted to its exact obstinate former position. Mr. Wilson said:

"Clemenceau has a kind of feminine mind; it works well on specific problems, poorly on general policies. He is like an old dog trying to find a place to rest. He turns slowly around following his tail, before he gets down to it."

I told him Lloyd George said that Clemenceau had failed much since the murderous attack upon him in February, and he agreed. He said Clemenceau had hard coughing fits; and repeated that he was the chief obstacle in pressing their negotiations.

Every time I saw the President during those days I urged that he make some kind of a statement to head off the criticism that the consideration of the League of Nations was holding up the peace settlement. This accusation was one way of attacking the League and delaying its organization. On March 27, the President evidently began to be convinced and asked me to try my hand on such a statement. I drew it up and when he came over to the Crillon that afternoon Colonel House and I got in the car with him and rode up to his house in the Place des Etats-Unis where he revised the statement I had written. In my draft I knew I was trying to tell too much truth. I laid the blame squarely where it belonged upon the "obstructionist groups" who were making "claims for strategic frontiers and national aggrandizement." "In pressing what they believe to be their own immediate interests, they lose sight entirely of the fact that they are surely sowing seeds of future wars." The President said he was not ready yet to make statements even so guarded as these; but he did use the last paragraphs of the statement, in which the League of Nations was exculpated of blame for the delay. He dictated it to Mr. Swem, and we got it out by cable and wireless that evening.

CHAPTER XLV

Efforts to Wear the President Down

FEW PEOPLE KNEW during the last days of March and early April how close the Four came, more than once, to an open rupture—with Clemenceau, Lloyd George and Orlando on one side and the President on the other. It seemed to those who were meeting the President every day that there was a deliberate effort being made to wear him out, break him down, by sheer unrelenting day-long argument. This effort was supported by the hammering of the opposition press in both Paris and London, which by innuendo, if not openly, was blaming the President for all the delay. And while they argued there in secret sessions, there came lurid reports of unrest and violence, some of which smacked of cunningly devised propaganda, emphasizing the steady drift toward Bolshevism in eastern Europe.

After a whole week devoted to conferences on reparations the French suddenly appeared with a wholly new plan. They brought in their claim to the Saar Valley and set forth their historical rights, reaching back to 1814. The President said at once, and plainly, that he considered the French claim to the territory and the people as contrary to the terms of the Armistice and to the Fourteen Points upon which they had all agreed. At this, he told me afterwards, Clemenceau broke out angrily, accusing Wilson of pro-Germanism.

"If such opposition to our just demands are made I must resign."

Upon this the President said he could make no comment, but suggested that if M. Clemenceau was not prepared to abide by the solemnly accepted terms of the Armistice, he (the President) might as well go home. He was evidently deeply disturbed; Grayson told me he could eat no luncheon. When the conference resumed in the afternoon he made a powerful speech to his three associates. He was not, he said, for an easy peace, but for a just peace, and he painted a vivid picture of what Europe would be like if the terms of the treaty were so harsh that the Germans would not or could not accept them.

Clemenceau, who during the luncheon period had evidently reflected upon what would happen if the Conference broke up, got up from his seat and with tears in his eyes shook Wilson's hand:

"I agree with you, Mr. President, I agree with you."

"And I, too," said Lloyd George.

I suggested to the President that the Four ought to issue some kind of communique, giving the world at least an inkling of what was going on. I told him that American correspondents, greatly disturbed by rumors of a disruption within the Conference and unable to find out what was happening, were growing extremely restless and critical.

"How can we say anything?" the President asked. "We have nothing to report. We have actually accomplished nothing definite and if we were to tell the truth we should have to put the blame exactly where it belongs—upon the French."

"Isn't it time that this situation be known?" I asked. "Why shouldn't you come out squarely and say what the trouble is?"

"The time has not come yet," he said.

"Then why not let some of our correspondents do it?" I asked, though I feared I was making a nuisance of myself.

"Well," he responded, "if some of them are indiscreet enough to tell the truth I shall have no objections."

I took this for a permission and told the correspondents how the land lay, and a number of blazing reports went across to America.

As a matter of fact, the Peace Conference was getting into deeper and deeper water—disagreeing about indemnities and reparations as well as boundaries, both Clemenceau and Lloyd George being fearful of accepting too little lest they be turned out by their own governments. Lloyd George was reaping the whirlwind of his election promises.

On the other hand, if they made the terms of the treaty too stiff, they had begun to fear that Germany would not sign.

It was also plain that the President was outrageously overworking. He was taking little or no exercise, not even the customary drives out through the Bois. On one day he had three conferences going on, all at the same time: the usual meeting of the Big Four; a conference with the financial experts in another room; and a separate meeting with Orlando, the Italian premier, on the impossible Italian claims. I had the feeling at the time that such a feverish pace could not continue.

On April 2, I found the President again profoundly discouraged. He looked very tired. He said it began to seem to him that the French were *intentionally* delaying the proceedings by endless talk.

During these days everyone I met was plunged in the depths of pessimism. When I asked the President if he wanted me to tell him exactly what I was hearing and seeing at my listening post, he said:

"Certainly."

So I told him about the bitter feeling that I was hearing expressed by delegates from all parts of Europe.

"I know it," he said.

I told him that he was being blamed on all sides for the delay.

"I know that, too," he said.

I again suggested cautiously that sooner or later he would have to show what the reasons really were for the delay.

"If I were to do that," he said, "it would immediately break up the Peace Conference—and we cannot risk it yet."

The unlimited greedy bargaining continued unabated with only the President growing grayer and grimmer all the time, standing upon principles of justice and right.

The break came on April 3.

Just at the close of the meeting of the Council of Four on that day, the President fell ill and Dr. Grayson put him to bed. He had a severe cold with a fever. It was not unexpected to those who knew what the conditions really were. Dr. Grayson had been shaking his head for several days; he said that the President could not much longer continue to bear such a strain.

There were other unmistakable evidences that the supreme crisis was at hand. That very evening Italian friends of mine rushed around with the story that Orlando and the entire Italian delegation were going to leave the Conference if they were not given Fiume. They were all wildly excited, predicting the fall of Orlando's Government. The Italians already had won back their unredeemed provinces with over one million Italians, and yet they were willing to endanger everything for twenty-five thousand Italians in the wholly doubtful city of Fiume which, even in the pact of London, they had not claimed. It sometimes seemed that the worst of all the imperialists were the weaker, newer nations—Italy, Poland, Czecho-Slovakia, Jugo-Slavia.

Even the Belgians were in a rebellious mood. The King of the Belgians flew down from Brussels to see the President; a tall, blond, youthful-looking man, handsome and engaging. All agreed that he was much more moderate in his demands than some of the Belgian delegates, but nevertheless insistent.

Before his illness I had told the President of the remark of one of the Italian diplomats who had come to see me. When I asked him whether he was for the League of Nations, he had replied naively:

"Yes, but we want Fiume first."

I observed that this seemed typical of the position of all the Allies—that they wanted first to be sure of their "grabs" and "indemnities" and then to organize a League of Nations to protect them in their possession. I told him how I had answered two Italians, aides of Orlando, who declared they were going home if they did not get Fiume.

"That is interesting," I had said. "It would relieve us of a great responsibility."

"How is that?" they asked.

"Well, we are now stabilizing your lira at 6:32. Of course, if you withdrew from the Conference, you could not expect us to continue to do that."

Their faces fell.

"And," I said, "our merchants are now shipping much wheat and other food to Italy. I presume they will not care to do this unless they are well assured of their pay."

"That was exactly what you should have said," the President remarked.

We had some talk of Lloyd George's position and the clear intimation that he was preparing to throw the blame for delay upon Wilson.

"Well," said the President sadly, "I suppose I shall have to stand alone."

I told him I believed the great masses of people were still strongly with him, but were confused and puzzled by hearing every case in the world but ours, and that they would rally again strongly to his support if he told them exactly what the situation was and the nature of his opposition.

"I believe so, too," he said.

I asked him what I could say to the correspondents, and he told me to tell them to read again our agreements on the basis of the peace with the other Allies and with Germany, and to assure them that he would not surrender on these principles. This I did, gladly, but it was far from being the "spot news" that the correspondents wanted.

I went to talk with Colonel House and found him sitting on his lounge with a figured blanket over his chilly legs—quite serenely dictating his diary to Miss Denton. More and more he impressed me as the dilettante—the lover of the game—the eager secretary without profound responsibility. He told me that if *he* had it to do, he could make peace in an hour. Were the Italians going home—well and good, let them go. Was Lloyd George going to issue a defense (as I intimated to him) which might compromise the President—all right, let him issue it. I told him of the President's illness and said that Grayson told me that the President had probably contracted his cold from contact with Clemenceau, who coughs fearfully.

"I hope," said the Colonel genially, "that Clemenceau will pass on the germ to Lloyd George."

Colonel House said that some of the correspondents told him that I was putting a dark interpretation on the situation, and he expostulated.

"The President does not seem cheerful," I said.

"No," he admitted.

"I do not see why we should try to smooth over the situation and imply that everything is all right."

"We are all together on everything but certain small details," he insisted.

"Have you decided the question of Fiume?"

"Not yet."

"Or that of Poland?"

"No."

And there you were!

Details, of course, caused all the trouble. In settling an estate it is often not the money nor the old home over which the heirs quarrel, but the family Bible and grandmother's alpaca shawl.

The President could escape no responsibility, and must go to punishment not only for his own mistakes and weaknesses of temperament, but for the fear and the greed of the world. I did not love him—but I believed and trusted in him beyond any other man.

I said in my notes, "He is the only great man here. Clemenceau is serious, but serious for smaller causes, immediate gains. Lloyd George is a poor third—who lives for the moment, is pleased with every new compromise, pledges reckless future benefits for each present gain. Orlando is an amiable southern Italian without depth or vision, playing little games of local politics while the world is afire."

CHAPTER XLVI

The Greatest Sensation of the Peace Conference

THE GREATEST SENSATION of the entire Peace Conference came on April 7. Early on that morning Dr. Grayson sent me word that the President, who was still ill in bed, had ordered the *George Washington* to sail for Brest. She was then in dry-dock in America, and was not expected to be out until the 14th of April. He said that the President desired that the bare statement of this fact, without explanation, be made to the newspaper correspondents.

It was, of course, news of the most sensational character. In giving it out I took pains to offer no interpretation, but the implication was perfectly clear—that the President had grown tired of the delay and the opposition and was determined to make an end of it. The correspondents made the most of the announcement.

Some such explosion had been in the making for several days. Conditions all over Europe seemed to be still further deteriorating. The papers were full of the most incendiary news. The Italians were continuing to threaten to break up the Peace Conference by going home; news was coming from northern Russia that the Bolsheviks were threatening the extermination of the American troops that had been sent up there; Bavaria was actually in the process of setting up a Soviet republic. Even in Paris the situation looked blacker than ever before. An enormous red-flag parade just at this time served to increase the general restlessness. It was a protest against the acquittal of the assassin of Jaurès, the French socialist, with extreme speeches by radical leaders, including Anatole France.

"If these old leaders only knew it," I wrote in my diary, "Wilson is the only strong bulwark left to the old order against Leninism: he would save the present democratic system by making it just, decent, honest. What they are doing with their greedy demands and selfish interests is to give new arguments, new force to Lenin and his following. They can't see this—and plunge on to their doom. . . . For what good will be a League of Nations unless the settlements upon which it rests are just? A League, the only purpose of which is to guarantee 'grabs' of land by France, Italy, Poland, etc., is doomed to speedy failure."

It can be imagined how the President's action in ordering the *George Washington* on the 7th cut through the dense gloom which had enveloped the Peace Conference. What was needed was *greatness* —greatness, boldness, courage—and at the critical moment Wilson had acted.

That evening I went up to see the President—the first time since he had fallen ill—and had a long talk. I found him fully dressed, in his study, looking thin and pale. A slight hollowness of the eyes emphasized a characteristic I had often noted before—the size and luminosity of his eyes. They were extremely clear, and he looked at one with a piercing intentness. In regard to the calling of the *George Washington,* he said:

"Well, the time has come to bring this thing to a head. House was just here and told me that Clemenceau and Klotz have talked away another day. They brought in a report which Clemenceau said he had not seen. There is the best of evidence that he had seen it. The unspeakable Klotz was called in to explain it. One mass of tergiversations! I will not discuss anything with them any more."

I then urged, as I had done before, that a statement be issued at once setting forth the specific applications of his principles. This we discussed, he being doubtful about too detailed a statement upon the specific issues. All that was necessary to say, he thought, was that he proposed to stand upon his principles.

"Then Italy will not get Fiume?"

"Absolutely not—so long as I am here," he said sharply.

"Nor France the Saar?"

"No. We agreed among ourselves and we agreed with Germany upon certain general principles. The whole course of the Conferences has been made up of a series of attempts, especially by France, to break over this agreement, to get territory, to impose crushing indemnities. The only real interest of France in Poland is to weaken Germany by giving Poland territory to which she has no right."

He said that a League of Nations founded upon an unjust peace could have no future. He was going to fight to the end. He had reached the point where he could give no further.

Of one thing I was certain, after my conversation with him. He was not "bluffing" in ordering the *George Washington.*

I saw Wilson again on the evening of the 8th. He was much more hopeful. In ordering the *George Washington* he had wonderfully cleared the air. The Four appeared now to be willing to drive forward toward a settlement. It was plain that of all things the French did not want Wilson to go home. There was a cunningly significant paragraph on the back page of the *Temps* that morning:

THE PEACE CONFERENCE

FRANCE'S CLAIMS

Contrary to the assertions spread by the German press and taken up by other foreign newspapers, we believe that the French Government has no annexationist pretensions, openly or under cover, in regard to any territory inhabited by a German population. This remark applies particularly to the regions comprised between the frontier of 1871 and the frontier of 1814.* We make it all the more willingly, as the *Temps*, in the political direction which it has followed, has always made it a point not to encourage any annexationist aims.

This cautious paragraph was clear indication that they were willing, if reluctant, to change their tactics.

The first great and vital result of Wilson's stubborn fight, which had culminated in the ordering of the *George Washington* to take him home, was to initiate a period of "high politics." It could scarcely be called a victory for the President, since he hated political compromise, but it did serve to place the Four on a new basis of give-and-take negotiation. This was promoted by a chastened understanding, based on fear, that a negotiated peace, if it were to be realized at all, must be made at once. It was becoming a race between peace and anarchy.

But the days from April 9 onward were not happy days for any of the negotiators, least of all for Wilson. Lloyd George was under fierce attack from his own Northcliffe press for his "kindness" to

* Of course the territories here meant are the Saar and the Rhine frontiers.

the Germans and his effort to work with the Russians. Incidentally, Northcliffe was hitting even more virulently, if indirectly, at Wilson. As for Wilson, he was again, as I noted in my diary, overworking terribly and getting almost no exercise or fresh air.

"Today, when I went into his study, he looked old and worn. Things are not going well. He had two conferences of the Big Four today, and the League of Nations Commission last evening until midnight. I saw him standing with Grayson close to the window. The sash had been thrown up and Grayson was exercising the President by standing with him foot to foot, and with clasped hands pulling him vigorously back and forth. The President turned to me with the remark, 'Indoor golf.' But what a wretchedly poor substitute. I don't see how he can endure such a life much longer."

I tried in every way possible in this crisis to increase my assistance. I knew how little he heard about what was going on in Peace Conference circles outside his own conference room—how much less of what was going on in Paris—and how much he needed to know. I was well aware also how impatient he was with long reports and rambling conversations. I tried therefore each day to set down brief memoranda of what I heard and saw—not mere gossip and rumors, but facts—boiled down to the fewest possible words. He could glance over them in a few minutes. I did not often offer suggestions or advice unless he asked for it; what he needed was not my opinions, but the raw material for his own swift and powerful mind.

While neither the President nor Mrs. Wilson cared for conventional social affairs, a certain number were "required"—even though they were a further burden upon the President's strength. I noted in my diary one such occasion:

"April 9. I attended a reception given by Mrs. Wilson tonight. Lloyd George, Clemenceau, Orlando, and a great party of others were there. It was a notable gathering—all the celebrities."

In the meantime the conferences of the Ten and the Five to discuss the minor problems that faced the delegates continued their heavy-footed, dusty courses. The plenary session to receive the Labor Report was held on April 11 in the big dining room at the Quai d'Orsay.

It was a miserably dull meeting in the fetid air of a dim room.

Worse still, the entire proceedings gave one an unhappy sense of unreality, perfunctoriness. It was *staged for a purpose,* to show the labor of the world—the unrestful proletariat—that the Peace Conference in Paris had not forgotten it.

My own dejection at the time is shown in my notes of April 12: "Nothing much counts any more. A treaty will be made, but it may never be signed, or if signed it will have little meaning. We are plunging inevitably into an unknown world full of danger."

On April 14, the President sent me the first official announcement of any kind that the Council of Four had made—although it had then been at work for many weeks:

Paris, 14 April, 1919

MY DEAR BAKER:

At the request of my colleagues of the so-called Council of Four, I have formulated the enclosed statement of the reasons for advising that the German plenipotentiaries be summoned, and the effect which this will have upon the rest of the business of the Peace Conference.

Will you not be kind enough to see that this statement is immediately put in the hands of all the press representatives of all the countries? It is official, and I am merely acting as the spokesman of the Conferences that have been held at the Place des Etats-Unis.

Faithfully yours,

(Signed) W. W.

I received the President's statement * about nine o'clock in the evening and we got rapid distribution by wireless and cable throughout the world. It set the date for the arrival of the Germans for April 25.

This crucial announcement was followed by even more whirling days. The treaty-making was drawing to a close—unsatisfactorily. The Four were seemingly hurrying to get it done before the world fell apart. The pressure fell heaviest upon the President since he was faced by the difficult if not impossible task of applying ideal moral principles to specific cases. Yet the principles remained and were everlastingly true. It was Wilson's great service that he announced them, and that he tried desperately to apply them.

* For the text of this statement see my *Woodrow Wilson and World Settlement,* Vol. II, p. 77.

I talked with the President about the matter of getting the treaty, when finished, distributed as news throughout the world. It would be a stupendous task—over one hundred thousand words, half as large as *Pickwick Papers*. He said the French and British would never let it out a day in advance, so we could not use couriers. He empowered me to call a conference of the British and French press representatives to see if we could not arrive at some co-operative method of distribution which would not hopelessly clog and swamp the cables and wireless stations of the world.

As for myself those breathless days, I did not live. I merely existed, one whirl of desperate work.

"Spring is coming in the country," I wrote in my diary, "and I am not there. I walked to Notre Dame last night and saw the moon between the towers and came back along the Seine and stood and looked long at the lights, like pinpricks in the old beauty of the dark buildings, and the glimmering water under the bridge arches—and ached with longing for time to live, to think, to feel. And not be lost in a sea of profitless talk. What is the use of all this? Why any longer waste life on such futility? A quiet place, a friend or two, and a little beauty—all so simple to be had—and yet I am here imprisoned in a mad-house of suspicion, fear, covetousness, hatred. We are swept resistlessly into the morass—we, too, talk wildly, wear ourselves out with footless meetings—we who know better, we who know well that reality is not here, nor truth, nor happiness. But who can do anything? Who can change the crazy world?

"April 18: I dined tonight with my old and dear friends Ida Tarbell and William Allen White. Dr. Westermann was there and talked of the Armenian problem and the need for America to take a mandatory in that part of the world. I lunched with Professor Pupin, the Serb genius, and others, including Beer and Shotwell, and heard Jugo-Slav claims presented."

The Italian question was still acute with neither the President nor the Italians giving an inch. Several Chinese delegates came in to talk about the Shantung settlement. The American Commission was torn within itself concerning the Russian question: the President held up the report made by Bullitt and Steffens upon their return from Russia; and Herbert Hoover, who would feed the Russians, was sharply critical of the Bolsheviks.

I took time out for a couple of hours with Charles R. Crane in the Bagatelle. It was beautiful with spring. American soldiers were playing baseball within sight of Marie Antoinette's little palace. But we talked China, Turkey, and other far places.

The next day I attended a committee meeting of the heads of the press at the Dufayel Club—Mair and Colonel Strode-Jackson for the British and Pueux for the French. Several technical cable and radio experts were present: Colonel Coan for the British and Walter Rogers for us. We arranged for the pooling of the cables and wireless apparatus of the world for sending the Treaty and the summaries we were then preparing. It was the first time, I believe, that there was ever such co-operation in communications. We also discussed at length the press arrangements for meeting the Germans at Versailles. It was a complicated business.

I had quite a long talk with Mr. Wilson after the meeting of the Four on April 21. He told me fully about the Adriatic negotiations which he said were at complete deadlock. I conveyed to him the message of Orlando sent through Tozzi, accounting for the attacks in the Italian press, which Orlando deprecated. Orlando wished to assure the President of his great personal respect and admiration. The President told me that he had always liked Orlando, had found him a gentleman and a man of his word. He thought, however, that the Italians had worked themselves up to the point of insanity. He said Orlando told him that a break meant the ruin of Italy. The President had prepared a strong statement of the case which he said he would put out if a break came. I was allowed to tell almost nothing to the correspondents that evening.

CHAPTER XLVII

The Great Battles over Japanese-Chinese Problems

COMPROMISE FOR A FEW DAYS was the magic wand at Paris. Why hadn't they thought of it before? With one High Negotiator giving away a city he did not own, and another High Negotiator accepting a strategic frontier he had never expected to get, there would be immediate peace in the world. Had not the Germans been summoned to hear their fate on April 25? The Treaty would be signed in a week, or possibly ten days, everything would be well with the world, and we could all go home. There were optimists in high places who told one another just that!

With some of this talk ringing in my ears I went up in the late afternoon of April 22 to see the President. I found him sitting by the sunny window in Mrs. Wilson's drawing-room. She was at work with her needles on a brightly colored scarf. A huge bunch of white lilacs perfumed the quiet room.

I thought I had never seen the President looking so utterly worn out. One of his eyes twitched nervously. He told me in a weary voice that the Four had spent the day discussing the Italian and Japanese problems. They had got nowhere with either of them.

"I have told them," he said, "that I will not sign the Treaty if the Italians are allowed to seize Fiume and the Dalmatian coast."

The time had come, he said, when Lloyd George and Clemenceau, who considered themselves more or less bound by the London Treaty, must either side with him or with the Italians. He now expected that the Italians would break away and go home. He would not care so much if it were not for the effect it might have in Germany. He spoke with a kind of still determination.

The situation regarding the Japanese settlements, he said, was no better. They had made their unjust demands and would stand on them. If they could not get what they wanted they also would go home. No, they were not bluffing. If both Italy and Japan should withdraw, what would happen to the League of Nations?

This did not seem to me at all like compromise. And as for the Treaty, would it ever be signed at all?

The President had talked with me several times "in the strictest confidence" about an appeal which he was thinking of making to the Italian people—without consulting their leaders. It would be a resort to his sovereign remedy; the kind of appeal which, from the very beginning of his political career, had been the basis of most of his triumphs. He believed, all but mystically, in "the people"; if he could get to them they would give him the necessary support, even against their own leaders. No doubt he was remembering the thundering, worshipful crowds which had cheered him in Rome and Milan.

He had read his proposed appeal to both Lloyd George and Clemenceau, who approved it, or said they did. It was like so many of Wilson's messages—extremely brief, but packed with implications that were as explosive at that time as dynamite. When I read it my heart sank. It seemed to me to come too late: and how could he be sure of the same kind of response from the Italian public as from the American? But the President did not ask my opinion regarding the appeal, and since he had already decided to make it, I did not venture to comment upon it. We put it at once on the wireless and cables, had it translated into French, and the *Temps* succeeded in publishing it that day in a special edition. It caused a terrific sensation and brought down upon us all the newspaper men in Paris.

The message, with its violent reverberations and responses, had a good French press and our own people, few of whom knew what was really involved in it, came up solidly behind the President. One of its results could have been expected, two were more or less unexpected.

1. It widened the breach between the Italian leaders and the other members of the Peace Conference. Orlando had gone home, but the Italian economists had remained.

2. It seemed to have little effect on the Italian people; probably they did not understand what it meant. There were even evidences that it increased their support of their own Government.

3. It seemed, however, to have one important result—perhaps it was what the President had chiefly in mind. It brought plainly to the surface the two forces which had so long been struggling in secret, placed the President's determined position irrevocably upon the record, and clarified the issues relating to the Adriatic.

The President's appeal settled nothing: and the Peace Conference was now weakened by the absence of one of the Allied Governments, at a moment when the Chinese-Japanese settlement was at an acute crisis.

Some of the Italian delegates evidently thought that when Orlando angrily left Paris and returned to Rome, the Conference would be shaken to its foundations. It might even break up. But nothing had happened. They began to be uneasy when they saw the Peace Conference sailing along without them. Two of them who came in often to see me asked one day:

"What are you Americans going to do?"

"Why, make peace, and go home," I said.

"What about the Adriatic?"

"You're settling that, aren't you?" I asked.

What they wanted was to be invited to come back.

"But," I said, "no one invited you to go away. You are still members of the Peace Conference, and the Americans, to the last man of us, want you here and think you ought to be here. You have only to come."

They then wanted to know whether they could get a mandate in Syria to offer to the Italian people. Trading to the last.

About that time I had a long talk with the President regarding the Chinese-Japanese problem, which he considered one of the most important of all. I asked him if he had had it in mind when he issued the Italian message, for many people seemed to see its application also to the claims of Japan.

"No," he said, "not specifically, but when you lay down a general truth it may cut anywhere."

It was plain that the Japanese problems disturbed him deeply.

"They are not bluffers," he said, "and they will go home unless we give them what they should not have."

"The opinion of the world," I said, "supports the Chinese claims."

"I know that," he said.

"Especially American public opinion," I added.

"I know that, too," he replied, "but if the Italians remain away and the Japanese go home, what becomes of the League of Nations?"

Those spring days for everyone at the Conference, not the weary negotiators alone, were among the most difficult and laborious of the year. I wrote in my notes on Sunday, April 27:

"This is the first day of let-up I have had for weeks. I got a car and took Ida Tarbell and Will White [William Allen White] to Fontainebleau where we had a fine visit with Jaccaci who is convalescing in the home of Tavanier, the painter. We ran on to Barbizon for luncheon at Charmette's and afterward saw the fields where Millet painted the 'Angelus.' We visited the homes of the Barbizon celebrities, Millet, Rousseau, Diaz, and others, and came back again for tea at Tavanier's: and then through the beautiful country into Paris. A fine trip, with spring coming on and good friends to enjoy it with—what in all the world could be finer? As we came rolling homeward we caught up with the President's car; he and Mrs. Wilson and the Admiral had also been in Fontainebleau."

In a conversation with the President on the next day (April 28) he asked me regarding several meetings I had been having with the Chinese delegates. He was anxious to know what their reaction to the various proposals for the settlement of the Japanese claims would probably be. I had already brought him several brief memoranda on the subject—in the preparation of which I had been greatly helped by Williams and Hornbeck, American experts on far eastern affairs.

Accordingly, I went over that evening to dine with Dr. Liang at 8 Rue Monsieur, one of the aristocratic old places of Paris. These are the notes I made regarding the talk we had:

"Dr. Liang is among the most distinguished writers and progressive leaders of China. Dr. Wellington Koo was there, and other members of the Chinese delegation. It was one of the best dinners I ever ate in my life. All the Chinese except Liang spoke English well. The Chinese I like; they are much livelier minded than the Japanese, and franker. The Japanese, those who are here anyway, are reluctant to take a position on anything. They seem unsure of themselves, but one can discuss anything with the Chinese. Also the Chinese do not invite you to dinner merely to badger you with propaganda. Go to lunch or dinner with the Italians, and from the moment you sit down until you escape with relief, you are battered and bruised with arguments for Italian 'rights,' made to feel Italian 'sufferings,' or assaulted with the 'glories' of Italian history. The same is more or less true with the French, but not with the British. The British have a superior air of assuming that their rights do not need to be discussed.

"Yet I did talk out the Shantung situation thoroughly with the Chinese.

"When I returned to the hotel about midnight, I found that the President's house had been repeatedly calling me. I immediately called Admiral Grayson and he said the President wanted me to secure certain information on the Chinese situation. I got Hornbeck out of bed and we talked until two A.M. I then came back here to the Crillon and worked on memoranda until six o'clock this morning. I lay down for an hour or so, but could not sleep, and soon got up and went at it again, in order to have the material ready for the President before his meeting with the Japanese. The Admiral called me again about eight-thirty and at nine I was at the President's house where I laid before him the notes I had made, together with various memoranda furnished me by Williams and Hornbeck and by Koo and Wei and others of the Chinese.

"I pinned up a good map on the wall of the President's study and made as strong a case as I could for the Chinese position, urging some postponement at least. The President listened with that intensity of attention which is sometimes disconcerting, and when I had concluded making my points—which I had written down beforehand, to make them as brief and clear as possible—the President said:

" 'Baker, the difficulty is not with the facts of the controversy, but with the politics of it.' "

I knew perfectly well where the President's sympathies were: he was for the Chinese. Probably the most immediately popular thing he could have done would have been to decide against the Japanese and go home. But it would have been temporary popularity—before the storm broke.

He pointed out to me that morning how inextricably the whole matter was tied up with old secret treaties, that Great Britain felt herself bound to Japan, and again expressed his concern that with Italy already out and Belgium bitterly discontented, the defection of Japan, not an unreasonable possibility, might not only break up the Peace Conference, but destroy the League of Nations.

The next day the President went over the whole ground with me at length. Said he had been unable to sleep the night before for considering the question. Anything he might do was wrong. He gave me a copy of a cablegram he had just sent to Tumulty, giving the gist of the decision. He said it was "the best that could be gotten out of a dirty past." He had considered every possible contingency. His sympathies were all with the Chinese. I found afterward that he had been fairly bombarded by pro-Chinese arguments by our own people, including a powerful letter by General Bliss, expressing his conviction:

"It can't be right to do wrong even to make peace. Peace is desirable but there are things dearer than peace—justice and freedom."

Bliss was strong for the Chinese view of the settlement. Often at Paris I heard him express himself strongly upon this subject. It was the simple, direct, honest, limited view. But could the "rights" and "wrongs" be so clearly blocked out? Every right involved some wrong as the President had said; and every wrong some right—in those complex decisions at Paris. And a right adhered to in one circumstance might involve a serious wrong in some other. There *are* things dearer than peace; but could they be had by more war? If we had stood for "justice and freedom" in the Chinese settlement, as the fine old General desired, and had delayed peace, or let Japan leave the Peace Conference as Italy had just done, would justice and freedom have been assured in China? The President saw farther and deeper, that real justice and freedom in the world was dependent not upon trying to right every wrong of every people, but upon securing a *new basis of unity in the world,* a new instrumentality for obtaining justice and freedom.

I gave General Bliss my heart; but I gave the President my head. The trouble was that the President had so little to build upon. I afterward found among his papers pathetic passages relating to his conferences with the Japanese in which he urged trustfulness between Japan and China! He was so sure that unjust settlements would bring their own punishments. He told the Italians this; he told the Japanese; he told the French; but he effected nothing. *There had been no change of spirit in the world.*

If President Wilson had made such a decision as the Chinese desired, the Japanese as he believed would have gone home. With Italy already out, and Belgium threatening, would Germany sign the treaty, or would she prefer to await certain chaos? It might mean that everyone would return home and begin to arm—wars everywhere. This would not force Japan out of Shantung; it would only encourage deeper penetration. The only hope of peace was to keep the Allies together, establish the League of Nations with Japan a member, and then try to secure justice for the Chinese, not only regarding Japan, but regarding England, Russia, France, and America, all of whom had concessions in China. If Japan went home, there was danger of a Japanese-Russian-German alliance—and a return to the old "balance of power" system in the world—on a greater scale than ever. He knew well that his decision would be unpopular in America, that the Chinese would be disappointed, that the avaricious Japanese would feel triumphant, that he would be accused of violating his own principles—but nevertheless he *must* work for world order and organization against anarchy and a return to the old militarism. More and more the President was coming to have a kind of mystic belief that the League, if he could get it accepted and organized, would save the world. He seemed ever more willing to compromise desperately to get it.

I urged strongly upon the President that I be allowed to announce immediately the exact terms of the settlement, lest it come out garbled through Japanese sources. To this the President finally consented, and sent me the following memorandum, which I am inserting here because I was sharply criticized in certain quarters for making the announcement at that time:

Paris, 30 April, 1919

DEAR MR. BAKER:

The President asks me to send you the enclosed copy of a cable message which we are sending today in cypher to Tumulty regarding the

Japanese-Chinese settlement. The President asks that you do not use any of the information in this telegram as coming from him but only as the basis of what is to be told the newspaper men. And he asks further that you use it only when you find that the general subject matter of the settlement is being given to the press from some other quarter.

Sincerely yours,

Gilbert F. Close

Confidential Secretary to the President.*

I went back to the forty or fifty correspondents who were awaiting me with one of the biggest "stories" of the conference, so far as the Americans were concerned. What a clacking of typewriters followed!

The next day the President asked me to see the Chinese and explain to them the exact nature of the problems he had had to face. At ten that evening I went over to their headquarters at the Hotel Lutetia and talked until midnight with Wang (the ablest of them) and Koo and a considerable group of others. I put the case to them just as the President put it to me. I have rarely seen a more depressed group of men. Some of the hot-heads (Cheng) were for issuing an immediate statement or even for leaving Paris, but this I urged them strongly not to do—to wait and see, to wait until the whole situation was clear. I tried to show them that the League of Nations would prove the first real safeguard that China had ever had, the only one that promised a reconsideration and reformation of all foreign relationships with China. For the first time, America would have a part in a covenant to preserve the integrity of China. But it was difficult, in the presence of sharp immediate disappointment, to argue the validity of future benefits. It was also bitterly hard, where one believed in the justice of a claim (as I did in the justice of the Chinese demands) to argue that they be disregarded in order to accomplish some farther-sighted purpose.

Wilson had for long been the prophet of the world; he had now to fight in the dust and heat of the arena in order to save from utter extinction even a small part of his grand plan. He must bargain and bluff, give way here, stand firm there. Miserable business—but *wise*.

* For the message referred to see my *Woodrow Wilson and World Settlement*, Vol. III, pp. 315–316.

How he would be hated by all the little ones who thought they could go away by themselves and be good.

I was able to put the situation in such a light that many of the correspondents really saw the President's problem and the need of some such compromise with the Japanese. Some of the factors I argued were:

1. The utter weakness of the Chinese government; both weakness and corruption. The very man, Mr. Lu, who as foreign minister had signed the disgraceful treaties with Japan, was now in Paris demanding help for the Chinese. To risk everything to bolster up a government which might tomorrow fall out from under us again—what good?

2. The Japanese, after all, were abominably crowded in their little islands. They also demanded *something* from the war—as France, Italy and Britain were demanding much.

3. If we stood by China, broke up the conference and went home, who would then put Japan out of Shantung? Our people, certainly, would never fight Japan on that issue. The only hope was in a world organization.

Wilson's Chinese decision caused a furor among the Americans in Paris. I found that no one of our Commissioners had known about it until I told them. All of them, except Colonel House, who was for smoothing everything over, were strong proponents of the Chinese, and declared that Wilson had made a terrible mistake. Williams, Hornbeck, and others of our experts were openly sympathizing with and helping the Chinese. I had a long talk with Secretary Lansing, while he drew his interminable grotesque pictures on a pad of paper, and found him quite inconsolable. He said he would not, under any circumstances, defend the decision. He would not attack it. He would remain silent. He was for the right of the matter, he said, regardless of consequences.

"And break up the Peace Conference?" I asked.

"Even that, if necessary."

Both General Bliss and Henry White sided with Lansing.

Later I saw several of the Japanese delegation, but they were as uncommunicative as Red Indians. Several of our ablest correspondents supported the President's decision. William Allen White was one of them, and Smith of the Associated Press, who had been long in the Far East, said that this, after all, however hard for the Chinese, was the only practical solution. On the whole, I think we got over the entire problem, both sides of it, including the sharp and strong reply of the Chinese; and that was my sole purpose.

On May 3, the Three put nearly the finishing touches on the Treaty so that it could go to the printer; but the troublesome Belgian and Italian problems remained unsettled. They were trying to force Wilson's hand on the Italian question; and after the Three adjourned, the Italian Ambassador to America, Celleri, appeared and nearly wore the President out with talk—delaying his dinner for half an hour. He was so beaten out that he could remember only with an effort what the Council had done in the forenoon.

CHAPTER XLVIII

I Watch the May Day Riots in Paris

ON MAY FIRST in Paris came the May Day riots. We watched from the window of my office on the Rue Royal just at the corner of the Place de la Concorde, and saw cavalry, soldiery, and police, aided by the fire department, take turns in beating, sabering, and wetting down the crowds of working men out for their annual demonstration. We saw many bloody heads and one man with a finger cut off by a sword. What folly! What unutterable folly! It only showed the weakness of the French Government, indeed the weakness of the old social order. The crowds of miserable looking workmen wearing little red *boutonnieres* with sprigs of white lilies-of-the-valley, came by our window shouting,

"A bas Clemenceau," and "Vive Wilson."

These were confusing and tumultuous days. Everyone was getting ready for the great ceremony of the presentation of the Treaty to the Germans although the exact date had not yet been fixed. The whole world indeed was awaiting the disclosure of the terms that would be imposed. When I read the first proofs of the Treaty as it was originally drawn, it seemed to me a terrible document; a dispensation of retribution with scarcely a parallel in history. Too hard? I thought the German delegation, which had then arrived at Versailles, would fall in a swoon when they saw it. I questioned whether they would sign it. "If they do," I wrote, "it will be with crossed fingers. I can see no real peace in it. They have tempered justice with no mercy."

Even the President said to me, "If I were a German, I think I should never sign it."

The problem of distributing throughout the world the news of what was in the Treaty had been under consideration for several weeks. The Treaty itself was a voluminous document which few people would read and fewer understand: and an attempt to send it in full would swamp all of the avenues of transmission. Even more important than this was the fact that it might be substantially changed when the Germans sent in their comments and criticisms. It was finally decided to let each of the three nations chiefly concerned—the French, the British and the Americans—make its own summary, afterwards submitting it for approval to the Four.

This task was undertaken by the three official press bureaus: represented by M. Tardieu for the French, Mr. Mair for the British and Mr. Sweetser for ours. It proved to be a highly difficult problem. We not only had to decide what should go into the summary and what should be left out, but there soon began to be fierce demands for various hours of release in America as well as elsewhere—the morning papers, the evening papers, the press associations, and the independent correspondents, all having different interests, and these had to be harmonized with the cable and air facilities. We had our hands full!

On May 6, I was summoned to attend the session of the Big Three for the discussion of the completed summaries. The British and Americans had worked in complete harmony, but our summaries differed considerably from the French so that it was necessary to get some decision from the Three as to what was to be considered "official." We were kept waiting in the anteroom of the President's study for a long time, for the Three were in the last throes of the treaty-making. We finally had our inning. The President helped greatly in securing favorable decisions regarding our release. Mr. Sweetser had done an excellent piece of work; we did not find it necessary to change a word in it.

We also arranged to send the American summary to all of North America, the western coast of South America, Japan, and China; the British summary to all of the British Empire except Canada; and the French summary to all of Continental Europe. It was at that time, I believe, the greatest co-operative undertaking in the distribution of news that had ever been attempted.

Before the Treaty itself was in type, even before the summaries were made public, the news of what it contained had spread like wildfire. Born with such agony of travail, it seemed to satisfy nobody. Everyone concerned began to demand changes, especially the representatives of the small nations who had been unable to make their piping voices heard above the clamor of Paris.

I attended the secret session at the Quai d'Orsay when Tardieu read his summary of the Treaty to the small nations. This was their first detailed knowledge of what was in the Treaty they must sign. The Portuguese representative made a hotly critical speech protesting against the inclusion of Spain in the League of Nations Committee; China made a temperate protest, and Marshal Foch attacked the military provisions of the Treaty, trying to prove that they were not strong enough to deal with the German danger. It was practically an attack on Clemenceau.

Another strange situation developed as soon as the text of the Treaty began to come under the fierce scrutiny of critical readers, many of them experts in their fields. We heard of it first in bated whispers—since the Treaty, fresh from the hands of the Three, was more or less sacrosanct, but these whispers grew louder and louder. There were "jokers" in the Treaty, and what was more, we Americans seemed to be the victims of most of them.

We had not watched the game as closely as the others had. It was the price we paid for having so few specific "material interests." When the Treaty was being finally revised—that crowded Sunday and Monday—the French and British experts were there on the job watching every turn; our own, with the exception of the conscientious Haskins of Harvard and one other, were not there. "Jokers" were the result. For example, the French and British wanted us committed absolutely to permanent membership in the Reparations Commission; we, however, demanded and got a provision that any nation might withdraw from the Reparations Commission on twelve months' notice. We in the Press Bureau had the original text of the Treaty and put this provision into our summary. When, however, the Treaty itself appeared, this particular clause was missing. Who left it out? How was it left out? When the omission was discovered, Lamont, Davis, and others rushed over to the President and the whole thing was brought before the Big Four and the earlier reading restored.

Another "joker" was discovered by the President himself. The words "for the mother country" had been added to the clause of the Covenant which provided for raising troops in colonies under mandatory, making it possible, for example, if France and Britain should go to war, for each to raise, say, Arab troops, for fighting the other. Thus Arabs would be fighting Arabs for no cause of their own. When traced down it was found that Clemenceau himself had added the words—though he was not on the League of Nations Commission and had nothing to do with the Covenant, which had already been adopted at a plenary session. It took all the influence of both Lord Cecil and Colonel House to get the French secretariat to make a change in the original text.

During this period, as the Peace Conference drew toward its close, I find that I was making many entries in my notebooks, trying to clarify my mind about Woodrow Wilson—trying to explain him to myself more clearly. These were not final judgments, but it seems worth while here to put some of them down as stepping stones toward understanding.

"I wonder," I wrote, "if Wilson has not recently been thinking too much politically. He took hold of the living soul of the world while he was its prophet; how much has he lost by becoming its statesman? Every time he has made the gesture of defiance—as in the Italian matter—the masses of the world have loved him; every time he has yielded to compromise—as in the Chinese settlement—the world has been cold. It is a great question whether it would not have been better for him to have stood upon his "points" more sternly and gone home. He has wanted his League of Nations more than anything else; has he sacrificed too much for it? No one else has really sacrificed anything. He will get his League, but can it rest upon such a basis of greed and injustice?

"It is noble in the prophet to assert that he has no selfish or material interests—it stirs the soul of man to its depths, starts an emotional tidal wave that may last for uncounted years—but when the prophet sits down with the poker players, each one of whom wants the jack-pot, the aura fades.

"Every one of the leaders here except Wilson has been a pleader for some special interest or interests; and by agreement among themselves have been able sometimes to overwhelm him. Great Britain, especially, has quietly got all she really wants.

"The President seems now to be losing the support he had among the liberal-minded people of the world, the idealists, the workers, the youth of all nations—without gaining the support of the conservatives. The great liberal and labor papers—the *Manchester Guardian,* the *Labor Herald,* the Italian *Secolo,* the French *L'Humanité,* and others, are now critical.

"Yet his principles remain. They are true; he has stated them once for all, but will he himself ever see the Promised Land?

"Let me try to be clear in my own mind. As the responsible head of a great nation, the chief leader in a world torn with suffering and anarchy—could he pursue his own way unchanged and unchangeable? Has he a right to choose the path which, proving his own faithfulness to his principles, yet leaves the world in frightful disorder? Having agreed to co-operate with other nations in making a peace, can he enforce everything the Americans demand, yield nothing to anyone else? Is this the way humanity moves forward? How far must one work with the forces of his time, however passionate, ignorant, greedy? If he compromises, accepts the best he can get, he may not acquire the crown of prophecy, which is crucifixion, but he may win the laurels which posterity at length bestows upon the wise.

"The alternative is not so simple as many facile critics here at Paris imagine; not between going home and staying here; it is between anarchy and organization.

"Never was I more in doubt as to my own course. This Treaty seems to me, in many particulars, abominable. How can I go home and support it, support the League of Nations founded upon it, support Wilson? Yet I cannot commit the folly of mere empty criticism, harking back to what might have been done. I know too well the impossible atmosphere of greed, fear, hatred, he has had to work in. I have felt it myself, every day, every hour. I have wondered many a time how it was that he could have held on so grimly with almost everyone here against him—not only with direct attacks, but with the most insidious, underhanded, cruel, indirect attacks. Has he not, considering the time and the place, considering the 'slump in idealism' which followed allied victory, got as much as any human being could get?

"American enthusiasm for the League may be the element that finally carries it through. Many of us feel that this League when it comes into being will not long be dominated by the elements which have allowed it to be created. Time will reduce passion; when reason begins to prevail, new liberal governments will everywhere spring up and take charge of affairs; they will dominate the League and furnish a rallying place for settling world controversies without war. I think this is Wilson's firm conviction; all that reassures him when he looks steadily at the settlements."

Many other men in Paris were also trying to explain Woodrow Wilson; as many will, for years to come, be trying to explain him. One afternoon, Jo Davidson, the American sculptor, gave me his opinion. He had made a bust of Wilson the year before—which pleased neither the President nor Mrs. Wilson. He called Wilson's "a hewn face"—cut out with strong strokes. Said that he admired the man, but found nothing in him to love, that the President seemed to be interested in no art, neither painting, sculpture, nor music, nor to know much about any one of them. He was a moralist, a great leader, a powerful personality, whom one *felt* in a room. He invoked fear and respect, like God, but not affection.

As the day approached for the presentation of the Treaty to the German delegates, who had been cooling their heels at Versailles since April 25, we had heated meetings of our correspondents (our newspaper "soviet," as they themselves called it) to protest against arrangements that were being made for them at Versailles. They demanded vociferously not only to see the Treaty presented, but also to be given the opportunity of meeting and interviewing the spokesmen of the German delegation. I was strongly with them in this effort. I felt all along that the greatest fault of the Peace Conference was the failure to take the people more fully into its confidence. It made me angry to think of it. If it had not been for the correspondents, the public would have got no chance at all—just the old private diplomacy. I had a hot argument with Lansing about it. He was all against any concessions—undignified, and so on. I met one of the experts of the State Department in the hall and he said:

"I hear your correspondents want to talk with the Germans and get in at the Session."

"Yes," I said, "why not?"

"Well, I'd see them all shot first. Spreading German propaganda!"

"Are you implying that our correspondents are any less loyal than the diplomats who are to meet the Germans? Or any less honorable? You let our correspondents go into Germany and send out what they will; why shouldn't they meet their representatives here?"

I'm sure I did not convince him.

Colonel House agreed with me on my arguments for better press arrangements at Versailles but thought I ought to take it up with the President, since no one else had authority enough to make any changes. I did so at once, and had really quite a sharp argument with him. Finally he admitted there was justice in our demand for admission to see the Treaty presented to the Germans, since the German correspondents would be there, but he was decidedly against the second proposal—permission to meet the German leaders. He said that in this he agreed with the French. He said there were two factions in the German delegation—the unbending and arrogant Brockdorff-Rantzau group, and the more amenable Melchior group, and while they were to be given free communication with Germany, he felt that the feeling was too intense to make it advisable for our men to talk with any of them.

When I brought up the subject a second time, the President told me he had discussed it with the Three, with no avail. They would let in a number of unneeded secretaries, and a few ornamental wives, but no working correspondents! At the same time German correspondents would be sending their despatches freely, making it probable that our news of the conference would come by way of the *Frankfurter Zeitung* or the *Cologne Gazette*.

As a matter of fact the refusal to permit our correspondents to meet the Germans resulted in there being any amount of unofficial interviewing. One of our press association men (Conger) had a room in the Reservoir Hotel, one wing of which was occupied by the Germans! When the German delegation arrived, the station was policed in the characteristic French way—the guard at one end of the train while the Germans got out at the other end. Result, our men and the British had quite free access to the Germans. What a farce!

All of the old political leaders at the Conference wanted to use the press—pursued it eagerly when they needed it, and neglected it, and avoided it at other times. The treatment of press correspondents is always the acid test of the democracy of any people, and the only way to have an honest and responsible press is to take it into the confidence of the leadership.

The editor of *Le Temps* told me one day that six of the most influential Paris papers were subsidized with Italian money—borrowed from America.

On May 5, I was delighted to learn that the Three were planning to go to Versailles to look into the proposed press arrangements, and to be invited to go with them. As a result of the visit they finally agreed to give space to forty-five correspondents, five American, five British, five British Colonies, five French, five Italian, five Japanese, five German, ten Small Countries.

I need scarcely say that this decision was gladly welcomed by the correspondents. While the number to be admitted was small, and scores of eager correspondents from all nations would be sharply disappointed, we all felt that the principle of press representation at the Conference had been established.

When these tempestuous matters had been settled, I went to dinner with William Allen White and his son, Bill, and afterward to the Theatre Antoine to see a really marvelous presentation in French of *The Taming of the Shrew.* Gemier played the Petruchio—and wonderfully played it. They took all kinds of liberty with Shakespeare's old play—made a laughing farce of it.

CHAPTER XLIX

Presenting the Treaty to the Germans

ON MAY 7, the great meeting for the formal presentation of the Treaty to the Germans took place in the Trianon Palace at Versailles. Everything had been done by the French, who beyond any other people possess the genius for staging such an affair, to make the event truly notable—as well as truly painful for the Germans. It was altogether the most impressive and indeed important and critical meeting of the entire Peace Conference—far more impressive than the crowded and over-staged later ceremony of the signing in the Palace of Mirrors. For this was the first tremulous, uncertain contact of bitter enemies. What would the Germans say? What would they do? At the last moment a rumor had spread throughout Paris that Brockdorff-Rantzau intended, after a bitter denunciation of the Treaty, to refuse dramatically to accept it.

The heads of the four most powerful nations of the world, a president and three prime ministers, and the leading men of many other nations, were seated at the table. The doors swung open. At the words "Les Plenipotentiares Allemands," the Germans entered. The entire assembly rose to its feet and stood in silence while the Germans took their places. The doors were closed.

Clemenceau, short, powerful, impressive, stood at the head of the table; President Wilson sat at his right, Lloyd George at his left. Count Brockdorff-Rantzau, surrounded by his eight or ten German delegates, sat facing him. Looking straight at the German delegation Clemenceau spoke with biting intensity:

"It is neither the time nor the place for superfluous words."

His address did not occupy more than two minutes. It was repeated in English; interpreted into German.

Count Brockdorff-Rantzau, tall, thin, black-clad, aristocratic in appearance, his face deathly pale, did not rise from his seat, thus offending the proprieties of the occasion and placing himself and the German delegation at a disadvantage. He spoke slowly, and sentence by sentence his words were interpreted.

Sullenly and defiantly he called into question the good faith of the statesmen who were facing him, he denied Germany's accountability for the war, he held the Allies responsible for the death of "hundreds of thousands of non-combatants who have perished since November 11 by reason of the blockade," and claimed the "right that is guaranteed by the principles of peace."

When Count Brockdorff-Rantzau finished M. Clemenceau spoke even more sharply than before, words like bullets.

"Has anyone any more observations to offer? Does no one wish to speak? If not, the meeting is closed."

The session had lasted a brief moment of a spring day. Through gardens of surpassing loveliness, past lilacs and chestnuts in the first burst of bloom, the Germans returned to their hotel behind its palings and its guards. The Allied leaders went back to Paris. It was over.

I had a talk with the President that evening. Whatever the problems in the future, he seemed much relieved at having the German Treaty off his hands. I asked him what he thought of the Brockdorff-Rantzau speech.

"Not frank, and peculiarly Prussian."

He also spoke of the speech as "stupid," which with him was a kind of crime. He meant, probably, that it was untactful. It had everything in it: explanation, appeal, defiance, and above all, harsh accusations of injustice—but it left in my mind a definite feeling that the inclination of the Germans was to sign the Treaty, which after all was the main consideration. The British criticized Brockdorff-Rantzau sharply for remaining seated while speaking; they called it an insult. To me he looked ill—very pale and worn; but he might have apologized or explained.

The next day was fine and warm and everyone was recovering from the heavy work of the past week. The Big Four had a brief meeting in the morning, but in the afternoon the President and Mrs. Wilson went to the races at Longchamp, and Lloyd George played golf. I saw the President, as usual, in the evening and found him unusually cheerful. He loved to look at people and the afternoon in the sun had been enjoyable to him.

Dissatisfaction with the Treaty and criticism of its terms continued to increase. Secretary Lansing defended the American Commissioners on the ground that they had been too little consulted by the President and did not really know what was going into the Treaty. He also charged that the great fault of the Conference from the start had been too little publicity. While I heartily agreed with him in the latter criticism, I recalled the fact that no one of the Commissioners, in practice, had been more hostile to any real publicity than he. He had been too long disciplined in the school of diplomatic timidity.

Bernard Baruch, one of the ablest men at the Conference, and a staunch friend of the President, said that the Treaty was unworkable because of the economic terms. Herbert Hoover agreed with him, fearing that if the economic terms were enforced, Germany would degenerate into Bolshevism. Smuts and Botha of South Africa, as well as many other Britishers, thought the Treaty, if enforced, would inevitably lead to future wars. There were, even at that time, at least eighteen little wars going on in the world, to say nothing of revolutions, strikes, famine.

"Who does like the Treaty?" I asked in my diary. "Are we not all disappointed to the souls of us? Did we not set out with high hopes of remaking the world? Are we not now lost on uncharted seas? A lot of poor, bruised idealists facing the hard, cold, ugly facts of human life! One of our Americans has taken himself easily away from the hard-beset ship and sailed off to flowery shores. An easy way out. How one is tempted to take that course and go to the hills and nurse one's happy plans for the human race. But it won't do; it won't do. What good are ideals not tested by the fiercest storms? One *cannot* desert the ship."

Along with the disapproval and the criticism, however, there was an evident relaxation of the tension, especially among the topmost leaders. For better or worse something had been done. I found the President in the best spirits in weeks. He and Mrs. Wilson took long drives in the afternoon and early evening. One day after luncheon the President suddenly decided to re-arrange the furniture in the gorgeous sitting room of the house. He said the colors of the chairs had been bothering him; they did not harmonize. So he and Admiral Grayson went at the purple and green French furniture and spent half an hour moving it about to suit the President's taste.

For the first time at Paris the President seemed willing to see visitors who were not directly connected with the actual negotiations. But he wanted to make sure that visitors would not wear him out with arguments based upon a defective knowledge of what the facts really were. Visitors often failed with him because they tried to use him for advancing their own interests or for airing their own prejudices.

Norman Hapgood, Henry Morgenthau, Felix Frankfurter, Lincoln Steffens, and other American liberals came to my office arguing that changes were necessary in the Treaty and that the President could still get the liberals of the world behind him in such a program if he wanted them. They suggested that I bring the matter to his attention, which I did at the first opportunity. I assumed quite frankly that the President would like the Treaty somewhat modified (which he never denied) and asked in what way the liberal groups could help him.

"Baker," he said, "it is like this. We cannot know what our problem is until the Germans present their counter proposals."

When I reported to Hapgood, Steffens, and the others what the President had said, one of them remarked:

"Apparently he wants no help."

"He never does," said another.

When a certain vehement visitor left him one day the President said wearily:

"I wish people would give me the credit of understanding what they say when they tell me once."

I made an opportunity in one of my talks with him, to suggest again that the Treaty itself be released in America, so that our people could be promptly informed. No one over there had yet seen anything but our summary. This he objected to, saying that it would hamper them (the Council of Four) in making changes. I did not quite see how, for Herbert Hoover brought me two copies of a German translation of the Treaty that he bought at Rotterdam for two francs (fifty cents) each. How absurd it was, under such circumstances, to make a mystery of the business. It was all coming out through German sources; and some time later the New York *Times* published the complete text.

The whole world at that time seemed to be disintegrating—like an apiary in which the bee colonies have begun to rob one another. Some of us began to wonder if organization had not become more important than any attempt at a perfect settlement.

Professor Philip Marshall Brown showed me his confidential reports on Hungary and the situation in Central Europe, which I took to the President. He read them carefully and then said sadly:

"They are like most of the reports we get: good enough in presenting the facts, but they do not tell us what to do. They all ask us to make more war."

The President seemed to me at this time to have been driven to his last line of defense. He was having to accept a treaty that represented many compromises; his faith must now rest upon the speedy approval and immediate organization of the League of Nations. He believed that when the League was in being, and the world recovered its sanity, the defects in the Treaty could gradually be rectified.

I was never quite sure when he began to consider seriously the looming problem of the enemies in his rear—that is, the attitude of the American Senate. He had certainly been long aware of it—he knew his American history—but his rock-like faith rested upon several considerations. First, he believed that the vast majority of his fellow countrymen were soundly behind him in the conviction that a strong co-operative world organization had become an absolute necessity. Second, that they would support him if he appealed to them—and would compel favorable action in the event that a struggle with the Senate should develop. He held this faith deeply, all but mystically—and his courage equalled his faith.

The tense interim between the presenting and the signing of the Treaty was among the most laborious and trying periods of the Conference. Many small but irritating problems had to be settled. The Four had in the Ukrainians and heard their story; a message was prepared for the Poles; the Syrian question continued to be exasperating. The President told me, with a kind of amused satisfaction—for once he had a little fun out of the Conference—of a red-hot conflict of view between Lloyd George and Clemenceau. It seems that Lloyd George calmly proposed to give to Italy (to induce a settlement of the Fiume question) a slice of Syria which Clemenceau on his own account had already decided to gobble down. This perfectly frank scramble for territory, which—in a moment of anger—was fought with all guards down, seemed to amuse the President vastly.

On May 21, a request came from the Germans for more time to present their objections to the Treaty. Another week was granted. The French urged the concession, for they were again fearful that the Germans would not sign the Treaty. So indeed was the President. I wrote in my notes, dated May 28:

"Everyone is now asking, Will the Germans sign? Up to noon every day I think they will; after lunch I am not sure; and just before going to bed I'm persuaded they will not. On the whole, I think they will—with fingers crossed."

Voluminous German notes and criticisms on the Treaty came in constantly, and the Four busied themselves with caustic replies. The French loved to make the responses as ironically cutting as they best knew how. The President used his influence to secure modifications, at least in language.

In these final struggles, the President seemed to have both extremes of opinion against him. On the evening of May 28, when I went up to see him, he looked much worn, and the left side of his face twitched sharply, drawing down the under lid of his eye. His chief difficulty just at that time was the exasperating Italian question that would not remain settled. He said he would agree to no arrangement which gave any people to Italy without their consent. He was deeply in earnest, and he wished me to present the situation to the Italian liberals.

"The United States does not own any part of the Dalmatian coast," he said to me, "and I have no right to join in conveying it to

Italy. Neither have France and Great Britain, for that matter. We cannot give away that which does not belong to us."

The problem of plebiscites in reality was very difficult indeed, so much depended on the units chosen and the ticklish problem of strategic frontiers. In trying to settle the matter of the "Polish Corridor" up the Vistula River, two of the Fourteen Points had come into conflict—"self-determination" and the "right of access to the sea." Evidently the President was himself puzzled by some of the difficulties which arose.

When I spoke of the Brenner Pass Germans assigned to Italy for strategic reasons, he said,

"I am sorry for that decision. I was ignorant of the situation when the decision was made."

"Is there not time to change it?"

"I am afraid not; but those Tyrolese Germans are sturdy people —and I have no doubt they will soon be able themselves to change it."

Still another extremely difficult problem arose at that time— though very little was heard of it outside the Council of Four. It concerned the "mandatory system," especially the proposal that the United States should accept mandatories in Turkey. What was a mandatory: was a mandatory an international responsibility, a colony, or a possession?

When I tried to argue out this problem with the Italians I found it almost impossible to arrive at any meeting of our minds. They had really no conception of what we meant by a mandatory. Their idea was that Italy should have a part of Asia Minor for the benefit of Italy: our idea was that America should take Asia Minor, or part of it, as a mandatory for the benefit of the people of Asia Minor. They argued that Italian occupation would result in benefit (incidental benefit) to the people, though this had scarcely been true in the past. We, on our part, admitted that an American mandatory might also be of benefit to us, incidentally. It was in either case a matter of emphasis: but an emphasis in which there was all the difference in the world.

I had a difficult task those days trying to explain even to myself what was going on, and why. I did not pretend to know how the criticisms of the Treaty were to be met, but I did try to remain as clear as possible in my own mind.

As to the reparations and economic clauses, I wrote in my notes: "The Treaty must not be judged by what it is *not,* or what it might have been, but for what it now is. I am arguing that it is as good a treaty as could be had, considering the atmosphere of hatred, fear, suspicion, greed, in which it was made. I am also arguing that it would have been far worse if Wilson and the Americans had not been here. If we now fight the Treaty and defeat the League, unsatisfactory as both may be, what is the alternative? What but present anarchy, and another world war as soon as the nations can get ready for it."

On May 29, when Admiral Grayson and I came down the heavily carpeted stairs we surprised a group of the President's secretaries and secret service men gathered in the lower hall. The doors to the study were open, for the President and Mrs. Wilson had gone for a drive. Suddenly out of the door of the President's room catapulted a young secretary, and turned a nimble handspring before the great mirror in the hall. He was greeted with cheers and his success was immediately challenged by another secretary with an equally acrobatic performance. A number of French servants in shiny shirt fronts and white cotton gloves were standing about smiling broadly at the incomprehensible Americans. I don't know what might have happened next if they had not discovered the Admiral and me coming down the stairs and the President and Mrs. Wilson entering by the outer door.

I told the President that it had been reported from British and French sources that the Four were preparing to recognize the Russian Government headed by Kolchak, provided he agreed to certain demands. This, I said, I had been denying. The President told me with some heat that there had been no talk at all of recognizing Kolchak. How did such reports find currency?

I also told him of a call I had had from Louis Marshall, American Jewish leader, and of his assertion that all oppressed minorities in the world, religious or political, would be for the League, and that the Jews in America would be among its most determined supporters.

"All the minorities except the Irish," said the President.

"Yes," I said, "the Irish seem unhappy. Walsh and Dunne are in my office every day with a new letter or manifesto."

"I don't know how long I shall be able to resist telling them what I think of their miserable mischief-making," said the President, almost savagely. "They can see nothing except their own small interest. They were at first against the League because it contained a reference to the interference of outsiders with the 'domestic affairs' of other nations, thinking that it prevented Irish-Americans from taking part in Irish affairs. Now, they are attacking Article X because they assert that it limits the right of revolution. As a matter of fact, Article X safeguards the right of revolution by providing that the members of the League shall respect and preserve the integrity of nations only against 'external aggression.'"

Sweetser and I dined at the Restaurant des Iles in the Bois, a beautiful night full of the scent of acacia blossoms. The pond was filled with boats carrying swaying red lanterns. We walked part of the way into the city and then hired an open hack of the old-fashioned sort, driven by a great Jehu in a varnished hat, and came down the Champs-Elysees in grand style. Another night we gave a dinner to the heads of the British and French press bureaus with Colonel and Mrs. House as our honorary guests.

CHAPTER L

The President Dedicates the Suresnes Cemetery in France

ON THE AFTERNOON of May 30, American Memorial Day, I drove to Suresnes and heard the President speak. The occasion was the formal dedication of the great new American cemetery. It inevitably recalled that other dedication, at Gettysburg in 1863, when Lincoln thought he failed. It was a hot, bright day, and dusty in the newly made cemetery. All about were thousands of people, mostly our soldiers, filling the acacia groves on the hillside from which one looks off so grandly upon the city of Paris.

Near at hand were the long rows of the American dead who had given their lives on the battlefields of France. Each had its little cross, and its name and number. A few had been decorated—not many, for loving hands were far away. The great of the world were there—statesmen, generals, diplomats. They came quietly, reverently.

It was a wonderful speech, so perfectly turned, so sure, so musical, so appealing at that hour. Never did an orator have more perfect command of himself and, without palpable effort either in voice or gesture, so infuse an audience with his very spirit. He had one of the great resources of oratory: restraint; so that when his voice rose and thrilled in the high passages in which he invoked the spirit of the dead, as in the last matchless personal dedication, it was with incalculable power and grace. I saw tears in the eyes of those around me, and felt them in my own.

It would be no profit to us to eulogize these illustrious dead if we did not take to heart the lesson which they have taught us. They are dead; they have done their utmost to show their devotion to a great cause, and they have left us to see to it that that cause shall not be betrayed, whether in war or in peace. It is our privilege and our high duty to consecrate ourselves afresh on a day like this to the objects for which they fought. . . . These men did not come across the sea merely to defeat Germany and her associated powers in the war. They came to defeat forever the things for which the Central powers stood, the sort of power they meant to assert in the world, the arrogant, selfish dominance which they meant to establish; and they came, moreover, to see to it that there should never be a war like this again. It is for us, particularly for us who are civilians, to use our proper weapons of counsel and agreement to see to it that there never is such a war again.

He put into his words, with great power, the intense conviction which lay at the foundation of his faith, that the people were with him, and that a new day in the world had dawned.

The peoples of the world are awake and the peoples of the world are in the saddle. Private counsels of statesmen cannot now and cannot hereafter determine the destinies of nations. If we are not the servants of the opinion of mankind, we are of all men the littlest, the most contemptible, the least gifted with vision. If we do not know our age, we cannot accomplish our purpose, and this age is an age which looks forward, not backward; which rejects the standards of national selfishness that once governed the counsels of nations and demands that they shall give way to a new order of things in which the only questions will be, "Is it right?" "Is it just?" "Is it in the interest of mankind?"

I thought it then, and I have thought it since, the greatest speech I had ever heard—greatest in its emotional power over the people who were present, greatest in the conviction it gave of the speaker's utter devotion to his inner vision, and his determination to realize it.

I had heard the President speak many times, often powerfully and persuasively, but never as he spoke that day at Suresnes, in the midst of his lonely struggle at Paris, where all the principalities and powers were against him. It was a speech in which the calculated sentences seemed to come hard and hot out of the volcanic depths of his being. It was not only the resting place of brave men he was dedicating, but his own life, his own spirit.

I sent these lads over here to die. Shall I—can I—ever speak a word of counsel which is inconsistent with the assurances I gave them when they came over?

I can never forget the impact of his final words, not merely the evidence of their power upon that audience of tearful faces, but in my own soul.

Here stand I, consecrated in spirit to the men who were once my comrades and who are now gone, and who have left me under eternal bonds of fidelity.

As we came away I saw the President lay a wreath on a soldier's grave; and a French woman with tears in her eyes run up to shake his hand; and Foch, the old Marshal, grip him hard with emotion that was strongly evident.

I drove back alone that afternoon with such a loathing for the evil forces at Paris that were defeating the President's high purpose as I had never believed I was capable of. What a den of iniquity —everywhere suspicion, greed, fear, hatred, everywhere lies and trickery. I knew it for what it was, I had lived in it myself for months. I even felt a kind of anger at the President himself of which I was afterwards ashamed. Why hadn't he fought harder, why didn't he die for his vision!

And yet, when he challenged the spirits of the dead, there on that day, calling them to witness, I saw and felt a great soul struggling with the bleakest forces of his time, I gave him all I had.

One thing that day did for me: it gave me a deeper and clearer understanding of Woodrow Wilson. A lonely man, outwardly cold and remote, inwardly molten passion, with an unparalleled tenacity of faith, an unequalled constancy of courage. He would make mistakes, he was making them, but I resolved then and there to help him as never before. For he was that rarity, a leader whom a free man could follow without surrender. He did not ask for personal allegiance, he had extraordinarily little personal vanity: he wanted you to join him unselfishly in devotion to the vision he had. You were not to flatter him or worship him: he was not to praise you: you were to work loyally together for a cause that you both believed in, and that was far more important than either of you.

CHAPTER LI

Struggle for Changes in the Treaty

WHEN THE GERMAN peace delegation had been summoned to come to Paris on April 25, there was great rejoicing. It had seemed probable that the Treaty would be signed and the Peace Conference concluded by the middle of May. We could all go home! But week after week passed, and the impasse seemed in early June to be graver than ever. Some of the demands for changes made by the Germans seemed to thoughtful men, after careful reading, not only realistic but necessary. Criticism from Allied sources, especially those made in England, were as insistent as they were embarrassing. But could any changes at all be made without letting in a flood of demands that might mean a rewriting of the Treaty? If the Allies stood upon the Treaty as originally presented, the grisly question again arose: Would the Germans sign? And if they refused, would it not mean a new outbreak of war, probably with the Russians?

The mercurial Lloyd George, especially, was seriously alarmed. He had Colonel House to lunch with him and told him in so many words that the liberal and labor criticism in England was reaching great strength and that he favored making changes, even considerable changes, in the Treaty. The next morning Clemenceau told the Colonel that he was against any changes whatever in the Treaty. He was for forcing it straight through. The Colonel told me he thought that the President would stand nearer to Clemenceau than to Lloyd George.

When I went up to see the President on the evening of May 31, I raised the urgent problem of possible changes, for the correspondents were making insistent inquiries. He asked me what my own opinion was, and in reply I could not help saying exactly what I thought: that it was an unworkable treaty.

"If the economic clauses are enforced, there is no hope of collecting the reparations. The two clauses are mutually destructive."

"I told Lloyd George and Clemenceau as much when we had it under discussion," he said, "but there was no changing them."

I observed that Lloyd George seemed now inclined to make modifications.

"Yes, he is hearing from his own liberals."

I said that liberals and working groups everywhere were attacking the Treaty.

"It has had good support in the United States."

"Yes," I said, "but they do not know what is in it."

"They have had the summary."

"But it gives no such cumulative impression as the reading of the Treaty itself."

He asked if I thought our people were interested in the details.

"Not now," I said, "but they will be later. When your enemies in the Senate, Mr. President, begin to discuss the League of Nations they will want to examine the basis upon which it rests and what it is they are guaranteeing—and that will mean a close scrutiny of the Treaty."

I am afraid I pushed the argument too far, for the President arose abruptly and made an end of the conversation. But I had at least cleared my own mind and expressed my own doubts.

It was plain that at every point the President was now thinking of American public opinion. I had letters about that time from Walter Lippmann, Ellery Sedgwick, and other Americans who were thoughtful critics of the Treaty and I had come to believe that the opinion in America was not so generally favorable as the President thought. I was afraid he relied too much on Tumulty. Moreover, I had been reading Brockdorff-Rantzau's letter of transmittal which came with the German counter proposals on May 31. It seemed to me a strong document which the Allies would do well not to treat too cavalierly. But it was evident that the President was beginning to share, strongly, the views of Clemenceau.

The Austrian Treaty, like the German, had been made largely without consultation with the smaller allied powers. The restless Balkan States, with their age-old problems, had been kept largely in ignorance of settlements which were of primary importance to them. Serious objections, reaching outright revolt, began at once to appear. Only a day or two before the Treaty was to be submitted to the Austrians at St. Germain, a secret plenary session was called at which it was read aloud to all the delegates concerned. All but riotous objections broke out, led by the Roumanians, who had assumed leadership of the smaller powers. The Roumanians had for some time been more or less in revolt against the tutelage of the Great Powers. One of the immediate points at issue was the provision in the Treaty for the protection of religious and political minorities (Jews especially) in the smaller states, such protection being guaranteed by the Great Powers. Roumania argued that it permitted interference by the Great Powers in the internal affairs of the weaker nations.

When the debate began to get out of hand—even Clemenceau seemed unable to control it—the President arose and made a short but extremely forceful speech. It seemed to some of those who heard it that he was enunciating a policy which had been developing from the beginning, but which he, in particular, had not hitherto clearly accepted, or at least adopted as his own. This was that the Great Powers, by virtue of their military and economic strength, must necessarily bear the chief burden of maintaining the peace of the world, until the League of Nations could be organized and take over this function. If they accepted this responsibility, they must assure themselves of the basis upon which it rested. He laid down the principle:

"Where the great force lies, there must be the sanction of peace."

This, in bald outline, was the position taken by the President, as he himself told me about it that evening. I asked him to let me put out a verbatim copy of what he said, urging its tremendous importance, but he was not yet ready to do it.

While this attitude had, of course, been implicit all along, it now appeared as a statement of policy: that the world, at least in the immediate future until peace could be firmly established, was not to be, and could not be, governed by a democratic society of equal nations (like the states of the American union). It must accept, for the time being, domination by a powerful group of great powers with supposedly benevolent intentions.

It thus became perfectly clear where the President stood. It was impossible to let the Conference degenerate into a riotous debating society, as the Germans plainly hoped that it would. Its findings must be sternly carried through. He knew well that mistakes had been made, but the only recourse was to make peace—enforced if necessary—and go home. His new policy as a statesman was to get the League of Nations accepted and promptly organized. As the passions of the war began to disappear, and normal associations were re-established, the League could listen to the demands of the little nations—or the big ones—and settle the problems calmly and justly, one by one.

The twofold importance of the President's position at that time was not fully realized. He was setting forth a vigorous policy for dealing with the current confusion and criticism; he was also outlining a comprehensive plan for the future.

The President evidently wished to test further the new formula he had in mind, and on June 3 he called a meeting of the entire American Commission, including all the advisers and experts. It was held in Secretary Lansing's office at the Crillon Hotel, and was the first of its kind in the entire course of the Peace Conference. It was interesting for the frank discussion of the German replies, and the expressions of view as to what should be done, if anything, in modifying the Treaty.

The President apparently stood for some minor changes, but not because the terms were hard.

"The terms *are* hard—nations should learn once for all what an unjust war means—we don't want to soften the terms, but we do want to make them just," he said. "Wherever it can be shown that we have departed from our principles we ought to have rectifications."

Two things he considered indispensable:

"The most fatal thing that could happen would be a break between the Allied and Associated Powers. . . . What is necessary is to get out of the atmosphere of war."

To keep the alliance firm, to get peace, and to build up a strong organization to deal with post-war problems—these were the prime needs. He was not inclined to make concessions, as Mr. Hoover suggested, as a mere expedient in persuading the Germans to sign.

In my notes made at that time I commented on the existing world conditions as they appeared to discouraged observers in Paris:

"All the world seems to be going to smash. Paris is wretched with strikes of all kinds—accompanied by a nameless fear that these strikes, which in France tend toward political action, may result in a revolution. We hear of bitter industrial struggles in China, widespread bomb outrages in the United States, deep-seated discontent in both England and Italy—finally, the apparently increasing determination on the part of the Germans not to sign the Treaty. This, with the mounting divergences in view among the Big Four themselves, makes the outlook indeed black. In many ways this is the most critical moment in the entire conference."

One day during this depression of mind which affected nearly everybody, I dined with an Old Calm Historian who had a fine way of saying comprehensively, "all wars," or "no treaties are ever satisfactory," or "after every important peace-making it has seemed impossible that the world would adjust itself, but it always does. It always returns to the normal." "Once get the ordinary processes of life going, and the readjustments will be swift." "We pay too much attention to what is written down in a treaty made while men are half insane with the suffering and losses of war, and do not realize how easily changes can be made when sanity returns."

It was a cooling experience.

On June 7, the President said to me:

"We have already taken up two-thirds as much time in examining the Germans' counter-proposals as we gave them to examine the entire Treaty. The British and the French can agree on nothing, and do not maintain the same position overnight."

It seemed at that time that the divergencies among the Allies were becoming more dangerous to the peace than their controversies with the Germans—especially those between Clemenceau and Lloyd George. The French demanded huge reparations, promptly paid, to help them start again; the British wanted the economic crippling of

Germany as a commercial rival. These were mutually destructive objectives, for if England ruined Germany economically, how could she earn the reparations to pay France? To add to the general confusion, disputes and even wars between the smaller countries were constantly breaking out and the Big Four were forced to pause now and then to stop a new leak in the peace of the world.

I decided that about the only thing left for an honest man was to go to the country and grow potatoes and turnips—or keep bees. That, at least, would be useful.

The President was being attacked all over the world as never before. He, personally, was being blamed for every provision of the Treaty that failed to satisfy the ambition, the greed, or the fears of the nation affected. His own Senate had also become highly critical and were urgently demanding that copies of the Treaty be sent on at once. He said that many of the provisions were still in process of revision and that treaties were never presented to the Senate in advance of their signing. He would not be forced by the demand. I think he was realizing for the first time the magnitude of the political problem which was facing him at home.

I tried every day to bring to the President as much good news as possible. I had heard from French sources that the Germans would be ready on Monday, June 9. I said it looked like good news.

"I think if I could have a really good piece of news I should fall dead."

It was one of the few admissions of his heavy personal burden that I ever heard him make.

Several times during the fine spring weather of the later days of the Conference, when I arrived at the President's house, Mr. and Mrs. Wilson invited me for a quiet drive with them in the Bois. This was a great pleasure to me: I found the President always at his best in such easy and informal meetings. One evening after our return I was taken back to the Crillon in a Commission automobile driven by a typical "dough-boy," who had been often with me before. He had an off-hand easy way with him, read detective stories while he waited, got off "toot-sweet" and "fee nee" with great unction, and gave me cold chills now and then by the way he dodged through the crowded street traffic in Paris. I asked him once how he liked the people of Paris.

"Oh, they ain't so worse—but they're so damned ignorant."

He thought Denver—he was from Colorado—a much more attractive city than Paris.

"There ain't a mountain to be seen anywhere around Paris."

And he didn't approve of the girls that flocked in the dusk of the Champs-Elysées.

"I tell you, they ain't no ladies."

We were spinning down the Champs-Elysées when I chanced to see, across the wide avenue, a French automobile which had just caught fire. It was standing near the far curb, with flames spurting out of the forward part, and an excited crowd gathered around. My driver gave it a single swift glance, and then to my amazement and alarm, turned his car instantly into the traffic on the other side of the street, nearly ran down two taxicabs, avoided a huge horse truck by a hand's breadth and, before I could utter a protest, was tooting his horn and driving straight into the crowd around the flaming French car. The people scattered in every direction. Two or three Frenchmen were excitedly throwing sand—by handfuls—into the flames, without the slightest result.

My driver leaped out with his squirt of a brass fire-extinguisher in his hand, and before he was well on the ground he began firing a stream of the mixture into the flaming machinery. He thrust his elbow into one man's stomach, gave another a quick shove with his shoulder—and the whole crowd stood away and let him squirt. He never said a single word; and no one said a word to him. In one minute he had the fire out. He gave the open engine a single, rather contemptuous, glance as though he were saying, "These dang French machines!" and then tossed his extinguisher back into our car, jumped in after it, and in two seconds more we were turning perilously back into our course. Not one word had been said by anybody. No thanks, no explanation; but the fire was out.

As I was beginning to catch my breath my driver half turned his head and said out of the corner of his mouth:

"These here Froggies are so damned excitable."

Later, when I told this story, I had a good hearty laugh from the President and Mrs. Wilson.

I also tried to see something, all too little, of the intimate life of the French people. It is easy to meet diplomats, statesmen, and business leaders; hard to know them in their own homes. I spent a Sunday in June at Fontainebleau and toward evening I called on my old friend Jaccaci who was stopping with the artist Tavenier at his home on the edge of the forest. We sat and talked quietly in the garden.

How little those who saw only Paris knew what the war meant behind the walled gardens of the homes of France. There were in this home four grandchildren of Tavenier, whose son had been killed at the front; only the old, the women and the children were left. A whole generation gone! The old artist was doing his best to be both father and grandfather. He had learned to play tennis: and came out with two of the children: a beautiful girl of eleven with long blond braids, and a boy of eight or nine, and stumblingly tried to teach them the game. Jac and I turned our seats around to watch: and presently out came the grandmother, the old aunt, and others of the household to watch this rather pathetic game.

"Are you ready there, my dear boy?" the grandfather would call out in English.

"Play," the boy would reply.

Most of the serves were "mauvais" and few of the returns were "bien."

Presently they would have it that I play too, and ran for soft shoes for me to use: and I joined them for a set or so.

It was a beautiful family. Tavenier was an old artist who painted wonderful hunting scenes, with horses and dogs, of the old lost times of 1815–30. He loved to make sketches in the forest—spring days with water pools among the trees, charming bits of bracken, chestnuts in bloom. He was a devout Catholic, a stout conservative, thinking that all radical leaders were rascals and mischief-makers, loved France passionately and was as simple and sweet as a child. He spoke English well.

I stopped with them for a simple dinner, a meal full of gay

banter—a huge loaf on the table which we all cut from, and cold meat and a salad and little new peas from the garden, and cheese and strawberries served by an old familiar servant with a face like yellow parchment who laughed and joked with the master while he opened the wine bottles.

There were beautiful things all about, beautiful bits of carving, pictures, statuary. A fine old French home, where Jac fitted safely in —a haven in a mad world there on the edge of the forest—but with only the old grandparents and the gay children left out of the wreck of war. I enjoyed every moment of that visit.

There had been many requests from the Belgians for a visit from President Wilson, and finally, on June 17, at the urgent invitation of the King, the President made the difficult trip. Since I had flown up to Belgium at the request of Mr. Wilson a few weeks before to make inquiries of Brand Whitlock, the American Minister there, the President asked me to be a member of the party.

It was one of the hardest trips I ever made, and one of the most interesting. Wednesday was devoted to an all-day motor ride over dusty and often badly broken roads through the battlefields and ruined cities of Flanders, including a most interesting visit to the Zeebrugge harbor where we were escorted by British naval officers, who showed us how the gallant British naval contingent had blocked the channel. At Nieuport and along the Iser Canal we covered the same territory that I had visited less than a year before in the midst of the war. Then shells were singing overhead and it was death to move one's head above the trenches. We arrived at Brussels Wednesday night about 9:30—and rode through crowded streets. I was up half the night seeing that our communications were open and the despatches of the correspondents moving properly.

Thursday was devoted to a paralyzing program of trips, receptions, a big luncheon, and in the evening the grand dinner at the Palace, given by the King and Queen to President and Mrs. Wilson. The President sat on the right of the King, then the Queen, then Cardinal Mercier in his red gown and hat. On the left of the King sat Mrs. Wilson. We entered between rows of red-clad flunkies and were relieved of our wraps but asked, such is the court custom, to carry our hats, which was a nuisance. The dining tables were profusely decorated with roses and the royal gold plate was displayed. The King, big, handsome, and boyish, looked the real monarch, and I lost my heart outright to the little, sweet-faced Queen, who was as unaffected as a schoolgirl.

The King read, awkwardly and in a low, embarrassed voice, a speech proposing the President's health, and the President responded —all of us standing. There was a most imposing array of guests in full diplomatic uniforms, bespangled with medals and gold braid.

Whitlock told me just before the train left that the President had completely won the Belgian people; and had, he thought, quite counteracted the effects of French propaganda. But they had nearly killed him with their strenuous program: they wanted to show him all their sores. They responded politely to his enthusiasm for the League of Nations and the reign of right in the world; but when he spoke of giving Belgium help in credits, raw material, and new machinery, one could fairly *feel* the electric change in the atmosphere, and there was a warmth in the response which left no doubt as to its complete sincerity.

CHAPTER LII

The Signing of the Treaty in the Hall of Mirrors

EARLY ON THE MORNING of June 23, the Germans sent in a note asking for further delay: but the Three met at nine o'clock and denied the request. I made close telephone arrangements with the French Foreign Office, our own Secretariat, and the President's house, for the earliest possible notification from the Germans of acceptance or rejection. Our office was full of correspondents all day long, and many visitors came in or telephoned to see if we had any news. It was at a few minutes after five that Mr. Grew called me up and said that the Germans had agreed to sign. Such a rush as there was to the telephones! Such a clatter of typewriters! We had a copy of the message itself, in French, half an hour later, and made fast work translating it into English and getting it off, "priority A."

There was much firing of guns that evening and blowing of sirens and a gala celebration in the boulevards, although it was a pale and artificial affair compared with the armistice rejoicing which I had seen in Paris the previous fall.

The council of Four had three sessions during the day with a throng of experts before them, but in the evening I found the President looking brisk and cheerful. He wanted an early signing and a quick departure for home.

A pleasant feature of the day was Colonel House's farewell conference with the newspaper correspondents. Paderewski happened in and shook hands, and Ambassador Page of Italy was there with the new Polish Minister to the United States.

The next day the President told me that the Four were going to Versailles and suggested that I join them. It turned out to be a wonderfully interesting trip. Clemenceau acted as showman and explained to the President the various treasures in the Palace as we passed.

We looked at Louis XIV's bed, and Balfour, observing its extreme height from the floor, said it would be dangerous for a man who suffered from bad dreams.

"It must have been dangerous, then," remarked the President, "for more than one Louis who slept in it."

We walked through the mirror-walled bedroom of Marie Antoinette and Clemenceau then took us into the exquisite little theater now used as a senate chamber, and told the President much of the history of the place, finally pausing reminiscently to say:

"I made my first political speech from that rostrum."

It was during the Commune—forty-eight years before. What an extraordinary old man he was!

Our principal objective was to visit the Hall of Mirrors and discuss the arrangements for signing. The room was ready and beautifully decorated, with a raised platform at one side covered with magnificent rugs of the time of Louis XIV. There was much joking about the signing. It seemed that seals were required and few of the signers had any. The President exhibited the gold ring on his finger and said it would have to do. Balfour, if any man there, had a seal, but he remarked that he never used one.

"I suppose there are several about my house. I will telegraph and see."

When they began calculating the time it would take for the signing they were staggered to discover that if the seals were put on during the conference, it would require several hours to get through. Baron Sonnino suggested that the seals be affixed in the morning, so that only the actual signing of the Treaty would be done at the conference. This was agreed to. As we passed the head of the long peace table Clemenceau turned to Wilson and remarked:

"You will sign first, Mr. President."

"How is that?"

"Etats-Unis: You stand at the head of the list."

When they were talking of the kind of delegation Germany would send, Balfour remarked:

"I suppose, now, they'll send us a few bow-legged, cross-eyed men to sign the treaty."

That evening Mrs. Wilson told me the story of the President's seal ring, about which we had all been curious. She said that when they were married, the State of California sent them a nugget of gold out of which it was suggested that a wedding ring be made. This they had done, and Mrs. Wilson was wearing it. Out of the gold that remained, a signet ring was made for the President. When a design was asked for, he wrote his name in full—Woodrow Wilson—in shorthand and combined the characters in a monogram which looked like an Arabic inscription.

While at Versailles we had a warm discussion over the admission of photographers: both Clemenceau and Wilson being sharply opposed to the making of any photographs whatsoever. I put up as good a case as I could. The decision was *no*, but no sooner had the Four departed than the French began making plans to have a moving picture man present. I learned also that the British had secured a favorable place in a window recess for their artist, Sir William Orpen, so I obtained an equal privilege for Jo Davidson, our American sculptor.

Our correspondents protested sharply against the French arrangements at Versailles; the press section was far too distant from the peace table, and the seats were too low: the correspondents could neither see nor hear what was going on. The British correspondents joined with us in a protest, which I presented to the President and they took to Lloyd George. The President told me he thought the arrangements were bad but he did not see how the Four could dictate changes in the completed French plan. We then went directly to the French foreign office and were promised some alterations, which were not made.

The correspondents were not the only ones who were having to struggle for representation at the Versailles Conference. I had a long and very interesting talk with Secretary Lansing, who told me about his efforts to get the South and Central American delegates admitted to the Conference. He had written two letters to the President strongly urging this courtesy and the President had taken it up in the Council of Four. Lloyd George was opposed to the admission of any but "effective belligerents" but had finally consented to admit China and Siam—no doubt because they were in the sphere of British influence. The President told Lansing that it was the best he could do, that the other two would consent to no more invitations—except to Brazil, which was regarded as an "effective belligerent." At the plenary session on the day before the Treaty was presented, Lansing told me he had renewed his argument. The President finally turned to Clemenceau and said that the American delegation strongly favored the admission of the South and Central American delegates. Clemenceau made some noncommittal reply and looked up at the ceiling in a way he had when he was opposed to a suggestion but did not want to argue it. At this point Lansing leaned over and said,

"Monsieur Clemenceau, the American delegation not only favors the admission of the delegates from South and Central America, but will feel offended and resentful unless they are admitted. Delegates from small nations in other parts of the world, to say nothing of delegates from the colonies of Great Britain, are admitted. Why not the South American delegates?"

Clemenceau referred the question to Lloyd George and after a moment's whispered conversation he said to Lansing:

"All right. I have no objection."

"And they will be invited?"

"Yes."

But Lansing, still skeptical, told Leland Harrison, diplomatic secretary, to go personally to all the South and Central American delegates and tell them to be there, whether they received invitations or not. They were there. And not one of them had received an invitation. Neither the French nor the British wanted them present. They went back to America as thoroughly disillusioned with European politics as we were. Several of them told the Secretary (they gave him a formal dinner) that they saw more clearly than ever that their future was bound up with that of the United States.

The signing of the Treaty was finally set for two o'clock Saturday, June 28, with arrangements for the President's party to leave Paris that same evening, and sail on Sunday.

On the day before, the President had gone down to Secretary Lansing's room in the Crillon and talked for over an hour with our correspondents. Too bad he had not done it oftener, for he invariably made a profound impression. In summing up the whole matter he outlined the position he was himself prepared to take upon his return to America.

"All things considered, the Treaty adheres more nearly to the Fourteen Points than I had a right to expect. Considering the incalculable difficulties we had to face, it comes remarkably near. Never forget that Germany did an irreparable wrong, and must suffer for it. . . . Think of the positive achievements of the peace—the newly liberated peoples, who had not before dared to dream of freedom, the Poles, the Czechoslovaks, the Slavs, the peoples of Turkey. The peace has given a new charter to labor, has provided for economic equality among the nations, has gone far toward the protection of racial and religious minorities, and finally and greatest of all, it has banded the peoples of the world in a new League of Nations. It is a colossal business. It is only on paper so far, of course, but it is up to us to see that it is made effective. There are great difficulties ahead of us and heavy burdens—but I never believed more firmly than I do now in our own people."

He said he would admit Germany to the League when she had proved that her new democratic government was firmly established.

Asked by a correspondent about the prohibition law then just going into effect in the United States, he laughed and said:

"Frankly, I'm stumped on that."

On the day of the signing of the Treaty at Versailles I took two automobile loads of correspondents out with me, as well as my secretary, Miss Groth, and a youthful soldier from South Georgia who had served as my orderly. He wore a broad smile all the way. It was warm and sunny and the fine ride through the Bois and along the river by way of St. Cloud was a joy in itself. Our automobiles were provided with yellow and blue cockades which took us through the police lines.

Every effort had been made to give impressiveness and beauty to the staging of the ceremony. I had seen the preparations the day before. The course into the Palace through the Court of Honor was brilliant with splendid lines of picked troops, both mounted and afoot, and there were gorgeously caparisoned guards on the grand staircases and along the royal passageway to the Galerie des Glaces where the signing was to take place. It could not have been better staged for Louis XIV.

It had indeed been staged in the spirit of Louis XIV. When the correspondents arrived, some four hundred of them from many nations—true ambassadors of the people, if any were there—they were directed to a side gate and through a back entrance, as Louis's servants must have been, into their end of the great Galerie. Thus the men who were expected to report all this grandeur for the democracies of Wisconsin or Vermont or Oregon, to say nothing of the miserable and hungry peoples of Belgium and Poland, never even saw it.

The places assigned to us were all but impossible. A row of Hussars in magnificent helmets with black manes was drawn up across the room squarely in front of us, and a large number of Frenchmen, who had crept in early, probably without permission, had crowded into the front seats which had been assigned to our working correspondents. It was little indeed that anyone could see over the heads of the ticketless Frenchmen and between the legs of the Hussars. Ridell, Puaux and I at once sought the commandant and had a stormy session with him. He finally agreed to remove the Hussars, but the correspondents themselves, almost at the point of fisticuffs, had to clear the aisles and seats assigned to us. We probably expected too much! There was no Fifth Estate to be provided for in the time of Louis XIV.

In spite of distance and obstructions we could see that the French had performed wonders of decoration in the body of the great hall. The peace table itself glowed with tawny yellow coverings, blending with the rich browns, blues, and yellows of the antique rugs and tapestries. We could get fugitive glimpses of a glorified group of generals and admirals, all in the most brilliant uniforms. General Pershing was there wearing the scarlet sash of the Legion of Honor.

At three o'clock the allied delegates, with Clemenceau, Lloyd George, and Wilson at the center, had taken their seats at the peace table. A few moments later a hush fell upon the hall. There had been unseemly shouts of "Sit down, Sit down" by irritated spectators in the overcrowded room. These ceased suddenly.

The German delegates— Dr. Hermann Müller, secretary for Foreign Affairs, and Dr. Johannes Bell, Colonial Secretary—had appeared at the farther end of the hall, and were advancing toward the peace table. We could see that they were holding their heads high. What we could not see was the pallor of their faces or the look of arrogance in their eyes, afterward reported by those who were nearer at hand.

The delegates of the Allied Powers did not rise from their seats to receive the Germans, thus sharply recalling the discourtesy of Brockdorff-Rantzau in not rising at the ceremony on May 7 when the Treaty was presented to the Germans.

Dr. Müller and his associates took their place at the table between the Japanese plenipotentiaries on their right, and the Brazilians on their left. Clemenceau's address (which we could not hear) was characteristically brief and biting, and after a tense pause the Master of Ceremonies escorted the German plenipotentiaries to the peace table, where they signed the Treaty.

President Wilson was the first of the Allied delegates to sign, and at three forty-five o'clock the momentous session was over.

No one rose when the German delegates made their way out of the Hall through the silent, but plainly hostile, crowd of French spectators. A few moments later when President Wilson, Premier Clemenceau, and Prime Minister Lloyd George descended from the Hall of Mirrors to the terrace at the rear of the Palace, masses of people swept forward shouting "Vive Clemenceau!" "Vive Wilson!" "Vive Lloyd George!" It was the one spontaneous outburst of the day.

There had been a plan to have all the Allied delegates march across the beautiful terraces of the Palace, where the historic fountains were playing, but the struggling crowd was too great. Even as it was, the three Allied leaders reached their car with difficulty, the people following and cheering, while guns boomed and low-flying airplanes filled the air.

We returned to Paris about five-thirty. The correspondents came in to say good-bye with a cordiality and friendliness that I deeply appreciated. I had made many enduring friendships among them. While I had undertaken the task at the Peace Conference with many misgivings, it had turned out to be a rich experience.

We left Paris in the President's private train at ten o'clock that night. All the celebrities were at the Gare des Invalides to see the President off—including the French President, Poincare, and Clemenceau. Everyone was happy.

We went aboard the *George Washington* on Sunday about noon and sailed at two o'clock. After wonderfully calm seas and pleasant weather, we arrived at New York on July 8, where a great celebration of welcome awaited the President.

My son Roger met me in New York and I arrived at home in Amherst about six o'clock the next evening, deeply glad to be on my own hillside again.

CHAPTER LIII

I Watch Wilson's Struggle with the Senate

LOOKING BACK along many years, I can recall no period in which life in America looked bleaker to me than it did during the half dozen years following the close of the Peace Conference at Paris in 1919.

At the end of the war itself I was full of hope: the long struggle had at last been won: the terms of settlement, including intelligent preliminary plans for a League of Nations, had been adopted by all the belligerents: the leadership of America, with Woodrow Wilson the dominating figure, had been as warmly welcomed as it had been commanding. A great constructive transformation in world affairs seemed possible, even probable.

During the long months at the Peace Conference these hopes, this faith, had gradually dwindled. There was a faint revival at the homecoming of the President. I recall the triumph of his entry in New York harbor—the accompanying dreadnaughts, the airplanes and dirigibles in the sky, the boom of great guns. I saw one excitable little tugboat, crowded with cheering friends that had flung out a streamer with the words:

"Honor to Woodrow Wilson, Peace Maker."

No homecoming American ever before in our history, I believe, had such a welcome. It seemed momentarily possible that Woodrow Wilson's leadership might still prevail, that America by its own power and prestige might yet save the peace.

The President laid the new Treaty before the United States Senate on July 10—two days after his arrival in Washington—with a strong and clear address of explanation. He told the Senate frankly that it was not "exactly what we would have written," for the difficulties often "seemed insuperable." "It was impossible to accommodate the interests of so great a body of nations . . . without many minor compromises." His chief emphasis, of course, was upon the League of Nations. He called it the "only hope for mankind."

"We can only go forward, with lifted eyes and freshened spirit to follow the vision. It was of this that we dreamed at our birth. America shall in truth show the way. The light shines upon the path ahead, and nowhere else."

The discussions of the Treaty began at once. On August 19, the President appeared before the Senate Foreign Relations Committee. The point chiefly at issue was the series of "reservations" to the proposed Covenant of the League, the general purpose of which was to nullify or weaken the commitments and obligations of the United States as a member of the League. We wanted, or said we wanted, the benefits of organized international co-operation, but if the Senate represented us, we were apparently unwilling to make any real sacrifices to obtain it.

In late August it became plain that the President was losing the battle for ratification, and he determined upon his usual recourse in meeting such situations—a recourse that had rarely failed him—an "appeal to the people."

In spite of the anxious warnings of Dr. Grayson that he was not physically able to endure the fatigue and hardship of such a campaign, in spite of the pleading of his wife and his closest friends, he left Washington on September 3, and spoke in cities from the Middle West to the Pacific coast.

"The only force," he told the people, "that outlasts all others and is finally triumphant is the moral judgment of mankind."*

It was as grueling a trip as any ever made in a political campaign; it resulted in the President's physical collapse on September 26.

I watched all these events with intense interest and anxiety. I had returned home well aware that there would be sharp fighting over the ratification of the Treaty—what important treaty sent to the Senate of the United States was ever ratified without a struggle?—but I had faith that the great majority of the American people wanted the League and would support the President in his efforts to get it; and I believed in Woodrow Wilson's tested powers as a popular leader.

I also found myself unexpectedly and deeply moved by solicitude for the man himself. In earlier years I had trusted and followed Woodrow Wilson because I thought him right, because the country

* At Salt Lake City, September 23, 1919.

needed such a leader, without feeling any deep personal attachment. He had often seemed to me a cold man, aloof, sometimes actually forbidding. Most men who met him were afraid of him. During the long hard months of the Peace Conference I had had unusual opportunities of seeing and knowing him at times when momentous decisions tested every faculty, commanded every power the man had. I knew him when he was the most acclaimed man in the world; I knew him also when he faced stark defeat. More and more he had seemed to me, not cold, not aloof, not arrogant, but intensely engrossed, absorbed, concentrated. He had been entrusted by the American people with the greatest duties and responsibilities of any man of his generation—he must do what they expected of him. He must devote every energy to the task in hand. So many men who came to him—demanding this or that trivial privilege, or favor, or honor, urging partisan expediency, or selfish national aggrandizement—had no understanding of devoted greatness, still less of a character dominated by stern inner principles, noble ideals, a sensitive conscience. So often we do not believe in admirable souls, as Emerson said, "because they are not in our experience." Again and again at Paris I saw men imposing upon his patience, small men stealing his precious hours and going away angry because he "would not confer." On the other hand I never knew any man who was his equal in willingness to reason with opponents if they knew what they were talking about, or with critics who really wanted to know the truth. I recall how at Paris he strove patiently to examine every related fact in several of the most perplexing world issues—for example, the Chinese-Japanese controversy. I also recall how rock-like he was when his decision had been made. So often, although not always, what was imputed to him as stubbornness seemed to me to be courage of conviction. He was far simpler, more direct, more naive in his honesty than most men gave him credit for being. What he said in public he meant in private. Not a few of the enmities he awakened grew out of his unwillingness to enter into secret agreements, or "personal understandings"—the currency of betrayal so beloved of politicians. When I was writing his biography I read thousands of his private letters, and I never discovered a single instance in which he told one correspondent one thing, another something contrary: and when he promised in one letter to write this or that to some other correspondent, I was sure to find that he had done exactly that.

While Woodrow Wilson had unusual intellectual powers, perhaps overrated powers, to awaken one's admiration, it was his sheer courage of conviction, his utter self-reliance, his faith in the highest ideals known to mankind, that lay at the heart of his power; they were the secret of the hold he had, and still has, upon the world.

When he replied to Dr. Grayson's warnings regarding the western trip in 1919, that his life did not matter if he could fire the people with the determination to support the new plans for world co-operation, I knew he meant exactly what he said.

Oh, I know well enough! He had temperamental limitations and defects, he made serious mistakes—I pointed out some of them in my *Life and Letters*—but in the inner qualities so necessary to great leadership, there was something that kindled the faith of men who loved their country, and will continue to kindle it. So often down the years I have thought of a passage in Wilson's noble tribute to the leadership of General Lee which so ably described his own:

"When you come into the presence of a leader of men," he said, "you know you have come into the presence of fire,—that it is best not incautiously to touch that man,—that there is something that makes it dangerous to cross him. You do not want sweetness merely and light in men who lead you. . . ."

I had tried in vain all that summer and early fall of 1919, to recapture the old magic of my garden at Amherst, my orchard, my meadow, my bee-colonies. "To-day I picked the Belle of Georgia peaches. . . . The Damson plums are ripe at last. . . . An immense business of canning in the kitchen. . . ."

I could write truthfully of my home in the country:

"I have tried many things, and am happy only here. Of all that I have seen in these troubled months nothing satisfies: nothing comforts the spirit of man like this."

But I could not get Wilson's struggle out of my mind. It seemed to me that the questions at issue were vital to the life of the world: that unless they were settled correctly there would soon be more dreadful wars, threatening the very existence of civilization.

"The world, it seems to me," I wrote in my notebook on October 1, "was never in such a state of disorganization and demoralization. All the passions of men seem to have been let loose; a far rebound from the discipline and sacrifice of war. At this moment in America we are facing a number of huge strikes: notably the steel strike. There have been fierce and brutal race-riots, only the other day one in Omaha in which the mob burned the court house and nearly killed the mayor. Troops have been called to put it down. During a strike of the policemen in Boston all the criminal class suddenly broke loose and as soon as the law turned its back began to loot, rob citizens, attack women. Never did the crust of civilization seem so thin. The tragedy here was not the strike in itself, bad as was the refusal of the sworn officers of the law to do their duty, but the demonstrated fact that there existed so many people prepared to riot and to rob the moment the actual fear of the police was removed. . . .

"Everyone is preaching rights rather than duties: each man is his own judge of what his rights are: if they are not instantly granted he tries to enforce them. No man thinks of sacrificing anything for any cause whatsoever. . . ."

This may seem an extreme expression of disillusionment and despair: it was nevertheless exactly what I felt at that time.

I watched Wilson's departure on his western trip with a kind of amazement. The sheer courage of the man! No doubt he saw the distracted world as clearly as I did, and he knew better than anyone else the power of the forces gathering to destroy all he had achieved at Paris, even to destroy him personally: and yet he continued to believe in the people. He still had faith that if he could get to them directly, they would listen to reason, and support him in his struggle. He had now no strong organization behind him: many of the leaders of his own party were lukewarm, if not opposed to him. He was setting out alone, risking his very life in a conclusive demonstration of his faith.

I followed with painful eagerness, every day, the reports of his trip. I read his speeches, reported all too meagerly in the eastern newspapers. To me there was something sublime about that tragic venture, something indescribably great, beautiful, in what seemed to me its futility. For even if right, and the people proved willing to support him, was it not then too late to influence a recalcitrant political opposition? Was he not attempting an enlightenment of the people that should have been started while we were at Paris? Had we all been too sanguine? Had we expected great fundamental changes in world relationships in too short a time?

What was there now to do but to get back to primary things, the old, slow program of education and growth? It occurred to me that Wilson's trip might not after all be so futile. Was he not trying to make the people understand? If he could not secure immediate support for his plan of world co-operation he was nevertheless laying the foundation for greater efforts in the future. *What he said was true: it could not die.*

I began to feel strongly that I must help the President in his struggle in the only way I knew, with my pen. I had also another, possibly lesser reason, for wishing to get into the fray. I was indignant regarding the personal attacks being made upon him. Washington in particular was full of the most outrageous and slanderous stories. Apparently there was nothing too low for his enemies to say; no traitor, no criminal, could have been worse maligned.

It made me boil when I thought of the President's cruel months of labor there at Paris, devoted to the true service of his country, doing the very best he knew how, trying to distill even a little good out of much evil. An American newspaper one morning reported that a petition to Congress for the President's impeachment for high crimes was being circulated in New York. On another page of that newspaper, I saw an account of the anxiety of the King of England to confer some notable honor on the British Prime Minister. Lloyd George had certainly been one of the most unpopular prime ministers of England in recent years, and yet the English people wished to recognize his devoted service. It made one ponder the differences between the American and British democracies—and our treatment of our great men compared with theirs. Wilson was not the only one. Lincoln had been scarcely less foully attacked and maligned. And in our case the kind of vile stories being circulated touched not only the men attacked but their wives and families. It made one blush for his country.

I packed my bag and took the night train to New York. I went to the managers of McClure's newspaper syndicate and told them I wanted to write ten or a dozen articles explaining clearly what Wilson had done at Paris and why he had done it: that I wanted them put out to the newspapers while the President was still on his trip.

"Are they ready?" Brainerd asked me.

"No," I said, "but I will have the first of them written by the time you can make arrangements with the publishers."

I could see that the prospect appeared doubtful to these experienced editors: they told me bluntly that the American people were "fed up" on the Peace Conference; they didn't want to be bothered any more with the woes of Europe.

Nevertheless I began at once to write the articles; and the attitude of the syndicate people completely changed as soon as they began to hear from the newspapers. There was money in it! On my first visit to New York after the enterprise was launched I was amused to have two of the men in the office jump up quickly when I opened the door, and shake me heartily by the hand. They had just that morning sold the series in Buenos Aires to *La Prensa* and had agreed to send each article as it appeared by cable, at $300 an article. They had also sold the series in Japan and in England, as well as to a well-assorted list of American newspapers.

I worked on the articles at high pressure, hoping to add my contribution while the President was making his speaking tour in the West. I did not aim at completeness; I tried to explain as simply as possible the half-dozen great critical problems the Peace Conference had to meet and the President's attitude toward them. I wrote the whole series in about four weeks. I had not the remotest idea of book publication, but Doubleday thought he could get a much wider circulation of my report, and brought out on November 24 the little book called *What Wilson Did at Paris*. It was said at the time to have made a record in speedy book publication.

I had been somewhat anxious about the response of the President to my articles, still more to the book. If I could have reached him beforehand I should have asked his advice, but he was then on the Western trip, and before the series was completed he had returned to Washington, a broken man. It was a great satisfaction, therefore, to hear from Mrs. Wilson and from Admiral Grayson who, I knew, would express the President's attitude. Mrs. Wilson thanked me heartily for making "such a splendid effort to interpret to the American people the stupendous difficulties that confronted the President in Paris." Admiral Grayson wrote me on November 1 that "the President is grateful to you for your interest and help in this matter."

The series reached a large number of people; Brainerd estimated a reader-circulation of 10,000,000. I heard from the articles from all sides: it seemed, when I went to Washington in early November, where the series was being published in the *Star*, that everyone I met had been reading it. Senator Owen asked permission to republish the entire series in the *Congressional Record,* and I heard of friends of the President who distributed many hundreds of copies of the little book.

On November 5, I lunched at the White House with Mrs. Wilson. The President was able to see no visitors. I find these notes in my diary:

"Mrs. McAdoo, Mrs. Sayre, and Miss Margaret Wilson, the President's daughters, were there; and Admiral and Mrs. Grayson. They were all very warm in their commendations of the Wilson articles. Mrs. Wilson looks worn and tired after her long vigil, but remains irrepressibly cheerful. Grayson told me he did not see how they could have gotten along without her. She has been up all hours of the night with the President and has never faltered in her attention.

"The Western trip must have been a terrible affair, as she and Admiral Grayson told me about it. The President was ill when he started. The western altitudes affected him; in Montana the hot dry weather and the dust caused an affection of the throat and he developed a kind of asthma. In Washington state he began to have terrible headaches—so blinding that when he got up to speak he saw double. Yet he would not give up. At several functions in California—one a dinner in which those present smoked inordinately—he suffered frightfully, but made a wonderful speech. He steadily refused the beseeching requests of Grayson to stop and rest.

"Coming eastward the Doctor saw a curious drag or looseness at the left side of his mouth, a sign of danger that could no longer be disregarded, and he and Mrs. Wilson took things into their own hands and called off the trip. No one knows yet how serious the attack was or what the President has been through. I spent the entire afternoon talking with Grayson; he went into every phase of the case and read me his secret reports. . . .

"The President will be much longer in getting up and about than anyone knows; and he may never get up at all. The Doctor has built a kind of chair back, with arms, for use in his bed. He has also a new wheel-chair in which, presently, he hopes the President may be able to get about. He is undeniably better, but the Doctor is guarding him closely, preventing, as much as possible, any business coming to his attention. This is hard to do because the President's mind is exceedingly acute, as good as ever it was, and he chafes at the inactivity. The President has never lost his sense of humor: nor ever failed, even at the worst, to have a witty response. When one of the doctors was taking a sample of his blood, he remarked: "That's what the Senate has been trying to do to me."

CHAPTER LIV

More About the Fight on the Treaty

WILSON'S STRUGGLE with the Senate, and his physical breakdown, however disheartening, were not the most immediately alarming aspects of those post-war months in America. The domestic crisis appeared to many observers even more threatening than the problems of international relationships. Difficulties of reconstruction seemed overwhelming; business was struggling with all but uncontrollable inflationary trends; hoards of the unemployed were walking the streets; labor was disorganized and rebellious. There seemed nowhere any vital leadership: the President lay helpless in the White House, Congress was worse than impotent, the leadership of both the great national parties was as usual absorbed—and paralyzed—by the oncoming presidential election.

Thomas W. Lamont, member of the firm of J. P. Morgan, had bought The New York *Evening Post,* one of the oldest and most distinguished newspapers in the country. He had brought in as its editor Edwin M. Gay, who had been dean of the Harvard School of Business Administration. Both of these men had been consultants during the Paris Peace Conference; both were well aware of the dangerous situation in America—especially from the point of view of the industrial and financial interests. I had letters from both of these men asking me if I would join the staff of the *Post,* at least temporarily, and help in an earnest editorial effort to clarify the situation. They willingly agreed that I should have complete freedom in reporting exactly what I found and in expressing my own views, wherever I might find it necessary.

I had a warm admiration for Dean Gay. I liked to think of my approach to great social and economic problems as closely similar to his own—that of the inquiring scientist, looking first of all for the truth of the matter.

I took hold of the task with hearty satisfaction. The *Post* arranged for syndicate publication, and gave the series unusual advertising and publicity, so that I might be assured of a wide reading.

I said in my introductory article:

"We are passing through much the same psychological process in getting a new understanding between labor and capital as we are in getting a League of Nations. Much the same forces are at work: the same obstinate reactionary elements, the same unreasonable radicalism. We are trembling upon the thin edge, in both problems, between organization and anarchy. . . .

"I felt over and over again at Paris that if one who had been there could sit down with a group of his neighbors and explain the whole situation, present the difficulties involved, describe the dangers of drifting without a constructive purpose, he could show them why, even though the Treaty was defective in many ways, it was profoundly necessary to get some organization at work, some league in being to steady the world.

"I have had exactly the same conviction regarding the present industrial situation in America. It is based upon the same solid faith in the essential good sense of the American people. If they can only *see* the situation, as it presents itself in some of the great industrial centers, where strikes have been raging; if they can only *know* what the issues really are as interpreted by leaders on both sides of the great controversy; if they can only *understand* how intensely human the problems are, how full of the common stuff of life; if they can be shown where the truly reconstructive experimentation is going on and who are the thoughtful leaders on both sides—if the American people can *see* and *know* and *understand* these things they will decide aright regarding them."

I traveled extensively about the country, I talked with leaders on both sides, and wrote about twenty articles. They were apparently widely read. The *Post* could not supply the demand for back numbers, and even found it necessary to issue reprints. Doubleday brought out the series in book form under the title *The New Industrial Unrest: Reasons and Remedies.*

But the public response seemed to me not only perplexing but unsatisfactory. I had written the articles with the same searching effort to secure authenticity as I had in the earlier so-called "muckraking" inquiries. I remembered how eagerly those studies had been received, the unmistakable interest expressed in letters and editorial comment—even the red-hot attacks of critics who did not agree with me. I had had a feeling at that time that I was speaking to men who had a real appetite for the truth, and that they intended to act immediately and vigorously to change existing injustices and wipe out official corruption.

I got no such feeling out of the articles I wrote for the *Post,* nor out of the reception of the book that followed. The reviews were generally favorable, but they seemed to me mild and tired—and worst of all, academic. I longed for one of the slashing attacks of the earlier years. I think I should have liked it if someone had called me names—as Theodore Roosevelt had done in 1906.

The plain fact was that the people were emotionally and intellectually exhausted by the war. They wanted to be let alone; they wanted to get back to work. They wanted what the nondescript President who followed Wilson aptly called "normalcy."

Well, the Senate rejected the Treaty, even derisively. They were proud of what they had done. I found these verses in a newspaper printed at that time:

THE INQUEST

Who killed the Treaty?
"I," said Hank Lodge;
"With my little dodge
I killed the Treaty."

Who saw it die?
"I," said Bill Borah;
"It got my angora.
I saw it die."

Who'll dig the grave?
"I will," said Sherman;
"They say I'm pro-German.
I'll dig the grave."

Who'll toll the bell?
"I will," said Smoot;
"At knells I'm a beaut
I'll toll the bell."

Who'll read the service?
"I will," said Moses;
"I'll water your noses.
I'll read the service."

Who'll be chief mourner?
"I," said Medill;
"I'll weep with a will—
I'll be chief mourner."

Some time later these men, probably incited by Senator Lodge—for it was like him—sent back the actual official copy of the Treaty to that broken-down old man in the White House. I here express my deliberate opinion that this was one of the cruelest, most despicable acts ever committed in American politics.

I was occasionally at the White House during that terrible winter. One day when I was there, Dr. Grayson told me of a conversation he had had with the President regarding the Treaty, and the fight in the Senate. After a pause the President had said:

"It would probably have been better if I had died last fall."

So deep did it go with him.

It was a thought that had sometimes occurred to me. Few men were as fortunate as Abraham Lincoln in the timing, or in the drama, of their death; but fate could have chosen a moment when Wilson's death might have radically changed the judgment of history—at least the immediate judgment.

The circumstances of that fateful moment have never been related in print. It was on the return of Woodrow Wilson from Paris in February, 1919: when he was bringing home the first, tentative draft of the League of Nations Covenant. During all of the stormy voyage the President carried that precious document in the inside breast pocket of his coat. Once when he was climbing the stairs to the ship's bridge and his coat blew open I saw it there. It was the most cherished thing in his life.

When the *George Washington* sailed from Brest its destination was supposed to be New York. After we had been out several days, we heard that, instead of New York, we were sailing for Boston. The President had been urgently asked to speak there before going on to Washington. I never knew exactly what happened on that stormy night of our approach to the American shore. I learned that it was an unfamiliar passage for the ship's officers of the *George Washington:* and that there had been—in that night of black weather—confusion as to the entrance to Boston harbor. When I went on deck early in the morning I learned at once that the ship was late. It was actually sailing almost south. In the night it had lost its course and had gone northward toward the rocks of Gloucester Point. One of the first men I met knew more about those waters, probably, than any other man aboard, not connected with the ship's command. His hobby from boyhood had been ships and sailing: he was then the Assistant Secretary of the Navy, and had been in that office for some half dozen years. I asked Franklin Roosevelt what the trouble was. He said he did not as yet know exactly, but that we had been far too close to the rocks of Gloucester.

I recall with what a shock it came to me: what if the ship had struck and gone down!

What if Woodrow Wilson, with the precious Covenant in his pocket, had gone down with her? Years later, I also asked what changes there might have been in our history if that able young Assistant Secretary of the Navy had also gone down with the ship. In writing to me in 1939, Mr. Roosevelt added a touch to the well-remembered incidents of that fateful night when, as he said, we had the "really narrow escape" near Gloucester Point:

"Do you remember," he asked in his letter, "the party given below decks by the ship's crew when the leading 'lady' with hairy arms and a rope wig kissed the President at the end of the play?"

Well, what *would* have happened, after that merry celebration, if the great ship had gone down? (I, too, should have been drowned and no one left to tell the story!)

Books were written about what Lincoln might have done if an assassin's bullet had not laid him low. Would he not have met and solved the problems of reconstruction? If he had lived would he not have healed the hatreds produced by the war?

Would the world have asked even more poignant questions if President Wilson, with the League of Nations Covenant in his pocket, had gone down with the *George Washington* at Gloucester Point? If he had lived, would he not have succeeded in organizing the League and preventing future wars? Would he not have saved humanity from the disasters that came in the next generation?

But he did not go down with the ship. He lived to struggle, and suffer, and fail. Few great Americans, I think, ever suffered more. But I wonder if, in the long years, the complete story of that struggle and that suffering and that failure will not be worth more to humanity than the implication that any one man, however powerful, could have solved the world's bitterest problems at that time. I am sure Woodrow Wilson himself would have said that solutions, to be effective, must rise out of the sufferings and defeat, the slow processes of education and of growth, the hard lessons of sacrifice, of humanity itself.

I was deeply concerned all along, during the Treaty fight, regarding the President's attitude. I knew well enough what the bitter Senate bloc led by Lodge was trying to do—but I wondered if the President was wholly right in his stubborn resistance to any changes whatsoever. On January 22, 1920, I was in Washington and lunched at the White House. I found that, under the doctor's orders, no outsiders were seeing the President, but that he was improving in health every day. Grayson had got him an Atlantic City boardwalk chair and provided a fur foot muff so that he could take his exercise in comfort. They told me he was as vigorous as ever mentally, and calm about everything except the Treaty fight.

"He tried some days ago," I said in my diary, "to write out his views in regard to the various reservations proposed, but soon gave it up.

"I had a long talk with Mrs. Wilson, who impressed me again with her good sense, her real understanding of the difficulties of the present situation, and her eagerness to help. I told her just what I thought the people felt—that while they were wholeheartedly behind the President in their support of the *spirit*, the *reality* of the League, they were profoundly disturbed by the differences over minor matters: and that they were inclined to blame Mr. Wilson as much as Mr. Lodge. I made the point as diplomatically as I could, but she came out quite bluntly:

" 'They think him stubborn,' she said.

"So much hangs on this issue," I continued, "possibly the very existence of a League."

" 'I know,' she said, 'but the President still has in mind the reception he got in the West, and he believes the people are with him.'

"That is the trouble!" I wrote afterwards. "He has been ill since last October and he cannot know what is going on. He sees almost nobody: and hears almost no direct news. This sick man, with such enormous power, closed in from the world, and yet acting so influentially upon events!"

I was so deeply moved by what I saw and felt during that visit that I determined that I would, if I could, present the situation to the President as I saw it. He had listened to me many times before, even when I was critical: possibly he would again. I thought I knew something of the real opinion in America. I had been traveling about the country for the past two or three months, while writing my articles for *The Post*. It had been more or less my business all my life to try to understand and estimate public opinion. I thought I could tell him honestly that the great majority of the American people were with him in his main contention—the necessity of a world league—but that many doubted his position in standing so firmly upon the letter of the Covenant.

I therefore wrote a long letter (on January 25) to Mrs. Wilson in which I set forth my honest conclusions.

My dear Mrs. Wilson:

Since our talk of Thursday, I have had the present situation very deeply upon my mind. I have the feeling that all the President went to France to fight for—for which he fought so nobly—is being swept away: that the chance for world reorganization, which is the President's high purpose, is more and more threatened. And I feel so strongly that if the President were not ill—if he were himself—he could and would save the situation. I believe the people of the country are just in the mood to respond to the kind of moral appeal which the President, beyond any other living man, is best able to make. The people want the League: they are for the reality—the spirit—which lives in the idea: but they are bitterly confused over the present minor disagreements. Their thoughts go straight to the heart of the matter—which is to get something started quickly, some going organization to meet the problems of the world, some group of men sitting in common council. They know that no document is or can be final, and that a real League will grow as it begins to function. . .

People in the future will forget about the minor disagreements, if the thing itself comes into being. . . .

In the conclusion I offered to help in any way I could by explaining the President's real position.

I knew well enough that this letter implied a criticism of the President's course, especially the references I made to the disagreements as being "minor." It might even break my long-standing and friendly relationships with him; and I was greatly relieved to have a response from Mrs. Wilson dated on January 26, in which she said:

I have read with great interest your letter which reached me this morning—and I am convinced that you have the right idea as regards the preservation of the "spirit" of the Covenant and if you bring out that idea, as you can do so well—it may help as much as your little book is helping.

I asked Dr. Grayson to tell you the day you were here how sincerely my husband appreciates your wish to help and now I am repeating it that you may know how sincere it is. . . .

I don't know positively that this correspondence had any part in prompting the President's letter to Senator Hitchcock* dated January 26 (but not made public until February 7), or in shaping the contents of it, but it followed so closely the suggestions in my memorandum that I thought it would only confuse matters if I wrote a semi-inspired article on the same subject. I was, in fact, pleased with what seemed to me the broadly conciliatory tone of the President's letter.

"I have once more," he wrote, "gone over the reservations proposed by yourself . . . and am glad to say that I can accept them as they stand."

This did not, of course, mean the acceptance of the far more serious reservations proposed by Lodge and his supporters. His letter, indeed, included a strong statement of his opposition to certain of the "destructive" reservations, the purpose of which he believed to be to secure the benefits of the League without accepting any real

* Senator Hitchcock was the Democratic leader in the Senate in the fight for the ratification of the Treaty.

obligation or responsibility on the part of the United States. Under these something-for-nothing reservations, the Lodge group in the Senate was asking that the great and powerful American nation be permitted to enjoy all the benefits of world co-operation without paying for them. The President, and every American with any pride in his country, who understood what was really going on, regarded these proposals as humiliating. So it was that the President took his position, finally and decisively, in his letter to Senator Hitchcock, against any reservation or resolution which stated that: "The United States assumes no obligation under such and such an article. . . ." He also said in his letter that it was "important not to create the impression that we were trying to escape obligations."

Here were clearly defined the essential positions of the two combatants. The Hitchcock reservations were acceptable. The Lodge reservations were not "minor" differences; in the President's mind, they went to the heart of the matter, and could not be accepted.

Some time later—I think in late February—I had a brief talk with the President in which the subject of the reservations came up again. The conciliatory letter to Hitchcock had, after all, done no good. I shall never forget the sad finality of the President's words regarding the situation:

"These reservations [that is, the reservations demanded by the Lodge group] are not made by thoughtful men to improve the Covenant; they represent a dishonorable attempt, on the part of leaders who do not speak for the people, to escape any real responsibility, so far as the United States is concerned, for world peace in future years. They are essentially partisan political devices. If I accept them, these senators will merely offer new ones, even more humiliating."

He paused a long moment and then said:

"These evil men intend to destroy the League."

Whether right or wrong, I believe that this was the President's conclusion regarding the matter, and the principal reason for his determined opposition.

CHAPTER LV

The Tragedy of Woodrow Wilson

DURING ALL THE months that followed the refusal of the Senate to ratify the Treaty, I could not get the thought of that tragical defeat out of my mind It seemed to me the downfall of one of the noblest aspirations of mankind: that, literally, it meant what the far-seeing President himself had prophesied.

"I can predict with absolute certainty that within another generation there will be another world war if the nations of the world do not concert the method by which to prevent it."*

He also said:

"Stop for a moment to think about the next war, if there should be one. I do not hesitate to say that the war we have just been through, though it was shot through with terror of every kind, is not to be compared with the war we would have to face next time. . . . What the Germans used were toys as compared with what would be used in the next war." †

What was a man to do who believed absolutely, as I did, in these direful predictions? Was there anything that any one man, especially if he held no public office, *could* do? The President himself had failed in his disastrous effort to reach the people in time to bring pressure upon the Senate. I had tried to help him with my little book, *What Wilson Did at Paris*—all to no purpose, as it seemed to me.

And yet what other recourse was there in a democracy than the "appeal to the people"? Had not the old, slow process of informing and educating the people to go forward? If one lost faith in that, what hope was there left for our noble system of government?

My mind began to turn, as so often in the past, to the problem of leadership. As a more or less well-trained follower—who regarded followers as quite as important as leaders in our form of government

* At Omaha in 1919.
† At Denver in 1919.

—what was there to do but to find a new leader? Although I knew that Wilson, old and broken as he was, had resolved to go on with the fight—he had even considered becoming a candidate for the third time, in the campaign of 1920—I knew that his official leadership was ended. There must be a new man, or new men.

I remember setting down the names of six or eight possibilities, each at the head of a sheet of copy paper, down the middle of which I drew a line, with the heading "Pros" on one side, and "Cons" on the other.

I recalled a remark that President Wilson had made to me on the last voyage of the *George Washington:*

"You think I have had a hard time of it," he said, "but my difficulties are nothing compared to those which the next president will have to face."

One of the chief qualifications that I put down in my survey of possibilities was "ability to take punishment."

Only two men on my list seemed to me, finally, to answer in any degree the requirements of the great office of the American presidency in such an emergency. One of these was Newton D. Baker, who had been the highly successful Secretary of War in Wilson's cabinet, and the other was Herbert Hoover.

I liked Newton Baker especially: I find I wrote of him in my notes at that time:

"If Secretary Baker had the presence, the 'front,' of Secretary Houston, he would be one of the outstanding figures in the coming presidential campaign. But he is so small, so light, so unimpressive, physically. Yet he is much the strongest man in the Cabinet. He has liberal ideas, he is a really fine speaker, he is a good administrator. He has a keen, direct mind, and the agreeable ability of placing himself at once in democratic touch with the man he is meeting, no matter who he is."

But upon consideration, I felt that Herbert Hoover came nearer to being the most available man, largely because of his knowledge of world affairs. I did not know what his politics were—I think he did not himself know at that time—but I considered that this was a "pro" item, not a "con." I had become personally acquainted with him at the Peace Conference. I liked his thoughtful and honest approach to problems he had to face. I knew and admired what he had done in feeding Belgium.

So, on September 5, 1919, I wrote letters to the New York *Times*, the Springfield *Republican*, and I think to other papers, to this effect:

"I see that Herbert Hoover, upon his return to America, disclaims any interest in politics. But there are many good reasons why he is just the kind of man we need in politics now in America, perhaps even in the very highest place. There are very few men who possess in such high degree the passion for disinterested service, combined with really great gifts of leadership. He is an able and skilled administrator, with years of training in large affairs. Is there anything more needed in public life to-day in America? . . .

"From this time forward, we are destined in this country, whether we like it or not, to play a larger and larger part in foreign affairs. There is no other public man in America who knows every phase of the foreign situation as comprehensively as Herbert Hoover, and none who has been able to deal more skilfully with complicated international problems. No one who saw him in action at Paris can doubt either his knowledge of these conditions or his genius for dealing with them. It must not be forgotten that his experience reaches far back of the commission for relief in Belgium and that for years he has been interested in large enterprises in Russia, South Africa, China and elsewhere. . . .

"Herbert Hoover has had five years of heavy work, without pay, and largely without honor, for great public causes, and wishes now to retire to private life. But can we spare him? . . ."

I was much pleased to have this response of October 6:

My dear Baker:

I did receive a copy of your letter in the Springfield *Republican*. Everybody likes words of commendation, more especially from people whom one esteems as highly as I do yourself.

On the other hand, I am convinced that you are somewhat on the wrong track, for I have a notion that what this country needs is a few private citizens, as well as aspirants for public office.

I am hoping to see you some of these days, as I am going back to the East, and I have a number of things that I wish to discuss with you.

Faithfully yours,

HERBERT HOOVER

Some time later I found this paragraph in Hoover's first statement to the public:

"If the Treaty goes over to the presidential election (with any reservations necessary to clarify the world's mind that there can be no infringement of the safeguards provided by our Constitution and our nation-old traditions) then I must vote for the party that stands for the League."

While this statement pleased me in its declaration that Hoover would "vote for the party that stands for the League," I was perplexed by his reference to the "reservations." What, precisely, did he mean by "infringements" of American "safeguards"? Did he, or did he not, believe that the American people, if they wanted the inestimable benefits of co-operation with a world organization, must be willing to make real sacrifices for it?

Sad to relate, when Hoover actually became the Republican candidate for the presidency, and set forth his political views—and still later, after he reached the White House—I was disappointed. While I continued to admire his many fine qualities, and his devotion to what he considered the public interest, I did not vote for him.

With the nomination of Harding in that summer of 1920, the whole political picture—like the industrial and economic situation—seemed to me to be near hopelessness. The movement for Hoover had been abortive: and the nomination of Cox by the Democrats seemed an admission of incompetency.

On August 11, I wrote a letter to my friend Brand Whitlock, who was still in Brussels as the Ambassador of the United States, which presented my own dark picture of the situation.

"It is a very great pleasure to have your letter. Curiously, I was thinking the other day how much I should like it if I could talk with you about the present conditions in Europe, which for me grow misty with distance and preoccupation.

"Over here, those of us who came back from Europe after the Peace Conference with any hope left—as I did—have had a sorry time of it. The whole struggle over the Treaty and the League, worst of all the apathy and want of knowledge and imagination on the part of our people, have been most discouraging. All that is narrowest and most selfish in the America which spoke out so nobly during the war, seems to have come uppermost.

"There was, for a time, an encouraging movement for Hoover, but it went to pieces against the impenetrable machinery of the old parties. Hoover himself lost a great opportunity for liberal leadership. . . . He somehow lacked the necessary vision. And finally, he actually added his strength to the most reactionary group of them all. He has utterly destroyed his usefulness in this field.

"I attended, last November, with some hope, the convention in Chicago that organized the new Labor Party. But it was without constructive leadership. The recent joint convention at Chicago of the radical groups was also a fizzle.

"I shall vote this fall for Cox and the Democrats, though without enthusiasm, because of their position on the League of Nations. At present, however, it does not seem that the Democrats can win. The reaction from the war, the present unpopularity of Mr. Wilson . . . the rampant appeal to the narrowest and most provincial spirit in our national life, are all helping Harding. . . .

"The grim old schoolmaster there in Washington still has power in the land, as the Democratic party contests in various states have shown. He is about the only unmovable thing left.

"I don't want to make too dark a picture—I am writing offhand just as it looks to me. It seems sometimes as though we were 'wandering between two worlds, one dead, the other powerless to be born.' "

During that fall (1920), I was from time to time seeing the "grim old schoolmaster." He was not only physically helpless, he was under fierce attack both for what he had done and for what he had not done.

In November, many of the liberals and progressives of the country voted as I did for Cox, because Harding seemed to us so palpably impossible. I had not yet lost faith in Herbert Hoover as a future leader, but I could write in my diary (August 14, 1920):

"There is hope in young Roosevelt."

Not a few progressives, even as early as that, had begun to think of Franklin D. Roosevelt.

The President himself, his powerful intellect undimmed, but his body broken and futile, who was watching with penetrating intensity the condition of the world, was often bitter in spirit and scathing of tongue. He had broken with several of his important associates and friends. He had not seen Colonel House in many months, and in early 1920, he parted company with Secretary Lansing. Concerning this unfortunate episode I wrote in my notes:

"Papers full today of President Wilson's summary discharge (for it looks like nothing else) of Secretary Lansing. It seems the petulant and irritable act of a sick man. Although I do not rate Secretary Lansing high or regard his judgment as sound, still this sudden and violent action, with the reasons for it, does not seem wise or politic. I do not think that the Secretary was ill-advised in calling Cabinet meetings. It is four months since the President fell ill, and he has himself been able to transact very little public business. It seemed to me as I went around Washington the other day as though our government had gone out of business. Both executive and legislative bodies are scarcely functioning. With enormous problems to solve, Congress is frittering away its time in fruitless discussions of the Treaty, and the President is ill. It makes one apprehensive to look forward to the next year or two."

I felt much the same way regarding the later break with his secretary and friend Tumulty—at the same time that I recognized how difficult Tumulty had sometimes been. While there had been no diminution of the President's intellectual powers, he seemed to have lost the elasticity of self-command and self-discipline with which he had met a thousand difficult problems of the earlier years of his administration. Unable to act and achieve in the higher realms, he seemed to give way, explosively, in meeting minor irritations. Some of Wilson's friends thought that the loss of resilience began with his illness at Paris in April, 1919: but no one could have followed the Peace Conference discussions in May and June—after the German replies came in—without being deeply impressed with the President's continuing energy and vitality. And think of the sheer intellectual vigor of his appeal to the people during his campaign through the country in September, 1919!

The real "letdown" seemed to me to have begun with the stroke at Pueblo on September 26. Judgment of everything he did after that must be tempered by the consideration of his physical condition.

One heartbreaking incident of that fall—just after the election of Harding—I recall with almost intolerable clarity. Mrs. Wilson had invited me to luncheon at the White House, and had suggested that I come early for the moving pictures.

While I waited in the parlor I saw the heavy red rug in the hall being lifted and laid aside. Then the President came shuffling slowly with a cane upon the smooth marble flags of the floor. He swung along heavily, his left arm inert, his left side drooping. To one who remembered vividly upon so many former occasions the alert, listening poise of the head, the singularly active step, it could not but be a shock to see him there—a shock of intense compassion, which instantly gave way to amazement at the indomitable spirit of the man. It was in every line of his face, sharpened and deepened with suffering, it shone in his extraordinarily large and brilliant eyes, it was in the strong pressure of his hand when we met, and in the jest with which he greeted me.

There he stood, a stooped, gray-faced, white-haired old man, and yet he gave such a sense of unconquerable will, of untamable life, as cannot well be described.

We passed down the hall into the great ballroom of the White House. That grand room with its faded glories was now wholly bare and empty except for half a dozen chairs placed in the middle of the floor. It was almost unlighted and resounded to our steps. The President took his seat in the first of the chairs, Mrs. Wilson next, then a niece of Mrs. Wilson, Admiral Grayson, and I.

The moving picture machine behind us began to click and sputter and a picture flashed upon a screen at the far end of the room. I had been told that it was the initial exhibition of the film record of the President's expedition to Europe.

With the first brilliantly lighted episode we were in another world; a resplendent world, full of wonderful and glorious events. There we were, sailing grandly into the harbor at Brest, the ships beflagged, the soldiers marshalled upon the quay, and planes skimming through the air. There was the President himself, smiling upon the bridge, very erect, very tall, lifting his hat to shouting crowds.

By magic we were transported to Paris. There he was again, this time with the President of France, driving down the most famous avenue in the world, bowing right and left. In the distance we saw the Arc de Triomphe, symbol too of this latest triumph, and caught a glimpse of the tomb of the great Napoleon guarding its dimmed glory.

The man back in the darkness of the great room sat bowed forward, looking at all this, absolutely silent.

We were crossing the English Channel, two nations disputing the glory of guarding our passage. The warships of France came half way with us, and gave over reluctantly to the warships of Britain. We were ashore. Were there ever such marching regiments of men, such bowing dignitaries, so many lords and their ladies! And there was the President, riding behind magnificent horses with outriders flying pennants, and people shouting in the streets, coming down from Buckingham Palace with the King of England.

The show was over, the film had run its course. It was only a film. All that glory had faded away with a click and a sputter. It was to us sitting there as though the thread of life itself had snapped, as though we had fallen from some vast height into the musty reality of this lesser world. We were again in the dim ballroom. We drew long breaths, and turned to see sitting there, quite immobile, quite silent, the stooped figure of the President.

Out of the surrounding darkness one came and placed his foot against the President's foot, so that he would not slip as he rose from his chair. He turned slowly, and shuffled out of the doorway alone, without looking aside and without speaking.

He was gone from the room, and I was left realizing more strongly than ever before that he was one of those men who, from the very beginning, and in whatever scene, had been appointed—chosen, doomed—to occupy the center of the stage. He was one of those corrosive men, a powerful reagent in clarifying fluid social conditions, and whether the president of a university, the governor of a state, the chief magistrate of a nation, or the supreme figure in a world conference, he was a kind of center of life and heat, causing the fiercest ebullitions, separating society into its elements, starting new combinations, and engendering everywhere the fiercest human passions, the whole gamut from sheer worship to deadly hatred.

He had never anywhere in his life been negligible; he could never be brushed aside or got around. The politicians tried their best to avoid him in the recent campaign. And though he was a broken invalid, they could not escape him. It was he and his policies that people fought about. It was he who was the supreme issue.

I knew well what he was doing on that election day of 1920 while thirty million people were voting for two puppets. With his cane in his hand, he was trying and failing, as he had been doing week after week, failing and trying again, to climb a series of three or four little low steps which Dr. Grayson had built in the White House for his exercise. They thought they had him beaten down at Princeton, they thought they had him beaten down in New Jersey, they said he had failed at Paris. I was watching him climb those little steps. What did it matter if the steps he climbed led only into history? He'd climb them.

What a man was this, as lonely as God—a titan struggling with earthly forces too great for him! At one moment, to those who were closest to him, he seemed the simplest, the most sincere, the most direct of men. At other moments he seemed utterly remote, aloof, unapproachable. At one moment he appeared a pathetically friendless and lonely human soul, longing for human love (as he once told a friend), but rarely achieving it, getting at best only wonderfully gilded husks of respect, the glorious outer accoutrements of admiration, the inverted recognition of the envious. At another time he appeared one of those insular figures not needing sympathy, that Matthew Arnold compared with the stars:

> These demand not that the things without them
> Yield them love, amusement, sympathy.

No—I thought there in the White House that morning—the tapestry of his life is yet too large to be seen in its entirety; I was beginning to know how much stitching and knitting had yet to be done. I could only here and there prick in a detail which would some time, perhaps, take its place where it belonged in the finished picture.

I followed that shuffling figure of the man walking painfully out of the room, with tears in my eyes. I felt a passion of anger at the personal and slanderous attacks (I do not refer to political opposition), of insect-minded enemies and soured friends and envious rivals, upon this broken man, this strange fated character, built upon heroic lines and set upon a heroic stage.

I did not dare to speculate upon what was going on in that powerful, active, intense mind now imprisoned in the ruin of a body with little but itself to feed upon. A man's capacity for suffering is in exact ratio to his power to think and to feel. What then must be the suffering here!

Later at the luncheon with the President, there began outside of the White House the slow, single-file parade of a group of sympathizers with Irish freedom. They were demanding of the broken old man that he straightway free Ireland. The pathetic faith of it; the pathetic faith of men in heroes and supermen. The idea that someone who has spoken true words can magically do for them what they can only do for themselves. This also was the very core of the tragic events at Paris; of the still persistent idea that the world can be made over by the word of one man of whom they would make a god, or perchance a president. And when their prayer is not answered, they turn upon him and rend him. The world could have used—perhaps—the tables which their prophet brought down to them out of Sinai, had they not already turned to the worship of the calf. And the tables fell and were broken—and who was there now to return to the heights and brave the anger of the Lord?

CHAPTER LVI

I Open the "Steel Box"

I HEARD only one comment by Woodrow Wilson regarding the election of his successor to the presidency, Warren Gamaliel Harding:

"How can he lead when he does not know where he is going?"

This was on December 1, 1920. The President did his best to indicate where *he* was going in his annual message when Congress convened on December 7. He took for his text the immortal saying of Abraham Lincoln:

"Let us have faith that right makes might, and in that faith let us dare to do our duty as we understand it."

While the message itself seemed to me far from being as able a document as many of his earlier ones, it should have convinced any honest observer that the President, although ill and bed-ridden, had still a commanding grasp upon public problems. It contained much wise and practical advice as to what Congress should do in its coming session; but in its essence it was a plea for a more thoughtful democracy in America.

> I have not so much laid before you a series of recommendations, gentlemen, as sought to utter a confession of faith, of the faith in which I was bred and which it is my solemn purpose to stand by until my last fighting day. I believe this to be the faith of America, the faith of the future, and of all the victories which await national action in the days to come, whether in America or elsewhere.

In a discussion I had with the President at that time I raised the question as to how this more thoughtful democracy could be stimulated and built up in America. I had always had an uncomfortable feeling, as I have pointed out before in this book, that faith in itself is not enough. It must rest firmly upon understanding: the people must *know,* even if it takes a long time to educate them. When the

President asked me what I myself had in mind I recalled the paragraph in my little book, *What Wilson Did at Paris,* in which I said that I believed the "great, solid, sensible, forward-looking masses of people" in America would stand behind him in his fight if they could be made to understand the "whole case."

I had written in that book that the "supreme failure of the Conference was the complicated failure in publicity."

I was somewhat embarrassed to reiterate what I had said so often in Paris: but it was the truth as I saw it.

"Many people seem to have read your little book," the President said.

"Yes," I said, "but, Mr. President, I am not the final authority. They want to hear directly from you."

The President asked me what I thought he should do.

"If you yourself could write a short account of the Conference and publish the documents and reports which are still secret, I think it would help more than anything else in promoting understanding—and support. What the people want is the truth. They haven't had it yet."

I learned later that a New York publisher had offered the President one hundred and fifty thousand dollars in cash if he would write just such a record as I was suggesting. He seemed never even to have considered it. Although he did not at that time respond to me, I found a week or two later that he had spoken to Admiral Grayson of what I had said. So I wrote him (December 16) offering to help him in any way I could. He replied (December 18) as follows:

"It is clear to me that it will not be possible for me to write anything such as you suggest, but I believe that you could do it admirably."

I responded on December 23 expressing my doubt as to my ability to attempt such an overwhelming and important task, but saying that I was willing to try it if I could be assured of his support, and be given full access to all the secret documents. The President replied (December 27) as follows:

My dear Baker:

Thank you for your letter of December twenty-third, which gave me a great deal of pleasure. I have a trunk full of papers, and the next time you are down here I would like to have you go through them and see what they are and what the best use is that can be made of them. I plunked them into the trunk in Paris and have not had time or physical energy even to sort or arrange them. I am looking forward with great satisfaction to the work you are purposing to do, and have no doubt that it will be of the highest value.

With the best wishes of the season,

Cordially and faithfully yours,

WOODROW WILSON

I was surprised at the sudden opening of this opportunity and not a little overwhelmed by it: but I wrote the President on December 30: ". . . The mention of the trunk quite takes hold of one's imagination. I shall search that trunk with far more interest than I should if it were treasure trove of the Spanish Main and contained pieces-of-eight.

"The more I think of it, the more certain I am that here is a great and useful work to do: to try to present, with the sturdy thrust of the actual documents, facts, reasons, the first really great clash of America and American ideals with world affairs, and this from the American point of view. . . .

"The preliminary trouble at Paris, so far as America was concerned (as I see it) was a blinding ignorance on the part of our people of foreign problems. It was an outgrowth, of course, of our traditional isolation. I saw this vividly symbolized by our newspaper correspondents, many of them exceptionally good men and the best of them as able as, or abler than, either British or French writers, but vastly inferior to either in knowledge of the history, politics and psychology, of Europe. I think a vigorous outline of what Europe was, as I saw it intimately during the year preceding the Peace Conference, would form a proper background for the picture of the Peace Conference. Only thus can we make clear the problems you had to face over there: the forces you met: the logic of your course. . . ."

Three weeks later I was at work in the White House. I had had an interesting preliminary talk with the President concerning the task ahead of me. I wanted to have it made perfectly clear as to where I stood with regard to the book, and just what I could and could not assume. Either I should write with his supervision and authority, or I should write my own book in my own way. It could not be both.

"If I authorize the book or even read it to criticize it," he said, "it would be the same as though I wrote it myself."

"Then it is to be my book, with my own interpretations and conclusions."

"Yes," he said.

I was glad to have this problem definitely settled. I could now go ahead and set down exactly what I found and what I knew. The great thing was not to defend or excuse every act of the President, but to present this strong, able, fallible man struggling with vast events in a chaotic world. I wanted to exhibit America in contact with Europe for the first time on a really vital scale: the clash of character, ideals, methods. It seemed to me a perfect opportunity for dramatizing all of the issues involved against the background of the Peace Conference. I recalled a quotation from an address by Elihu Root which I often quoted at that time: "A democracy which undertakes to control its own foreign relations ought to know something about the subject."

Looking back after many years to these hopes, I can see how far short the achievement fell from the brave plans I made. I did not realize the immensity of the task I was attempting; the book I dreamed has not yet been written.

I shall not forget that day in January, 1921, when I went up with the President to his study on the second floor of the White House. He was somewhat better in health, but he walked slowly with his cane, his left side drooping painfully.

One of the men accompanied us carrying the shiny steel cabinet-box which I had so often seen on the desk of his study in Paris. He had kept his important papers in it, and I recalled just how he shut and locked it every night.

"I knew," he said, "that certain of the servants were paid spies: and I left no important papers around anywhere."

I then learned that there was not only the "trunkful" of Paris documents to which the President had referred in his letter but *three* trunkfuls, besides the steel cabinet, and a precious smaller box which Mrs. Wilson had kept in a bank vault.

I began working at once, for a time in the President's own study, but presently in one of the White House bedrooms, where I had more room to spread out the papers and could have a stenographer to help me.

I have no intention here of recording the long labor that followed. There is little outward excitement, or incident, in the life of a writer. It is mostly lonely, endless labor. I find in my notes innumerable passages such as this one:

"Work, work work. Not going anywhere or doing anything but work. I study forenoons, dictate afternoons, and am too tired evenings to do much of anything. Keeping two stenographers busy most of the time."

I should have surrendered on the spot if I had known that I was to work on the life and times of Woodrow Wilson for more than twenty years.

But what most people know nothing about, because most of his experiences, his excitements, his adventures are invisible, is the grand inner life the student lives. It is difficult for me to convey the intense interest I had, the keen appetite, in opening that steel box, and those heavy, close-packed trunks, that still bore the seals of the President or the State Department. When I had accepted the President's appointment to the Peace Conference, I had exacted the condition that I should be allowed full access to all that was going on at Paris. I should be a real insider. It was only thus, I thought, that I could function intelligently in the position I held. But what an ignoramus I had really been! Every third document I turned over revealed wheels within wheels, the tortuous fatuities of secret discussions, that I had known little or nothing about. I soon began to discover that the President himself, to say nothing of Lloyd George and Clemenceau, did not begin to know all that was going on in that cave of the winds. "Where is Prinkipo?" asked Lloyd George innocently. "I never before heard of the island of Yap," remarked the President. Who could understand or cope with all the problems of the world in the space of four or five tumultuous months?

It may seem ridiculous, but I occasionally became so absorbed and interested that I actually forgot to go out at noon. Several times Mrs. Wilson, who had the thoughtful and hospitable ways of the South, appeared at my doorway, and brought me to myself with an invitation to lunch there at the White House.

As I read the documents, I was impressed as never before by the difficulties faced by leaders in a real democracy in dealing with leaders who were not so bound and limited by the slow processes of democratic action. How inform such a multitudinous electorate as that of the United States? How secure the "assent of the governed"? I had long believed that all reformers were too much in a hurry: and the more I studied those documents in the White House, the more thoroughly settled I became in this opinion. One day the President asked me about Alexander Meiklejohn. He had known and admired Meiklejohn and wondered why he had failed as President of Amherst College. I told him I thought Meiklejohn had many good ideas, but that he had tried to impose them far too rapidly upon a fine old institution devoted to its many richly ivied traditions. I was considerably surprised by the President's reply:

"That was one of my troubles at Princeton; trying to change an old institution too fast."

Could he not have said the same thing regarding his effort to change an old and wicked world? But what a heritage of principles and ideals he left for the nourishment of forward-looking men who would carry the banners of progress after he had left the field.

One of the incidental developments of those early weeks of work that I found mildly irritating was the blast of criticism in certain quarters called forth by the news of my new task. I was being attacked and prejudged by certain men and certain newspapers that were chronically bitter toward Wilson. They were assuming that I would necessarily write an ex parte account because I was a friend of the President, that I would not be "coldly historical" and "unprejudiced."

"Well, I *am* a friend of Wilson's," I wrote in my diary, "and it is only by a friend that any man can be understood. No man who was wholly 'cold' or entirely 'unprejudiced' ever wrote a good book: or an understanding book. I admit the charge of being a friend of Wilson's, of being vastly and deeply interested in him: but I am also vastly and deeply interested in the age and the people of which he is a symbol, and in the people he has served. I see him moving against that background: at one moment his figure vivid against the sky, at the next fallen to the earth, a broken heap. We are interested in men, we love them, not because they are perfect, for we know they cannot be perfect, but because they are greatly human, because they are themselves. Merely to defend a friend, thick or thin, is silly business, and raises him in the estimation of no one: but by trying to understand and explain him we infect others with our interest; sometimes we are even able to communicate our love. My attitude is not one of defense but of explanation. Wilson is no longer a political figure: he has now stepped into history."

One single incident of those weeks impressed me so strongly that I noted it in my diary:

"Coming out of the White House grounds today two young fellows stopped me, and said, 'We are newspaper reporters. Do you know what Secretary Colby is doing at the White House?'

"It struck me all in a heap: 'What an absurd method of getting at the doings of a great state!' Here were two boyish looking reporters probably as ignorant as mud of any knowledge of foreign affairs, or government policies, lying in wait like beggars for a chance visitor from the White House—I was a total stranger to them—to get at what was being done by the Head of the Nation and his Secretary of State.

" 'I am sorry I cannot tell you,' I said. 'I think there ought to be a better way for you to get this information. I do not know anything about the conference.'

"As I walked on I felt a peculiar sense of shame for my profession. Here were the representatives of an honorable calling—one of the most important links in the democratic system—snooping around alleys, waiting at gates, begging of chance passers, for what was necessary for the life of the Nation. A miserable business."

I recall with keen pleasure those long quiet days in the White House. I was rarely interrupted, and almost every forenoon I was regaled by a concert by Miss Margaret Wilson, who practiced in her room across the hall. But one day, as I went out, I came upon a porter with a bird cage in one hand and a family portrait under his arm, on his way to the moving van—and I knew that the Wilsons were soon to leave the White House.

Mrs. Wilson gave me a little comfortable room in the President's new home in S Street to work in. On my first visit there she showed me over the house. It was really a delightful place: with a small breakfast alcove giving upon a terrace-garden then green with new grass and bright with tulips. Mr. Wilson's study also opened upon this quiet and roomy garden. In the large front room Mrs. Wilson had hung the magnificent Gobelin tapestry presented to her in France. It covered all one end of the room and was so long that nearly half of it was rolled up at the bottom.

The little windows of my workroom opened on S Street and I could often see the public automobiles and sight-seeing wagons go by the house—the caller-out shouting: "Just below on the left—not the house on the corner—is the new home of Ex-President Wilson." Sometimes the cars would stop entirely and there would be much pointing and craning of necks.

One of the advantages of my change of location was a greater opportunity of meeting Mr. Wilson. I find this notation in my diary for March 22:

"After luncheon I went upstairs for a talk with Mr. Wilson. He was in bed, propped against a huge pile of pillows and looking inconceivably old, gray, worn, tired. His hair seemed unusually thin: and his face a kind of parchment yellow, with the skin drawn down over the temple and cheek-bones, bringing into new prominence the fine aquiline modelling of his face. Only the eyes seemed undimmed: very bright, clear, piercing: burning like living coals in the ashes of a spent fire.

"He had a couple of electric flashlights on the stand near him, a book of detective stories, and some chocolate. A very much worn Bible lay on the desk near the head of the bed; he reads it every day. He could look out from where he lay across a pleasant, quiet room to the garden, where spring is now breaking with rare beauty. Mrs. Wilson says the cardinal birds come to sing there: and just at the foot of the garden is a wondrous red-blooming shrub, like fire against the wall.

"But he is bitter at heart. I told him of the change which was coming in the country toward him, but he was inclined to be skeptical and want cases: which I was abundantly able to give him. When I mentioned the superior applause with which his picture was greeted at the moving picture houses over that of Mr. Harding, he said:

" 'But that was discourteous to the President of the United States.'

" 'It showed how people felt,' I said.

" 'I remember, in the early days of my presidency, being at the theater, and hearing Roosevelt's picture much more cheered than mine—although I was present.'

"He seems lonelier, more cut off, than ever before. His mind still works with power, but with nothing to work upon but memories and regrets. He feels himself misunderstood and unjustly attacked: and being broken in health, cannot rally under it. He has not read Lansing's book in which his course at Paris is sharply criticized, and does not intend to. He said to me, 'I think I can stand it if Lansing can"

All that bright spring in Washington I worked every day, harder, I think, than ever before in my life. I find this notation under the date of May 25:

"Dictated a good part of the day: lunched at the Wilsons', and in the later afternoon, as I was starting to walk, friends hailed me from the street and would have it that I get in their car with them and ride through the park, which I did with delight. In the evening, working again on these infernal documents until late. I am suffocated with paper: I flounder in it, sleep in it, get my nose out two or three times a day for a breath of air and a bit of food, and then down I go again into that dusty confusion."

If it had not been for many good friends and much delightful conversation, it often seemed to me that I could not live through it. So many entries in my notebooks refer to delightful visits with various good friends, familiar dinners at the Cosmos Club—and so on and so on.

"March 25, 1921. It was a great joy to find Victor Clark at the Club. We went out late this afternoon for a tramp to see the Japanese cherries in bloom, but they were not yet out: and we came back footsore. How we railed at the world! We nearly made up our minds that western civilization was on its speedy way to degeneration (citing Spengler) and that it was well enough for seasoned and knowledgeable observers like ourselves to accept the downfall. Let

Demos go to the 'movies' while Rome burns! They cannot see that they are doomed, as we can. And so, walking in the fading light of the spring evening, with the scent of flowers in the dark, and the breath of the tide rising cool from the river, so walking, we enjoyed our melancholy—and came home to the Club with a sharp appetite for supper."

"April 19, 1921. I lunched at the Capitol with Senator Hitchcock. Senator Henderson of Nevada and Mrs. Borden Harriman were also there. Met Ernest Poole and his wife. The Senate was discussing the Colombian Treaty. Calvin Coolidge slipped in through a crack in the door and had a frugal glass of milk and a sandwich—alone, saying not a word to anyone."

"May 27, 1921. Dinner with Justice and Mrs. Brandeis. Arthur Bullard and his wife were there, also Senator Ladd, and a Dr. Erickson who is helping to draw up the new constitution for Albania. If he draws it according to all the directions he got from us, Albania will be the jewel among nations. There will be no sin, sickness, nor suffering: no wheat rust, nor bone-spavin: no bald heads. Much good talk of a pessimistic turn: there is no pleasure in optimism these days!"

"May 30, 1921. Hard at work. Dropped in for tea at Brandeis' and afterward the Justice and Norman Hapgood and I went for a walk in the Park south of the White House."

"July 28, 1921. Arrived in Washington after a burning night in the sleeper. To the Cosmos Club for breakfast, where I fell in with Professor Ripley of Harvard. Afterwards Secretary Wallace (of Agriculture), who is an old friend, came over and invited me to dinner. Also met Judge Anderson of Boston and Professor Cummings, who are on their way to Geneva to study the League of Nations.

"Went out to S Street and worked hard nearly all day on the documents. Lunched with Mrs. Wilson: much good talk. Dined with Secretary Wallace. Professor Ripley and Judge Davis, Director General of Railroads, were of the company. Afterwards, the evening being hot, the Secretary took us for a fine ride through the Park, where it was deliciously cool."

As the work progressed Mr. Wilson's interest in what I was doing seemed to increase: and he helped me greatly in deciphering some of his stenographic and other notes. One day about noon, I found him sitting in his bedroom and having his luncheon, attended by Mrs. Wilson. Once during the meal he looked up at her and then over at me and said, "You see how well I am cared for!" Mrs. Wilson smiled and patted him on the head. She seems most happy these days: and I never saw her looking more beautiful. She went about the house whistling like a boy. The President wore a purple velvet jacket and his left hand was curled down and hidden by his side. He could not use it. His color I thought much better, more wholesome, than when I last saw him, and his voice was stronger. Grayson told me afterward that he was in the best health since he fell ill eighteen months before. He was apparently expecting to get well: went at his exercises with boundless tenacity and courage.

We fell presently to talking about the Peace Conference: and finally, though I was fearful of unduly tiring him, I went and got the Inquiry Report of 1918 with his stenographic notes on the margin. He deciphered all of them for me—which I much desired. He even seemed to enjoy it and readily promised to read any others I might find. I was delighted to clear up quite a number of difficult points, as to the origin of his position on the mandatory system, and his view of the rights of small nations.

We got to talking about a title for the book and he had the same idea I had had: to express the contact of American ideals with European realities.

"Why don't you call it *America Meets Europe at Paris*?" he said.

Presently Mrs. Wilson and I were called to luncheon, but had hardly got well started when Mr. Wilson sent down his Negro attendant, Scott, to ask me to come up to see him. He was now in bed propped high with pillows. As soon as I came in he said, without preface:

"In my notes on the Balkans [which he had previously interpreted for me] I speak of the relationships of the several Balkan states to one another as being determined by friendly council along historically established lines of allegiance and nationality. This is important. I was thinking there of the great value of tradition and habit in the settling of these problems. Habit is the basis of order. I am not an impractical idealist, nor did I, at Paris, want everything torn up by the roots and made over according to some ideal plan. I recognized always the importance of habitual relationships in cementing all of these allegiances."

The President quite warmed to the enthusiasm I expressed in telling him of my plans for the development of the book, and of the service we might do with it in arousing a better consciousness in America regarding international problems.

"It is the biggest work I ever attempted," I said.

"It is the biggest any American writer ever attempted," he said.

It was as near enthusiasm—warmth—toward me as I ever saw him get: not so much in the words as in the intonation of his voice and the expression in his eyes. But at the last the barrier never breaks quite down. One never quite gets to him. One feels like standing up as I did through all this conversation—at the foot of his bed!

As time passed it became more and more difficult for me to do my work properly in the little room in S Street, or in the Washington hotel apartment where I lived. I had now a research assistant,* and a stenographer or two—and it was difficult to arrange and organize the accumulation of documents and books I was working with. More even than this, I did not feel comfortable or happy in that crowded way of life. I longed for my own hillside and my garden.

One Sunday in May I wrote in my diary:

"I came home to Amherst Friday morning. The spring here is at its golden moment: There is a richness, a fullness, an exuberance about the coming of spring in Washington, but it lacks for me the magical charm of May in these northern hills. Here the spring comes slowly, reluctantly, coyly. It reveals its growth with modesty: awaits maturity with a kind of mystic enticement. I looked out of the car window in the morning coming up the Connecticut Valley, and across the sunny water saw the old green hills: and the filmy golden mist of the deciduous trees against the darker greens of the pines and the hemlocks: and could not keep from crying. The new soft foliage of poplars: the reds and tans of the maples: the warm browns of the elms.

* Dr. Joseph V. Fuller, who was of the greatest assistance in analyzing and digesting the documents.

The lilacs and honeysuckles are coming into bloom, the apple trees still hold their blossoms, the dogwoods are white upon the hillsides.

"Yesterday I worked nearly all day with my honeybees. A swarm went out and rested thick and brown among the currant bushes. I cut them out and hived them. The new grass of my seeded field is coming in: the oak trees are beginning to leaf out—when an oak leaf is as big as a squirrel's ear it is time for the corn-planting!—and upon the trellises the new grape foliage—is there anything more exquisite?—is coming out.

"It seems to me I have lost the spring this year. I have not been here to live it. I shall never get it back again."

When I presented my sad case to Mrs. Wilson—and indeed to the President—they readily agreed that I should take all the documents and books I needed home to Amherst, with occasional visits to Washington for consultation. From that time forward the work became far more bearable, and I found I could make much better progress. In October my manuscript was so nearly finished that I made arrangements for its serial publication in the newspapers. I wanted to get the facts before as many people as I could, as soon as I could. The New York *Times* was to use the narrative in the East, and began in December with a tremendous campaign of advertising—using entire pages in the newspaper itself and, having thought of expedients of which I had not dreamed, plastered the signboards of the city and the surrounding country with posters five by ten feet, or more, containing a huge picture of Woodrow Wilson's "secret steel box," now to be opened to the people. The men who managed the syndication also placed the series in many other American papers and made contracts for publication in Japan, Mexico, South Africa and Canada—and "rights" in Germany and France, but not, I think, in England. Altogether a great hullabaloo, to me often embarrassing. In 1922, Doubleday brought out the book, *Woodrow Wilson and World Settlement,* in three volumes, two of exposition, and a third devoted wholly to documents.

I said of it in my introduction:

". . . there is no more instructive failure—if it was failure—than the President's at Paris, for when we approach it with a desire not to condemn or defend, but to understand, it reveals, as nothing else could, the real elements of the struggle which the liberals of the world have yet before them."

The book was translated and published in Germany in January, 1923, later in France, Poland and Austria: the British edition came out on January 18 of the same year. It was widely discussed in all these nations, as it was also, in America.

I like to think that the book increased even slightly that understanding which, above everything, I longed to instil.

CHAPTER LVII

Era of Confusion: Harding and Coolidge

THE HARDING administration and the years that followed, when we were "keeping cool with Coolidge," seemed to me then, and have seemed to me ever since, one of the darkest, most hopeless periods in recent American history. To a follower like me, eagerly seeking a leader with a constructive program, whom he could trust, it was a time of confusion and dismay. I could not see where to take hold or what to do.

In February, 1923, I went to Washington to attend one of the famous dinners of the Gridiron Club, the chief attraction of which had always been the warranted license, for one hilarious evening, to satirize the notable men of the American scene. No one there could be wholly sure he would not be singed on that undiscriminating griddle. Even I, who was congratulating myself upon being a mere invited guest, had one terrifying moment when I heard my name called and I was asked to face that great company. Fortunately for them as for me, I was not asked to make a speech. It was altogether an interesting occasion: even those who suffered most were able to endure, if they did not wholly enjoy, the proceedings. Since the great ones squirmed upon the gridiron without publicity and the speeches were elaborately unreported, it furnished an unusual opportunity for an inquiring follower like me to discover what his superiors were made of.

I had not yet met Warren Gamaliel Harding, and while I knew Calvin Coolidge slightly—he was an Amherst man—it was the first time I had seen him meet the tests of a critical audience. He sat through the entire dinner with solemn decorum, withdrawn into himself; the hotter the gridiron sizzled, the chillier he looked.

The chief subject of discussion on the floor was the prohibition law and how to get around it—as many of those present, including numerous honorables, were doing with considerable and plainly evident success. Irvin Cobb made the hit of the evening by observing that since the passage of the Volstead Act over the veto of Woodrow Wilson, the world "had been made safe for hypocrisy."

My own chief interest was in hearing and seeing President Harding. He was not called upon until near midnight. A large, benevolent-looking, vague, tired human being he appeared; there seemed to me to be nothing sure, strong, clear, about him or his speech. His voice dripped with good intention pleading for sympathy. What he seemed to resent most were the satirical references in the earlier part of the evening to the "spy-glass diplomacy" of the nation and the fun poked at "unofficial observers." He declared that a new war in Europe was an utter impossibility: the people would not stand for it. And this at a time when the French were in the Ruhr and the Turks laying mines off Smyrna. Like so many Americans, he simply closed his eyes to disagreeable facts and bolstered his optimism with gushing enthusiasm about the greatness of America. Not a word of vitalizing leadership, not a suggestion of courage, vision, power. It was pathetic; you were sorry for the man, sorrier still for the country.

I noted that his speech was little applauded, even by enthusiastic Republicans. I wondered what was going on in the minds of men like Herbert Hoover, Henry Wallace, and Gifford Pinchot, who sat listening there.

I had also wanted to see something of Secretary Hughes, but he did not attend the Gridiron dinner. While he had been defeated as a presidential candidate by Wilson in the election of 1916, he remained a commanding figure, now in the powerful position of Secretary of State in Harding's Cabinet. He might again be the leader to whom the country would turn in its need.

So I went to a small luncheon, given a day or so later by the Overseas Club, which was addressed by Secretary Hughes. His speech was to be a "confidential explanation of his course in foreign affairs."

It was Hughes at his best: and Hughes at his best could be very good. He was no vague figure, uttering platitudes, like Harding, but a sturdy, vital, erect personality, with a gift of vigorous and often pungent English, and no mean wit. I sat close to him where I could see his profile: his shiny bald pate with a roll of gray hair at the neck, his substantial forehead, shaggy brows, capable nose, complete chin.

A man's outward eyes are often symbols of his inward vision. Wilson's glowed, burned, penetrated: were wide open and clear. Hughes's seemed to me dull, small, guarded.

The next day when I went to see Mr. Wilson I told him about Hughes's speech.

"A greatly overestimated man," he said. "When he was nominated I expected a hard fight: you remember what happened. He has certain qualities of industry in a prepared course, but goes to the core of nothing."

I thought then that Wilson underestimated Hughes, as he usually underestimated the cautious, traditional, legalistic mind, which in its place is truly valuable. Hughes had some of the strong qualities of Wilson—Roosevelt called him a "whiskered Wilson"—qualities of lucid and forceful exposition, but without the flair, the spark of genius, which lifted Wilson's best into the unforgettable.

A policy of drift, of "watchful waiting" is tenable only if supported by real arguments and based upon established facts. At the Overseas Club Hughes presented cogently every possible reason for doing nothing. His description of the attitude of the administration could be boiled down into one of his own phrases; the important thing for us now was "to mind our own business competently."

The plain fact was that Hughes, the great legalist, was the impressive advocate of Harding's weakness and fear. Harding wished to offend nobody, no congressional group, no economic group, neither France nor Germany: he was doing nothing either to help settle the desperate situation in Europe or to tell America what was wrong with its soul. He wanted to be *safe*. Hughes, the lawyer, also wanted to be safe, but in a crisis such as then existed, as in war, leadership goes to the man who has vision and daring, and is willing to make the great adventure. Hughes's leadership just wouldn't work.

In short, it was clear enough to me that I could not accept Hughes, let alone Harding, as my leader. I could not accept Coolidge; he did not know where he was going. All through the years I had been eagerly looking for leaders; not so much the men themselves, as the principles they lived by, the ideas they stood for. Some of the men I found were of a limited greatness, "inadequate heroes, not heroic enough." While they sometimes accomplished notable results, especially in lesser places, their own personal fortunes too often became the test of their activities. They began to consider themselves indispensable to the causes they were promoting. Those around them, the most devoted followers of the flag they flew, were too often swept into an almost irresistible personal allegiance. The price of criticism or disagreement was usually the loss of friendship. To a follower with a free mind, and convictions that went deeper than the personal fortunes of any leader, however great, the position ultimately became intolerable. I learned much from all of the men I followed—the greatest lesson of all being that I could depend on nothing not in my own soul.

In those sad days of Harding and Coolidge, I was not only disillusioned with the leadership I found in Washington and elsewhere, but I had a severe attack of disgust with politics in general. I was afterward ashamed of it, for politics in its essence is the method by which men work together to govern themselves. It can become hopelessly inefficient and corrupt, but it is like life itself, it cannot be abolished, it must be lived and used.

In moments of depression I sometimes recalled a remark that Ida Tarbell had made many years before, during the so called "muckraking" period. It was at one of our editorial discussions—I think Lincoln Steffens was also there. We had been "viewing with alarm" the state of the nation. Miss Tarbell was then exposing the iniquities of the Standard Oil Company, Steffens was uncovering the shame of the cities, and I was working on the problems of labor and capital. It was a bleak world we saw that morning: nowhere in America any great leadership; nowhere, apparently, any vision.

Ida Tarbell said earnestly:

"Remember that we have had great leadership in the past: we shall have it again in the future. Keep looking back to Abraham Lincoln."

It was what she herself had long been doing. She had written a life of Lincoln which we had published in our magazine, and whenever the world looked black she would write a little article or story about him. One, I remember, was called "He Knew Lincoln." Lincoln fortified her spirit with his greatness and his humility.

If we had not, momentarly, the leaders we needed, we could turn with confidence to our American heritage of greatness. Where was there anywhere in the world such a tradition of constructive leadership? Not only Lincoln, but George Washington, Thomas Jefferson, Andrew Jackson, and many others. Once I spent many weeks reading, a little at a time, Jefferson's letters. What a respect these leaders had for human personality, which is the essence of democracy, what faith in the "improvability of man," as Jefferson phrased it in a letter to his friend Joel Barlow. These men are still the leaders and prophets of our race. They are more than that, they have become leaders and prophets in countries where men are still not free. When I was in Italy in 1918, I found one of the ablest scholars of that country studying the papers of Jefferson and Hamilton.

"I am trying," he said, "to find out how you Americans have come to be what you are."

It seems strange to me now that I had for so long been a devoted follower of Woodrow Wilson before I realized fully how completely he was of the great American tradition. It came to me with a sense of surprise and deep satisfaction when I began to read straight through all of his books and public papers.

In 1924, Professor William E. Dodd of Chicago University * and I had discussed the idea of bringing out an edition of Woodrow Wilson's public papers. Mrs. Wilson liked the idea, and Harper and Brothers wished to publish the volumes as they appeared. We began our work at once, and the first two volumes, called *College and State*, appeared in February, 1925—a year after the President's death, the second two, called *The New Democracy*, in July, 1926, and the third two, *War and Peace*, in July, 1927.

We found it a much greater task than we had anticipated, since many of the addresses, especially the earlier ones dealing with the Princeton and New Jersey periods, were not easily obtainable. I recall the triumph we felt upon discovering the first published article by Thomas Woodrow Wilson, written when he was a sophomore at Princeton University and signed "Atticus." It was a laudatory sketch

* Professor Dodd had written one of the earliest short biographies of Woodrow Wilson. He was afterwards United States Ambassador to Germany.

of Prince Bismarck. We were glad to be able to include his "last public statement," written from his sick-bed less than a month before his death. It was a bold challenge to his own party in which he demanded the "redemption of the nation from the degradation of purpose into which it has in recent years been drawn." He concluded by saying: "I shall be glad to take part."

No other part of the task interested me so much as the evidence we found everywhere of Wilson's intellectual heritage. He had been nourished on the daring ideas, the glowing aspirations, of the founders of the republic. He said of a history of the United States upon which he had toiled for years that he wrote it primarily because he wished to understand the origin and spirit of American institutions. He had studied deeply the life of George Washington as a basis for the biography he wrote. No other president ever entered the White House so well grounded in democratic principles as he, or so determined to act upon them. Lincoln was one of his greatest heroes. Although he himself was a Democrat with a Southern background, and Lincoln a Republican and a Northerner, there are few finer tributes in the language to the greatness of Lincoln than those to be found in Wilson's public papers. Read also what he says of Thomas Jefferson, and General Robert E. Lee. If you wish to understand how he fortified his own spirit at the fountainhead of American idealism, and applied that idealism to the problems of his day, examine what he says in an address, given in 1914, called "Be Worthy of the Men of 1776."

"Have you ever read the Declaration of Independence, or attended with close comprehension to the real character of it when you have heard it read? . . . It was a vital piece of practical business, not a piece of rhetoric, and if you will pass beyond those preliminary passages which we are accustomed to quote about the rights of men and read into the heart of the document you will see that it is very express and detailed, that it consists of a series of definite specifications concerning actual public business of the day. Not the business of our day, for the matter with which it deals is past, but the business of the first revolution by which the Nation was set up, the business of 1776. . . . Liberty does not consist, my fellow-citizens, in mere general declarations of the rights of men. It consist in the translation of those declarations into definite action."

Most collections of presidential papers are of a deadly dullness, all but impossible to read. Wilson's are full of the very stuff of life, and will continue to be a storehouse of inspiration for those who believe in the democratic way of life. His papers are nearly all brief, nearly all bear the touch of a master craftsman in the English language. Woodrow Wilson never used "ghost-writers": everything he said was his own.

In editing the Wilson papers, Dodd and I had to read critically nearly a million words, practically the entire product of Woodrow Wilson's mind, except his published books, and to prepare the papers for printing in six volumes of about five hundred pages each. We had to write introductions, and to supervise the making of bibliographies and indexes. I cannot forget the weary months we spent, nor the slogging labor, and yet it proved later to have been of inestimable value to me. It gave me a fundamental grasp of Woodrow Wilson's development and career, which I could have attained in no other way.

CHAPTER LVIII

The Death of Woodrow Wilson

WOODROW WILSON DIED on the morning of February 3, 1924. Dr. Grayson told me that the last sign of responding life which he gave was on Friday, February 1. He had ceased to speak: he was acutely weak, but when Grayson told him that Senator Glass of Virginia had just called and said: "Give the Chief my love," the eyes of the dying man opened and gleamed and there was a slight movement of the fingers of his right hand. The "Chief" was fond of Senator Glass.

He had been slowly failing for many months. His last brief message to his countrymen had been written in the summer of 1923. It was called "The Road Away from Revolution," and it contained this final conclusion of all his thinking:

"The sum of the whole matter is this, that our civilization cannot survive materially unless it be redeemed spiritually."

I was asked to come to the funeral, on the sixth. The day was not cold but it broke dark and murky, with a few flakes of snow in the air. When I arrived I found all the streets blocked by cars and crowds of people, with police and soldiers keeping the lines. The whole of the little hill-side opposite the house was black with the crowd. I was shown upstairs to the hallway. Most of the guests were already there, distributed between the library and dining room at the back. The body lay in the large room at the front of the house, the doors of which were opened when the President and Mrs. Coolidge arrived.

The service was brief and simple, and noteworthy only for certain passages from Mr. Wilson's book of devotion which he had been reading on the last day before he fell ill.

Six men in uniform—two army, two navy, two marines—bore the coffin out to the street. Fine-looking young men they were, of the kind the President loved. The Chapel at the Cathedral was crowded. It was the most notable gathering of Americans I had ever seen on any one occasion: for Mr. Wilson was not only a statesman but also a distinguished educator and writer.

He was at rest at last: after a career of struggle and disappointment his body lay there under the stones, his spirit was marching onward. As I walked back into the murky city, I found myself repeating a passage I had recently found in *The Brothers Karamazov*:

"The just man passeth away, but his light remaineth: and it is after the saviour's death that men are mostly saved. Mankind will reject and kill their prophets, but will love their martyrs and honor those whom they have done to death."

I went to Europe that summer with a family party, trying to re-orient myself and to discover what I was to do next. There had been tentative discussion of an authorized biography of Woodrow Wilson, but no decision had yet been reached. I was doubtful whether I was the man to do it—whether I had the qualifications to make the most of such a venture.

I find in my notes this entry, dated January 2, 1925:

"I lunched with Mrs. Wilson and Mr. Bolling,* and talked with them the entire afternoon about the proposed *Life and Letters*. She said she felt that I was in grave doubt about doing the work, that I seemed to have changed and lost enthusiasm since last spring. I told her frankly that this was so; and that the reason lay in my clearer perception of what the task involved, the immense labor and the responsibility."

I had talked over my plans with old and dear friends—Ida Tarbell, John S. Phillips, and others. All of them urged me strongly not to un-undertake the Wilson biography.

"It will swallow up your whole life," Phillips said, "and just at a time when you are prepared for your best creative work."

John H. Finley, another old friend,† told me of his invitation to write the biography of Grover Cleveland, who had been his warm friend and neighbor at Princeton, and of his final refusal to attempt the task.

I had many long and anxious talks with Mrs. Wilson. I raised all

* John Randolph Bolling was Mrs. Wilson's brother and secretary.
† Afterward editor of the New York *Times*.

the problems I could think of—most important of all, my own complete freedom as a writer. If I should undertake such a task, I must put down exactly what I found, and take my own time in doing it. I found her as level-headed and far-sighted as I could wish. The truth was best, regardless of consequences.

It was as difficult a decision as I ever had to make, and I am not sure that I should finally have agreed to take on the task if Mrs. Wilson had not shown me a letter written to me by Mr. Wilson only a few days before his death. It was dated January 25, 1924, and was the last letter he ever wrote to anyone. He was too ill to sign it. Here is the text:

MY DEAR BAKER,

Every time that you disclose your mind to me you increase my admiration and affection for you.

I always dislike to make, or even intimate, a promise until I have at least taken some step to facilitate my keeping it. I am glad to promise you that with regard to my personal correspondence and other similar papers I shall regard you as my preferred creditor, and shall expect to afford you the first—and if necessary exclusive—access to those papers. But I have it on my conscience that you should know that I have not made the smallest beginning towards accumulating and making accessible the letters and papers we have in mind. I would rather have your interpretation of them than that of anybody else I know, and I trust that you will not think it unreasonable that I should ask you to accept these promises in lieu of others which would be more satisfactory but which, for the present, would be without practical value.

Pray accept assurances of my unqualified confidence and affectionate regard.

Faithfully yours,

I could write an entire book regarding the adventures I had in getting together and organizing the Wilson documents. I was at first appalled by the sheer volume of the collections, then partly stored in the house in S Street, and partly in sealed storage rooms in a Washington warehouse. Woodrow Wilson's records, covering the eight years of his administration including the First World War and the peace negotiations which followed it, exceeded in volume that of any other president of the United States up to that time.*

* For a more detailed description of this documentary material, see my introduction to Volume I, *Woodrow Wilson: Life and Letters.*

When I thought that I had discovered all of the various files, trunks, cabinets, steel boxes, and wooden cases, I was completely bowled over one day by hearing of a large file of Wilson records that, even after four years, remained still in the White House. When I went down into the catacomb-like corridors underneath the executive office, I found a solid row of steel cases, sixty-seven in number, containing five thousand five hundred and sixteen folders, a total of some two hundred thousand letters and documents. It was positively terrifying to think about it. It had been the practice of American presidents, all along, to take their papers with them, but Mr. Wilson was ill at the time he left the White House and apparently overlooked this accumulation. While these documents were more or less routine records, I found later that it was necessary to examine them thoroughly, since they furnished monumental evidence of the burdens and responsibilities of the executive head of a nation of one hundred and twenty million people, each one of whom, if he feels aggrieved, or thinks he knows better than anyone else how momentous problems are to be solved, considers it a God-given privilege to write to his president. No one seemed to have the power to let me remove these dusty steel boxes. I had to go to President Harding himself, explain the situation, and get his personal approval.

We decided to remove the entire collection of Wilson documents to my home in Amherst. The great van in which they were shipped arrived on March 6, 1925. I wrote to Mrs. Wilson on the following day:

"I wish you could have seen the commotion caused yesterday upon the appearance on the quiet streets of our town of that gigantic van. It was no mere incident, it was an event! The driver arrived with a long face—as long a face as any good-humored colored man holding such a position of importance could draw—for he had been stopped in Connecticut for driving an overweight truck. It tipped the scales at something over eleven tons (the limit being six tons) . . .

"When I saw the bulk of this material, I had a sudden renewed sense of the overwhelming responsibility and difficulty which it truly involves. If it were not for the assurance I feel of your unqualified support and your understanding of the fundamental requirement of the work—that is, time to do it thoroughly—I should certainly be staggered."

Amherst College generously provided a secure place to store a part of the collection until I could get ready to use it. Later, these boxes and cabinets were removed to the fireproof study rooms at the top of the Jones Library.* I also built a large fire-proof vault in the basement of our house, where I kept, under lock and key, the most precious of the files.

I spent all of the first year in organizing the documents, and in a widespread correspondence with old friends of the President, seeking information regarding their association with him. While this resulted in the accumulation of much valuable new material, it increased the labor of studying and digesting it.

I devoted several months trying to visualize more clearly all phases of Woodrow Wilson's life by visiting the places where he had lived in his earlier years. I spent a night in the very house where he was born at Staunton, Virginia; I poked my head up into the dusty loft of his father's barn at Augusta, Georgia, where, at the age of about ten, he organized the Lightfoot Club, his first "government," and wrote a constitution for it. He was always writing constitutions! At Columbia, South Carolina, I talked with many friends who had known him well as a slim, quiet, backward, studious boy who wanted to go into the navy. Here it was that I heard the story of his religious conversion in a little one-story chapel built out of an old stable. When I visited Atlanta, Georgia, I tramped out from his law office in Marietta Street, up Forsyth to his boarding place in what was then the outskirts of the town—in Peachtree Street—and found myself turning over in my mind the very problems he was then so diligently considering.

Later, I went up to the University of Virginia, where I lunched with President and Mrs. Alderman, who had in Professor Dabney, a classmate of Mr. Wilson at the University of Virginia. Professor Dabney walked around with me to the spots he and "Tommy" Wilson knew as students. We called on Mrs. King, who sang with Woodrow Wilson in the college choir. I found rich treasures of letters every-

*I wish to acknowledge warmly the courteous assistance of Robert S. Fletcher of the Converse Memorial Library and Charles R. Green of the Jones Library.

where. I spent the afternoon in the library examining records connected with the Wilson tradition.

I visited Wilmington, North Carolina, where Wilson's father was pastor of the principal Presbyterian church, and Davidson College where "Tommy" was briefly a student and wrote another constitution, and then to Princeton where I found floods of new material. I talked steadily for eleven hours one day with Stockton Axson, who was Wilson's brother-in-law and who had been with him at Princeton University—and left so many things still undiscussed that on the following day we talked seven hours more.

I soon began to feel as though I knew the young Wilson personally, inside as well as out. I could all but see and hear him—and pity him.

It is no wonder that I could write in my diary on January 1, 1926:

"Looking back, it seems to me that the past year has, in many ways, been the most interesting of my whole life. I have been crowded with work, but have enjoyed it all keenly."

I was soon well aware that I should need assistance in organizing and digesting the documents. I recall a review I wrote of an excellent biography of Daniel Webster, in which I compared in my own mind the task I had with the task of the writer whose subject has been dead for seventy years. He could bring together all the necessary books, diaries, comments in one room, and sit down and read them. All those who had known Daniel Webster were thoroughly dead, all the memoirs published, all the stories told. How I envied such a writer! For the harder I worked, the more documents and letters I uncovered. There were many friends and associates of Wilson still living who had voluminous material as yet undisclosed, important incidents still unclarified, common rumors unexamined, cock-and-bull stories undisproved. Some of his associates already had memoirs in the making. Most of Wilson's friends were more than willing to tell me all they knew, show me all the documentary material they had—my cup of gratitude often overflowed—but I could think of some others who might be ambushing my innocent progress, and eager when I made a mistake to pop me over with letters or other evidence I had never seen. I had not only to know what I had, but what I had not. Thinking of these many difficulties I often quoted a comment of Woodrow Wilson in one of his early essays:

"It is a wonder that historians who take their business seriously can sleep at night."

If there had been only one ton of the documents I could perhaps, with the assistance of good secretarial help, have struggled through with the work myself, but there were about five tons of them. What was to be done?

I already had, in Katharine E. Brand, an invaluable secretary and later research assistant, who was with me for fourteen years, and has since become the special custodian of the Wilson documents in the Library of Congress, but it was also clear that I must have special research assistants, and these I was most fortunate in being able to secure. They were all excellent collaborators, and became my warm friends.*

The financial aspects of the work had also to be discussed and settled. I knew well the pressure which would be exerted by publishers to secure the rights to the serial and afterwards to the book. They had already made dazzling offers, but I dreaded above everything else being asked to sign contracts which, if they provided for the advances I needed for necessary expenses, might also require a specific date when I was to furnish copy. I had already had bitter experience with the Peace Conference book. For the objectives of the salesman, who appears to be the crowning product of our age, are not always those of the craftsman.

In the very week in which I wrote so happily of my work during the first year of my biographical labors, the editor of one of the most important American newspapers wrote offering a positive guarantee of two hundred thousand dollars with advance payments and monthly allowances for the syndicate rights of the book. He added that he would also turn over eighty per cent of everything the series earned beyond two hundred thousand dollars. Mrs. Wilson wired asking me

* Dr. Joseph V. Fuller, of the Department of State, who had helped me with the Peace Conference book, assisted me also with the *Life and Letters*. Dr. A. Howard Meneely, later professor of history at Dartmouth College, and now president of Wheaton College, was with me for several years. Dr. Harley A. Notter, who was a devoted student of the writings of Woodrow Wilson and who is now with the Department of State, came to me later.

to come to Washington for a conference. I remember walking out to S Street that dull January morning feeling as low-spirited as I had in many months. I could see only more trading for work I had scarcely begun—and in the end, limitations and commitments I could not accept.

Bernard Baruch, who had long been a devoted friend of both Mr. and Mrs. Wilson, was there when I arrived. I had become acquainted with him during the Paris Peace Conference and had regarded him as one of the ablest men there.

We discussed the whole subject of the publication of the biography. I had decided beforehand upon one thing: I must have complete freedom to do the work as I saw fit, without being hurried. I presented my problems as a writer as clearly as I knew how: and was greatly pleased and relieved to find that Mrs. Wilson fully understood my position.

"We must let nothing," she said, "interfere with the work itself."

Mr. Baruch warmly agreed with her. Just before he left to take his train, he called me aside and said:

"See here, how are you going to live while this work is being done?"

"I'm all right for a year or so," I said.

"Well, I want to do this: I want to have you let me make you an allowance of, say one thousand or fifteen hundred dollars a month—and have you forget about it. I want to do it for the same reason you are writing—to honor Woodrow Wilson's memory."

What could possibly have been finer or more generous! I thanked him heartily and said that it was a great comfort to know that there were friends who would see me through, but that I'd rather go ahead for the time being on the old basis. I felt that I had to have complete freedom.

Well, I sat down in my home in Amherst to write the life of Woodrow Wilson. I sat there most of the time for fourteen years. I had many ups and downs. I had times of keen enjoyment, thinking I was doing a great and useful work, and times when I realized acutely my own limitations and deficiencies. There were times when the monev came pouring in, more than I had expected, and times when the returns from my Wilson writings scarcely equalled the wages of a day laborer. There were times when my health seemed absolutely perfect and I turned off the daily work on the biography with an ease and relish that warranted the joy I felt during the long afternoons and evenings, in looking after my honey-bees, and my meadow, and my apple and peach and plum trees. There were gray days and weary months when I was ill, once so ill that I thought I should never be able to finish the life and letters of Woodrow Wilson. Everything happened in those fourteen years!

Looking back, weighing the life I lived, I find the balance tipping strongly toward a sense of satisfaction. It was not that the work itself satisfied me, or reached the vision I had of it, but that it was, somehow, what I wanted to do—passionately wanted to do—and that, after all, I was doing it as well as I could, considering the man I was and the talents I had. I was paying the tribute of a follower to the greatest leader I had ever known.

A man must somehow learn how to live as well as how to work. I had one abiding source of comfort in all those years. I was living in a small town where I had many friends and a bit of land of my own upon which I could work with my hands. I had long before adopted the country way of life: but I had never learned what a perfect foil it could be for the studious concentration to which I was now committed. It had adventure, variety, endless beauty.

But it is not enough to live in a country town: one must also live with it. Little towns are shy, not easily taken by assault. Their acceptances are often slow; but they are genuine. Nothing much is said about democracy: but we manage to get a good deal of it into our common affairs. We somehow know that the core of democracy lies not in being able to make something out of the town, but of contributing something to the town.

I had thought at first I would write of my friends—the Town Patriarch, the Town Philosopher, the Town Financier, the Town Reporter, the Town Poet and many others—but I found it would take the whole of a little book to do it. In a small country town such as I live in, one can come to know, in time, the good that men do secretly.

Another element in my life, during all the hard-pressed years, in many ways the most important of all, I have said the least about.

I have read many autobiographies: most of them leave out the things that go deepest, that mean most to the writers of them. This is because such things are either too difficult or too casual or too commonplace or too intimate to set down in cold type. As I look back it seems to me that I owe more to a satisfying and uneventful family life than to almost anything else. A writer must usually work at home, a difficulty in itself, and he must above everything have quiet—long hours of quiet—with a minimum of interruption and disturbance. It seems to be a selfish necessity! I did not fully recognize at the time how exceptionally favored I was in these genuine beatitudes; we often fail to appreciate a machine that runs smoothly, how much more a life. In this intimate regard, my life, especially in the years when I was most driven, ran smoothly.

My work on *Woodrow Wilson: Life and Letters* ended in 1939. The last volume, number eight, was published June 23 of that year. I speak of the work as "ended": I was unable to finish it as I had planned. The early volumes were issued as syndicated serials in many newspapers, but the later ones, the element of timeliness having evaporated, and the interest in Woodrow Wilson having reached its nadir—at times it seemed as if I could positively hear the hush-hush which accompanied any reference to him—the later volumes appeared only in book form. I could not complain of the reviews of each volume as it appeared, both in America and in England, although I had times when I wished that some of the later commentators would consult Roget for a synonym for "monumental." What pleased me most was the conclusion set down by the London correspondent of *The New York Times.*

"Most of the reviewers seem to have risen from their study of this volume with a higher opinion of Wilson's personality than when they sat down to it."

A reviewer in *The Scotsman* of Edinburgh said of the Wilson who emerges from the book:

"If not a great, he was a great-minded man and President."

Such comments as these, coming at a time when Wilson was sadly neglected and disregarded, gave me deep satisfaction: for they commended me for doing what I had set out most earnestly to do.

I think the deepest satisfaction of the later years of my life has been to see Woodrow Wilson coming into his own, being recognized for the pre-eminent man he was, as the true inheritor and prophet of the great American tradition.

> Curious, in time, I stand, noting the efforts of heroes:
> Is the deferment long? Bitter the slander, poverty, death?
> Lies the seed unreck'd for centuries in the ground?
> Lo! to God's due occasion,
> Uprising in the night, it sprouts, blooms,
> And fills the earth with use and beauty.

Index